EX LIBRIS

THE POETS'
DAUGHTERS

DORA WORDSWORTH

AND

SARA COLERIDGE

KATIE WALDEGRAVE

HUTCHINSON
LONDON

Published by Hutchinson 2013

3 5 7 9 10 8 6 4

Copyright © Katie Waldegrave 2013

First published in Great Britain in 2013 by
Hutchinson
Random House, 20 Vauxhall Bridge Road,
London SW1V 2SA

www.randomhouse.co.uk

Addresses for companies within The Random House Group Limited can be found at:
www.randomhouse.co.uk/offices.htm

The Random House Group Limited Reg. No. 954009

A CIP catalogue record for this book
is available from the British Library

ISBN 9780091931124

The Random House Group Limited supports the Forest Stewardship Council®
(FSC®), the leading international forest-certification organisation. Our books carrying
the FSC label are printed on FSC®-certified paper. FSC is the only forest-certification
scheme supported by the leading environmental organisations, including Greenpeace.
Our paper procurement policy can be found at
www.randomhouse.co.uk/environment

Typeset in Janson Text by Palimpsest Book Production Limited,
Falkirk, Stirlingshire

Printed and bound by CPI Group (UK) Ltd, Croydon, CR0 4YY

To Mum, Dad and Indro

The Wordsworth and Hutchinson family tree

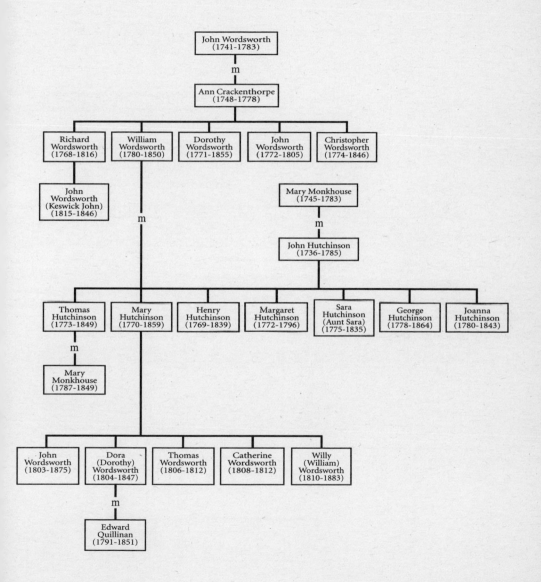

John Wordsworth
(1741-1783)

m

Ann Crackenthorpe
(1748-1778)

Richard Wordsworth
(1768-1816)

William Wordsworth
(1780-1850)

Dorothy Wordsworth
(1771-1855)

John Wordsworth
(1772-1805)

Christopher Wordsworth
(1774-1846)

John Wordsworth
(Keswick John)
(1815-1846)

Mary Monkhouse
(1745-1783)

m

John Hutchinson
(1736-1785)

m

Thomas Hutchinson
(1773-1849)

Mary Hutchinson
(1770-1859)

Henry Hutchinson
(1769-1839)

Margaret Hutchinson
(1772-1796)

Sara Hutchinson
(Aunt Sara)
(1775-1835)

George Hutchinson
(1778-1864)

Joanna Hutchinson
(1780-1843)

m

Mary Monkhouse
(1787-1849)

John Wordsworth
(1803-1875)

Dora (Dorothy) Wordsworth
(1804-1847)

Thomas Wordsworth
(1806-1812)

Catherine Wordsworth
(1808-1812)

Willy (William) Wordsworth
(1810-1883)

m

Edward Quillinan
(1791-1851)

The Coleridge and Southey/ Fricker family tree

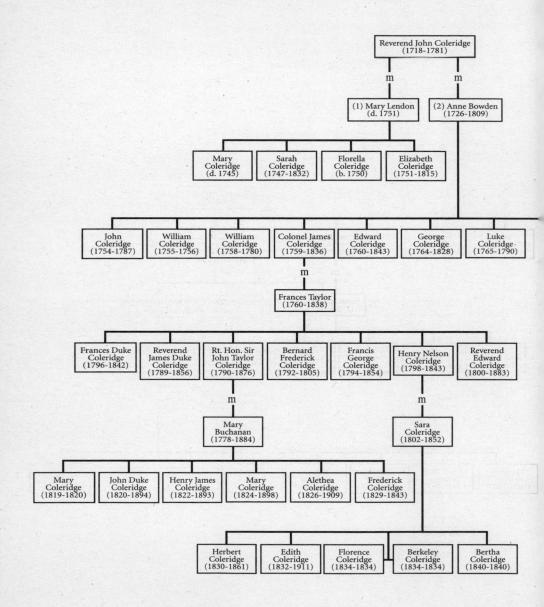

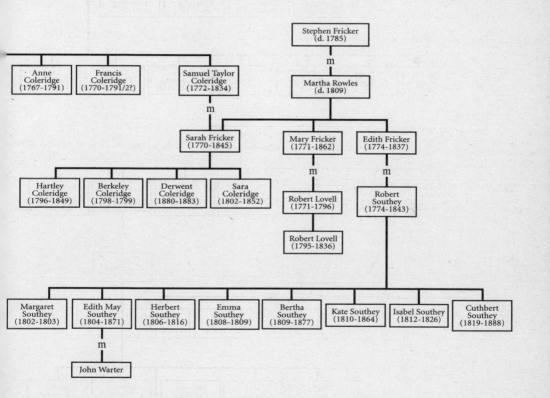

Stephen Fricker
(d. 1785)

m

Martha Rowles
(d. 1809)

Anne
Coleridge
(1767-1791)

Francis
Coleridge
(1770-1791/2?)

Samuel Taylor
Coleridge
(1772-1834)

m

Sarah Fricker
(1770-1845)

Mary Fricker
(1771-1862)

Edith Fricker
(1774-1837)

m

m

Hartley
Coleridge
(1796-1849)

Berkeley
Coleridge
(1798-1799)

Derwent
Coleridge
(1880-1883)

Sara
Coleridge
(1802-1852)

Robert Lovell
(1771-1796)

Robert
Southey
(1774-1843)

Robert Lovell
(1795-1836)

Margaret
Southey
(1802-1803)

Edith May
Southey
(1804-1871)

Herbert
Southey
(1806-1816)

Emma
Southey
(1808-1809)

Bertha
Southey
(1809-1877)

Kate Southey
(1810-1864)

Isabel Southey
(1812-1826)

Cuthbert
Southey
(1819-1888)

m

John Warter

CONTENTS

LIST OF ILLUSTRATIONS

FOREWORD

Father! – To God himself we cannot give a holier name.
William Wordsworth,
'Sponsors', Ecclesiastical Sonnets XXI

Dora Wordsworth and Sara Coleridge led parallel lives in the
shadows of monumental fathers who were the greatest poets of
their day. Between 1797 and 1807 William Wordsworth and
Samuel Taylor Coleridge worked, and often lived, together. They
wrote poetry which established that period of literature we now
call the Romantic and in their wake came Byron, Shelley, Keats
and a host of others. Theirs was one of the greatest literary
friendships in English history. Its high point was 1797–8, a year
in which they jointly produced the *Lyrical Ballads*, the most
important single volume of poetry of the Romantic period.*
Twelve years later, in 1812, when the lives of their families –
including their daughters – were intertwined, the relationship
between the poets was destroyed by a bitter quarrel.

Living in the blinding reflection of such epic events, Dora

---

* The point about Coleridge and Wordsworth is that they made their greatest
poetry together – more or less as a joint enterprise – particularly duing their
'*annus mirabilis*' of 1797–8 which culminated in the publication of the *Lyrical
Ballads*. Harold Bloom once wrote that 'it remains the most important volume
of verse in English since the Renaissance, for it began modern poetry, the
poetry of the inner growing self' (*The Oxford Anthology of English Literature*,
edited by Harold Bloom and Lionel Trilling, Oxford University Press, 1973,
II, p. 125.)

and Sara's lives were eclipsed by their fathers and neither daughter left anything but the most fleeting of reputations. Certainly both women would have been surprised at finding themselves subjects of a book, and not wholly pleased. Both had seen at first-hand the damage a biographer's pen could wreak. Yet the stories of their lives and their friendship are every bit as fascinating as the stories of their fathers. This is an attempt to finally tell those of Dora Wordsworth and Sara Coleridge in their own right.

Virginia Woolf – herself the daughter of a great man – once wrote a biographical essay about Sara Coleridge, describing her as a 'continuation' of her father's mind. Her 'years were lived in the light of his sunset, so that, like other children of great men, she is a chequered dappled figure flitting between a vanished radiance and the light of every day. And, like so many of her father's works, Sara Coleridge remains unfinished.'[1] She might as well have been writing about Dora.

PROLOGUE

In early January 1804, two poets set out to climb a mountain. Samuel Taylor Coleridge and William Wordsworth left Wordsworth's Cumberland cottage and, some hours later, the pair reached 'the highest and outermost of Grasmere' from where they could see the Lakelands they loved spread out before them.*[1] Wordsworth had moved to the village of Grasmere at the end of 1799 and Coleridge had followed him north in 1800. Since then the men had been living half a day's walk away from one another. Now Coleridge had left his home in the village of Keswick to stay with Wordsworth for a month. It had been a visit filled with symbolic last moments: each knew a chapter in their lives was ending. Coleridge was about to leave the country to go anywhere at all as long as it was far away. He hoped for a lengthy absence in an unknown place: 'Cornwall, perhaps, – Ireland perhaps – . . . or Madeira, or Teneriffe. I don't see any likelihood of our going to the Moon, or to either of the Planets, or fixed Stars.'[2] He was keen to seek out Indian Bhang (cannabis); he was desperate to escape. His stay with Wordsworth had gone some way towards repairing a once great and now increasingly strained friendship, but it had not been easy – Coleridge was

---

* Adam Sisman suggests they may have climbed to Hause Riggs which is a couple of miles from Grasmere and the last point from which Grasmere Lake can be seen (in *The Friendship: Wordsworth and Coleridge*, London: Viking Books, 2007, p. 368). Duncan Wu suggests it may have been Easedale (*A Companion to Wordsworth*, Oxford: Blackwell Publishing, 2001, p. 187).

dependent on opium and brandy and his wild way of living had vexed and harried the whole household. Yet before Coleridge left, Wordsworth wanted him to know he had taken up the challenge his friend had set him some five years earlier, when things had been easier. Looking down at the view, Wordsworth read Coleridge 'the second Part of his divine Self-biography'.

In 1798, Wordsworth had promised he would complete a project which Coleridge had entrusted to him: he would write verses to save mankind. It was to be an epic, 'the *first* and *only* true Phil[osophical] Poem', and it would be called 'The Recluse'.[3] The lines Wordsworth read Coleridge, as the men looked down on Grasmere, were the latest instalment of its prelude. Their theory was that since the French Revolution had failed, people would have to turn to poetry for salvation.* 'The Recluse' would give pictures of 'Nature, Man, and Society' and lead man to a new state of enlightened being. Coleridge thought Wordsworth was, quite simply, the greatest poet since Milton and so, although the vision for the poem was his, and he promised to provide the structure, he decided Wordsworth should do the actual writing. In retrospect it was not a good arrangement. Wordsworth began in 1798 and reckoned it would take 'at least a year and a half to come'. It was an ambitious target given that he had said: 'I know not anything which will not come within the scope of my plan.'[4] Five years on Coleridge was disappointed that Wordsworth had merely succeeded in working on the 'preamble' and wished that his friend would progress faster. Inspired by the walk, Wordsworth once again vowed to live up to Coleridge's ambitions for him. It was as solemn a promise as any wedding

---

* STC wrote to tell WW, 'My dear friend, I do entreat you go on with "The Recluse"; and I wish you would write a poem, in blank verse, addressed to those, who, in consequence of the complete failure of the French Revolution, have thrown up all hopes of the amelioration of mankind, and are sinking into an almost epicurean selfishness, disguising the same under the soft titles of domestic attachment and contempt for visionary philosophes. It would do great good, and might form a part of "The Recluse", for in my present mood I am wholly against the publication of any small poems. STC to WW, 10 September 1799; *STCCL*, I, p. 527.

vow and on the eve of Coleridge's departure, when neither man could be sure he would see the other again, it was their pledge to the power of poetry and the mind to change the world.

From the heights above Grasmere the poets walked home and into very different futures. While Wordsworth would stay put in the Lakes until the end of his life, Coleridge would depart several days later – for Malta, as it turned out, rather than the moon. He would leave his wife and their three children, including a baby girl named Sara, and not return for several years. Mrs Coleridge and her children would remain at their home, Greta Hall in the village of Keswick. When Wordsworth descended the hill it was to a baby son and a house full of women, including his wife Mary, who was pregnant with a daughter who would be named after her aunt Dorothy and known to all as Dora.

PART ONE

CHAPTER 1

'THE SHADOW OF A SHADE'

1808

'What Phantoms Hover Round'

On 7 September 1808, a carriage wound its way to the top of a hill just outside the village of Grasmere in Cumberland. The horses pulled up in front of a large white house and two men and a little girl descended, stretching their cramped legs. It had taken them several hours to travel the thirteen miles from Keswick. The first man, William Wordsworth, was tall and wiry; the second, Samuel Taylor Coleridge, always known as STC, was shorter and heavy with a pale, bloated face and thick dry lips.* The girl was sprite-like, with blonde hair and enormous blue eyes.

Sara Coleridge, aged five and three quarters, stood and regarded her friend Dora Wordsworth's new house, Allan Bank. Behind her, at the bottom of the hill, was Grasmere Lake; in front of her, the house, large and white, beneath a craggy fell. Her father had promised she would be happy staying here: Allan Bank was his home now. When the men were ready, she took her father's hand and walked towards the front door. A shriek of joyful recognition pierced the air and John Wordsworth, five and a quarter, bounded out of the house and into the garden. Sara knew the Wordsworth children – John, Dora and two-year-old Thomas – well, but as they approached John disappeared back

---

* When Southey saw STC in 1808, he declared him to be 'about half as big as the house' (Holmes *DR*, p. 146).

inside, suddenly shy. Dora's two spinster aunts, and finally Dora herself, emerged to greet the travellers. As the adults embraced, the girls made a striking contrast to one another. Sara wore her best lace cap over blonde curls and a frilly dress. Dora, just turned four, was a stocky, ruddy-cheeked child in a simple dress, already nearly as tall as her older playmate.

Wordsworth rushed into the house and up the stairs to where his wife Mary had the day before given birth to a girl. The baby, whom they would christen Catherine, and usually call Cate, brought the number of little Wordsworths to four. Meanwhile John had fled into the house and hidden under the kitchen table as Sara approached. When she came near, he 'peeped out at her, then all red with Blushes crept back again, laughing half convulsive yet faintly – at length he came out, & throwing his pinafore over his face with both hands upon that, he ran and kissed her thro' the pinafore'. The adults laughed, delighted. By the end of the day the young sweethearts were engaged and John had pledged to carry her all the way to the church and back – just to be sure.[1] Sara danced, spun and twirled, basking in his admiration. Dora's Aunt Dorothy, watching Sara on such an occasion, said 'the exquisite grace of her motions, her half Lady, half spirit form, and her interesting countenance made her an object of pure delight'.[2] Dora was not so much of a one for twirling.

Until six months before, Wordsworth had lived with his family at Town End Cottage, Grasmere (now known as Dove Cottage).* He and his sister Dorothy, separated in childhood, had established a household together in the beloved Lakeland District of their youth in December 1799. Though more stable than STC's, Wordsworth's had not been a conventional household. To outsiders it seemed highly eccentric. From the start, Dorothy and Wordsworth and their friends and relations kept strange hours and wandered the hills and vales appreciating what we now see as the picture-postcard-pretty landscape, but which

---

* Dove Cottage currently receives almost 100,000 visitors a year from all around the world.

was then mostly viewed as a place of poverty and isolation. His family despaired – they had hoped he would become a lawyer or a clergyman.

Then, in 1802, Wordsworth married Mary Hutchinson, a childhood friend whom he had met again with STC in 1799. Wordsworth's marriage was a difficult change in circumstance for Dorothy and speculations about conflict and incest remain to this day. Frances Wilson's *The Ballad of Dorothy Wordsworth* provides the most subtle and intelligent reading of their relationship: the bond between brother and sister was extraordinarily close and soon adapted itself into a bond between husband, wife and sister that was almost as close again. Mary moved into Town End Cottage and in the July before STC and Wordsworth's *Recluse* walk, she had given birth to her first child, John. Town End's – and later Allan Bank's – domestic tasks, including bringing up the children, were shared by Mary, Dorothy and, when she was there – which was often – Mary's sister Aunt Sara Hutchinson.*

Since Sara's father, STC, had returned to England from Malta in 1806, he had lived mostly with the Wordsworths rather than returning to his own family. Now he was bringing Sara for a visit, her first to Allan Bank, the Wordsworths' new house. She quickly decided she didn't like it. Her own home was refined by comparison to this cold smoky place and she was homesick. She was also nonplussed to find there were no nurseries, no routines and no discipline. 'We children sometimes left our beds at 4'O clock and roamed about the kitchen before there was anyone to dress us,' Sara remembered years later. They drew on the walls and 'were chid and cuffed freely enough, yet far from kept in good order'. The Wordsworths had two servants to help – Fanny and a 'backward girl' called Sally, who was little

---

* The three Saras make telling this story particularly complicated. Throughout, therefore, Sara Coleridge, STC's daughter, is called 'Sara'; Mrs Coleridge, his wife, (also a Sarah) is 'Mrs STC'; and Dora's aunt, Sara Hutchinson, is 'Aunt Sara'.

more than a child herself – but disorder still reigned.* Sara found
bath-time particularly upsetting – it was carried out 'in a tub in
the kitchen, in an exposed sort of way' and frequently 'some
men or man came in during the operation'.³ Allan Bank house
was cold as 'a well & made us shiver' even in summer, but it
was almost impossible to heat. Whenever they lit a fire, the
downwind from the fell filled the rooms with 'horrid smoke' or
blew it out of the grate altogether.⁴ Sometimes the women were
forced to cook in the study, the room with the best chimney
– but even then they could barely see one another through the
smoke.⁵ At other times Aunt Dorothy's bedroom was the only
chimney which drew and they would be forced to huddle together
there. The walls were black to the touch and soot soon covered
Sara's pretty dresses.⁶

Her own childhood world was the cheerfully ordered chaos
of her uncle Robert Southey and his large family. They lived at
Greta Hall, twelve miles over the Dunmail Raise from Allan Bank
and on the edge of the town of Keswick. Uncle Southey considered
no house complete unless it contained 'a child rising six years, and
a kitten rising six months', and Sara and the others lived in a place
of fairy-tale and fantasy. The names they gave their cats give some
idea of the landscape of their imagination and the books which
created it: Madame Bianchi, Ovid and Virgil, Pulcheria, Zombi
and Rumpelstiltskin wandered around house and garden.⁷ To the
end of her life Sara would look back on the mountains and lakes
of Keswick as an Edenic landscape to which she could never return
lest it not live up to her memories, but she yearned for it all the
same.⁸ At Allan Bank, she was away from her mother for the first
time and, especially at night, the dark corners of the house were
frightening. The presence of her father only made things stranger.

* Sally was the daughter of George and Sarah Green about whose tragic deaths
in March 1808 Wordsworth and Dorothy wrote a great deal. She'd been kept
on when her parents died but was not well suited to the job. See also
Wordsworth's 'Elegiac Stanzas Composed in the Churchyard of Grasmere,
Westmorland, A Few Days After the Interment There of a Man and his Wife,
Inhabitants of the Vale, Who Were Lost Upon the Neighbouring Mountains,
on the Night of the Nineteenth of March Last'.

Little Sara idolised STC but she hardly knew him; he was separated (though not divorced) from her mother and had been mostly absent from her life.* When, in 1804, after STC and Wordsworth's solemn walk, Coleridge had fled from his wife and family and travelled to Malta, Sara had just turned one. He remained abroad for several years and Sara just remembered him reappearing at her house when she was almost four.† She also recalled, following that, tears and blazing rows between her parents. Mrs STC had tried her hardest – she nursed her husband when he was sick and loved him more than ever; yet the harder she tried, the more STC felt she was making 'an exact and copious Recipe' for '"How to make a Husband completely miserable"'. Eventually he decided his long-suffering wife had failed him: 'Ill-tempered speeches sent after me when I went out of the house . . . Ill-tempered Speeches on my return, my friends received with freezing looks, the least opposition or contradiction occasioning screams of passion.'[9] He had complained bitterly to the Wordsworths and they sympathised with him and persuaded him to leave Greta Hall, his wife and his children. And so Sara's father left again, first for the south of England and later to move in with Dora's family.‡ The Allan Bank household, particularly Dora's Aunt Dorothy, who had never liked Mrs STC, was confident they could provide him with the love and stability his wife could not. Sara's uncle, Robert Southey, was furious. The

* Even had STC wanted a legal dissolution of their marriage it would have been virtually unobtainable in England at this time. Only a very few, very wealthy people sought or were granted a divorce in any given year.

† STC returned to his family in October 1806. Sara turned four in December 1806.

‡ For an excellent account of STC's itinerant life, see Holmes *DR*, pp. 80–145. Between December 1806 and April 1807 the Wordsworths and STC (with his son Hartley) stayed with their patron, Lord Beaumont, near Leicester. In April 1807 they all went to London for a month, after which the Wordsworths returned home. Between May and September, Mrs STC tried to follow STC around with her children – to the West Country and London – but eventually she gave up and returned to Greta Hall. At the start of 1808 STC began giving lectures at the Royal Institution in London; the series continued until June 1808. He returned to Grasmere on 1 September 1808.

Wordsworths, he said, had 'always humoured . . . [Coleridge] in all his follies, – and listened to his complaints of his wife, – & when he has complained of the itch, helped him to scratch, instead of covering him with brimstone ointment, & shutting himself up by himself'.[10] Thus the lines of opposition were drawn up: Greta Hall with Mrs STC and the Southeys vs. the Wordsworths with STC at Allan Bank.

Sara didn't understand all the complex and unexpressed adult tensions at Allan Bank, but she was nevertheless conscious of them. What she could not know was that STC's relationships were influenced by the great quantity of opium he took. His way of behaving with all the Wordsworth family was confusing, but most strange was the way he acted around Dora's Aunt Sara. Little Sara would later discover that shortly after marrying, STC had inconveniently fallen in love with Aunt Sara. His love for Wordsworth's sister-in-law was almost an extension of the love he felt for Wordsworth; in his poems she became the immortal 'Asra', the object of a series of exquisite love poems.*

Nearly ten years later, STC's ardour for his Asra showed no sign of cooling. In the midst of his opium addiction, she was the unattainable and therefore infallible object of his adoration. STC believed himself to be passionately in love. Young Sara would later learn that, at her own birth, one of the few signs of interest her father showed was in the spelling of her name. He 'bore her sex bravely' and insisted on naming her 'Sara' like his beloved, not 'Sarah' like his wife.[11] Aunt Sara Hutchinson's name was spelled either 'Sarah' or 'Sara' by her family, but Coleridge always addressed her as Sara, i.e. with a long first 'a'. His wife was always Sarah. In every sense, Aunt Sara was Mrs STC's rival.

---

* One symptom of morphine addiction is that maintaining close relations with one's immediate circle becomes impossible. The sufferer will accuse these people of neglect and cruelty and in the meantime seek what Molly Lefebure has described as a 'small handful of "in-group" persons upon whom he can rely for uncritical sympathy and condolence'. Inevitably, when this group becomes too close, too human, they fail. See Molly Lefebure, *Bondage of Opium* (Worcester and London: The Trinity Press, 1974).

Yet even without knowing any of their history, Sara took strongly against Aunt Sara during her 1808 stay. She experienced her antipathy in the terms of a five-year-old: the woman was objectionable, plain and dumpy. Meanwhile STC waxed lyrical about Aunt Sara's kind eyes and soft hair. Begrudgingly the little girl acknowledged Aunt Sara had beautiful hair.[12] The image is strange – a father extolling the virtues of his would-be lover to his infant daughter who forms her own, very different opinions. It is particularly poignant given that Sara's mother wore a wig because her (once beautiful) hair had fallen out after the death of her second child, Berkeley, in 1799, when STC was absent in Malta.

Sara could see her father already had good relationships with the Wordsworth children, particularly Dora. The fact they all found it easy to hug and kiss him made Sara profoundly anxious. She could not do the same. Dora was STC's great pet – he called her his 'beautiful Cat of the Mountain' – and together they would romp and shriek on the stairs, in defiance of Aunt Dorothy and Dora's father who pleaded quiet for their headaches and poetry respectively.[13] The naughtier Dora was, the prettier STC thought she became.[14] Sara was unable to love her father as he wanted, since 'truly nothing does so freeze affection as the breath of Jealousy'.[15] When he approached her, she instinctively recoiled. STC reproached her and told her to be more like Dora with her ready caresses. She slunk away and hid in the wood behind the house. John was the only one to find and comfort her. Years later, recalling that September stay, she vowed never to say to her children: '. . . "Alas – why don't you love me?" . . . for love is an emotion and cannot be compelled.'[16] She knew, in the way children do, that there was something off-kilter about her father's desire to win his daughter's affirmation. As an adult, she could see that in the war between STC and his estranged wife that autumn, Coleridge's motives 'at bottom must have been a wish to fasten my affections on him'. At the time, it only served to intensify her loneliness at being separated from her home and her mother.

Wordsworth was no easier to please. Early one evening Sara

was playing with Dora in the garden. Wordsworth, looking proudly at his daughter, exclaimed at how lovely simple sleeveless dresses looked on little girls: their bare arms lent any scene an air of rustic simplicity. Sara was wearing a grand long-sleeved lace-trimmed dress and smart scarlet socks. The barb of the comment still stung forty years later – the feeling she always got things wrong. Wordsworth was not entirely consistent, but he had strong and often pioneering theories on the subjects of children's health, appearance and education.* He believed in the importance of allowing children to roam the countryside 'wild and free' in order to grow and learn. He had strong opinions about what wild and free children looked like. They should appear picturesque – a romantic version of the peasant children who peopled the *Lyrical Ballads*. Wordsworth favoured Prussian Blue for dresses. Coleridge broadly agreed with him but preferred simple white smocks. Neither was in keeping with Sara's elegantly fussy clothes. At home, Mrs STC dressed her children with a 'taste for the grand'.

Dora's Aunt Dorothy endorsed all the Allan Bank views. Children ought to not only appear wild and free but also be sturdy and healthy. Sara felt she was constantly letting her father down. By comparison with Dora, she was 'timid' with a 'little fair delicate face muffled up in a lace border and muslin'. Sara was brought up to see herself as weak and fragile, despite being a perfectly healthy child. Her mother raised her on the story that, as a toddler, she had fallen into a river and been sickly ever since. At Allan Bank she continued to make the wrong impression. With the scarlet socks, grand clothes and lace cap her mother had sent her in, she irked her father. STC was so under the Allan Bank spell that he could only see Sara through their eyes, and he was not above using her as a conduit through which to express his antipathy towards his wife. One day, wearing a smart new 'stuff frock', she ran to meet him: 'he took me up and set me down without a caress. I thought I had displeased

* Wordsworth's great autobiographical poem, *The Prelude*, can be read as his defence of natural education.

him.'[17] Only later did it occur to her that it was her clothes he had disliked.

Everyone favoured and admired Dora for her long golden ringlets, never cut and kept in curling papers which were – as Sara later noted – slightly against the poetic philosophy of the household. Wordsworth described her as having 'angelic hair'.[18] Early in Sara's stay, STC, wanting to endear himself to his host, asked Sara if she did not think Dora and her locks beautiful. Sara refused to perform. 'No,' she said bluntly. For this, she 'met with a rebuff which made me feel as if I was a culprit'. The Wordsworths and her father 'boasted that [Sara] was rosier after a month's stay at Grasmere' but being moulded into someone else's idea of a good shape is never a comfortable experience.

New insights into the adult world apart, it was the painful feeling of extreme homesickness that Sara remembered most from her visit. She missed her mother and found the dark terrifying. Her father was only partially helpful. When he came to bed at midnight or one in the morning, he would wake her up and tell her fairy-tales. The imagination that created the Ancient Mariner and his slimy things and the flashing eyes and floating hair of Kubla Khan's poet-narrator is not the one most of us would choose for bedtime stories and gave her nightmares. She hadn't yet heard of 'goblins, demons, devils, boggles, burglarists, elves and witches', so instead she dreamed about lions, the ghost in Hamlet and 'the picture of Death at Hellgate in an old edition of Paradise Lost' which she'd found in the library at home.[19] As an adult, Sara's inner world would both torture and fascinate her. At five, this strongly felt conflict between inner and outer world – fear and calm – was mostly the contrast between night and day. Adults saw a pretty little thing, charming all she met, wide-eyed and curious, who repeated fairy-tales to the servants and played with John and Dora in the garden of Allan Bank. But at night she suffered from nightmares and sleeplessness. As Sara grew up the split between the light and dark remained just as intense and became a constant theme in her writing.

How gladsome is the child, and how perfect is his mirth
How brilliant to his eye are the daylight shows of earth!
But Oh! how black and strange are the shadows of his sight,
What phantoms hover round him in the darkness of the
    night![20]

Sara wrote her poem almost thirty years later; by then the
phantoms were different but she would never make the common
adult mistake of downplaying children's feelings. She always
recognised that though pleasures and horrors may change their
childhood forms, they retain their impact. In the autumn of
1808, though Sara was not yet six, she was already aware of a
darker world hovering beyond her own. Later, she saw in her
time at Allan Bank 'the shadow of a shade'. By the start of
October, Sara had had enough; when her mother arrived to
collect her, she clung to Mrs STC's skirts and wept for she had
experienced a 'good deal of misera'lity'.[21] Her father, of course,
was furious at this unWordsworthian performance.

'Mild Offspring of Infirm Humanity'

What must Dora, just turned four, have made of Sara who was
twenty months – and half a lifetime older? Unlike Sara who left
a memoir of this period, Dora left no record of her thoughts.
She was, in any case, almost too young to be able to form opinions based upon experience. Psychologists make a distinction
between the kind of friendships made before and after the age
of five. Before five it seems that friends are quickly made and
forgotten. A convenient, amenable playmate is a friend, while
strong antipathy is felt towards those who disrupt the child's
world in any way – and Sara was disruptive of Dora's world.
    Before Sara arrived in September 1808, Dora was the only
girl at Allan Bank and beloved of mother, father, aunts and STC.
Now Sara was a rival for the attention of these heroes. Sara
slept in STC's bed and it seemed to be her reaction he looked
for when he played with them. When STC settled down to tell

the children a 'wild tale', it was the sight of Sara's 'large eyes
[which] grew almost as large again with wonderment' which
pleased him.[22] John was apparently going to marry her.
Meanwhile, Dora's parents and aunts turned their attention
towards the new baby girl, Cate.

Dora's first four years had been spent, as all who visited
could see, as 'the apple of her father's eyes'.[23] She was born on
16 August 1804 in Town End Cottage. Sara and her mother
and brothers were staying at the house at the time, so Sara and
Dora's relationship had begun at birth. Town End, Dora's home
until the move to Allan Bank, is nestled in the hills above
Grasmere in Cumbria. It has been skilfully preserved by the
Wordsworth Trust and appears today much as it did then, a tiny
whitewashed cottage, with exquisite views over Rydal Water and
a small tumbling garden. As far as Wordsworth was concerned,
it was 'sweet paradise' until 1805, when the view was ruined by
a new building called Allan Bank. Afterwards, the view from his
cottage included 'staring you in the face, upon that beautiful
ridge that elbows out in to the vale (behind the church and
towering above its steeple) a temple of abomination'.[24] The
abominable Allan Bank did not conform nearly so well to the
rustic idyll of the *Lyrical Ballads*. It was a sad irony that within
three years the need for a larger affordable house had driven
Wordsworth to live in the abhorrent temple.

Despite the view, Town End, – a 'little white cottage gleaming
from the midst of trees' – charmed Wordsworth just as it charms
tourists today. The main room had a single 'perfect and unpre-
tending cottage window, with little diamond panes, embowered
. . . with roses; and, in the summer and autumn, with a profusion
of jessamine and other fragrant shrubs'.[25] But the cottage was
small – considering the number of people living in it – and, even
when the sun shone, dark. The kitchen was dank and gloomy
and the sleeping arrangements crowded. The house had six
rooms, four upstairs and two downstairs, plus the back kitchen.
Normally Aunt Dorothy had a downstairs bedroom and William
and Mary the main one upstairs. The children shared a tiny room
which Aunt Dorothy had lined with newspaper for warmth. This

left a single bedroom besides Wordsworth's study. Staying with them at the time of Dora's birth were Mrs STC and her three children plus Dora's Aunt Sara Hutchinson who arrived the day afterwards and became a more or less permanent member of the household. Some of the children may have been farmed out to neighbours – if not, they had ten people in three bedrooms. Either way, housekeeping the poet's home cannot have been much fun. For children, however, it was an idyllic place. The steep garden is just the size to be a perfect knowable world.

When the children played outside it gave Aunt Dorothy and Mary a chance to manage some of their own tasks. For the early part of the children's lives they were also helped by an old lady named Molly Fisher. Molly scoured the dishes, washed clothes and ironed for three hours a day.[26] After she left in 1804 a younger girl took over and stayed with them until Dora was four. Even with this help the amount of work was tremendous. They had a weekly wash for small items and every five weeks a 'great wash'. Great washes took four days; Molly – and later her replacement – did the bulk of the work, but another girl would be hired for a few days to assist. All the women helped with the business of ironing and starching and laying the clothes out to dry. Whenever it was wet – which was often – drying clothes had to be pegged up inside and around the small fires. The house steamed and the windows fogged up. There was endless sewing and repairing. All women were taught needlework, but Aunt Dorothy was considered to be particularly talented and made everything from dresses for the children to mattresses created out of sacking bought in Ambleside. She was a good thrifty housekeeper and when the children showed her torn clothes, they were allowed to choose a patch from her bag of rags. Between the washing of dishes, brewing of beer and cooking of meals, activity in the kitchen was constant. The larger household tasks, such as grinding paint and whitewashing walls, also fell to the women, assisted – or impeded – by the various children.[27] But all this domesticity was put aside when Mary went into labour on 16 August.

Dora entered the world as the second child of a poet with a complicated reputation. The popular version of literary history tells us the *Lyrical Ballads* were instantly recognised as a revolutionary challenge to all that had gone before and as such were savagely criticised.[28] In fact, the first volume was published anonymously and, before Dora's birth, the reviews were mostly positive. *Lyrical Ballads* did not cause an overnight sensation; no one seemed to notice the Birth of the Romantic Era of Literature, but there was general agreement that the volume was significant and interesting.[29] (Ironically, Southey wrote the most critical article.) *Lyrical Ballads* sold respectably and in 1800 the publisher Longman printed a new edition. (The 1800 version of *Lyrical Ballads* actually appeared in January 1801 but delays in the printing meant the title page says 1800.) In this second edition, Wordsworth's name alone appeared on the title page, but despite this he remained a reasonably obscure poet: by no means a household name. What he was doing was highly experimental. Wordsworth wanted to be able to write about the poor and the humble in language that was simple and true rather than grand and 'poetic'. The second edition received only one serious review (in the *British Critic*), which was at least broadly positive.[30]

By the time Dora was born in 1804, the tide of criticism had begun to turn. In 1802 Francis Jeffrey, a Scottish lawyer and critic, used the newly created *Edinburgh Review* to savage what he saw as a new sect of poets.[31] His article was nominally a review of a new volume by Southey, but his targets were clearly Wordsworth and Coleridge who had, in his view, overturned the old rules of poetry without creating any new ones of value. It was the start of a popular movement against Wordsworth (and to a lesser extent Coleridge) which only increased as the years went by. Not, of course, that toddling Sara or the newborn Dora would have been aware of any of the affairs of high poetry. And nor perhaps, on 16 August, was Wordsworth, as he saw his new daughter for the first time, loosely wrapped, but not swaddled, which was considered dangerous, and lying beside Mary.[32]

Somehow it was Dora, rather than his first child John, who

made Wordsworth feel the miracle of childbirth. 'She is her father's darling,' Dorothy had written in 1804, 'I think he is more tender than ever he was over her brother.'[33] Dorothy herself took a different view. In her opinion, fourteen-month-old John was 'extraordinary', while Dora was merely 'a nice baby, healthy enough'.[34] But Wordsworth was instantly besotted and wrote countless poems about her or inspired by her. This 'Mild Offspring of infirm humanity' – his daughter – was 'the second glory of the heavens'.[35] He was proud of his paternal love which, it seemed to him, was somehow more extraordinary, even more civilised, than the instinctive love of the mother. It was all this love which Sara's presence in the autumn of 1808 seemed to disrupt.

Dora began to throw tantrums. Aunt Dorothy, filled with disapproval, described Dora's temper and her 'abominable' habits which included the unpardonable sin of clicking her tongue against the roof of her mouth.[36] The aunts deemed her stubborn and ungovernable. Dora's family may have thought Sara Coleridge acted too much the little lady; but her manners only threw Dora's into sharper relief. Tantrums, Dora's instinctive response, showed a passion that she spent much of her life attempting to subdue, with tragic results.

Dora was good at being wild and free and this was a Good Thing – as far as the amateur child psychologists of Allan Bank were concerned. Sara's presence, however, reminded them all that she was less able to behave in an appropriately feminine manner. Her family, and Aunt Dorothy in particular, decided she needed to be 'broken' – perhaps she should even be sent away to school. It was probably with relief that she watched Sara depart after a month.

Sara's father lived with the Wordsworths for the next eighteen months. Young as Dora was, it was clear STC was not an easy house-guest. He shut himself up his room and was cross and depressed. He took too much laudanum and couldn't sleep. He suffered from horrific nightmares and would frequently wake the children from their sleep with shrieks. Dora's Aunt Dorothy

would be despatched to calm him. He would demand complicated food at odd times of the day and night and complain about
his living arrangements. Aunt Dorothy grumbled – she had his
parlour to clean, his fire to light and 'his bed always to be made
at an unreasonable time'. He would sleep all morning, exclaimed
Dorothy in self-righteous astonishment, even in 'this beautiful
valley'.[37] Cooking for him – even simple dishes like boiled eggs
– was a nightmare. The eggs had to be 'kept in boiling water
one minute, folded up in a napkin for a minute and a half, &
then put into the boiling water which is now to be removed and
kept from the fire, & kept there with the saucepan covered from
4 to 6 minutes, depending on the size of the eggs'.[38] Finally, not
content with salt, he needed to sprinkle cayenne pepper over
the eggs, which he ate from a tea-cup. STC suffered from
constipation and stomach aches; one moment he was cheerful,
the next distraught, and the children found the changes frightening. Aunt Dorothy was crestfallen. 'It has been misery enough,
God knows, to me to see the truths which I now see.'[39]

Coleridge was supposed to be writing a journal called *The Friend*.
To do this he locked himself in the parlour with Aunt Sara and
dictated to her for hours on end. He seemed to be finding this
harder and harder. Aunt Dorothy, never a particularly cheerful
person anyway, was distraught. 'We have no hope of him,' she
told her friend Catherine Clarkson. 'His whole time and thoughts,
except when he is reading . . . are employed in deceiving himself,
and seeking to deceive others. He will tell me that he has . . .
written, half a *Friend;* when I know for a fact that he has not
written a single line.'[40] STC was no longer fun.
      Later Dora and Sara would learn that the friendship
between STC and Wordsworth was strained and complicated.
The decline had begun around 1800, when they planned the
second edition of the *Lyrical Ballads* in which both had intended
to include poems.* The first volume included Wordsworth's

* Often referred to as a second edition of *Lyrical Ballads*, this was a strange
publication. Its full name was *Lyrical Ballads, with Other Poems, In Two Volumes,*

famous Preface – a defence of his poetry. STC's contribution
was to be a long supernatural ballad called 'Christabel'.
However, after much deliberation, Wordsworth rejected it and
'Christabel' was not included. Historians disagree over whether
this was a brutal assertion of dominance by Wordsworth, or a
mutual agreement that the poem was discordant with the rest
of the volume and, perhaps more to the point, that it was
unfinished. Whatever the truth, their relationship had begun
to deteriorate. In the end, the edition included one new short
poem by Coleridge ('Love') and many new poems by
Wordsworth. After much debate this edition still included 'The
Rhyme of the Ancient Mariner', but Wordsworth printed a
dismissive note about the poem, apologising for its 'great
defects'. STC had allowed himself to become subservient to
Wordsworth, while Wordsworth depended on STC's belief that
he, Wordsworth, was the greatest poet since Milton. A rot had
set into the friendship which damaged each man professionally
and personally. The unease, mistrust and distance would
become a central thread in the pattern of their lives, and the
lives of their daughters.

Nearly a decade later, STC still adored Wordsworth. He
adored him as much as he denigrated himself. 'That there is
such a man in the World as Wordsworth,' he had sighed to a
friend that year, 'and that such a man enjoys such a Family,
makes both my Death & my inefficient Life a less grievous
Thought to me.'[41] In his adulation he created a myth which
both men and their families had to live with, for better or worse,
until Dora and Sara began as adults to unpick the story.
Meanwhile STC could do nothing to lessen his hopelessness as
a house-guest or his own misery.

Despite the strain of living together, from time to time
Wordsworth and Coleridge would rekindle their former passion
in conversation. The pair were often joined by Thomas de
Quincey, a young admirer and acolyte, who had recently moved

---

but the first volume was also described, on the title page, as a second edition,
while the second volume was not.

to the area expressly to be near his hero Wordsworth. In the evenings, the three men paced up and down the rooms putting the world to rights. On the frequent occasions when Sara came to stay, she and Dora would, unnoticed, trail their fathers and de Quincey. The children 'understood not, nor listened to a word they said' but longed to interrupt. De Quincey's handkerchief poked out of the back pocket of his trousers and Sara itched to pull it out. She was disgruntled for he had promised to marry her and now she thought he behaved 'faithlessly' in not claiming her hand. Sara was keen on weddings at this stage in her life, not unusual in a little girl, but poignant when one considers the parlous state of her own parents' marriage. Hour after hour the girls watched and listened as the men paced, gravely and earnestly 'discussing the affairs of the nation, as if it all came home to their business and bosoms, as if it were their private concern!'[42]

More often the men quarrelled, often about money. Sara's father had a large appetite but at Allan Bank everyone was expected to eat porridge for at least two meals a day. The Wordsworths had never been renowned for their hospitality: Sir Walter Scott famously used to climb out of the window and escape to the nearest inn when he was fed up with eating nothing but oatmeal.* The Wordsworths had stopped buying tea, because Aunt Dorothy had realised that the previous year they had spent £15 on Twinings – the same amount as their Allan Bank rent.[43] STC, however, refused to stop drinking tea. He told anyone who would listen that for him tea was 'an absolute necessary, if not of Life, yet of literary exertion'.[44] He also made a secret arrangement with the public house to have a supply of spirits delivered to him. But even with the tea and the alcohol he stopped writing *The Friend* and spent whole days in bed. Eventually Aunt Sara – whom Dora adored – drove away to stay

---

* This story originated with Ralph Waldo Emerson, who visited Rydal Mount in 1833 and 1848 and heard the story from a local mill owner. Emerson recorded it in letters and included the tale in a book he wrote called *English Traits*.

with cousins. She could not manage him and once she left STC collapsed altogether.

Dora's father was no less gloomy than Sara's. 'London wits and witlings lack the capacity to respond to poetry' was his constant grumble. The problem was that 'these people in the senseless hurry of their idle lives do not *read* books, they merely snatch a glance at them that they might talk about them'.[45] Wordsworth was beginning to fear his greatest poetry was behind him. The pressures (and the noise and activities) of being the head of a large and expanding household were significant. When Wordsworth had moved to a cottage in the Lake District (to the despair of his relations who had wanted him to be a lawyer), he was a romantic young man with only a sister to support. By the time he was installed at Allan Bank, those days were over. Now he had four children plus Coleridge to support and Mary was pregnant again. Sara's older brothers, Hartley and Derwent, who were weekly boarders at nearby Ambleside, spent the weekends at Allan Bank, and had to be fed. The problem was his poetry was not selling well: he did not have enough money.

In 1807, Wordsworth had published a new book: *Poems in Two Volumes*. It contained poems we now consider near-perfect, 'To the Small Celandine', for example, and 'Ode. Intimations of Immortality from Recollections of Early Childhood'.

> Whither is fled the visionary gleam?
> Where is it now, the glory and the dream?
>
> Our birth is but a sleep and a forgetting:
> The Soul that rises with us, our life's Star,
> Hath had elsewhere its setting,
> And cometh from afar:
> Not in entire forgetfulness,
> And not in utter nakedness,
> But trailing clouds of glory do we come
> From God, who is our home:
> Heaven lies about us in our infancy![46]

It was savaged by the critics. Francis Jeffrey in the *Edinburgh Review* described it as 'illegible and unintelligible'.[47] Byron, just nineteen years old and beginning to build his own reputation as a poet, considered the book 'namby pamby'.[48] Jeffrey twice called it 'trash'.[48] The consensus was that Wordsworth had not lived up to the expectations of the *Lyrical Ballads* (a volume which they all belatedly now agreed was brilliant). Again and again the critics said he stuck too rigidly to his new 'system' of writing which was an 'open violation of the established laws of poetry'.[49] He wrote about trivial topics and he made himself ridiculous.

Wordsworth was devastated. He grew ever more convinced that the reading public needed to be re-educated, but the response – including that of friends – was almost unbearable. A saving grace was that he also attracted passionate admirers: men and women, such as Thomas de Quincey, who had understood how to read his poetry and who represented the way poetry would be received in the future. These people recognised his genius and sought him out. He became a cause célèbre, a tourist attraction for fans and for fashionable London travellers keen to meet the poet who, from a cottage in Cumberland, was dividing the literary establishment.

Notoriety did not translate into income, unfortunately, and STC's presence made the atmosphere ever more tense. Sara continued to make visits to see her father and Dora and as time passed the girls became close. However, despite the fact Sara worshipped her brothers and her father, it was always a relief to leave Allan Bank and return to Greta Hall. And, given the troubles at home, Southey's household at Greta Hall became a sanctuary for Dora too.

CHAPTER 2

'THE AUNT-HILL'

1810

Sara was really the reason the Southeys lived at Greta Hall. In August 1803, Robert and Edith Southey's baby Margaret had died at their home in Bristol. Even before the child was actually dead, Southey hit upon the idea of going to Keswick to visit Edith's sister, Mrs STC. He thought he could 'try and graft' her baby Sara 'into the wound while it is yet fresh'. As soon as Margaret died, they rushed off to Greta Hall, where the Coleridges were living, for a short stay. In his desperation to flee his personal tragedy, Southey hadn't reckoned on how Sara would 'sting' them all.[1] Nonetheless Greta Hall suited and Southey invited his wife's third sister, Mary Lovell, a widow with a young son named Robert, to come and stay too. Their visit extended on, all through the most turbulent years of the Coleridges' marriage. Southey always intended to leave. It wasn't until 1807 that he decided to make Greta Hall his permanent home. That February STC had written from Town End to his estranged wife, to say that, as soon as the Southeys left, he planned to move into Greta Hall bringing all the Wordsworths. With typical thoughtlessness, STC thought it the perfect solution to the fact that Wordsworth needed a bigger house. Mrs STC and Sara – whom he apparently did not see as part of the new household – would have been homeless. Mrs STC was 'almost frantic' with worry.[2] Southey, hearing about the plan, was furious: 'It is out of the question', he reassured Mrs STC and promptly took up the lease himself.[3] Southey had always had dreams of returning, one day, to Portugal. In that moment, he gave them up.

This gave Mrs STC and her children a secure home, but it also placed them in an awkward position of dependency. It meant too that Southey became a more real father to Sara and her brothers than Coleridge, and it brought Southey permanently into the orbit of the Lakeland poets. Subsequently the trio of men and their households became a literary centre that attracted satellites from around the world. Their wives and families merged into an extended family: a spider's web of relationships built on love and envy, rivalry and fierce loyalty.

Southey called Greta Hall the 'Aunt-Hill' since it was a hive of industry, filled with aunts and governed according to a strict routine. The older children had lessons with Mrs STC or another of the aunts from 9.30 in the morning until 4 in the afternoon – when they all had dinner together.[4] Within this time half an hour was set aside for dressing and one hour for walking. Walks were an important part of daily life at Greta Hall; Southey went out every day between dinner and 6 p.m. dressed in a blue cap and a fawn coat with a book in his hand (in winter it was always a 'bottle-green great coat').[5] Local people had great respect for his orderliness. 'I never seed him wi' a button off in my life' said one old man who knew him. Sara and the other children, one of them on the Greta donkey (known as the noble jackass), often accompanied him. Southey couldn't pass a child without stopping to pat it on the head and exchange a few words. He returned at 6 o'clock for tea with the household, after which he would write letters in his library while the children were readied for bed.[6]

In the summer of 1810, Keswick's calm was briefly interrupted; following eighteen months at Allan Bank, Sara's father returned to Greta for a stay. It was not an easy time for anyone. STC behaved most oddly. He washed his hands a hundred times a day, even when they were perfectly clean, even when Sara had already seen him wash just minutes before.[7] Southey could hardly stand to be in the same room as him anymore. Yet Sara had been brought up on tales of how STC and Southey had once been the best of friends. She knew that as young men they had dreamed of building a utopian world. He and Southey and a number of

other friends and their wives were going to become 'Pantisocrats';
they would sail away to America, to the banks of the Susquehanna
River in Pennsylvania, and there they would create a model society:
a commune, where all would be equal. Their womenfolk were
to come with them, and it was really in preparation that STC
had speedily married Southey's sister-in-law. It was a beautiful,
unrealistic idea; they chose the Susquehanna as a suitable location only because STC liked the sound of the word. Southey
was the first to acknowledge it was all a dream – and that was
the beginning of the end of their friendship.

By the time of STC's summer visit in 1810, Southey, the
responsible King of the Aunt Hill, thought that STC's habits
were 'murderous of all domestic comfort'. It seemed he did 'all
things at all times except the proper time – does nothing he
ought to do and everything which he ought not to'.[8] STC was
still trying and failing to write *The Friend*; Mrs STC was reduced
to tears by the sight of the journal – she was growing increasingly terrified that STC would never be able to provide her and
her children with a secure income.[9] Sara was just beginning to
understand there was no guarantee Uncle Southey would always
look after her as he would his own children.

Throughout that summer, while Sara's brothers were home
from boarding school for the holidays, STC made an effort to
be as cheerful as possible. He was convinced Hartley was a
genius and found Derwent – whom he nicknamed Stumpy
Canary for his yellow breeches – a source of great pleasure and
amusement.[10] But once they returned to Ambleside he became
restless; try as she might, Sara's presence was not enough to
keep him at Greta Hall. He admired her 'Kalligraphical
Initiations' and wrote her a dialogue on the Italian language.[11]
But he was bored. Greta was damp; he was unhappy. (In fact,
he was feeling suicidal, but with considerable effort he disguised
this from his wife and children and the Southeys.)[12] A few weeks
into the autumn term, STC left for London. Sara studied calmly
in preparation for his return, but once again, Greta Hall settled
back into a more normal routine. Southey did not think STC
would manage in London. He thought he should come back

and try three months without opium, but Coleridge ignored him and even left his letters unopened, and so that was that.[13]

While Sara's world had been upturned by STC's presence, Dora had an equally turbulent time after his departure. In the months after STC went to London, Dora and her siblings caught the whooping cough. Just before STC left Allan Bank, Mary had given birth to a baby named William (known as Willy), which brought the total number of children to five. They all had to be taken out of Allan Bank to recuperate in another house (with less smoky chimneys). They stayed for a few weeks and had more or less recovered when they returned home to find the dreaded scarlet fever on their doorstep. So almost immediately they set off to stay with a friend of Dora's father, John Wilson, at Elleray House on the shores of Lake Windermere, eight miles from Grasmere.* He was another of the men who loved Wordsworth and moved to the Lakes to be near him.† He had spent his inheritance on a cottage and estate in Windermere and over time his home became a literary haven. Guests included not only Wordsworth and Southey but also Charles Lloyd, Sir Walter Scott and John Gibson Lockhart.

Dora liked Mr Wilson. The mood always lightened when he was nearby. Aunt Dorothy and her mother teased him; they

* John Wilson, poet, scholar and man of letters, is now most famous for presiding over the influential Tory *Blackwood's Magazine*. The magazine was founded in 1817 and Wilson became its principal writer soon after, though never, officially, its editor. Using the pseudonym Christopher North, he grew notorious for his often vicious reviews. Wilson wrote prolifically and was a key personality in the nineteenth-century literary scene. The picturesque Elleray House, on the shores of Lake Windermere, is currently Windermere Preparatory School.

† Initially the Wordsworths took to Wilson; Dorothy described him in 1808 as a 'very amiable young man, a Friend and *adorer* of William and his verses'. (DW to Catherine Clarkson, 28 March 1808; *WW LMY*, II, p. 206). For many years the family was close to the young bachelor Dorothy nicknamed 'The Beau'. But their friendship did not last; in the end both Wordsworth and Wilson felt betrayed by one another (see Mary Gordon and Mackenzie Shelton. *Christopher North*).

despaired at his inability to ever have a good pen and ink or clean hands. Dora knew he had harum scarum friends – 'The Windermere Gentlemen' – and her aunts thought he was impossible to manage and obstinate, but she knew too they smiled when talking about him.[14] He was excellent at boats and picnics and, sickness permitting, took her and her siblings out on Lake Windermere. He made the children laugh despite their whooping. But, even with the best efforts of their host, there were not many smiles to be had at Elleray. The whooping cough dragged on. The children reinfected one another again and again until it reached a point where nobody had slept through a night for months.

Eventually they returned to Allan Bank in time for Christmas 1810. Dora, John and baby Willy had just about recovered, but Tom and Cate remained sickly. Their ceaseless coughing and vomiting meant they were under-nourished: Cate had been 'worn to a skeleton' until she took on the 'appearance of a child raised in Gin-Alley'.[15] In the end their mother took Cate and Tom away to lodgings in Ambleside to be nearer their physician, Dr Scambler. It was an agonising time for Wordsworth. Whooping cough killed thousands of children every year and his had been unwell for some time. He was so busy – and so anxious – that Coleridge's movements barely registered. It was this preoccupation with the children, as much as anything else, that meant Wordsworth was quite oblivious to what everyone in literary London was talking about: his 'quarrel' with STC.

What nobody in the Lakes knew was that as soon as STC had reached London, he had fallen out of love with Wordsworth with all the passion, hatred and self-loathing of a spurned lover. His drama had begun in the summer of 1810 when STC told Wordsworth about his plan to stay in London with mutual friends named Montagu. It had seemed a sound enough plan to Wordsworth, but he felt duty-bound to warn the Montagus about STC's living habits. What he did not know was that Montagu (and one has to question his motives) told Coleridge the gist of Wordsworth's comments. Between Montagu's telling and Coleridge's hearing, the criticism and hurtfulness of what

Wordsworth had said (in confidence) was exaggerated, the result being that Coleridge felt Wordsworth had betrayed him. 'W. authorised M. to tell me, he had no Hope of me!' he recorded in his diary with despair.[16] He could not believe this was how fifteen years of friendship had been rewarded. As he understood it, Wordsworth had told Montagu that 'for years past [I] had been an ABSOLUTE NUISANCE in the Family'.[17] STC sank into an opium-fuelled despair from which he intermittently wrote devastating accounts of Wordsworth's behaviour to anyone he thought would be interested and sympathetic. Gossip spread – the quarrel was *the* topic of London drawing rooms and drinking clubs. Yet with all the illness in his family, Wordsworth had troubles of his own and simply did not notice.

On the other hand, relationships between the two houses, Greta Hall and Allan Bank, eased with the departure of STC. Once again, sickness permitting, children and poets flowed back and forth across the Raise. By now the Southeys had four children: Edith, Herbert and the little ones, Bertha and Kate. Their baby Emma had died the year before – Dora and Sara's first shocking encounter with death. Dora's brother Tom was best friends with Herbert Southey; Edith was between Dora and Sara in age; all the Southey, Coleridge and Wordsworth children formed a gang, constantly in and out of one another's houses. The three girls – Dora, Edith and Sara – were bosom companions. Even Mrs STC and Dora's aunts were becoming friends. Mrs STC asked Aunt Sara to come and visit her at Greta Hall; during the course of the visit, in 1811, the two women quarrelled about STC. Aunt Sara offended Mrs STC by criticising STC's behaviour. Mrs STC sprang to her husband's defence, outraged that Aunt Sara should speak ill of him. When Aunt Sara confessed 'everything that I say to you *have I said to himself* – and all that I believe of him now I believed formerly' some of Mrs STC's anger was assuaged.[18] Ultimately, it was clear her love for STC was greater – it had survived the betrayals where Aunt Sara's

had not – and it enabled the two women to make their peace
with one another. Besides, with STC away, any rivalry was a
moot point.

Whenever Dora stayed at Greta Hall she enjoyed an order
and discipline which was entirely lacking at home. Where Allan
Bank had smoking chimneys, a pig, a cow and chickens, Greta
had a well-organised library and an ever-increasing number of
cats. Meals at Keswick were different to those at Allan Bank.
At home, Wordsworth would appear at the table untidy and
distracted. He read and murmured lines between mouthfuls of
toast while slicing uncut pages in new books with a buttery
knife.[19] If he asked his wife or sister – or later Dora – the
expectation was that she should leave her porridge to get cold
and rush to scribble down whatever it was he said. The other
women would fetch his tea and find the sugar. Wordsworth's
nephew, Christopher Wordsworth, had a point when he said
later, 'If Providence had not blessed him [Wordsworth] with a
wife, a sister, a wife's sister, and a daughter, whose lives were
bound up in his life . . . and who felt that his poems were
destined for immortality, and that it was no small privilege to
be instrumental in conveying them to posterity, it is probable
that many of his verses, muttered by him . . . would have been
scattered to the winds.'[20] At Keswick breakfasts, by contrast,
Southey, always immaculately dressed, superintended the
making of the toast. He invariably spent most of the meal
coaxing his wife to take 'this or that dainty morsel, stirring her
tea for her, sweetening it to her taste, buttering her toast or
joking with the children'. His own breakfast went untasted until
it was cold.[21]

Southey's married life, like Mrs STC's, ought to have been
sad. After baby Emma's death, Edith Southey had begun a
decline into madness which would eventually see her sent to
an asylum. Yet, like Mrs STC, Southey remained loyal to his
spouse and determined to build a safe and happy childhood for
the brood of children under his care. Together, he and Mrs
STC were an indomitable force and life at Greta was built on

the solidity of their relationship.* Mrs STC, aided and abetted by Southey, invented a ridiculous 'Lingo Grande'. It was Mrs Coleridge's creation, but everybody used it with great enthusiasm. Sara taught Dora that at Greta, children's feet were 'trottlykins', mist was 'fogrugrum' and when a dog misbehaved they would holler 'dogrorggarum' at it. Mrs STC (known as the Venerable) addressed Southey as a 'detesty, a maffrum, a goffrum, a chatterpye, a sillicum and a great mawkinfort' and he accepted them – though he made a great show of complaining to the children that she ought not to call him names, since he was a 'serious man' and it was 'not decorous in a woman of her age'. When he whidgetted her chair it made her cross and she red-raggified him in full comfabulumpatus. The childerōapusses shrieked with laughter. 'She called me a Tomnoddycum,' he complained, 'though my name, as she knows, is Robert.'[22]

When the weather was warm enough for them to play outside, the girls 'went to the grove/and picked purple bilberries near the bright lake'. Later, fingers stained purple, they made 'excellent' pies.[23] Or rather, as Mrs STC trilled, 'pie-ie-ies' and 'pudding-udding-uddings'.[24] Standing on stools to mix the pastry they made a good mess before rushing outside to climb to the top of a favourite beech tree.[25] When it rained they spent their time on the top floor of the house. Here there were 'six rooms, a nursery, nursery bedroom, landing place, maids bedroom . . . a lumber room, and a dark apple room, which used to be the supposed abode of a boggle'. To escape the boggle was a 'way out upon the roof, and a way out upon the leads over one wing of the house'. From here they could see as far as Penrith Road, Brow Top and the Saddleback of the region.

Entering from the kitchen garden rather than the front door, Dora and Sara skirted the drooping laburnum and took off muddy outdoor clogs. The house was divided into two. The

---

* Indeed, such was the closeness and affection with which they addressed one another that it is interesting to speculate whether, following the deaths of Coleridge and Mrs Southey, they might have married. As it was, the law prohibited marriage to a wife's sibling until 1907.

landlord, Mr Jackson, and his wife lived on the right; Sara and the Southeys lived in the larger left-hand side. In the yard Dapper, Southey's dog, and Cupid, Jackson's, might be worrying the cats. In the large, stone-flagged kitchen, Wilsy, the children's beloved nurse, might be found, wearing her white neckerchief across her breast, rolling pastry or feeding a baby – a tabby cat purring at her ankles. From the kitchen, a passage led the girls past the parlour (where poor gloomy Aunt Lovell sat), past the dining room (which they called Peter), the breakfast room (Paul) and the sitting room to the mangling room.

Everything at Greta had an order. In the mangling room, 'clog shoes were arranged from the biggest to the least & curiously emblemed the various stages of life'. Presiding over the order (besides Mrs STC, Southey and the various Southey aunts) was Wilsy, who scolded and petted all the children who came through the house. Dora and Sara placed their clogs amongst the lanterns and ice-skates, rugs, coats and general paraphernalia of picnics and outdoor activities and, returning, took the staircase to the right of the kitchen, which you climbed from the passage and which led to a landing place filled with bookcases. Every day from breakfast until 4 p.m. Southey sat in his study at the end of the landing and was not supposed to be disturbed (though when he was he might be persuaded to mimic all the animals of a farmyard for the amusement of the children). Southey made up the tale of the Three Bears for them, played boisterous games and commanded picnics and expeditions.* All the children loved Southey's study, known as the Cottonian Room, where they were allowed to help put little cotton coats on all the books.

A few steps beyond the Cottonian took Sara and Dora to the little room Sara shared with her mother. This room had a view over Greta River and, beyond, the mighty Skiddaw

---

* Southey's original 'Three Bears' tale has a very different plot to the version we know today. Southey's protagonist was a little old lady, not a golden-haired girl. Over the next fifty years, the 'crafty' old lady turned into a pretty young girl. She settled as Goldilocks in 1904.

Mountain. From her bed, Sara could hear the river flowing and sometimes the forge hammer in the distance.[26] From her birth to the day she left Greta Hall to marry, Sara shared this small room with her mother. The other children lived upstairs and the room was symbolic of her different status in the house. It was, however, one of the few quiet spots where Sara could spend hours reading to her heart's content. Dora could already see that Sara was different to the other Southey and Wordsworth children, particularly the girls. Whenever the opportunity arose, Sara would retreat to her bedroom and study the Italian and Latin her father had taught her. Edith and Dora complained about their lessons; Sara never did.

It is hardly surprising that Dora's learning was mediocre at best. Where Sara had the routine of Greta's schoolroom, Dora had suffered under all the interruptions of sickness and disorganisation. But where once Aunt Dorothy had clucked and frowned over Sara's 'theatrical and conceited manners', she now began to be more impressed by them, and to wish Dora would emulate her friend. 'Sara', Aunt Dorothy reflected, 'is an admirable scholar for her age. She is also very fond of reading for her amusement – devouring her Book.' Once again, the comments the Wordsworths made about Sara give us an indication of the things Dora was and – most tellingly – was not expected to be. With regard to her attitude to books and education, Sara was both praised and criticised. To be diligent in study was good; to excel was not. In manners, Sara's combination of frailty, delicacy and smart dress won her the accusation of 'theatrical and conceited manners' – she had none of the 'natural wildness of a child'.[27] But Dora's propensity to express anger was also frowned upon. Dora, by all accounts a naughty and strong-willed little girl, was just learning to tame the wildness her parents professed to admire into a more acceptable feminine role. Clever, but not too educated; ladylike, but not vain; hardworking, but not ambitious: these were the demands made of her. Praising her niece one day, Dorothy unwittingly summed up the difficulties that lay ahead of Dora. She described her face as 'very elegant. I never saw so much elegance combined with so much wildness in any face.'[28] The struggles to fulfil the irre-concilable duties of being wild *and* elegant would dominate Dora's life.

Finally, in the summer of 1811, Aunt Dorothy declared her niece was too wild and needed to be 'tamed'. However, she argued the village school could not keep her 'regularly and steadily to work, which is absolutely necessary for a learner of her airy dispositions'.[29] She would have to be sent away, to Miss Weir's school in Appleby on the other side of the Helvellyn Mountain range. On being told of the plan, Mrs STC strongly disapproved. Putting boys in boarding school was not unusual, but it was far less common to hear of girls being sent away, especially when, as in Dora's case, their brothers remained behind to be educated in a local school. John had a cheerful daily routine, carrying a tin can to Ambleside School. He was now a day boy where Hartley and Derwent were weekly boarders and on Fridays the boys came home to Allan Bank together.

In May 1811, just before Dora was due to leave for school, the lease expired on Allan Bank and Wordsworth moved his family into a cheaper house, the derelict Rectory on the other side of the village. Less than two months later, and two days before her seventh birthday, Dora was sent to school. Perhaps if Aunt Sara – always Dora's champion – had been at home when the decision was made she would have discouraged it. But after being driven away from Grasmere by STC in March 1810 she did not return to the household until after Dora went to Miss Weir in June 1811. Once her niece was at school, she went to visit regularly and 'thought her the most beautiful Creature I ever saw in my life . . . *bewitchingly* so – for your life it seemed most impossible not to admire her – there is such life and variety in her countenance as I never saw – then she was so modest & so pretty-behaved that it gave her face a milder & sweeter expression than I had thought it capable of'.[30] At home, Wordsworth suffered from headaches in the absence of his daughter, but did not challenge his sister's deci-sion. Instead, he drew her and his wife into his schemes to improve the village school and they busily tutored other people's children.

To modern sensibilities the idea of little Dora travelling alone to boarding school is pitiful. Yet the school her family had selected for her was no 'Lowood'.* It was one of the many informal schools in existence at this time; it had only twelve pupils, several of whom were cousins on the Hutchinson side. Dora knew Miss Weir, and the Wordsworths believed they were doing their best by her. Aunt Dorothy persuaded Dora it was all a great adventure and on a hot summer day in August, a colleague of Miss Weir's, Miss Jameson, came to collect her. Dora and her aunt spent a long half-hour waiting for the coach at Ambleside, the little girl clutching her suitcase and a box of seed cake for her birthday. When Miss Jameson arrived, and Aunt Dorothy bade her farewell, Dora burst into tears. There were no inside seats, so she was hauled up onto an outside one. A pair of drunk sailors sat themselves down opposite her. Aunt Dorothy cheerfully cried out, 'Do not fear they will take care of you.' Dora, her face white with terror, watched as the figure of Aunt Dorothy disappeared into the distance.[31]

* The school Jane Eyre attends in Charlotte Brontë's novel.

CHAPTER 3

'AN AGONY OF TEARS'

1812

'Airy Castles'

On a cold February morning in 1812, Sara was finally told her father was on his way back to Greta. STC had not been home since leaving the Lakes for London – and literature – a year and a half before. While her forty-year-old father made his way by stagecoach through smoke-stacks and newly built factories, nine-year-old Sara huddled over the lessons he had given her, a candle at her side, and awaited his arrival.

On Wednesday, 19 February, a chaise drew up outside Greta Hall. Sara was reunited not only with a dishevelled-looking father but also, to everyone's surprise, with both her brothers. Their father had gone to Kendal on his way to Greta to find a printer, but he could not find the man with whom he had business. So, with typical impetuosity, he had hired a chaise for 5 a.m. and that very morning had appeared at his sons' boarding school in Ambleside midway through the first lesson of the day.

Derwent had quite a tale. Their headmaster, Mr Dawes, called him and Hartley out of the classroom. Derwent, aged eleven, 'came in dancing for joy'. He was not a fan of Mr Dawes's and the antipathy seems to have been mutual. Derwent thought his headteacher favoured his older brother Hartley since 'he [Derwent] can't help crying when he is scolded, and because he ain't such a genius as Hartley, and Mr Dawes *only looks* at Hartley and never scolds him and that *all* the boys think it very unfair – he is a genius!' Derwent, not much keener on his books than he was on Mr Dawes, was delighted by an unexpected holiday and the return of his father. In contrast Hartley, fifteen, 'turned pale and trembled all over – then after he had taken some cold water instantly asked [Coleridge] some questions about the connections of the Greek with the Latin'.[1] Derwent thought this most peculiar. But whatever they, and indeed Mr Dawes, may have felt, the boys and STC all set off together in the chaise. STC was flea-bitten and full of stories about his travels. He had barely slept for forty-eight hours, having been kept awake by the coach clattering over potholes, his own nightmares, vermin and the need to prevent a fellow passenger from pick-pocketing him.[2]

The end of the journey was to Derwent and Hartley – and to Sara when they told her about it – most distressing. After a short cold drive, they arrived at Grasmere, which lies on the road to Keswick. As they approached the lane to Wordsworth's house, the boys looked out expectantly. Coleridge drove straight on. When his sons realised they were not stopping, Hartley was speechless with astonishment. Derwent's eyes 'filled with tears' and Coleridge turned his face from his children. Wordsworth was like a father to them; they spent all their weekends with him. They believed their father loved him like a brother. It was left to their mother to explain to them, some time later, that their father and Dora's had had a great quarrel. On hearing the news, Hartley 'turned white, as lime'.[3]

In fact, by this time the quarrel had – to Coleridge's mind at least – been going on for close to two years. They were two years in which Wordsworth had remained blithely unaware he had caused Coleridge grave offence. When Wordsworth's friends eventually realised something was wrong, they had helpfully written to tell him all about it. 'My dear friend! There has been downright *lying* somewhere,' Catherine Clarkson told Wordsworth with barely disguised relish, 'not mere misrepresentation and dressing up of facts,' she continued, just to be sure the arrow had struck, 'but inventing against you.'[4] When Wordsworth heard, in February 1812, that STC had returned to Keswick, he was relieved. STC would come and see him and the misunderstanding would be cleared up. It was only when

STC did not call that Wordsworth understood how upset his old friend was.

It was immediately obvious to all at Keswick that STC had undergone some sort of collapse in London, and his spontaneous return was not a sign of recovery. Southey grew more and more frustrated and the atmosphere in the house was horribly tense. Everybody, in the Lakes and in London, tried to persuade STC and Wordsworth to make up. Southey tried to talk 'common sense' to Coleridge.[5] Surely STC must see Wordsworth would never have told Montagu he despaired of him? Well, in that case, retorted a furious STC, Wordsworth was calling him a liar.[6]

Sara slaved away at her Latin and Italian, desperate to please her father and restore him to his former self. To his credit, STC was suitably amazed. 'She reads French tolerably and Italian fluently,' he boasted to friends in London. One evening, as Sara read to her father, the word 'hostile' came up. He quizzed her as to its meaning. Unfazed, Sara thought for a second and replied: 'Why! Inimical: only that inimical is more often used for things and measures, and not, as hostile is to persons and nations.' He was utterly enchanted – 'she is such a sweet tempered, meek, blue-eyed Fairy, & so affectionate, trustworthy and really serviceable!' he exclaimed with surprise and delight.[7] He began to make noises about taking her back to London with him for four or five months. He told his wife he was now beginning to make money with his lecturing and writing in London, and hoped they would all be able to come and join him soon. Mrs STC was not convinced and listened 'with incredulous ears, while he was building these "airy castles".'[8]

Sara did not know her father well enough to distinguish his airy castles from his solid ones. It was a horrible surprise when, one morning, after only six weeks at Greta, Coleridge upped and left without warning. Nothing had been resolved; Wordsworth was shocked to hear from Mrs Coleridge that STC had gone. It was April 1812 and Sara would not see her father again for ten years. She had hugely impressed him, but it was not enough.

'Surprised by Joy'

While Sara waited for her father to return, Dora waited to be summoned home. Finally, in the middle of June 1812, Dora, by now one of Miss Weir's sharpest and most amusing pupils, was called out of her classroom. She was not unhappy at the school – discipline was not harsh and she had grown to love Miss Weir – but it was not home. Furthermore, she knew that her departure had helped make space and time for the new baby. Dora must have experienced at least a moment of pure joy on learning she was going back to Grasmere before she was told the devastating news: her beloved little sister Cate, just three years old, had died. Dora's schoolmates watched as she clambered into a pony trap with all her bags and began her slow sorrowful journey to the Rectory. At home Aunt Dorothy holding baby Willy, and Aunt Sara, both dressed in black, greeted her. John – as well as Derwent and Hartley Coleridge, who still spent weekends with the Wordsworths – spoke in hushed tones. The house she walked into felt nothing like home. Between the convalescent holidays of the year before and the time at boarding school, Dora had spent little more than a couple of months in the Rectory and she could barely even remember her way around it. Cate's toys and clothes were there, but no Cate.

To the end of her life, Dora carried the fear that Cate's illness and subsequent death had been her fault. Some months before she had gone away to school, Dora and John had been making carrot bullets for their Burr-tree guns.* When slow Sally Green looked away to make their porridge, Dora didn't stop Cate eating three bullets. Later that day, Cate suffered a fit. It was not the first fit she'd had, but it was the worst and did the most damage. With good intentions but cruel treatment, the doctor scrubbed the tiny girl in mustard, subjected her to an enema and had her

---

* Burr is a North Country word for an elder tree. A Burr-tree gun was formed by hollowing out the soft pith of an elder branch. The leaves and raw berries of the elder tree are poisonous and, if eaten, more likely than carrots to have made Cate sick.

gums lanced, but she never fully recovered. Afterwards Cate's right arm and leg wouldn't work properly. Dr Scambler pronounced he was in 'no doubt but that these carrots were the cause of her illness'.[9]

Nine-year-old John told Dora what had happened the day their sister died. That evening Cate had seemed particularly well. At suppertime she had even managed to use her lame arm, feeding herself with a fork almost as steadily as her brothers. She was excited because the aunts had said she was allowed to sleep in her mother's bed. John went to look in on her when he went to bed and saw she had been sick. Her eyes were fixed and glazed. He shouted for Aunt Dorothy who sent the servant, Sarah, rushing for the doctor. His little sister lay in the bed fitting while Dr Scambler gave her an enema, but nothing could be done. By six in the morning, she was dead.[10]

By the time Dora returned home from school, Cate's funeral had already taken place. John and Willy as well as Derwent and Hartley Coleridge, the aunts and the servants had made up the funeral procession. Dora wanted her parents and little Tom, but no one knew when they would be home.

Wordsworth was on his way from London to find his grief-stricken wife in Wales. Wordsworth himself had gone to the capital a few months before, partly on business and partly to try and resolve the 'vile business' with STC.[11] Mary, leaving Cate for the first time in her life, had taken little Tom to visit her brother on his farm in Radnor. Dora's family would later learn – when it hardly seemed to matter anymore – that Wordsworth met STC several times in London. After tortuous negotiations they eventually struck a truce: STC and Wordsworth went for a long walk on Hampstead Heath and peace, if not friendship, was re-established. Wordsworth decided, out of loyalty, to stay in London until June: he would attend a series of lectures Coleridge was delivering at the fashionable Willis' Rooms in the West End. Wordsworth regretted the decision until the day he died. Shortly after 4 June, he received a letter from Dorothy telling him Cate was dead. He rushed to Radnor to be at his wife's side.

Dora's mother and father did not return for almost a month. Though Dora did not know it, Mary fought desperately to return to her surviving children, but she was weak and ill with grief and everyone counselled against travel. So it was Aunt Dorothy who was holding the fort when Dora arrived home. When Dora rushed to greet her aunt, in her usual affectionate manner, she was admonished. Her aunt declared she was both shocked and 'surprized at her joyfulness' when she arrived home from school.* Despite recognising Dora had always been 'particularly fond of Catherine', Dorothy displayed a curious lack of sympathy towards her niece. When Dora went to bed, Aunt Dorothy explained to a friend, 'she knelt down before me to say her prayers and, as usual, prayed for her Brothers and sister, I suppose without thinking of her. I said to her when she had done – My dear child you have no Sister living now – and our Religion does not teach us to pray for the dead. We can do nothing for them – our prayers will not help them – God has taken your sister to himself.' Dora 'burst into a flood – an agony of tears – and went weeping and silent to her bed'. Aunt Dorothy left her alone to cry and 'so she fell asleep' on her first night at home. When Dora had been back only a couple of days, her aunt tried reading to her and her brother. The exhausted little girl fell straight to sleep. Aunt Dorothy disapproved, as she so often did.

Aunt Dorothy's manner of grieving damaged Dora. Almost as soon as Cate died her aunt began to talk of the differences between Dora and her sister in ways which were hard to bear. She eulogised the dead girl by comparing her to the living: 'There was no variety in her [Cate's] ways, she having been kept back by so much illness and this has made her the most rememberable child that ever I was separated from. When Dorothy is absent it is difficult to call her to mind as she is – she puts on so many shapes; but sweet Catherine is and ever will be the

---

* It seems possible that this expression of Dorothy's was the inspiration for Wordsworth's later and great poem 'Surprised by joy' (Sonnet XXVII) on the subject of Catherine's death.

same in our remembrance as when she was alive.'[12] Of course Dora had been away so it was genuinely harder for Aunt Dorothy to remember, but it was also because ever since the seizure which had rendered Cate more or less speechless and lame, she had ceased to grow up in the normal way.* While Cate went from illness to illness, Dora started at the local school and was cheeky and naughty. She learned to read, was led astray by other children, grew taller and went to school at Appleby. She became, in short, a normal, bright little girl. Cate, meanwhile, had regressed. For a long time after the fit she could no longer say any of the words – like 'mama' – which she had learned. Instead, she'd invented her own word: 'kisleca' and it was 'kisleca', when she was angry and, if she was happy, she went about singing 'in the archest prettiest manner you can conceive "ah! Kisleca, ah! Kisleca" for five or ten minutes together'.[13] She needed constant attention and because she was innocent and dependent she was always, even in life, a 'little darling', 'the spirit of infancy', a 'dear Innocent', 'uncommonly good-tempered' and as pure as 'the purest spirit in heaven'.[14] After her death she remained suspended in time, unable to disappoint. Dora regularly disappointed. She had 'abominable habits' like clicking her tongue and throwing tantrums, whereas Aunt Dorothy said Cate's disposition had always been perfect. 'She had a temper never ruffled – there seemed no seed of evil in her – and she was so loving that the smallest notice or kindness shewn to her by those with whom she was well acquainted used to draw from her the fondest caress and expression of love.'[15] Dora felt the need to fill the shoes of her angelic little sister; it was of course an impossible task.

It was not only Dora's family who mourned Cate. For several years Thomas de Quincey had been living in Grasmere. In fact

---

* Muriel Strachan and Grevil Lyndop have recently suggested that Cate may have suffered from Down's syndrome. Wordsworth referred to her as his 'little Chinese maiden' – and he may have been describing the epicanthic fold of skin which gives some Down's children an unusual shape to the eye (DW to De Quincey, 1 August 1809; *WW LMY*, II, p. 365).

a year after they moved out of Town End Cottage, he moved in, expressly to be near the 'deep, deep magnet' of Wordsworth, and he was an almost daily visitor to the Rectory.[16] He was fond of all the children, but Cate especially. When he could, he used to carry her off to his cottage where she slept the night in his bed. Today this might ring alarm bells but in an age that worshipped children as innocents, it was peculiar in the extreme but made slightly more sense. De Quincey believed the three-year-old had a 'radiant spirit of joyousnes'; all he wanted was 'her blithe society'. He loved her for 'filling from morning to night the air with "gladness and involuntary songs," this it was which so fascinated my heart'. He became 'blindly, doatingly, in a servile degree' attached to her. And now he grieved most astonishingly for her. It is hard to imagine what Dora must have made of his behaviour. It is hard to know what to make of it now. 'Never,' he speculated, 'from the foundations of those mighty hills, was there so fierce a convulsion of grief' as when she, 'the impersonation of the dawn', died. De Quincey had not actually been at home when Cate died but, on hearing the news, he paid for his servant Mary Dawson to be put into mourning clothes and he came rushing up to Grasmere. Later, he would lie on her grave at night in the church in Grasmere, beating his fists and weeping in an 'intensity of sick, frantic yearning after neighbourhood to the darling of my heart'.[17] He took to having visions of her, carrying a basket on her head, in the fields around about. He was not shy about sharing the description of what he had seen. Romantic imagination is perhaps best left to mountains and waterfalls.

When Dora's parents did finally arrive home, their appearance, particularly her mother's, was shocking. In her grief Mary had grown terribly thin. Years later Wordsworth would write several poems about Cate's death. Ironically the first of these, 'Maternal Grief', is amongst his weaker poems. In his grief, he was still attempting to live up to Coleridge's dream of the philosophical purpose of *The Recluse*, yet he could not comprehend any possible purpose for Cate's death. He asks God to 'teach me calm submission to thy Will' but it lacks the authenticity with which Wordsworth's best writing explores the human mind. His later poem 'Surprised by joy', also about Cate's death, is one of his best, because it simply considers the emotion of grief rather than trying to make sense of the event. The horror of what had happened remained with him to the end of his life, but also served to undermine his faith in his abilities as a poet in the face of death.

Nobody, not even Aunt Dorothy, thought of suggesting Dora should return to Appleby. She stayed at home in the horrible now too-big Rectory to be given lessons when and if it occurred to one of the adults. She taught as much as she learned: Johnny, though older than Dora and bright, was a poor reader. It's likely he was dyslexic. The adults could see he was not stupid in 'spirit' but could not understand why he progressed so little at school despite being touchingly studious. He muddled words like 'stores' and 'stories' and 'requite' and 'require' and suffered agonies within what was surely one of the most literate families in the country. His schoolmaster beat him and Aunt Dorothy took to referring to him as the Dunce – or even the 'greatest Dunce in England'.[18] Dora helped make school life bearable for him. She was, in all ways, patient with him and kind to him. The two sat side by side for hours while Johnny laboured at his letters. Dora's only respite that summer was when Mary and William agreed to leave her at Keswick for a week. Then she was 'happy . . . almost wild with joy in the company of Sara and Edith'.[19] Greta Hall was full of people, including an artist who drew with the girls.

Back at home in the winter of 1812, Dora, John and Tom all caught the measles. Tom, aged six and a half, was the first to succumb. It began, on 26 November, with a catarrhal cough, a runny nose and conjunctivitis, and by the third day he was covered in red spots and running a high fever. Like the rest of the children, Tom had caught the whooping cough the year before and he had never fully regained his strength. Once again the adults were engaged in round-the-clock nursing. On the fourth day Tom seemed to be recovering and they relaxed their guard a little, but two days later, on 1 December, his fever climbed frighteningly high. Dr Scambler was called. He arrived at eleven in the morning, decided the child was stable and left the house with assurances all would be well. An hour afterwards the little boy was violently sick and in the next hour his temperature rose, he was racked with coughs and crying out in pain. Dora watched her father as he rushed to fetch Scambler back from Ambleside, but her brother's strength was fading. His family bled him, but to no avail, and Dora heard him exclaim 'I shall die, I shall die.' By the time Wordsworth returned with the doctor, Tom was barely conscious. He died, quietly, at 5 p.m.; his last brave words to his mother were 'I am getting better.'

Once again the family was plunged into mourning. And for Dora, comparisons with her dead brother were again devastating. Aunt Dorothy said Tom was, like Cate, 'guileless – the very emblem of innocence and purity and infantine sweetness'; in short, he was marked 'as not of this world; but chosen by God himself – to augment the number of blessed Spirits'. She told her friend, Catherine Clarkson, she wished any one of the living children 'was more like Thomas', for '*his* were heavenly graces – and Catherine's temper was as sweet as his – in *her* temper too there was no seed of evil'. The surviving children, claimed Aunt Dorothy, had 'wayward humours' but they had never quarrelled with Tom because of his 'ardour of soul'. John and Dora, Aunt Dorothy thought, were opposites: Dora quick and restless, John slow and dull. 'Thomas was between them – he had not the faults of either.'[20] She came to think that 'Thomas was of all the Children that one who caused us the least pain'.[21]

Following Tom's death, Mary, always slight, grew even more wraith-like. Both she and Dorothy avoided food at times of misery or anxiety. She claimed to have no appetite and was 'thinner than ever and evidently weak, though enabled by the power of her spirits to go through more exertion than many a strong and healthy woman'. Dora watched and learned. Mary had always had a habit of 'disregarding herself' – now she would barely eat at all, but nonetheless she was the strong one who comforted Aunt Dorothy, Wordsworth and the children 'with the calmness of an Angel'. By the start of January, however, her composure collapsed and she wept bitterly, night and day.[22] For the first and only time in her long life Mary Wordsworth seemed to be at risk of a total collapse. Aunt Dorothy and Wordsworth talked of leaving the Rectory. Mary grew so 'miserably thin' that it was 'melancholy to look upon her'.[23] For months neither John, Dora nor Willy were enough to draw her out of herself, try as they might. By February 1813, her face was so hollowed out it seemed she had a 'black complexion'.[24]

In the acute phase of its grief, the Wordsworth family coiled in on itself. It became rare for the children to leave their parents. Since Dora would not return to Appleby, they decided that the aunts would educate her, a duty which Dorothy embarked upon with steely determination but little pleasure. 'Sometimes', she confided to Clarkson, 'we have great Battles – and long confinements. I hope that perseverance may conquer her, and the sense will come that it is wiser not to make herself miserable. Poor Kate',* she sighed, 'had no ill humours!'[25]

Early in the New Year, the Wordsworths began to make definite plans to get out of the Rectory and the memories it held of Tom and Cate. Mary simply could not bear 'all those objects continually present in which the Children used to delight'.[26] They found a house, a few miles to the west, called Rydal Mount, on the edge of the village. It was a large white building, originally Tudor but enlarged in the Georgian period, and it overlooked Rydal Water. It was a step towards building a new life and on May Day they slept in their new home for the first time. Aunt Sara moved back in on a permanent basis to help with Dora, John and Willy. The family that was used to changing shape, adding a child here, subtracting a lodger there, moving from one house to another, now settled into something approaching a lasting, permanent form.

* Catherine was referred to as Kate and Cate.

CHAPTER 4

'THESE DARK STEPS'

1816

Keswick – 'To Be Young Was Very Heaven'

At the start of February 1816, Aunt Sara took her eleven-year-old niece to Keswick for a month. She had a hunch Dora needed a better education than she was getting at home. It was not only the lack of rigour that concerned her but also the lack of art or music. She planned to make use of the Latin master whom Southey had engaged at Greta, as well as their resident artist, Miss Barker, who had agreed to teach Dora drawing and the harpsichord.

Aunt Sara probably had a motive other than friendship for taking her favourite niece from the tightly knit household seething in its own grief at Rydal Mount. Throughout the past year, as the Napoleonic Wars came to an end, there had been a flurry of anxious correspondence between Rydal Mount and Paris. Dora was a sharp, perceptive child. She would have noticed letters hurriedly stuffed into a pocket when she entered unexpectedly, or low voices making their way through her bedroom floorboards late at night. It was becoming difficult to keep a secret from her; particularly one that required so much conversation: Dora had a sister in Paris.

Dora believed she was Wordsworth's eldest and – since Cate's death – only daughter. But two decades before, the father she knew as a celebrated poet – fast becoming a national institution – and a devoted paterfamilias had been a wild young man drunk with the excitement of the French Revolution. 'Bliss was it in that dawn to be alive,/ But to be young was very heaven!'[1] He was passionate about the politics, and passionate about a woman he met named Annette Vallon. She became pregnant. When the revolution failed, Wordsworth was distraught. In despair, and in some personal danger, he fled, promising to return.

It took him ten years, but in 1802 he and Dorothy had travelled to visit Annette and his then nine-year-old daughter, Caroline. The slightly shabby, certainly anxious, English brother and sister met the woman who called herself Madame Wordsworth or sometimes Madame William and walked along the beach near Calais. There he broke the news that, though the war was over, he was about to marry an English woman named Mary. He would do what he could for them but Annette must give up all hope of marriage and he would never be a true father to Caroline. Dora knew the sonnet Wordsworth had composed during this visit: 'It is a Beauteous Evening, Calm and Free'; in its serenity and tenderness it is one of the best he ever wrote. But Dora had no idea the poem's subject, the 'Dear Child! dear Girl! that walkest with me here', was her half-sister.[2] Since the meeting in 1802, Wordsworth had not seen either Annette or Caroline, though he corresponded with them regularly and provided for them financially. He could not have treated his two daughters more differently. Since Cate's death Dora had barely been out of his sight; he would not have recognised Caroline if he had passed her in the street.

For years the Vallons were quiet. But now this flurry of correspondence announced things had shifted. Two years before, at the age of twenty-one, Caroline had told her father she wanted to get married. Her fiancé, Jean Baptiste Baudouin, was a poorly paid civil servant in the Mont de Piété, the French government's pawnbroking institution. Despite the fact that Wordsworth had done nothing for her but pay her mother an allowance, she needed his consent.* Baudouin's low salary initially made Wordsworth nervous of giving his approval. He prided himself

---

* In France parental consent was necessary for women under the age of twenty-five.

on how strongly he took his responsibilities to Caroline – and to be fair he could have got away with doing less. He did not want a marriage that might leave her financially insecure. But he eventually consented 'on the supposition that they would obtain an increase of income' as Baudouin's government career prospects seemed good. Once the ceremony was imminent, the Vallons wanted one of the Wordsworths to go to France for the wedding. World events had intervened, however, when Napoleon escaped from Elba in 1815. Not only could the brother and sister not travel, but Wordsworth withdrew his consent: Baudouin's future had become too uncertain; now they should 'wait for a change'.[3] Only Napoleon's defeat at Waterloo rescued the situation – Wordsworth relented and gave his consent again.

Ever since there had been endless communication, which Dora could not but have noticed. The Vallons were desperate for someone from the family to travel to France. Aunt Dorothy was keen to go – but should Wordsworth? They had many anxious discussions. Mary, Aunt Sara and of course Aunt Dorothy all knew about the affair, and it must have become increasingly difficult to ensure that Dora did not. She was quite old enough to see that something other than politics and poetry was preoccupying everyone. At the very least, her education had become a low priority. Aunt Sara's offer to take Dora to Keswick suited them all.

Greta Hall was full to the brim, so Dora and Aunt Sara stayed with Miss Barker, the artist, in her house just down the road. Almost as soon as they arrived, Aunt Sara fell ill and took to her bed. Dora began her Latin, drawing and music lessons none the less, but when not studying she spent her time with Sara and Edith and the other Southey children. They were often joined by Mary Calvert, daughter of a friend of Southey's who lived nearby. It was a cold winter, but whenever the weather permitted, they were outside. The lake had frozen and a heady treat was to put on their wooden clogs and dig skates out of the mangling room. The gang of children would run as fast as they could, following Greta River, down to the banks of Derwent Water to 'sport on the Ice in high glee'.[4]

They were deliciously naughty. Thirty years later Sara was still proud of how they hid their tricks from the adults. As the waters began to thaw, Edith, Dora, Mary and Sara paddled, 'with shoes and stockings off – in Cumbrian streams'. One memorable day they went 'all the way from high up in Stonethwaite to Miss Barker's house at Rosthwaite, through the streams left by a flood', without any of the adults discovering them.[5] Sara was a ringleader. The other children had 'a certain respect for me, mingled with a contrary feeling'. They admired her power of 'running and leaping' and they were well aware she outshone them all in the schoolroom. She could also hold her own against boys. Once she had put crumbs into the porridge of two of Mary Calvert's cousins in retaliation for being beaten in a 'trial of strength'. Sara had instigated the revenge; as the cousins said 'it was all that little vixen, Sara Coleridge; M[ary] was quiet enough by herself'.

But they didn't always escape getting into trouble. An old lady lived in a hut near the Calverts who all the children thought was a witch; they dared each other to run up to her front door. Sara was caught one day and the 'morose, ugly, withered, ill-conditioned, ignorant creature' complained to Mrs Calvert, which Sara thought most unfair.[6] Adults and children saw Sara very differently. She was famed amongst the young for her agility, she was cleverer than any of the boys and yet all the grown-ups considered her delicate. Her diminutive stature (Dora, though younger, was both taller and heavier) and enormous eyes had something to do with this. Sara's beauty was becoming astonishing; years later Mrs STC would confess that a visiting gentleman had 'proposed for her daughter at thirteen'.[7] Dora knew Aunt Dorothy had her criticisms of Sara's learning – as did Aunt Sara – but the adults at Greta did not see bookishness in a girl as something of which to be ashamed. Even so, it gave Dora pause for thought.

For the first time in her life, Dora worked hard without being told. At home she had disappointed her mother with her inability to make 'regular progress'. Mary thought nothing could be done 'until her own hope and pride bring her to it – her temper is so much against her improvement'.[8] It was a tough assessment given that when she did attend school in Ambleside – which was irregularly – she was taught music and languages by a Miss Fletcher whom none of the adults realised was stone deaf.[9] It was also a relief to be away from Aunt Dorothy. Dora and her aunt continued to have great rows – 'terrible Battles' – whether about Dora's refusal to take a cold bath every morning, or her unsteadiness at her books, or her 'fits of obstinacy with pride'.[10] In frustration Aunt Dorothy wrote of Dora, 'she is extremely wayward and is desirous to master everybody. It is a woeful thing that so sweet a creature should be capable of seeking the perverse delight of making those who love her unhappy.'[11] With a flash of that astuteness of which she was unsettlingly capable, when Aunt Dorothy heard how well Dora progressed at Keswick, she wondered whether, if they had all been less anxious about her, 'and taken less pains she would have done much more for herself'.[12] Dora had been taught Latin by any of the adults at home who had a spare moment, but being under the regular instruction of the Latin master at Greta was quite different. It was perfectly obvious to her that she would never be as good as Sara, but she began to make steady progress. Sara's ability in French was enviable and Dora redoubled her own efforts at the language.

Dora was happy to admit she was not such a scholar as Sara. Together with Edith and Mary Calvert, she teased Sara for being a bluestocking (a term that had been in use now for forty years to depict an intellectual woman). Sara bore the label well. She began to enjoy it; 'cerulean' was a better word, they decided, and she became 'Ceruleanite' Sara.* Other mothers roundabout sniffed and disapproved. Mrs STC was compelled on several occasions to protest that she didn't push her daughter too hard: 'the *wise* Mamas, forsooth, insist upon it, that she is killed with study', wrote Mrs STC to a cousin, Thomas Poole, 'but although

---

* The original Blue Stockings Society was founded by Elizabeth Montagu around 1750, but by the nineteenth century the phrase was generally a derogatory term applied to intellectually minded women.

she is fond of improvement – she is far *fonder* of play'.[13] Dora's aunts were unambiguously on the side of the wise mamas. Mrs STC felt the need to keep making the point. 'Sara is almost half her time at Greta-Bank with Miss Calvert,' she wrote a little while later, 'where she rides on horseback often and plays more than half her time: I trouble you with these trifles to show you that she is not made ill by books; for I have not the slightest doubt that if anything ill should happen to this dear child there would not be wanting persons to say that she had been kept too close [at her studies].'[14] While Sara was cast as the scholar, Dora took up the role as counsellor. Sara valued Dora's quiet common sense and intuition. Though younger, Dora became Sara's wiser 'adviser'.[15]

The little Southey children were sometimes permitted to join their games. Herbert, aged nine, was a favourite with all the girls, perhaps because he was still small enough to be bossed around, dressed up, babied. He even met with unconditional praise from those at Rydal Mount, where he was considered 'the perfection of a child loving Books and learning, he is all a *Child* at play, and has all the simplicity of a child in his attainments'.[16] It was a combination of qualities that none of the rest of the children ever managed to achieve. That February he was poorly, so they were admitted into the sickroom with red noses and laughter and firm instructions not to over-excite him. They petted the little boy and showed him the mosses they had collected.

At Keswick Dora discovered two things she was good at – better even than Sara – which would give her pleasure all her life: music and drawing. Music and drawing were, par excellence, the two 'accomplishments' that middle-class girls were expected to display. Neither of these was much valued at Greta – at least not by Mrs STC or her daughter. Sara was clever at the piano and learned quickly, but was not really interested in music. She forgot how to play and 'never could make any hand of drawing' – she didn't particularly try.[17] Dora was slower in progressing but would eventually outshine her friend. She enjoyed the harpsichord, but what really made sense to her was the instruction she received in drawing. Miss Barker thought she had an eye. She certainly had the patience to begin to be a truly accomplished draughtswoman. Compared to Sara she was no linguist. She walked and ran 'most awkwardly' and was stout and tall.[18] She was not charming like Edith, but with a pencil, she far outshone the other children. Sara had been taught to think little of such skills, but still she and Edith were impressed. Oddly, for a girl who had been brought up to be 'natural' and 'wild', Dora happened to find she enjoyed 'lady-like' accomplishments.

March 1816 came in 'like a lion'.[19] The snowdrops gave way to celandine and daffodils. Chiffchaffs sang above green-robed larches, and Dora's stay at Keswick was extended because of Aunt Sara's illness. Wordsworth walked over to visit his daughter, but agreed she should stay put and so her lessons – and her play – continued. Herbert was getting better; the ice on the lake was beginning to thaw. As the weather grew warmer, they were outside constantly. They gathered primroses and filled baskets with fruits and flowers to make primrose wine. They climbed trees, jumped across Greta stream and fed Herbert and the others their pie-ie-ies. On occasion Sara grew upset for it seemed that Dora favoured Edith. Sometimes Dora felt that Sara's brothers and mother idolised her too much, but this was play-ground stuff. For the most part it was a charmed spring.

In the middle of April, however, it became clear that Herbert, far from recovering, was dangerously ill. The household prayed. The doctor was called. But it was no good. He fell into a fitful sleep, sank into a coma and died. Southey, who had been 'palsied' throughout his son's illness, was utterly distraught.[20] He felt weak as a child, his limbs trembled, he wanted to leave the country; he knew there was no escape from a lifelong grief. That afternoon he sent the stricken girls – Sara, Dora and Edith – off to Rydal with Aunt Sara.

By the time they arrived, Caroline, unbeknownst to Dora, had safely married her man without a representative from her father's family.

Rydal – 'On the Right Path'

Home for Dora was now the distinctly grand Rydal Mount, and the three miserable girls arrived on the day after Herbert's death. Usually the start of May brought maypoles, roast mutton hash, dancing, garlands and wine. This year, summer slunk in and no one noticed its arrival. Wordsworth, who knew too well what Southey was suffering, was desperate to help his friend. 'The head and flower of my happiness is cut off,' Southey told him.[21] Apart from writing a letter of condolence, which he did, all Dora's father could offer was to look after Edith and Sara for as long as required. Abandoning his study, he heard their Latin lessons every day. Sara was really astoundingly clever and the poet had a glimpse of her potential. In her, more than in any of STCs other children, he recognised the brilliance of his old friend's mind. He did all he could then – and ever after – to further her intellectual development. He took her for long walks and they talked about books and poems, nature and pictures. Sara was not a natural artist, but she was a natural student and she always felt Wordsworth had set her 'on the right path for understanding art as well as literature'. Where Southey was her guide 'in matters of heart and conscience', to Wordsworth she owed her 'intellect and imagination'.[22]

Rydal Mount was the start of a new era for the Wordsworth family. When they moved in, Wordsworth was just about to be formally appointed 'Distributor of Stamps for Westmorland'. Essentially this was a tax-collecting role and not one to which the younger Wordsworth would ever have aspired. But it carried with it a salary and security. Rydal was a short distance but a world away from the simplicity of the Town End household into which Dora had been born. Now they had Turkish carpets, new curtains and a beautifully landscaped garden.[23] Wordsworth delighted in the terraces, which he paced when composing. With its spectacular views, the house was, as they boasted, 'a *crack* spot and the envy of the whole neighbourhood'.[24] They worried, slightly, that people might think they were setting themselves up as 'fine folks', but after the horror of the deaths of Cate and

Tom, Wordsworth took his paternal duties more seriously than ever: hence the salaried job and the smarter house.[25] The man who, when young, had abandoned one family now hugged this second one even closer. They were to have all the security and comfort he himself had once spurned. And if it took being a tax collector to manage it, then he would risk the scorn of others and even, sometimes, of his deepest self. Wordsworth intended to support and protect his surviving children – especially his only surviving (and acknowledged) daughter, Dora – to the best of his abilities.

Spending time with Sara made Wordsworth more infuriated than ever by his erstwhile friend, her father. He saw that with all her attainments 'should it be *necessary* she will be well fitted to become a governess in a nobleman's or gentleman's family in the course of time'. But he desperately hoped it would not come to that for the 'remarkably clever' girl of whom he was so fond.[26] It seemed all too likely however: her father was still absent and her brothers, at the very least, would need to work out a way to live independently. If ever we need a reminder about the reality of women's lives in the Romantic age – an age that hymned equality of the sexes – it is this: clever girls, exceptionally clever girls, the cleverest girls in the country could, if they had neither father, husband nor brother to support them, look forward to a life as a governess.

When the time came for Sara to return to Greta with Edith, there were tears all round. Two things had become apparent when Herbert died. First, how seriously Wordsworth took Sara and how much she admired him. Where once Wordsworth's houses had been places of fear and muddle, Rydal Mount was now a place of refuge, 'steeped in sunshine'.[27] Second, Sara's precarious family life. She was not a part of the Southey family. Herbert was not her brother and she was not quite included in the mourning in the same way. Southey's grief was unbearable to witness. For some weeks he fantasised about selling all his furniture and leaving the country. He went so far as to calculate his expenses, but he considered these, and the size of house he would need, based only on his own surviving children. Southey loved Sara, she could be a useful tutor and friend to his children, but she was not his child.

While it was beginning to be apparent that one day Sara might have to work as a governess, another path was becoming apparent to Dora. Shortly after Herbert's death, Wordsworth suffered an eye infection which caused him, temporarily, to go more or less blind. This was not Wordsworth's first episode of near blindness and he began to fear – as some newspapers reported – he would permanently lose his sight. Terrified of the darkness, he now wrote a poem addressed, in the manuscript, 'To Dora'. He began by quoting the opening lines of Milton's *Samson Agonistes*:

> A little onward lend thy guiding hand
> To these dark steps, a little further on!

His words immediately summon a host of uncomfortable ideas. Milton in his blindness famously depended upon his daughters' eyesight to complete his work. In *Samson Agonistes*, a drama with another blind hero, he drew on the story of that most discussed of all father–daughter relationships, Oedipus and Antigone, and conjured the image of Antigone leading her blind father. When Wordsworth eventually published his poem in 1820 it was entitled 'To Antigone', but he never disguised its true dedicatee at Rydal Mount, and in later editions he replaced Antigone's name with Dora's.

In its own right, the poem is powerful and moving. Any critic would warn against too autobiographical a reading of the text, but Dora was twelve years old and a literal child. She did not understand all the classical references, but the plan her father had for his only surviving daughter seemed clear enough. If and when he needed to 'lean/Upon a living staff, with borrowed sight', it was not John or Willy but 'my own Dora, my beloved child' whose sight he intended to borrow and whose shoulder he would lean on. Milton was, as everyone knew, the greatest poet since Shakespeare. Her father was the greatest poet since Milton – she must be prepared to take on the role assumed by

Milton's daughters. If Wordsworth's future was headed both 'To heights more glorious still, and into shades/ More awful', then he would need Dora so that

> . . . advancing hand in hand,
> We may be taught, O Darling of my care!
> To calm the affections, elevate the soul,
> And consecrate our lives to truth and love.

Twelve-year-olds, or at least middle-class nineteenth-century twelve-year-olds, are just at the age to begin day-dreaming about love and marriage. From the start, Dora's adolescent day-dreams had this poem as a backdrop. One day it might be necessary to forgo love and, hand in hand with her father, consecrate her future to the truth of poetry. Her job would be to help Wordsworth complete *The Recluse*.

Dora knew *The Recluse* was to be the most important poem ever written, but a decade after Wordsworth's promise to STC, it was still far from finished. Two summers earlier, Wordsworth had published what he described as 'a portion' of *The Recluse*, under the title *The Excursion*. Within it appeared the character of a widower with six children. One daughter is her father's handmaiden. This girl, 'Her Father's prompt attendant, doth for him/ All that a Boy could do; but with delight/ More keen and prouder daring'.[28] She, like the girl in 'To Dora', is a perfect dutiful and virginal daughter.

The reception *The Excursion* had can only have made Dora more determined than ever to live up to her father's hopes. Wordsworth had always garnered hostile reviews, but those for *The Excursion* were astonishingly vicious even by the standards of the day. Lamb, Hazlitt and, most damagingly of all, Francis Jeffrey of the *Edinburgh Review*, ripped it to pieces. 'This will never do,' Jeffrey began in what is now an infamous article.[29] In painful contrast, Byron had just triumphed with *Lara, A Tale* which was selling faster than it could be printed. Wordsworth was scornful of 'somewhat cracked' Byron.[30] The 'man is insane; and will probably end his career in a madhouse'.[31] The rest of the country disagreed. In his lifetime Byron was probably the most famous poet the world has ever seen. At his funeral procession in 1824, crowds would line the street in an unprecedented outpouring of grief. He was a celebrity, and his popularity galled Wordsworth, who grew more depressed than ever about the state of the public's appreciation of poetry.

If all this were not bad enough, STC had written to him full of his disappointment on reading *The Excursion*. He confessed he could not now see how Wordsworth would complete *The Recluse*. 'I supposed you first to have mediated the faculties of men,' STC began and then gave Wordsworth several dense pages of what else he had 'supposed' he would do. He ended, disillusioned and disappointed, 'Such, or something like this was the Plan, I had supposed you were engaged upon.'[32]

Once again all the critics slated Wordsworth for not having lived up to the promise of the *Lyrical Ballads*. None the less, his reputation was still in the ascendant. Daily he was becoming a more renowned figure, and more than ever before, he attracted ardent fans and followers. His circle *knew* he was extraordinary. Southey thought he was the 'most original genius of his day'.[33] Hazlitt (first an admirer, fan and radical friend, afterwards a critic) later summarised what they all believed: 'Mr Wordsworth's genius is a pure emanation of The Spirit of the Age.'[34] Dora took all these signs to heart, but the truth was that when STC stopped believing in *The Recluse*, so, to some extent, did Wordsworth. On the other hand, his family maintained their faith. Dora decided her role would be that of the Widower's daughter in *The Excursion*: she would be his dutiful handmaiden.

Dora's education, meanwhile, continued haphazardly. At this point in his life, Wordsworth talked about little other than education. His theories about how the Madras system (a system where older pupils taught younger ones) might transform the working classes had become an obsession. And yet he continued to allow Dora to have the most unstructured time, picking up scraps of learning where she could. His thoughts about education were not entirely logical. In them one can see in the ageing bard the dreams of youth colliding with the realities of being a responsible father. Wordsworth still liked to see wild and natural qualities in little children, but he hoped his sons would go to Oxford or Cambridge. He admired Sara Coleridge's aptitude, but he was perfectly clear his own daughter would need to be fully equipped to manage housewifely duties. Indeed, too much learning in a girl could be gravely injurious. A craving for knowledge would 'be most pernicious to herself, preying upon mind and body'. It would lead to a 'want of dignity' and all kinds of strange fits of passion. Out-of-the-way knowledge of manufacturing and such topics was downright 'evil' and would lead to vanity and self-conceit. Dora was particularly at risk: as 'the only girl of brothers' she might be dangerously idolised. So far, so conventional, in a man of his times. On the other hand, those 'drawing room' accomplishments in which Dora had begun to excel might lead to 'complacence from conscious exertion of the faculties and love of praise'. He felt it was best for a girl to be put 'in the way of acquiring . . . such knowledge as will lead her out of herself, such knowledge as is interesting for its own sake'. This 'nourishment', he felt, was to be found in 'fairy tales, romances, the best biographies and histories' and so on.[35]

The problem for Dora was how to distinguish the good kind of knowledge from the bad. It had been perfectly obvious her father admired Sara's learning, and yet he and her aunts were at the same time critical that she had too much of it. Either way, the hope Dora would 'feed' on the right kind of education of her own accord was not working. At Keswick she had been given a taste of a broader, more structured education and it had suited her. Dora never complained – it was not her way – but she began to go into a decline. Nobody noticed to begin with, but a year later Aunt Dorothy would write with some despair to a friend: 'She has no particular ailment; but is excessively thin and pale – rather say black and yellow often times, and has had no appetite for some weeks.'[36]

Back at Keswick (Southey did not in the end leave the country), Sara realised Greta Hall would never again be as happy a home as it had once been. Herbert's death had sent Mrs

Southey skittering into madness, while her husband seemed now to be fixed obsessively on the past. By this time, Southey had become part of the establishment – mocked sometimes, to be sure, but solid. In 1813, the same year Wordsworth was made Distributor of Stamps, Southey had been named Poet Laureate. This was the greatest imaginable poetic honour, and no one could know then that Southey's poetry would barely be read two hundred years later. STC, meanwhile, continued on, apparently determined to avoid any kind of public honour. Brilliant but tortured, he was still living in London and that was about as much as anyone knew. Sara wrote to him; Mrs STC wrote to him. He did not reply. Sara was reading her father's poetry, philosophy and politics and beginning to understand his genius. She grew intensely jealous of his reputation, particularly in comparison to Southey and Wordsworth.

Still, since Genius did not provide, Sara began to tutor her cousins. It was all very informal but she was conscious she was earning her keep. Her brothers were beginning to think of university and careers, but were uncertain if they could afford to go. Her family seemed to be spiralling outwards and at risk of dispersing altogether. The one good thing which did seem to have come out of the year was a new closeness between Dora and Sara. They had always had a relationship akin to that of siblings. Now, like sisters sometimes but not always, they chose to become friends. They recognised admirable qualities in one another and their mutual affection and respect drew them closer. When apart from one another, they would send teasing letters across the Raise. 'Vile Doro,' Sara's would start after too long a gap, 'Your base neglect of me is intolerable, and I can endure it no longer' and then Sara would fill Dora in on all the Aunt-Hill gossip.[37]

CHAPTER 5

'LIKE THE GRACES'
1821–1822

Winter 1821

The last moments of Dora's and Sara's childhood might be said
to have begun on the evening of Friday, 28 December 1821.
Dora was seventeen and Sara just nineteen, ages that, before
the 'invention' of teenagers, caught them suspended between
their adult and child selves. That evening, on Kirkstone Lane
on the north side of Ambleside, in a small whitewashed school,
a dance was held. Outside were snow-covered stone cottages
and dark mountains; inside, light and warmth and the smells of
dancing bodies and hot food. Chairs and tables lined the room.
The tables were loaded with meat pies, tarts, creams, confec-
tionery and fruit, while the chairs supported the older and stouter
aunts and fathers.[1] The occasion was a school ball thrown in
honour of Dora and her friend Jane Harden, who were leaving
Miss Dowling's, where they had been 'parlour boarders' for the
last three years. Dora had eventually been sent back to boarding
school in Ambleside at the age of fourteen in 1818, when the
elderly Miss Fletcher had retired to be replaced by the more
capable Dowling. Dora had struggled with the 'confinements'
of schoolgirl life to begin with, but the teachers had nurtured
her artistic talent and she had grown in confidence. Ambleside
was just a couple of miles away and she could return to her
home and family regularly enough to be reasonably happy. She
left with competent French and good friends. Forty-eight adults
plus assorted children attended her party: 'all the Beauty and

Fashion of the neighbourhood'.[2] The dance was led off by Dora with Jane Harden's father, while Jane danced with Wordsworth.

Dora was now a tall – unusually tall – and healthy girl on the cusp of womanhood. Her adolescent spots were still troubling her (and her sharp-eyed aunts), but her bust had developed after a late start and her figure was full and strong. She had recovered the weight lost after her decline at Greta. Nobody would pretend she was beautiful; she had inherited her father's nose which was just a little too large for her, her eyebrows were just a little too thick and her mouth too wide, but her huge grey eyes were kind and she was quick to laugh and smile. Dora's wavy hair – fair as a child, now decidedly mousy – was scooped up to reveal her neck and a slight flush.

The ball itself was a good traditional country affair – none of the modern waltzes which would corrupt any virtuous maid in a moment. Lascivious quadrilles and waltzes might be all the rage in the cities, but in Ambleside the dancing was the hops and skips of country dances rather than the 'voluptuous intertwining of the limbs' so beloved of the French.*[3] Men stamped, women were spun and they all threaded energetically through one another, up the room, back around and down again.

Sara's childhood prettiness, on the other hand, had matured into true beauty. She must have been aware of the impression she made on all who saw her. With her enormous blue eyes, tiny frame and fair hair, she captivated men and women alike. Lady Beaumont, Wordsworth's patron and landlady, was

---

* After the Prince Regent introduced the waltz at a ball at court in July 1816, the editor of *The Times* decided something needed to be done: 'We remarked with pain that the indecent foreign dance called the Waltz was introduced . . . at the English court on Friday last. This is a circumstance which ought not to be passed over in silence . . . it is quite sufficient to cast one's eyes on the voluptuous intertwining of the limbs and close compressor on the bodies in their dance, to see that it is indeed far removed from the modest reserve which has hitherto been considered distinctive of English females. So long as this obscene display was confined to prostitutes and adulteresses, we did not think it deserving of notice; but now . . . we feel it a duty to warn every parent against exposing his daughter to so fatal a contagion.'

enchanted by her and described her as 'such a delicate little sylph, so thoughtful, yet so active in her motions. She would represent our ideas of Psyche or Ariel. Juliet would be too material.'[4] Hartley, who called her 'dear Namput', 'the Snimpet' and the 'dust of a butterfly's wing', adored his little sister almost as much as Derwent.[5] Three years earlier she had been painted by William Collins (Wilkie Collins's father). She became *The Highland Girl* in the portrait he exhibited at the Royal Academy Summer Exhibition in 1818. The picture caused a sensation in its own right but also in terms of speculation about the real-life subject of the piece. Who was this girl? Why had no one met her? Was she really the infamous Coleridge's daughter? London society nicknamed her 'The Flower of the Lakes'.

The full set of stately middle-aged Rydal matrons and spinsters – Aunt Dorothy, Mary Wordsworth and Aunt Sara Hutchinson – went to the party. The three women had all been as involved as one another in Dora's upbringing. Whether they danced themselves is not recorded, but they stayed until four in the morning gossiping at the edge of the room.

Aunt Dorothy, watching her beloved brother dancing with his daughter, could have reflected that she had done her best by her niece – wrestling to cure her tantrums, nursing her through childhood sickness and persuading Wordsworth to send her away to school again. It had been all very well for William to talk about his darling girl gathering an education at home, but she needed more tutoring than any of them had time to put to the task. They had their work cut out scribing and working for him, and in any case had no aspirations to run a schoolroom like Greta's.

Aunt Dorothy would have preferred Dora to be just a little less 'puffy' than she was.[6] She was 'almost twice as bulky as Sara, and considerably taller'. A year or two before Aunt Dorothy had compared Dora to Sara and declared, 'I wish she were half as studious; and perhaps both would be the better for such a division of property.'[7] The intervening years had only confirmed her opinion: Sara was a delight to teach and 'often do we wish that Dorothy was like her in this respect – *half* like her would do very well, for with all Dorothy's idleness there are parts of her character which are much more interesting than corresponding ones in Sara, therefore as good and evil are always mixed up together, we should be very contented with a moderate share of her industry'. Still, she had good reason to hope that Dora, dancing off her school days, had every chance of a bright future. Of pretty little Sara Coleridge she was less sure. She had always thought Sara wanting in 'the wild graces of nature'; nonetheless she admired her scholarship, indeed she almost envied it.[8] Dorothy could not but recognise a glimmer of her younger self in the clever young woman who, it seemed, would also need to look to her brothers for support in the future. For the second dance, Wordsworth claimed his daughter and, with mutual adoration, they took their turn around the room.

Aunt Sara watched as Dora's simple white frock and Wordsworth's best dancing shoes spun together. To her mind, Dora was just what she should be and 'as nice a creature as ever breathed'.[9] She was the only person who had never had any doubts that Dora, in every way, surpassed Sara Coleridge. Dora was healthy and her slight plumpness was, thought Aunt Sara, 'nothing but the fatness of health & content'.[10] There had been a worrying time, just before going to Miss Dowling's school, when her niece had grown very thin. The same thing had happened when she had studied too hard for the midsummer prizes earlier that year, but fortunately each time the weight had returned. She was a 'great *strapping* Lass now & very pretty'.[11] Sara Coleridge, beautiful as she was, was far too thin – and too interested in the admiration of others.[12] Aunt Sara was not impressed by prettiness. She congratulated herself for 'never having been a beauty' (despite what STC thought) and was appalled by the importance Mrs STC placed on looks.[13] Dora was a kind girl and usefully clever. In Aunt Sara's opinion Sara Coleridge had been spoilt by too much learning. She seemed to have no interest in anything 'but when she has a classical author in her hands'. She took no part in conversation 'but what relates to books, and personal beauty'. It was an undesirable combination and rendered her 'perfectly useless & helpless as regards the ordinary occupations of life'. Her future, after all, was by no means certain. Mrs STC had done her daughter no favours by allowing Sara to believe with her mother and brothers that there was 'not such another Being on earth'.[14]

As Mary Wordsworth watched her husband and daughter dance together one imagines her happiness for Dora was tinged with regret for the children she had lost. If she was in a reflective mood, standing with Mrs STC and the aunts, she might have thought about the past they had shared when the girls were babies. In those days they had lived so simply – and so far outside the accepted norms of sensible society – and now here they were (except STC, of course) at a refined little dance, considering marriage prospects for the girls. Mrs STC in her wig and her false teeth waddled like a 'stuffed turkey', while STC's slip of a child lit up the room.[15] Mary could not abide overeating; abstemiousness was a great virtue – Sara at least had that.

Mrs STC, now aged fifty-one, certainly did not dance (she felt far too fat) but she had every reason, as she watched, to feel pride. Her Sara had just completed a three-volume translation from the Latin of Martin Dobrizzhoffer's *Account of the Abipones, an Equestrian People of Paraguay*. She had spent most of the previous year slaving away at it. Southey had initially suggested Derwent might want to do it to earn some money to go to university, as poor old STC was unable to pay. Derwent barely began before he gave up, and Sara, just eighteen, took over. In a month her book would be published by John Murray. The tenacity with which she had tackled it was testament to her work ethic. The skill with which she had completed it paid tribute to the education her mother, Southey and the 'Aunt-Hill' aunts had given her. Derwent helped a little but Hartley had only ever teased her: 'Latin and celibacy go together' was his ceaseless chant.[16] But they were all proud of their clever, pretty 'Sariola' now on the dance floor with Dora.

Dora, though no fool, was barely acquainted with the classics, despite being educated so expensively. Was it not ridiculous, thought Mrs STC, that 'such clever people' had not been able to 'educate the daughter, at least, without paying 60, 70 pounds a year at a Boarding School?'[17] And this when Wordsworth had for years talked more about education than anyone she knew. He had grand theories, but had allowed his little girl – now a woman – to join the ranks of his female attendants; with her spots and her bad posture, poor too-tall Dora was going to struggle to attract a husband.

Amongst the men at the ball, the most dashing was dressed in the Dragoons' red and black uniform with distinctive bright blue facings. Thirty-year-old Edward Quillinan was a recent arrival to the Lakeland scene: until six months before he had served in the 3rd Dragoon Guards. But despite his soldier's garb, he considered himself a poet at heart and, six months before the ball, while stationed at Penrith, had persuaded a friend, Gillies, to write him a letter of introduction to his hero, William Wordsworth. Gillies duly complied and furthermore went out of his way to get a message to Wordsworth telling him to expect a letter. Edward's next step was to ride over and call at Rydal. To his consternation, nerves overcame him and he could not summon the courage to knock on the door. Several times he made the long ride to Rydal and each time returned without having delivered his letter. Wordsworth's poetry and celebrity were extraordinary. Sensible men, men who had fought in the army, could be reduced to trembling wrecks at the thought of speaking to him. Edward, like de Quincey, was prepared to uproot his life and family in order to be closer to his hero. But he could not summon the courage to walk to the end of the garden path. Plenty of audacious trippers were perfectly happy to come and peer through windows in the hopes of seeing Wordsworth in action – Edward was not among them.

It wasn't until a few months before the ball – and on his third attempt – that Edward had finally made it as far as the front door. Wordsworth received him in a great huff. He had been waiting for his letter for months. Now this nervous-looking man had arrived without it: at the last moment Edward had decided Gillies' epistolary praise would make him too self-conscious so he left it behind. Wordsworth worked himself up into a temper and hurled a chair about the room. Edward had just decided, reasonably enough, that the poet was 'most dis-agreeable' when Dora – home for a holiday from school – rushed into the room, summoned by the noise of the chair. 'Then it was', Edward confided to his diary, 'that I saw the poet's coun-tenance to advantage – All the father's heart was thrown into his eyes and his voice as he encouraged her to come . . . It was a timely interruption, I have loved that sweet girl ever since.' He described Dora, after that first encounter, as 'rather tall, of good features perhaps, not handsome – but of most engaging innocence of aspect'.[18] Dora had brokered the peace with Wordsworth, and Edward would always be grateful to her. She stayed for a moment to soothe her father and then rushed off to find Aunt Sara, who laughed the poet out of his mood, took the abused chair to sit on and forced her brother-in-law to receive his visitor cordially. The misunderstanding was soon resolved and after an inauspicious start, a friendship was born.

Sara and Dora both half fell in love with Edward Quillinan. Born in Portugal of an Irish mother and Portuguese father, he'd been brought up Catholic. To the young women he was an impossibly romantic figure. He had fought in the Peninsular Wars and acquitted himself well in a number of duels. He was tall and dark-haired with heavily lidded eyes and just a passing resemblance to Wordsworth. The good-looking Dragoon-turned-poet would have been much in demand at a ball. He had the appeal of an Austen hero without the risk that anything more than flirtation could be expected: he was safely married, with a beautiful but tragic young wife who had recently been despatched to a hospital in Lancaster. In October 1821, she had given birth to a second child named, at Wordsworth's sugges-tion, Rotha, after the 'stream upon whose banks she was born'.[19] The poet took a keen interest in her and he was asked to stand as godfather. Ever since the birth Mrs Quillinan had been to a greater or lesser degree 'deranged'.[20] One assumes she suffered from an intense form of post-natal depression, hence the hospital in Lancaster. Edward was looking after their children and would take them to her early in the New Year. Meanwhile, he danced.

A shout goes up, the final dance is called – the Roger de

Coverley perhaps – and the fiddlers tune up. Down the hall, cakes and glasses are abandoned, partners hurriedly scooped up and rushed into place and hands crossed and held in readiness. Dora and Sara now side by side, now speeding past, smile at each other. The men swing Dora, then Sara, round and round one another, weaving their way to the other end of the room. Sara might be a bluestocking but Dora is Sara's wiser adviser. Robert Southey watches. It is four in the morning and the triad of girls, Dora Wordsworth, his niece Sara, and Edith his daughter, are all about to spin off in different directions, dancing 'like the graces, hand in hand'.[21]

Spring 1822

A few days after the dance, Edward went to Lancaster to collect his wife, who, though still ill, had been deemed well enough to come home. Dora, helped by Sara, wrote a ridiculous rhyming letter to her 'Man of the Moon'. If he did not make 'haste dear dragoon', why then she would

> . . . fly to Lake Lune,
> For a bright honeymoon
> With my own sweet baboon.[22]

Edward kept Dora's letter carefully and returned quickly with his wife in tow.

Edward had become an almost daily presence at Rydal. Soon after meeting the Wordsworths he left the army and took up the lease at Spring Cottage, Loughrigg. Within months he moved even closer, to Ivy Cottage just minutes away from Rydal Mount.* He made himself useful from the start by lending the Rydal household his gig and horses whenever they required

* Spring Cottage was bought by Willy (Wordsworth's son) in 1881; it is now a holiday home known as Stepping Stones Cottage. Ivy Cottage is now the Glen Rothay Hotel and Badger Bar.

them and acting as another scribe for Wordsworth. His wife, Jemima, however, did not become a part of the household – even once out of hospital she was still unwell. A routine swiftly developed whereby Edward would settle his wife at home and then bring his children, Jemima (Mima) aged two and baby Rotha, down to Rydal. While the women, happy to have babies in the house again, looked after the children, the men spent their time 'versifying' in the garden or in Wordsworth's study.

In early 1822 Sara's *Abipones* translation made its way from John Murray's office in Albemarle Street to Greta Hall. In the same month they received the January edition of the *Quarterly Review*, which contained an anonymous review full of praise for the translator's 'judiciousness' and skill.[23] How many of them knew the article was by Southey is not clear; one hopes Sara did not. Charles Lamb was amazed by the Herculean scale of the undertaking: 'to think she should have had to toil thro' five octavos of that cursed . . . Abbeyponey history, and then to abridge them to 3 . . . At her years to be doing stupid Jesuits Latin into English when she should be reading or writing Romances . . . How she dobrizhoffered it all out, it puzzles my slender Latinity to conjecture.'[24] Sara's name was not on the frontispiece; she assured the Rydal aunts she did not wish to be 'ranked among Authoresses'.[25] Aunt Dorothy approved of the anonymity; she herself was toying with the idea of publishing one of her own journals anonymously. Aunt Sara wrote to all her friends and relations telling them to buy copies. They hoped it might make dear Sara a little money. If it should, she intended quite rightly, as far as Rydal Mount's inhabitants were concerned, to put the money towards Derwent's university education.

In the spring of 1822, flushed with the success of her *Abipones* translation, Sara spent a great deal of time at Rydal Mount. She was almost as fond of Edward and his girls as Dora; he was bearing up so stoically as he cared for his sick wife and tiny children. Edward enjoyed flirting gently with them both. He talked books and translation with Sara while Dora made him roar with laughter. And, strange to say, the fact there was only one man, and a married man at that, brought Dora and Sara closer than ever. Perhaps it was *because* he was married and therefore unattainable;

perhaps it was their joint love for his children. When Sara had to go home, Edward often accompanied Dora over to Keswick to see her. There the young women and Edward played with the surprising, and joyful, new addition to Southey's family, little Cuthbert, three years old and full of health, life and naughtiness. They showed Edward the see-saw in Greta's garden, the new-fangled kaleidoscope they'd been given and the Cottonian library. On one of the days that Edward took Sara home from Rydal to Greta on her own, Sara sat straight down to write to Dora. 'I hope you will answer this as soon as you have anything to say, & mind you tell me everything you can rummage up about Mima and Rotha: I grow fonder of li'le barns every day of my life.'[26] Dora hung a picture of them on her bedroom wall. Aunt Sara thought the whole thing delightful. 'Mr Q flirts with Dora and plays with Willy . . . Doro and he have had a poetical correspondence since he went to Lancaster,' she told a cousin with amusement, 'and Sara Coleridge who is here is quite as fond of him as Doro – So you may guess what a nice good-humoured creature he is.'[27]

Edward helped Wordsworth to be unusually productive that spring. Two years earlier, in 1820, Wordsworth had been on a tour of the Continent with Mary and Aunt Dorothy and he'd returned with a great deal of poetry. With Edward's help he was able to complete his revisions of the poems which went to the press as *Memorials of a Tour on the Continent*. Aunt Dorothy and Mary busily wrote up their journals. Edward's presence served to lessen the intensity surrounding all the transcribing. Perhaps it meant Dora did not notice anything awry, but it's hard to imagine she had no inkling there was something peculiar about the *Memorials* and journals. Her parents and aunts had kept a great secret from Dora: on that trip they had all visited Caroline, his French daughter, for the first time in her adult life. They had met in the Louvre amongst the throngs of casual tourists. Caroline now looked uncannily like Dora, which must have come as a shock.* She was with her new husband and their

---

* In a surviving portrait of Caroline as an older woman, the resemblance to both Dora and Wordsworth is clear. Dora and Caroline shared the same

two little girls (Wordsworth's first grandchildren) – one aged three, the other just nine months old. The three-year-old was called Dorotheé; a third to add to the string of Dorothys whose lives were defined by Wordsworth. This particular Dorothy would never see her grandfather again; none of the French family did. The Rydalians hurried home to write thousands of words about the tour without a single one touching upon its most momentous event.

Dorothy and Mary and Aunt Sara (as well as Southey's and Wordsworth's great friend, Henry Crabb Robinson, and a surprisingly large circle of friends who knew what was going on) considered Wordsworth had behaved perfectly with respect to Caroline. What is maddening is that, partly because of later descendants' attempts to cover the whole affair up, there is little surviving documentation. Certainly, however, nobody told Dora. What is intriguing is that at some point Sara *was* told. Southey had known unofficially about Annette and Caroline for years, but when he went to Paris in 1817, Wordsworth gave him Annette's address. One wonders if Sara picked up on a strange tension at Rydal Mount that spring and went home to interrogate Southey about it, but for the time being Dora continued in blissful ignorance and she and Sara had fun. It was more apparent than ever that Sara lived for her books; Dora did not and never would, but when Dora could prise Sara away from Horace or obscure Italian romances, they 'romped' together and played duets on the piano.[28] If Sara noticed strange undercurrents in the conversation at Rydal Mount, she didn't mention them, and if Dora sensed Sara's reluctance to return to Keswick, it seemed quite natural with all the attractions Rydal had to offer.

narrow chin and wide, almond-shaped eyes. Caroline and Wordsworth have the same shaped mouth and prominent cheekbones. Southey met Caroline in Paris in 1817 and he too was struck by the strength of the familial resemblance. (The photograph of Caroline is printed in Emile Legouis, *William Wordsworth and Annette Vallon*, London and Toronto: J.M. Dent and Sons, 1922, p. 106.)

Summer 1822

The spell broke in the second week of May when Mrs Quillinan had a shocking accident. The official version was that while standing too near to the kitchen range her clothes caught fire. She suffered horrific burns all over her body. Edward was in London at the time on business and so she was brought to Rydal to be nursed with brisk affection and efficiency by Aunt Dorothy. Given her history, it is hard to imagine the injuries were not self-inflicted. Perhaps with the children always at Rydal she felt unwanted and unneeded. As if all this were not dramatic enough, a few days after the accident Wordsworth fell off his horse while staying with a friend. Dora and Mary, thinking Jemima was on the mend, rushed off to tend to the bruised Bard. Just days later, and still being nursed by Dorothy, Mrs Quillinan died. By the time Dora returned, after only nine days away from home, Jemima was dead and buried in a grave in St Oswald's Churchyard in Grasmere and Edward, in a frenzy of guilt and grief, was packing up his house. He would leave England and tour the Continent. He would deposit his bereaved little girls with relatives in Kent. Within two weeks he had left Ivy Cottage, the home where he had been, briefly, so happy. Aunt Sara and Aunt Dorothy sorrowfully and meticulously prepared his accounts, arranged to sublet his cottage, sorted out the funeral expenses and sent love.

Edward's departure hit Dora especially hard. She went into a decline and nothing her aunts, or even her father, said could shake her out of it. She was 'neither well nor ill – that is – she complains of nothing: but looks wretchedly and, when not excited by pleasure, is apt to be dull in spirits – and sluggish in motion. Poor thing!' Dorothy wrote to Edward. 'Many a time have I seen her turn away to hide her gushing tears at the mention of your Dear Wife's name.' They all assumed her illness was down to how shocked she was by Mrs Quillinan's horrible death. Aunt Dorothy did not comment on the fact that, actually, Dora could talk of Jemima 'not only with composure but pleasure'; none the less she was desperately downcast.[29] After several weeks of moping, Aunt Dorothy scooped up her niece and took her off to visit Borrowdale, Buttermere, Wastdale and Keswick with the intention of cheering her up. Dora agreed with little enthusiasm: at least she would see Sara at Keswick.

Dora and Sara's reunion at Greta in June had none of the high spirits of the spring. Sara, having completed and published her translation, felt 'quite at a loss'.[30] It did not help that other than Southey's article, her book received only one not-very-positive review. She wrote ruefully to Dora: 'The Literary Gazette is rather severe upon poor old Dunderhoffer and "his ponies": they say the book can have been translated by none other than Dr Prolix.'[31] STC himself would later say the translation was 'unsurpassed for pure mother English by anything I have read for a long time'.[32] But in the summer of 1822 there was mostly silence. Sara wondered whether she ought to have published at all; Dora's Aunt Dorothy had not made her journal public in the end. *She* had decided that it was not appropriate – for a woman.

It was obvious to Dora, visiting Sara, that her friend's life was not easy. Sara spent her days tutoring her younger Southey cousins: this was now an explicit way of earning her keep – in the house that was her only home and in the service of a family she had always regarded as her own. Hartley described Greta as 'a house of bondage . . . Tho' she could not but know, that both she and her mother were doing daily services, much above the price of reciprocal favours, and that their presence was a perpetual motive of good and kindly feelings . . . an uncomfortable sense of obligation, always lay like an incubus on their gratitude.'[33] Sara's brothers were both desperate to get to a position where they could support their mother and sister, but neither was yet close. Dora would never need to think about her future in this way.

Keswick had been an ideal home for small children but it had a dark side. The aunts of the 'Aunt-Hill' did not even pretend to be industrious any more. Mrs Southey's spirits – and her appetite – had been in a decline since Herbert's death; she was emaciated and unwell. Southey cared for her with devotion, encouraging her to eat just a little at mealtimes, but the struggle took its toll. Something in him had died with Herbert which even Cuthbert's birth could not heal. Mrs Southey was not the only one whose emotions dictated her eating habits. Sara, too, was finicky about her food and Dora began to pick up some of her habits. Aunt Lovell, still in her dark parlour, was morbidly depressed. But perhaps saddest of all, the relationship between Southey and Mrs STC was strained.

That was Hartley's fault really. He had always been brilliant, but it was a mad kind of brilliance. He more or less held things together through his undergraduate degree at Merton College and gained a second-class degree. To everyone's delight (and surprise), he was subsequently elected a fellow of Oriel College. One year later, he lost the fellowship. His behaviour was not worthy of an Oxford don: he was dishevelled, he did not attend chapel regularly enough, his opinions were controversial and worst of all he was often drunk. In short, he was like his father. Having been asked to leave at the end of 1820 he had, ever since, been in London, often with STC, attempting to write but in fact doing as much procrastinating and drinking as working and even less earning. STC's landlords were fed up – he had to leave. STC chose this late moment to get involved in parenting. He decided Hartley should go back to Greta and work at Ambleside School under Mr Dawes, his former headteacher. Southey would not hear of it. 'The scheme of sending him to be under his mother's eye is preposterous,' he wrote to a sympathetic Wordsworth. 'As to his living under my roof . . . I certainly will not suffer any such disturbance of my peace or comfort as such an arrangement will inevitably bring with it.' He petitioned Wordsworth to remind STC that 'Mrs C has no establishment in which H can be received.'[34] Mrs STC understood, but it made her and Sara all the more acutely aware of their grace and favour position at Greta. Derwent was away at university (he went to St John's College, Cambridge, in 1820) and Sara felt increasingly alone.

During Dora's brief visit, she and Sara comforted each other as best they could. Dora, Sara's childhood 'adviser', listened and sympathised. Sara wanted to go to London. She wanted to go and find her father. His reputation as a philosopher, poet and teacher had been gradually rising in the past few years. STC was now 'the Sage of Highgate', and his home had become something of a magnet for young men of an intellectual persuasion. Thomas Carlyle, John Stuart Mill and Ralph Waldo Emerson joined the throngs who flocked to meet him. At Greta and Rydal, by contrast, he was still mocked. Aunt Dorothy had merely sighed over 'Poor Coleridge!' when she noticed that STC had recently put an advert in the paper for students.[35] Sara wanted to go and make her mind up for herself. A trip to London was an expensive and difficult undertaking, however, and nothing had been decided by the time Dora left for home at the end of June.

All was not well at Rydal Mount. Wordsworth had not composed a single verse since Edward's departure. Dora's father had come to depend on the younger man for everything. He was, in a sense, an ideal replacement for STC. Edward had the necessary honour and respect for Wordsworth and just enough talent to understand the older man's genius. But he was – or at least he had been – steadier in his habits, a mediocre poet, and just a little dull. In fact an ideal – and reliable – companion and aide. It is perhaps no coincidence that critics judge Wordsworth's most productive years to have well and truly ended at about the time Edward departed. On publication in 1822, *Ecclesiastical Sketches* and *Memorials of a Tour on the Continent* garnered some very hostile reviews. The *Edinburgh Review* declared that *Memorials* indicated that 'The Lake School of Poetry' was 'pretty nearly extinct'.[36] Many subsequent critics have agreed. Yet as quickly as Wordsworth's popularity amongst the literati declined, his general popularity increased. His celebrity was still nothing like Byron's but he was fast becoming a household name. In fact the only universally well received – and lucrative – volume which Wordsworth published at this time was his handbook for tourists called *Guide to the Lakes*.[37] (There is a famous story told by Matthew Arnold, which one hopes is true, of a young ecclesiastic who asked him if he had ever written anything else.)

Dora had grown up in the shadow of the unfinished *Recluse*. She and her aunts had hoped that now it might be brought out from its 'long sleep'. But Wordsworth was convinced he could not do it: 'at present I cannot face them', he pronounced of his 'ill-penned', 'blurred' and illegible notes.[38] Aunt Dorothy feared he would never write a word again and indeed, it was thirteen years before he published any new poetry. Dora did not know how to help. Wordsworth was anxious about his landlord who would not repair the roof and he was worrying about money again. You might, if you had been in Grasmere that winter, have noticed that Dora Wordsworth, the sturdy country girl from the dance, was beginning to look positively slender. Aunt Dorothy approved and told Edward, 'She is like *herself* again (which you hardly ever saw her) – Nothing remaining of that dullness and heaviness – that inactive appearance she had.'[39] It was not obvious what the next step was for Dora. Somehow, after the excitement of the dance, life had failed to begin.

CHAPTER 6

'PRIME AND PRIDE OF YOUTH'

1823

'Bluestocking Abroad'

In the end, Sara had not needed to spend the profits from the *Abipones* on Derwent's degree – a friend of STC's, J. H. Frere, paid. Instead she decided to spend the money on a trip to London. She felt not just a desire, but a need to visit her father. Her mother agreed to take her and they set off in November 1822. They travelled very slowly, in a combination of public stagecoaches and hired chaises. Having stopped at countless points en route, they visited friends in East Anglia and called on Derwent in Cambridge, but finally on Friday, 3 January 1823, mother and daughter knocked on the door of Moreton House, Highgate.

STC had lived at Moreton House for the past seven years, in an attic room of the surgeon James Gillman. Gillman, and his wife Anne, had taken in STC in 1816 at the height of his opium addiction and the kindly couple had more or less succeeded where the Wordsworths and others had failed. Instead of opium-filled nights with 'horrors' and daytime regret, he took 'delicious' walks round Hampstead Heath and annual holidays to the seaside with them. Perhaps something of his 'wild originality' was lost, but he was healthier and happier than he had been since childhood. Coleridge never stopped taking opium completely, but with Gillman's care it became a more or less manageable habit and he remained with them to the end of his life.

Most biographies of Coleridge have ended shortly after the point at which he washed up with the Gillmans. He lived on, however, well into the Victorian era. He was only fifty when Sara found him in London and it was not unreasonable of her to expect she could look forward to making up for lost time. It is all too easy to imagine her awkward anticipation as she stood on the threshold. Sara, just turned twenty, had not seen her father since she was twelve; her initial reaction was surely disappointment, even shock. The short, fat, grey-haired man who reintroduced himself had a 'flabby' face with a perpetually confused expression. She would have remembered the full lips and large grey eyes, which she had inherited, but he bore little other resemblance. STC's friends and even STC himself thought his face was too 'feeble', 'puffy' and 'weak' for a serious poet'.[1] In short, and unlike Wordsworth and Southey, he did not look the part. Wordsworth's Roman nose and Southey's rugged good looks lent each a suitably elegiac and distinguished gravitas. Indeed, Byron, decidedly not a fan of Southey's poems, thought the Laureate's face 'epic' and once said 'to have his head and shoulders I would almost have written his Sapphics'.[2] STC stooped when he approached his daughter, making himself seem even shorter than he was. His body, never trim, was now large and his breathing laboured and noisy. Wordsworth and Southey were both nearly six foot. Years of daily walking in their beloved mountains had given them tanned, lined faces and vigorous, upright physiques. Still, if Sara was disappointed she seems to have hidden it well. Later that same evening, STC began a letter to a friend in which he described his daughter as 'a sweet and delightful girl'.

While she was in London, swathes of upstanding Coleridge relatives – men of the church, army and law courts and their wives – came to inspect poor, reprobate STC's daughter and see how the girl, who'd drawn such a pitiful lot, had turned out. Amongst the earliest were two of Sara's first cousins, Henry Nelson Coleridge (twenty-four) and one of his brothers, John Taylor Coleridge (aged thirty-two). These two sophisticated young London lawyers were wild with curiosity about their long-lost relative – the Highland beauty and renowned scholar.

Sara was nervous. She wrote, only half in jest, to Derwent to tell him: 'My bluestockingism is gone abroad' and she was unsure how she would be received. She feared her reputation was causing a 'scandal' and claimed 'one gentleman expatiated most pathetically on the <u>fright</u> he was in when he first approached our house, the den of the monster'. Henry, meeting her for the first time, was prepared to dislike this bluestocking intellectual. All he knew about her was that she had recently published a staggeringly complex translation of a seventeenth-century Latin memoir. And she was, of course, Coleridge's daughter.

When Sara and Henry first met, he was soaked to the skin and freezing cold, having walked all the way from his brother John's house, in Hadlow Street, to Highgate – some four miles – in the pouring rain. (Hadlow Street no longer exists; it was destroyed to make way for the British Museum.) He and John had come to inspect this new cousin. Afterwards he told his sister Fanny with relief: 'She does not seem at all formidable; you need not alarm yourself.' The young lawyer with rather too much of the 'Eton Bronze' (according to Southey and his friend General Peachey) boasted to his sister: 'You would split to hear the way I <u>romanced</u> Sara! It amused me so myself, that once I slightly tittered, which she took for a nervous and enthusiastic token.' Sara later wrote about that first encounter:

> Yet Henry, when those eyes I first beheld,
> Their burning glance my spirit almost quelled,
> And, too intense, imparted to my mind
> A nameless dread, – a feeling undefined; – [3]

It was not an auspicious start to a relationship.

Henry had just begun to practise as a barrister after what was generally agreed to have been a brilliant career at King's College. He and his older brother John, in whose shining legal footsteps he was treading, felt themselves decidedly superior to this poor relation without, as Henry commented, 'a shilling to cross her palm'. Both found her extremely attractive but Henry, after his first meeting, downplayed her intellect. He wrote to tell his sister (who was as curious as the rest to hear about the 'sylph of Ullswater') that she was 'very ordinary in her wishes and thoughts'. Nevertheless, and because he could, he teased Sara on parting with 'the most affectionate prolonged diminu-endo and crescendo squeeze with both hands'. The brothers jested and jostled with one another: John (who was married) had sworn to Henry that he would kiss her, but, teased Henry, he 'quailed in the moment of trial'. One would pity Sara, the object of their mirth, more or less penniless, more or less father-less, and in London for the first time, were it not for the fact that she was to engineer the most astonishing change in the unsuspecting Henry.

Whilst at Highgate, Henry was fascinated to investigate how STC and Mrs STC were getting on: 'He and his wife are kind,' Henry reported back to his sister Fanny, 'but I suppose it is all surface work.' He managed to discover the sleeping arrangements and, despite all that had passed, was surprised that 'Mr and Mrs C do not use the same sleeping room. Hum!' Sharp-eyed Henry thought Coleridge did not seem 'very affectionate towards' his daughter.[4] He was right. For a day or two everything was as Sara had hoped it would be. STC wrote to tell Hartley and Derwent how delighted he was with their sister. She and her father had long and interesting conversations and she was confi-dent enough to disagree with his opinions. But one day, Charles Lamb came to call. He observed Sara for a while and then, at a pause in STC's dialogue, he mimicked her tone: 'But my Uncle Southey doesn't think so . . .' he began.[5] Coleridge was not amused; and Sara was mortified.

Shortly after the episode with Lamb, STC took to his bed and could not be persuaded out of it. He was sick, he said. Perhaps he couldn't stand the strain of living once again with his wife. Perhaps he was irritated by Sara's interruptions or the feeling she was endlessly weighing him up against Southey and Wordsworth. Perhaps he was actually ill. In all probability, he simply didn't know how to respond to this daughter – in his

memory a twelve-year-old child and now a beautiful woman –
who was desperate for a father. She was a complicated, intelligent
adult and, unlike Dora Wordsworth, he had never really known
her.

Lamb was not the only literary man not to see what ought
to have been obvious: Sara's intelligence. At Greta, later on, in
1825, she met Sir Walter Scott, his daughter Anne and his son-
in-law, the writer John Gibson Lockhart. Sara talked earnestly
to them all and found Anne particularly interesting. Lockhart
went away thinking her a 'lovely vision of a creature, with the
finest blue eyes I ever saw, and altogether, face, and figure and
manner, the very ideal of a novel heroine'. But, he added dismiss-
ively, 'They say she is very clever and accomplished. We see
nothing except extreme ignorance of the world . . . she talks
about books, bards and "the literary females of Edinburgh".'[6]
Unlike Lockhart, Sara's father always saw her brilliance – he
just couldn't see how to relate to her.

Three weeks later Coleridge was still in his bed, so Sara and
Mrs STC accepted an invitation to go and stay with John Taylor
Coleridge, his wife Mary and their two little children. Henry
was a frequent guest at their house in Hadlow Street and, though
they asked Coleridge to dinner on many occasions, he refused
to come, telling them, crossly, he was far too ill. Instead, Sara
was introduced to a new set of cousins: John and Henry's three
brothers, James Duke, Francis and Edward, and their adored
only sister, Fanny.

John, Henry and their siblings represented the respectable,
orthodox side of the Coleridge family. The grandfather they
shared with Sara, the Reverend John Coleridge, had been the
vicar and schoolmaster in the town of Ottery St Mary in Devon.
Their father, James, was the eldest surviving son of his ten
children; their uncle Samuel Taylor, the youngest. Even as a
child, STC had been the black sheep of the family and, while
he pursued his chaotic career in poetry, his brother James –
eighteen years his senior and the hero of his youth – rose up
through the ranks of the army to become a colonel in 1809.
Having married an heiress, he lived, as STC commented, 'most

respectably', and brought up his six children. This side of the family never understood STC. A generation later the colonel's great-great-grandson would explain to a scholar: 'Old Sam was only a poet, you know, never did anything practical that was any good to anybody, actually not thought much of in the family, a bit of a disgrace in fact . . . Now at least I know something about beef cattle . . .'[7] Of John and Henry's three brothers both the eldest and youngest, James and Edward, became vicars.

It wasn't just sundry Coleridge cousins who had heard about Sara Coleridge. It turned out fashionable London knew all about her too. One evening Sara walked into a theatre and, in recognition of her beauty, everyone present rose from their seats and fell silent. This was the 'Flower of the Lakes' whose face was already famous from Collins's portrait. Wherever she went people were struck by her rare beauty – large, pale-blue eyes, fair auburn hair and minute figure – and her piercing intellect. It was a heady mix. The reputation which preceded Sara had created a good deal of disapproving gossip in Coleridge drawing rooms. In fact, she charmed everyone. The men all fell half in love with her and with her position: 'surely it is hard to conceive a girl whose situation now and prospects hereafter can excite a more lively interest', wrote John in his diary '– so unfit to struggle with the world, & yet so likely to be thrown upon it. Her patrimony nothing, her father separated from her and in fact no father, Hartley' – he continued, getting quite carried away – 'of ruined character, unprofitable habits and in indigent circumstances, Derwent but little better and quite insensible of the degradation of dependence.' He resolved dramatically to offer her 'asylum' if she should ever need it. Most of the uncles and aunts left Hadlow Street promising one another they would try and club together to give Sara and her mother a small annual allowance. They invited them to visit country houses and to attend teas, suppers and balls. Only one uncle and aunt – Edward (another of STC's brothers) and his wife – were not convinced. They thought 'Sara brought up too finely, and that she ought to look out for a governess's situation'.[8] Sara was no fool, and both reactions reminded her of her position of dependency within her family and upon Southey. Despite the tactless comments, the sidelong looks, the whispered conversations and her failure with her father, Sara enjoyed London. She was introduced to a metropolitan social life which was a world away from the country dances and picnic expeditions of the Lakes: theatres, dioramas, the opera and all the entertainments London could provide. Most of all, she liked Henry.

Henry was a link with the father she had barely seen, but longed to know. He had read STC's poetry and his philosophy as a young adult at Ottery and when he arrived in London had made his pilgrimage to Highgate with so many other aspiring poets. Henry's father disapproved. The Colonel was firmly of the opinion – had been for years – that his brother Sam was mad as a March hare, in thrall to opium and 'a humbling lesson to all men'.[9] His infamously chaotic lifestyle, the way he had abandoned his wife and children, and some of his frankly shockingly non-conformist religious ideas did not endear him to his more sober and upstanding relatives. But Henry was not cast from the same metal as his father, despite his Eton bronze, and he was torn between the philosophies of his father and his Uncle Samuel. He would later declare Coleridge to be the greatest and the most imaginative man since Milton. He was proud of his slightly rebellious relationship with their uncle – he acknowledged his genius. His brother John understood – indeed, as an undergraduate he had felt something very similar himself. Henry was utterly enraptured by STC.

Henry's admiration for STC mirrored Sara's own and, having grown up with the disapproval of Southey, and the disappointment of the Wordsworths regarding her father, it was a joy to be with someone who did not pity her for being STC's daughter. Despite the links (familial and intellectual) with her father, however, Henry was from a stable, close and successful family that Sara could only envy. He was good-looking and though he may have presented his brash side to disadvantage, he was also genuinely clever: both a promising lawyer and critic and a competent poet.

By the time Sara and her mother moved to Hadlow Street,

the condescending law student had become the love-struck devotee of his poor relation. After just days he told his brother that Sara was 'the most lovely girl'. And in his private diary he reported he intended to marry this 'lovely creature' for 'I never can meet any woman so exquisitely sweet again'. Henry found it refreshing that she lacked the fashionable air of boredom beloved of most London ladies of his acquaintance. He compared her to the other girls he knew: 'She talks with much anticipated pleasure of seeing a play or an opera, or any such mundane divertissement [sic] which your Miss Bertha kind of creatures think beneath their exalted ultra personified stupid sensibilities.' He soon saw he had underestimated her intelligence and, like everyone, he was struck by her beauty. On top of all this, she was a flesh and blood representative of Coleridge. He was falling in love.

Sara understood Henry. She saw how the would-be-lawyer, diligent as he was, faced an internal conflict as he studied. He yearned for poetry and theology and those disciplines which 'call for a general admiration of the beautiful, a sense of what is just and pure in taste and execution, expansion of thought rather than attention of thought. Width rather than depth.' He buckled down to the 'long strait causeway of law' and felt his mind 'sharpen like a grindstone as it narrows'. The simile is aptly poetic. He longed for intercourse with his uncle's 'just and original views'. Sara, who had grown up amongst the Lakeland poets he so admired, possessed an intellect which might itself, in another age, have been well suited to the law. Their conversations were stimulating and impassioned.

Since his early teens, Henry had been an ardent admirer of his uncle; until now, however, he had not had much chance to get to know him. After a successful academic career at Eton – where he once wrote a long tribute to his uncle in a school magazine – and King's College, Cambridge, he had just begun to study law in London. On getting to know him, the poet felt great affection for his nephew who was between Hartley and Derwent in age. The relationship had developed more quickly and easily than the one between Sara and STC. The more

Henry conversed with Coleridge, the harder he found it to keep
his nose to the grindstone: 'It is an agony to me to read a stiff
case,' he told his brother James, 'my head is not sufficiently
analytic. Even this early in life I know my strength to be in
discourse and not in <u>tension</u> of mind. Accordingly I am fond
of, and understand History, Poetry and Criticism.' He fell in
love with STC and Sara simultaneously. He wrote to James
breathlessly of his feelings towards both: 'She really is an acqui-
sition to our family, it is a mechanical[?] delight to feel that it
is all ain fluid in yourself and a being of so much loveliness,
sweetness and intellect. Her mother I do not much like. My
uncle talks like no one else in this world, on all subjects whatever and at all times, he pours forth more learning, more, just
and original views, and more eloquence than I ever expect to
witness again.' Sara was part of STC and throughout her adult
life dedicated herself to being his daughter and aligning her
mind with his. Henry found that Sara seemed to return his
feelings.

From the start Henry knew his family would disapprove, so
he held back for a while from even admitting to himself that he
wanted to marry her. Had their approval been plausible, he
would have considered himself 'downright in love' within a
fortnight. 'One reason only' prevented him.[10] There were, in
fact, several pressing reasons. Sara was his first cousin, and while
marrying your cousin was not illegal (nor is it now), it was no
longer considered as desirable as it once had been. Next, neither
Henry nor Sara had money, although Henry at least had the
prospect of some future income. It did not help that Sara was
accompanied by her 'unbecoming mother' in whose eye Henry
thought he read 'design'. John agreed with Henry's assessment.
Mrs STC was 'weak and garrulous, and fidgety, & not genteel'
– a 'tyrant' even – and had ambitions to make the most of
London and marry Sara off.[11] The most significant problem,
however, was that Henry knew his father, the Colonel, would
not want his son to marry STC's daughter – given his opinions
about his poet-brother, she was hardly what he would choose
for a daughter-in-law.

Sara and Henry were so quick to declare their love – to each other at least – that the attraction must have been sudden, powerful and intensified by the knowledge that Sara's visit was short and the affair had to remain secret. Sara's impression of 'nameless dread' from his burning glance had gone. Instead, 'now thy gentle heart I better know/ 'tis but a warm yet soft and steady glow'. Ten weeks after they had first met, Henry gave Sara an engagement ring set with locks of her own hair. She took the coral necklace she always wore around her neck and fastened it around his throat. She did not do this lightly. She was, as Hartley later said, like Desdemona: 'When she loved, the fate/ Of her affections was a stern religion.' On 21 March, Henry confided to his diary that he and Sara were 'solemnly engaged to one another'. He wore her corals as he wrote. It had been a swift journey from rakishness to solemnity.

Sara had left Greta full of hopes and expectation about building a relationship with her father. Three months after arriving in London she set off for home having failed to do that. Instead of a father she had gained a fiancé. Henry was left to pine, to write devoted love letters and spill out his secrets to his trusted sister, Fanny. Sara had nobody to whom she could confide her feelings. London had strained her relationship with her mother. Sara found herself sympathetic to her brothers who were increasingly irritated by Mrs STC. The siblings felt their mother grew more and more 'Job-ish': that is to say, she always gave the impression she laboured under endless persecutions and difficulties. Sara knew Mrs STC would not have supported the marriage. It would not be the question of consanguinity, but money. Having lived a life without financial security, she had always hoped Sara would not have to do the same. If she had 'designs' in London, they were simply that Sara should marry well. She could not feel confident marriage to Henry would suit her brilliant but impractical daughter. She looked 'with an eye of apprehension, if not censure on all matrimonial engagements, where aught is left to be provided for by the bounties of Tomorrow' and worried about how Sara could possibly manage life on a low income.[12] 'I daresay they will *now* in the prime and pride of youth agree to live on hope; but, how will it be when youth and charms are fled?'[13] It was a tragic account of her own marriage, if nothing else.

On their way home, Sara and her mother were invited to Ottery to stay with the Colonel and his wife and yet more respectable Coleridge cousins. She did well with the Colonel. 'Sara is a sweet Girl,' wrote the bluff old man, 'and she has attached herself to me, and indeed to us all. Fanny [his wife and Henry's mother] is delighted with her.'[14] He took a strong dislike to Mrs STC but for Sara's sake he decided to increase the stipend he paid her. Had he any idea of the promises Sara and his son had made he would certainly not have been so affectionate or so generous. From Ottery, Sara went to Exeter, Bristol and Nether Stowey, and she and her mother arrived back at Rydal to her 'Father-in-spirit', Wordsworth, in the third week of June 1823. Despite referring to her as 'The Maid of Paraguay', Aunt Dorothy was surprisingly complimentary about Sara. She wrote to tell Edward: 'The young creature has returned to her native mountains unspoiled by the admiration that has been showered upon her – indeed I think her much improved. She is a sweet girl to look upon and is truly amiable.'[15] If Dora had been at home, Sara would probably have told her everything. But Dora had left, just days earlier, for Harrogate.

'Parisian Steps'

All through the spring and early summer of 1823, Dora's relations had been absorbed by the great drama of Dora's skin – she had spots! They summoned the doctor and he prescribed six weeks in a spa town. The aunts settled on Harrogate, where Mary had a cousin, and Dora was duly packed off, with little enthusiasm. She had hoped she would not have to stay the full six weeks so she could be back by the time Sara returned from London.

Harrogate was a dull end to the dull twelve months which had begun with Edward's departure in June 1822. Then Dora had been so gloomy that her aunts took her on various trips to try and lift her 'heavy spirits'. In the autumn they visited nearby Coniston Water and Stockton-upon-Tees, but there is a limit to how interested you can be in trees and water, even if you are a Child of Nature, and the expeditions had done little more than pass the time to Christmas. Meanwhile everyone else was having fun. Her parents went off on a continental tour (this time to the Low Countries); Edith Southey followed Sara to London. Aunt Sara visited friends in Boulogne from where she wrote a cheerful letter full of her adventures and excitements. It included a good paragraph, full of advice about how to remove her acne: 'wash <u>not only your face</u> but generally with sand'. Dora's spots became a very public conversation topic. Everybody wrote to tell everybody else how they were coming along. Aunt Dorothy wrote to all her friends about them and her parents inquired about them from guesthouses in Antwerp and Bruges.

Dora occupied herself through the spring of 1823 trying to read Horace, 'most industriously', keeping up a conscientious correspondence and sketching, but nothing could disguise her boredom.[16] Aunt Dorothy's spinster future beckoned. She began to sign her letters to Edward 'Old Maid'. Given she was not yet twenty it was a joke, but one that disguised a very real fear: someone was going to need to look after her parents, and it would not be her brothers. For most of the time, it was just Dora and Aunt Dorothy and Willy in the house. Her elder brother, John, was at Oxford. Only her younger brother Willy, deemed too sickly to attend school, was at home. She did her duty uncomplainingly, but silently she languished.

Hartley Coleridge had started his new job teaching at Ambleside in the autumn of 1822. (A compromise plan had been agreed: he took up the post but instead of living at Greta, took his own cottage in Ambleside.) He came to stay at Rydal from time to time, but he was bitter about having been made to resign his fellowship at Oriel, and was still inclined to drink too much. He found Willy 'a bore' but thought – as he always had – that Dora was 'a sweet, good humor'd girl'. Dora, who had more or less grown up with him, loved him like a brother and tried to help him. She found his conversation as bewildering as his father's, but when he was not there she had even less to occupy her. In May 1823, when Aunt Dorothy caught a 'most severe cold', Dora was 'a tender nurse and faithful housekeeper' – but all the time Edward was on her mind. 'She never lets half a day go by without talking of you all,' Dorothy wrote to tell Edward. Compared to the noise and bustle his family had brought to Rydal the year before, it was a sad and empty house and the emptiness made Dora miss Edward and his girls all the more. Her unhappiness did not increase her enthusiasm for the spa cure for her spots, but she set off obediently at the end of May.

William and Mary returned in June and went straight to Dora in Harrogate, where they stayed a week or two to fulfil her doctor's prescription. To Dora's frustration, by the time they arrived home Sara, having waited a week at Rydal, had returned to Greta. Only the drama of the spots remained. On the very day Dora reached Rydal, Aunt Dorothy wrote to update her friends Elizabeth Crump and Mary Laing with the sad news that they were 'as fresh as ever'. Crump and Laing replied with their advice. The summer – and the spots – stretched out in front of her.

Then, still before Dora had a chance to see Sara, she received a letter from Miss Eliza Dowling, her former schoolmistress at Ambleside, explaining that Eliza's two sisters were in Paris and the school was therefore in need of a replacement teacher: could Dora oblige? There is no record of the debate that broke out in the Wordsworth house at this request, but we can be certain there was one – and bad-tempered too. This was not *done*. The people who taught, even at such genteel institutions as Miss Dowling's, were much to be admired for their industriousness and virtue, but they were equally to be pitied. These were women who needed to work, who were in the sad position of having neither a husband or father or brother who could support them. All the Wordsworths were fond of Miss Dowling; nonetheless, the idea that Dora should take up paid employment was disturbing. She was hardly in Sara Coleridge's position. But Dora wanted to go, and, to everyone's amazement, the girl whose spirit Aunt Dorothy was sure she had broken answered back. For the first time since she was a small child, she stood up to her family.

And so she went; quite probably with warnings from her parents and Aunt Dorothy that she would soon return, exhausted by the drudging realities of being a schoolmistress, and perhaps with even more spots. How surprising, then, to learn Dora was not only managing, she was actually excelling. Aunt Dorothy in particular was forced to recognise a more adult and independent Dora. 'You will be surprized to hear of Doro's present engagement,' she told Mary Laing, and went on to explain her niece had thirty-seven or thirty-eight students under her care who were evidently very fond of her.[17] Six or seven slept in her bedroom every night and Dora was quite content. Miss Dowling begged her to stay on permanently. Dora had always had a natural affinity for children, but since the departure of the Quillinan girls she had only had ageing relatives to care for. What Aunt Dorothy found most surprising – alarming, perhaps – was Dora's evident pleasure at being away from home. On 31 August she came back for dinner but returned to Ambleside straight afterwards. Aunt Dorothy had wanted her to write to various of her old acquaintances, including Elizabeth Crump, but instead was obliged herself to write and say: 'she sends her very best love to you and says the first thing when she comes home shall be to write to you'. But she went on, crossly, 'you must not expect her letter in less than three weeks, for I find that she intends staying on a while after Miss M Dowling's return to have the benefit of the fresh import of Parisian steps'.[18] This was a new side to Dora.

Ambleside, in 1823, was hardly more than 'a paltry little market town' less than two miles from home. In terms of the excitement the place could offer a young woman of Dora's age, it was a far cry from London. But compared to the quiet of Rydal Mount, it was full of life. Every Wednesday, traders transformed the marketplace into a wool fair, which attracted large numbers to the town. Ambleside's Salutation Coaching Inn was full of travellers from miles around. Mr Dawes ran his boys' school – where Hartley taught – and several schools, like Miss Dowling's, provided a very different education for girls. There were shops, a post office and bustle. In July, when Dora arrived, the people gathered to watch the traditional rush-bearing cere-mony and the wrestling at Ambleside sports.* A couple of months later she heard the music drifting through the town as the end of the harvest was celebrated. This was actual country living, as opposed to romantically constructed country living. It involved other people in all their noisiness and wilfulness, but in all their liveliness too. It wasn't about being solitary but about being constantly assailed by smells and sounds and the busy details of every day. If you were looking for an antidote to Rydal Mount's stagnation, this was it.

In fact, the teaching role continued even after the return of Miss Dowling's sisters with their dancing steps because – so Dora told Aunt Dorothy – the elder Miss Dowling fell sick and Dora had to wait until she had recovered. All Aunt Dorothy could do to get over her continuing distaste that there was something essentially déclassé about what her headstrong niece was doing was to emphasise to everybody the dutiful side of her engagement and the gratitude of the Miss Dowlings, not to mention the novelty of the situation. She told her friends Dora looked forward to her 'release', and made it as clear as she could that the enterprise had not been taken up for money. In the meantime a bored Sara Coleridge sent Aunt Dorothy regular letters from Keswick saying she would like to visit as soon as Dora came home. Dora stayed away, however, until the begin-ning of October and, miracle of miracles, her spots disappeared. This, finally, seemed to reconcile Dorothy to the whole thing as a rather peculiar health trip.

* Rush-bearing ceremonies were once a common ritual involving the replace-ment of rushes on church floors. Ambleside's was particularly famous; young children carried rushes in ornate designs, there was a band and a procession. Ambleside is unusual in continuing the tradition today.

PART TWO

CHAPTER 7

'BUDDING, BILLING, SINGING WEATHER'

1823

Dora did not have long to enjoy her brief interlude of independence. By the start of the winter of 1823, her family decided her days of schoolmarm drudgery were over. It was time to return to the path mapped out for her. She needed to 'come out' and be presented to society. This was not a grand affair – no being presented at court and paraded through debutante balls – but a series of country-dances. Suitable curates and the daughters of the local attorneys and more prosperous farmers would gather in assembly rooms for some well-supervised flirtation. Once again, the Wordsworths seemed to have abandoned all their wild and 'natural' ideals and settled for something stiflingly bourgeois. Without even a moment to visit Sara at Keswick, Dora's parents whisked her off to Penrith for the first of the dances.

Penrith was a metropolis compared to Ambleside. Built in the shadow of Beacon Pike, along the route between Kendal and Carlisle, it was a considerably larger and more prosperous town. The Duke of Devonshire was 'Lord Paramount' and the town was surrounded by other wealthy estate owners including Lord Lonsdale, a patron of Wordsworth's. Penrith's economy, originally built on cotton, had survived even when that industry began to decline at the end of the eighteenth century. When Dora arrived, it was an important trade route with busy inns, shops and staging posts. The market square did bustling trade with fairs as well as the ordinary market every Saturday. On the north side of the town was a magnificent new racecourse which formed an integral part of the entertainment for those who, like Dora, came to the balls.[1]

Penrith's finest Assembly Rooms were in the red sandstone George Inn. They were widely considered to be amongst the most elegant and best proportioned in the north of England. William, Mary and Dora all went together to her first ball. 'Many persons told me that no one looked so happy in the ballroom as they,' Dorothy told Catherine Clarkson. Disgruntled, she continued: 'I was left at home with Willy.'[2] These gatherings were very different to the only other dance Dora had attended – the private party given when she left school. They were public balls, held with the implicit purpose of allowing young men and women to meet. Dora did not pick up any admirers, despite her French steps and lack of spots. She was quite happy for her father to steal the show. '"Father" was the gayest of the gay in spite of his eyes – made the agreeable to every lady in the Ball room, & notwithstanding the <u>lights</u> was all the better for his exertions.'[3] From Penrith, Dora sent her cousin Joanna Hutchinson a lively letter full of 'gay tea parties' and 'pretty young ladies, their dress' and the various other novelties she was witnessing.[4]

As soon as she returned home, Wordsworth told Aunt Dorothy that Dora was leaving again. She was to be allowed to go on her first trip to London. Aunt Dorothy was infuriated. Once again she had to make excuses for local visits Dora would not now be able to make. 'Her going was very sudden – a most pressing invitation came:' she explained, 'at the same time a Companion was ready, and the opportunity could not be resisted, though we (and especially her Father to whom she is very useful) were loth [*sic*] to part with her.'[5] Despite the opposition of both Wordsworth and Aunt Dorothy, Dora packed her bags and left.

It is hard to ascertain who was the driving force behind the visit. The travelling companion was one of the Dowling sisters and the invitation was from a young woman, Charlotte Lockier, whom Dora had befriended several summers before when the Lockier family had visited the Lakes. In all likelihood therefore, Dora, energised by Penrith, had laid plans to avoid another long

Rydal Mount winter. Her only sadness was that things were arranged so quickly she did not have time to say goodbye to Sara. After a brief stay with the Lockiers, Dora actually spent most of the winter with family friends, the Gees, at Hendon on the edge of London. It was a cheerfully relaxed and family-centred time, punctuated with occasional visits to town.

In the spring, William and Mary and Aunt Dorothy came south to stay with friends in London, and Dora met them there. Reunion with his daughter made Wordsworth as happy as a child. He had barely seen her in the past year and was determined to show her London without leaving a single pleasure unturned. In the subsequent whirlwind, Aunt Dorothy was the only one to attempt to keep up her correspondence, but even her letters are far more breathless than normal. Dora had never seen her father in town before; it was a revelation to encounter the reality of this whole other life and set of friends. They stayed with relatives in Gloucester Place, and one of these wrote to another: 'I wish you could be here with us now – when the Wordsworths are here you would find more entertainment in a week than a month at another time – They are such seekers out of Pleasure and you would see so many interesting people – They are in full tide of enjoyment from Morning to Night . . . The poet is in high Feather, never more agreeable – and Dora is of so contented a nature that she is always happy.'[6] London was the centre of an expanding global empire: not something one gained an impression of in Ambleside. In high excitement, Wordsworth took them off to the Diorama (which actually Dora had already seen with the Gees). The attraction was the height of fashion. Mr John Arrowsmith of Air Street, just off Piccadilly, had received the patent for his optical show only in February.* On another day they visited the Mexican curiosities, in the Egyptian Hall, also near Piccadilly. Aunt Dorothy found the human exhibits especially fascinating: she declared she found the 'live Mexican' the most interesting 'object'. Dora

---

* Arrowsmith's establishment was part of the vogue sweeping London and Paris at the time for shows that combined optical illusions with pictorial entertainment.

was less sure, and, when her aunt suggested a visit to the famous 'Swiss Giantess', she refused to accompany her.

On one day they went from Piccadilly to Somerset House on the Embankment, walked over Waterloo Bridge for the sake of the view and still were not tired when dusk fell. They embarked on an endless round of dinner parties – everyone wanted to pay court to Wordsworth. They saw the Lambs and the Lockiers and any number of the London literati. Several times she saw Sara's father. Despite everything, STC loved Dora like a daughter, and for her he stayed healthy and out of his bed. At several dinners Aunt Dorothy and her niece were the only ladies. Aunt Dorothy lapped up the attention but Dora was less sure – as she was with the whole of London. Dora went with her father to visit Edith. She was not certain what to make of her friend's new London lifestyle: 'I tell her she is quite spoiled for she is become a real London Lady enjoys parties dances Balls &c.'[7] Aunt Dorothy was quite indefatigable; she trudged through the rain from one end of the day to the next, paying calls and visiting the sights. Dora, by contrast, used the excuse of a cold to miss several engagements and earn herself an evening on her own. She was deciding whether or not to release herself into the excitement and declare herself in favour of the city.

Most fathers offer their daughters advice. Most fathers do not, however, publish the advice as poetry, for the entire world to read and wonder over. But in the year of the London visit, Wordsworth wrote a poem addressed to Dora in which he called upon his daughter to choose between the life of the parrot – 'By social glee inspired;/ Ambitious to be seen or heard, / And pleased to be admired!' – and the shy wren whose home is the 'moss-lined shed, green, soft, and dry'.[8] The parrot, like Sara Coleridge, 'shrills her song with tutored powers' and is a 'dazzling belle'. The wren has never visited 'strange places', she is 'self-contented' and a creature of nature. 'Say Dora, tell me!' he asked. 'If called to choose between the favoured pair/ Which would you be?' By the end of her time in London, Dora was well on her way to understanding she did not want to 'exchange my mountain dwelling for all the wealth & grandeur this city has to offer'. She struggled to explain why: she was not a 'butterflyish' character, for, if she was, the 'world would be too attractive'.[9] Instead, she was impatient to get home to Rydal, the mountains, the doves and Neptune, her beloved Newfoundland dog. On the way home, however, she wanted to go and visit Edward and his girls at Lee Priory, Kent.

It is tempting, at this point, to begin the story of a love affair between Dora and Edward – or at least of Dora's romantic hopes. Once upon a time there was a girl called Dora who loved a soldier-poet named Edward. Edward's wife had died tragically years before and Edward had fled from England. The story begins on his return. When Dora heard he'd come home, she travelled the length of the country – on the pretext of visiting friends – to see the man she had loved since childhood. His return from mournful exile was the only thing that could have drawn her from her home in the mountains. Dora's father did not want her to leave his side, and usually she was the most obedient daughter a man could hope for. But Dora kept her secret from him and left. Throughout the winter Dora and Edward wrote letters, which became increasingly romantic, though they always took care to destroy their love notes. When her father came to collect her, Edward invited Dora and her father to come and visit for a week. Edward would declare his love and ask for her hand in marriage, and they would all live happily ever after . . .

But, in truth, we do not even know whether she had timed the visit to the south to coincide with Edward's return to England. Robert Southey and his daughter Edith were in London, as was Aunt Sara, and those were the reasons Dora gave in defence of her rapid departure from Rydal. Sara had been to London the year before – now it was Dora's turn. In all probability, her journey had nothing at all to do with the old widower friend of her father. Dora was only nineteen – and a young nineteen at that: even if she harboured a schoolgirl crush, neither she nor anyone else would have imagined anything could come of it. It is hard to piece together much of what Dora did while at Hendon, whether she saw Edward in London and what she hoped for from the visit to Lee. We know the pair were in touch regularly while she was in the south, but we don't know whether they also met as none of the letters survive.[10]

Whatever else is true, Dora was keener on the visit to Lee Priory than Wordsworth, but with Edward's help she set to work on her father. They managed him beautifully: 'Mr Quillinan and Dora got my Brother persuaded to go,' Aunt Dorothy soon reported.[11] Edward urged them to travel on the fastest coach (the Tally-ho). On this point only did they disappoint him, travelling instead by one of the steadier coaches from Charing Cross on Friday, 23 April.[12] Edward's brother-in-law, Thomas Barrett-Brydges (brother of his dead wife Jemima), owned Lee Priory. Some years before, he and his father, Sir Samuel Brydges, had established a printing press in the grounds. It operated mostly at a loss but nevertheless established the house as a literary hub of sorts. A couple of years before, they had printed a volume of Edward's verse (though shortly afterwards they were forced to shut the press down). It was a great coup to have Wordsworth and his family stay.* The weather was beautiful all week. Wordsworth, Mary and Aunt Dorothy settled down to enjoy the sunshine in the Kent gardens after their exertions in London. Dora was delighted to see Edward's children Mima and Rotha again; she loved them without question.

The setting could have come from the pages of a popular novel. Lee Priory was a house in the Gothic style, complete with spire, turrets and dome. (It was demolished in 1953, though one room originally at the entrance of the library has been preserved at the V&A Museum. The style of this 'Strawberry Room' is typical of the whole place: painted panelling, an exquisite tracery ceiling and a carved wooden mantelpiece designed to look like the stone of a Gothic cathedral.) It was built for theatrical effect: nothing is quite what it seems. Walpole, the great champion of

---

* As well as being a bibliophile, Sir Samuel was a notorious snob. He had a tendency to claim he had more right to the throne than the monarch. He was publicly humiliated when the House of Lords turned down his claim to the recently extinct barony of Chandos. There is some evidence that Jane Austen based the dreadful Sir Walter Elliot in *Persuasion* on Brydges.

the Gothic revival, bestowed upon it his highest possible praise
when he said 'if Strawberry Hill [his home] were not its parent,
it would be jealous'. Lee was, he said, 'the most perfect thing
ever formed'.[13] Dora, whose entire being was steeped in the
Romantic culture her father had helped to create (in part in
opposition to the mock Gothic fashion of the late eighteenth
century), was overwhelmed by it. She and Edward spent the week
enjoying nightingales in the garden and transcribing poetry.

By now Edward had overcome his grief to the extent that
he let Dora's aunts tease him about the prospect of re-marriage
– they were forever finding suitable rich widows for him. And
Dora was no longer the awkward seventeen-year-old he had last
seen in 1821. The time spent away from her doting parents,
first teaching and, after that, with the Gees, had made her more
self-assured. Her complexion had improved and her figure was
no longer 'stout'. Dora doted on Edward: 'the most agreeable
man I ever met'.[14] In all probability she never thought of him
as a lover, yet if he never questioned her devotion he must have
been strangely naive for a man of thirty-three.

By the end of the visit, Dora had revealed insecurities to
Edward which she would never have confessed to her own family.
She was meant to be going – at the vehement behest of both
Aunt Sara and Aunt Dorothy – to Ramsgate with some
Hutchinson cousins. She confided to Edward that she was
dreading the visit because of the Miss Hutchinsons, two sophisticated young women about her own age. Dora was convinced
they did not want her to come and would consider her a 'spoil-
sport in their contrivances'. 'Nothing', she told Edward, 'could
be more disagreeable than to feel yourself where you know you
are not wanted.'[15] Dora felt at home amongst people of her
parents' generation; she could happily hold her own with Samuel
Taylor Coleridge, Sir Walter Scott or the Poet Laureate, but
with fashionable young women, she was apt to be miserably
uncomfortable. She knew it was possible she might see Edward
again in Ramsgate, but even this was not enough to tempt her
to brave the cousins. A delicate battle began.

Recruiting her father as an unwitting ally in defiance of the desires of her aunts, she fought to flee to the safety of home. Wordsworth was not part of the Hutchinson trip so she told him she could not bear the idea of separation. He was so touched that 'he yielded' to her demands. Aunt Dorothy was furious, but presented with a fait accompli, she was forced to write and cancel. 'I assure you this arrangement does not please me,' she fumed.[16] All the explanation she was able to proffer in her letter was that Dora and her father could not bear to be parted from one another. Wordsworth and Dora's mutual adoration would eventually entwine Dora unhealthily within her family, but for the time being she could employ his feelings to her own ends. Wordsworth had been rude to the Hutchinsons and risked a serious family rift – not to mention the disapproval of his sisters-in-law and wife – but he left them to deal with the mess and he and Dora drove home together in triumph.

By May Day, when he bade the Wordsworths farewell, Edward had begun to fall in love. For the first time he had seen Dora as a woman, and the fact she was Wordsworth's daughter gave her an allure no other woman could attain. Edward was undergoing an experience strikingly similar to that of Henry Coleridge the year before in London, with regard to Sara. Unsure what to make of his feelings, he sent Wordsworth a love poem. He would never have expressed his love for Dora anything like so ardently as he did towards her father; Dora would have responded with horror if he had. The verse in question, entitled 'To The Poet', is a terrible poem, but a double love poem for all that. (Wordsworth declared it to be 'very pretty' which, if he was genuine in his praise, suggests his aesthetic judgement could be severely swayed by flattery.)[17] Edward compares Wordsworth to a solitary nightingale, and the refrain mourns that 'he has gone away'. Dora, who was increasingly acting as Wordsworth's secretary, opened the letter.

> Wordsworth, the nightingales are come!
> They love the pleasant groves of Lee;
> 'Tis budding, billing, singing weather;
> 'Birds of a feather

Flock together.'
And where they are 'tis fit that you should be.[18]

And so on for several more verses, until it ends:

Yet he is gone away
Upon the very day
They flock to greet the bard, and welcome in the May.

Dora read it aloud to her father on their way home.

In the middle of June 1824, the kitchens of Greta Hall and
Rydal Mount were unusually busy. A great picnic expedition was
planned to the summit of Causey Pike, a good-sized fell a couple
of miles from Keswick. At Greta, from where the walkers would
depart, Betty, Mary and Hannah (Southey's ' ladies of the
kitchen'), presided over by the inimitable Wilsy (the children's
nurse), had been baking breads and cakes for several days. On
the morning itself, they packed these, along with cold roast
meat, cheese and punch, into cases and boxes. The entire household hunted out tin cutlery and tartan blankets, cooking pots
and kettle-pots. Countless trips were made to rummage about
in the mangling room. Southey's youngest children were decked
out in clogs and coats and given little baskets in which to carry
out lunch and bring back 'treasures of mosses and lichens'. Isabel
was twelve years old and Cuthbert just five. Sara, at twenty-one,
and Bertha and Kate aged fifteen and fourteen were probably
too old to collect mosses, but, with Mrs STC and Aunt Lovell,
they helped the little ones get ready.

Picnic expeditions were a speciality of Southey's. Indeed, his
picnics, like the legendary ones of his great friend, Sir Walter
Scott, were a defining part of the Romantic culture. In his
younger days, Scott had made a practice of taking his family
every summer Sunday after prayers. Like Southey, he planned
things meticulously to create a picture of rustic spontaneity.
Scott would sink wine in a well under the brae, chilling it in
water instead of ice. His lavish picnics (complete with his pet

pig) became a feature of the way he socialised – as they did for both Southey and Wordsworth. This particular expedition to the peak of Causey Pike was for the extended families of Keswick and Rydal. By good luck or good planning, Southey arranged the expedition for just a week after Dora's return. Finally Dora and Sara would be reunited. Because one or other of them was always travelling, they had not seen each other for almost two years – not since the miserable autumn of 1822. They had sketchy outlines of each other's movements from letters, but they could not judge if time had altered the friendship.

Sara was delighted to hear about Dora's flight from the Hutchinsons but aware of the impropriety of her friend's behaviour. She wrote with delight and amazement to tell Derwent the news: 'You know she has given all her friends the slip and returned home many months before she should have done.'[19] Mary referred to Dora's flight with her father as an 'elopement' that she did not want to talk about because of all the 'discussion' it had caused. There is just a hint that Mary found the unusually intense relationship between father and daughter troubling.

The Keswick walkers met the Rydalians and the group of thirteen set off for the summit. Sara, scrambling as fast as she could, reached the top long before the rest. She might have been delicate, but she was determined. She was joined on the peak by most of the party, who shortly afterwards descended a little to eat their meal, gypsy-style, around the campfire by the stream. Perhaps she and Dora sat a little apart, looking down on the views of Derwentwater, Skiddaw and Blencathra, and talking. Perhaps Sara shared with her the details of her new diet. Perhaps Dora silently observed the way Sara ate. Sara had discovered the irksomeness of the days could be staved off by leaving off butter and cakes. Breakfast should be small – an egg with perhaps a piece of dry bread. All the Rydal and Keswick women (including the Keswick aunts) seemed to have disordered eating patterns if not eating disorders. In fact, the only women of the whole group who did not seem to lose weight at difficult times were Mrs STC and Aunt Sara. Sara's thinness was just on the healthy side of fashionable. Aunt Dorothy – herself obsessively abstemious – did not go so far as to praise, but could not quite conceal her admiration. Sara was not sickly or bony but instead a 'Lily flower to be snapped by the first blast'.[20]

As they sat chatting quietly and looking out over the peaks and lakes, each girl faced an equally difficult immediate prospect. It is hard to imagine they did not discuss their worries. Sara's love affair was progressing tortuously. It had been more than a year since her London visit, and she had not seen Henry since. They had stuck determinedly to their engagement but, if anything, the likelihood of their ever marrying seemed to have diminished. Sara was still reeling from the shock of a series of letters she'd received from the Ottery Coleridges. Just that month, Henry had eventually plucked up the courage to tell his father about Sara; the reaction was worse than either had feared. The Colonel flew into a rage and demanded an end to the relationship. Henry, believing he acted for Sara's sake, had agreed. The Colonel then gave poor John (Henry's brother) the unenviable task of writing to tell Sara she should consider herself 'entirely disengaged'.[21]

Dora could do little more than sympathise with Sara's plight. She herself was relieved to be home again. She almost certainly did not speak about Edward. Nor, despite the coy hints from various aunts, was there anything to say on the general topic of marriage prospects. Her immediate future, as far as she was concerned, involved persuading her father to work on *The Recluse*. Sara called it her 'Rydal Mount career' and Dora took it seriously. But Sara grew increasingly worried that Dora would sacrifice herself on the altar of poetry – Dora was 'all tenderness and attention to others and self-postponement'.[22] The party stayed on Causey Pike until the sun began to set; then they made their way down and back to their separate homes.

At Greta Hall, Sara sat down to compose a letter of furious, controlled dignity to the Coleridges. 'According to current notions of honour, I may be disengaged, but my own feelings will never permit me to think myself so: in the eye of the world I might be justified in bestowing my affections elsewhere, since Henry cannot assure me of his hand as well as his heart; but after what has passed between us,' she continued bravely, 'after the vows that we have interchanged, I must ever think that for either of us to make a transfer while the attachment of the other party remains undiminished, would be a faithless and falsehearted thing.' She followed logically through what she had thought, felt and done and concluded: 'No! When I gave my heart to him I gave it for good and all, and never will I take it back till I perceive he is weary of the gift.'[23] Having made her decision, she considered herself as good as married. So she waited patiently at Greta.

Unfortunately, when it became clear to Henry's family that the lovers were going to be stubborn, the Colonel hit upon a new plan. In September 1824, Henry wrote to tell Sara he was obliged to travel, with his cousin William Hart Coleridge, to the West Indies.* His mother hoped the climate might improve Henry's poor health. His father hoped it would cure him of his love for his cousin. Sara told him she would wait but her own health suffered; she could not sleep. Henry wrote Sara passionate letters, which she read wandering alone in Greta's garden, the mighty Skiddaw mountain in the background. A letter in her hand, she would walk through Greta Hall's not-very-productive orchard, into the wood and down towards the river where she was out of sight. She replied to Henry in elegant sonnets: 'O, how, Love,' she asked, 'must I fill/ This dreary, dreary blank?'[24] She began to use opium with greater frequency to deal with the 'exhaustion produced by so many disturbed uneasy nights'. She did not like taking the drug, but persuaded herself she would find 'no difficulty in leaving it off'.[25] Her diet became ever more rigorous, partly to try to regulate her opium-deranged bowel movements. For both Dora and Sara, marriage was the only realistic alternative to dutiful spinsterhood or, perhaps in Sara's case, paid employment. Either seemed a bleakly distant prospect.

* William was the first Anglican bishop to be appointed to a foreign diocese and was Bishop of Barbados from 1824 to 1841.

CHAPTER 8

'THE PARROT AND THE WREN'

1826

'Bird of the Saloon'

In the years Henry was away in the West Indies, Sara grew increasingly committed to him, if occasionally nervous.

> And when I dwell on Henry's raptured strain
> I almost dread lest we should meet again,
> Lest closer ken the dear deceit remove,
> And I less please, and he more warmly love.

To her relief, as soon as he returned from the West Indies in the summer of 1826, Henry wrote to reassure her that two years abroad had only made him long all the more for his 'loved form'.

She had spent the intervening years fending off unwanted advances from hopeful local youths while writing him poetry. It seemed the Colonel's plan had failed – until Henry almost ruined everything. While abroad, he had kept a journal. When he returned he published it. The book, *Six Months in the West Indies*, did not go down well with Sara's relations. In the first place it was all about 'Eugenia', an absent heroine: 'My cousin . . . almost my sister, ere my wife', whose 'fair and languid shape rose ever and anon between the foamy crests of the purple waves . . . beckoning and speaking, though I could not hear'.[1] STC (he of the failed marriage, Asra love poems and countless infatuations) thought the book was 'ruthlessly indiscreet' and he was troubled: people might be misled into imagining that Henry loved Sara!

By now, Henry and Sara's engagement was an open secret amongst their closest friends and family – STC, however, had not been told a thing. Having read Henry's book he complained about it to his landlady Mrs Gillman. Embarrassed, she confessed she had heard rumours the pair were, in fact, engaged. Coleridge wrote to Greta immediately and demanded to know if the rumours were true. Sara confessed all and her father replied to say that though he did not feel he was in any position to withhold permission, he disapproved. Apparently without irony, he expressed hurt that she had not felt able to confide in him.

Even worse, for Sara, than exposing the secret were some of the more racy passages in Henry's book. These filled Sara's brothers with doubts. Hartley was disgusted by the book's 'flippancy' and 'vulgarity'. Henry had given detailed accounts of his interaction with the Creole people, in particular with Creole women. He described 'the soft dark eyes' of Creole girls at dances which seemed to speak 'such devotion and earnestness of spirit that you cannot choose but make your partner your sweetheart of an hour, there is an attachment between you which is delightful, and you cannot resign it without regret'. Hartley read the book with horror and decided Henry would not 'accord with the exquisite tenderness and susceptibility' of his sister's 'moral and physical constitution'.[2] Even reviewers of the book expressed sympathy for the fair Eugenia, doubting the 'allegiance and fast fealty' of its narrator. It was a testing time for Sara. She became the subject of gossip – the fall from Maid of Ullswater to poor pitiable Eugenia! She didn't know who knew what. Cousins must be talking, tongues clacking behind closed doors; even the girl who served in the Royal Oak inn and Otley the clockmaker in Keswick had probably heard all about it. She didn't want to doubt Henry for 'babbling' (as the critic put it) 'about making his fair partners in the Antilles the sweethearts of the hour'.[3] But had she really been deserted, as they suggested? She decided to travel to London again. She would see Henry, and she would consult STC.

Sara's mother was not keen on another journey to London, and not wildly keen on Henry either, so Sara had to find another escort. Wordsworth came to her aid and persuaded his friend Mr Gee, who was staying at Rydal Mount and about to return south – to wait for her. Sara disliked long journeys and could never sleep on the road. She was an awkward travelling companion, since most people preferred to travel at least partly at night for the sake of speed. Kindly Mr Gee, however, agreed to hire the most comfortable carriage he could, a barouche, and he promised they would spend every night en route comfortably with friends.* But, in the first week of July, just as Sara was about to leave, Isabel Southey, aged fourteen, was taken ill. She had a sore throat and kept being violently sick. Sara had tutored Isabel along with the other Southey children and Isabel was the great pet of Edith, Bertha and Kate Southey, as well as of Dora and Sara. Sara hung back, unwilling to leave while the house was in such a state of anxiety, and Mr Gee agreed to wait a little longer.

On the evening of 16 July 1826, Southey called his entire family into the drawing room and told them Isabel had died. At the end she had been so sick that Southey got down on his knees beside her and begged God to release her. She had died quite peacefully 'as if she were falling asleep'. While Sara, Bertha, Kate, six-year-old Cuthbert and the adults reeled from the shock, Southey read a passage from Corinthians. His words resonated through the still library in which, just weeks before, Isabel had acted as assistant to the older girls who had been commissioned by Southey to catalogue his 6,000 books to while away the days. 'Therefore, my beloved brethren, be ye steadfast,' read Southey, 'unmoveable, always abounding in the work of the Lord, forasmuch as ye know that your labour is not in vain in the Lord.'4

Sara did not know what to do with herself. Three days after Isabel's death, Southey wrote his eldest three children – Kate,

---

* A barouche was a good way to travel in the summer because it had a collapsible roof so did not get too hot. It was a particularly expensive, luxurious vehicle, however.

Bertha and Edith – a moving and loving, if brutally honest, letter about life and death. 'My Dear Daughters,' he began, 'I write rather than speak to you on this occasion, because I can better bear to do it, and because what is written will remain . . . When your dear mother and I were last visited with a like afflic- tion, you were too young to comprehend its nature. You feel and understand it now; but you are also capable of profiting by it, and laying to your hearts the parental exhortations which I address to you while they are wounded and open . . . Who may be summoned next is known only to the All-wise Disposer of all things. Some of you must have to mourn for others; some one for all the rest. It may be the will of God that I should follow more of my children to the grave; or, in the ordinary course of nature and happiest issue, they may see their parents depart.'[5] Southey gave a copy of the letter to his three girls, but he did not give one to Sara. He treated her as a daughter in many ways, but Isabel's death served to remind her, once again, that her future was not at Greta. As before, Southey thought about leaving. This time he went so far as to allow his landlord to place an advertisement in the paper to sell Greta Hall. [6] Sara's chief occupation at Greta had been hearing Isabel's lessons. The next surviving child, Cuthbert, was not yet six and didn't need much beyond the basic 'ABC' and one of his sisters could provide that.

Sara was not needed in this house of tears, so packed her bags quickly and set off for Rydal, where Mr Gee was still waiting. Dora understood her misery. So much of her own childhood had been bound up with the Southey children that she grieved for Isabel almost as much as Sara did. Perhaps mindful of her own ambiguous situation, she urged Sara to resolve the affair with Henry once and for all. Some of the other inhabitants of Rydal Mount gave Sara a cooler welcome. Aunt Sara was shocked to learn of the affair and thought the whole thing scandalous. 'I am sorry to tell you (but it is a secret) that she is engaged to one of her Cousins – he who has written the conceited work about West India,' she told Edward Quillinan. (Aunt Sara pre-empted Lord Franks's definition of an Oxford

Secret: something you tell one person at a time.) In addition, she thought Sara had woefully inconvenienced Mr Gee by making him wait. But the affable Gee seemed to think a death in the family a perfectly reasonable excuse for delaying the trip. A couple of days later, Dora waved Sara farewell. Sara and Mr Gee – and Mrs STC who would travel with them as far as Kendal – set off in their barouche.

Just four weeks later, Dora was disturbed to hear that Sara had abandoned her trip to London. She was terrified by the journey and unable to sleep for thinking about it. Despite Mr Gee's best efforts, she only managed to get as far as Kendal. She had developed what we might call travel phobia. Aunt Sara felt vindicated in her judgement and excitedly reported all the details to Edward. 'The Celestial Blue set off for town with Mr Gee about a month ago – but unluckily her mother accompanied her to Kendal & there persuaded her she was not fit for the journey, dosed her with Laudanum to make her sleep at a time when she could not have been expected to sleep if she had had the feeling of a stone . . . and brought her back – leaving poor Gee to go alone – after having waited 17 days for her convenience & procured a Carriage in which she could travel at ease – & have the advantage of staying on the road at night.' Sara, Aunt Sara Hutchinson went on, was 'in despair – Her father disappointed – Her Lover too (but why does he not fetch her)'. She felt vindicated in her view that Sara had better hurry up and 'turn out something useful before she ceases to be ornamental'.[7]

Unable to get to London, and sick with worry about Henry, Sara stopped eating. She grew thinner and she still could not sleep: her mother became frantic with worry. She was certain that if Sara remained at Greta 'all the winter brooding over the impossibility of being able to take the journey', she would become seriously ill.[8] Eventually, with the help of a good amount of laudanum and plenty of tears Sara managed to get to London, accompanied all the way by Mrs STC. It had taken her almost two months.

From his lofty perch in Highgate, STC was quite clear he

thought this marriage idea was a terrible one. 'I exceedingly
regret,' he wrote in his notebook, 'that the attachment between
her and – [Henry] – ever took place, for four momentous
reasons.'[9] Presumably his four reasons were: the lack of money,
Henry's weak health, the disapproval of the Colonel and the
issue of consanguinity. And, of course, he disapproved of Henry's
West Indies book.

Nonetheless, if Sara was hoping STC would tell her what
to do – or what not to do – she was to be disappointed.
Despite his opium-addled brain, he was quite clear he would
not give her advice. All he wanted was for her to be content:
'to know her to be unhappy would be deeper than regret',
and if that meant marrying Henry he would not stand in her
way.[10] Besides which, he did not feel it was his place to offer
her advice. He believed that 'up to the age of twenty-one, I
hold a father to have power over children as to marriage;
after that age, authority and influence only'.[11] Today the
sentiment is admirable enough, but it was not the standard
position of the time, particularly where girls were concerned.
To anxious Sara it must have sounded like the get-out clause
of a man who did not care.

In London, in the autumn of 1826, Sara saw as much of
Henry as she possibly could. She told Derwent that although
she had thought it would be 'impossible to love him better than
I did in absence . . . I feel the chain grow tighter and tighter
every day'. She stayed, for much of the time, with Henry's elder
brother John and his family. Once again, the smart side of
Coleridgean living – dinners with bishops and lawyers; trips to
the opera and theatre. Sara did not resolve her relationship with
Henry, but she at least came away without the slightest doubt
he was passionately in love with her and determined to wait as
long as need be. She fell in love with Henry's family, his circle
and his city, and though she declared that she could have wished
all the society she enjoyed at the bottom of the Red Sea if it
would have united her with Henry, unlike Dora she wanted to
belong in London. It was squalid and dirty and often dangerous,
but it was filled with the most fascinating people. She was a

'bird of the saloon' and by the end of her trip had chosen the exile of the parrot's 'gilded cage'; she was determined to 'dwell 'mid smoke and pent up nooks' with Henry.[12]

'Because I was Wordsworth's daughter'

While Sara headed away from Cumberland for London and love, Dora, wren-like, turned down a possible lover. It was not the only time she'd had a suitor. The first was Tom Robinson, a second cousin, who had come to stay at Rydal the summer before. Towards the end of his visit he proposed to Dora. In a great fluster of embarrassment, she asked her father to turn him down – and Wordsworth obliged with alacrity. Poor hopeful Tom was a practical problem that needed to be dealt with efficiently. Wordsworth wrote him a kindly letter advising him to 'look out for some lady with sufficient fortune for both of you'. Tom obligingly disappeared and Dora was free to remain and pursue her career in Rydal's 'moss-lined shed, green, soft, and dry'.[13] Only the observant would have noticed her diminished appetite meant she had begun to lose weight slowly but steadily.

Dora's second suitor was Reverend William Ayling. That summer, while Sara was struggling to get to London, he and his sister Emma had become the new tenants of Edward's old home, Ivy Cottage. Soon Dora and Emma were great friends. Dora's aunts and mother were not entirely sure about Emma. She seemed to have 'bewitched' the whole neighbourhood, and nobody was more under her spell than their Dora. When Emma played Handel after dinner the company, both men and women, were smitten. Dora had 'neither eyes nor ears' for anyone other than her 'Syren friend'. Mary, in particular, distrusted the beautiful and accomplished Miss Ayling. She would rather Dora's attention had been fixed on home: Wordsworth's eyes were bad again and there was a great deal of writing to be done.[14] Instead, the two young women walked and talked for hours on end. Ayling often accompanied them on their rambles and joined them for tea and gossip. Dora so loved Emma that she tolerated Ayling's company for her sake. Dora had a propensity for intense female relationships. The year before, she had made friends with the poet Maria Jane Jewsbury. Because Jewsbury lived in Manchester and Dora actually saw her only a handful of times, Dora's voice is captured in her letters. She wrote with regularity, describing herself as 'Your most faithful, loving & devoted friend'. Her letters to Maria were intimate and frank: 'my heart is with you long before I reach you . . . & yet – . . . I don't feel half sure you will like me . . . I am far more of a child than when you knew me', she would confess in 1929.[15] Evidently Dora's conversations with Emma (and indeed Sara) were equally passionate.

Dora may have tolerated Ayling for Emma's sake, but Ayling decided he had fallen in love with Dora and would like to marry her. When he proposed, the question 'burst upon' Dora as a horrible shock. Exactly when Ayling asked the question is unclear, but on 1 October Dora was stricken with a 'bilious fever' so intense her family were terrified for her health. She was confined to her bedroom for the next six weeks and when she emerged she was still 'ill and weak'. She remained poorly for the entire winter, so most likely he had proposed at the end of September, just before – and perhaps causing – the fever. Unlike Robinson, Ayling 'chose not to take Dora's word for truth when she said [she] could not return his affection'. He remained in the area until December in the belief he could change her mind.

When they finally realised she was not to be persuaded, both Emma and Ayling took the rejection as a grave offence. They – and Emma in particular – talked bitterly and publicly of the affair. Miss Ayling 'turned against' Dora, saying she had led her brother on and thus behaved most cruelly. Worse, Ayling 'went about and told everyone that Mr W would not let his daughter marry him & that she was breaking her heart in consequence'.[16] It was a cruel accusation and all the more devastating because it was plausible. Any visitor to Rydal could see Dora's love for her father was of an unusual intensity. Years later, Emma Ayling's version of the story was still doing the rounds in London's dining rooms.*

Dora was distraught, not only by the way Emma threw 'black clouds over my *moral* character' but by the dawning suspicion that she herself was 'the only one of this bright triad that ever was in love or they <u>could</u> not have behaved as they have done'. Dora could not turn this into a great joke, as she usually would, for what happened played to her greatest insecurity: 'the fear that they only wanted me among them because I was Wordsworth's daughter'.[17] She may have been naive about her effect on men but, like the children of all famous people, she was acutely aware of the powerful effect she could have on fame-hunters, senti-mentalists and the simply curious.

Aunt Dorothy was away when Dora's bilious illness began, and when she arrived home in the middle of November she was shocked by her niece's appearance. Even before the proposal and fever, Aunt Sara had noticed Dora was growing thinner and weaker. As early as August she told Edward, Dora 'looks like a Ghost . . . Seriously Her Looks are sufficient to make one anxious – but do not notice this when you write'. Dora blamed her loss of appetite on her teeth. Like so many of her contem-poraries, she suffered agonies in an age when the only alternative to the pain of tooth decay was extraction without anaesthetic. According to Dora, nothing was the matter beyond being 'plagued with the tooth ache'. Aunt Sara told Edward, however, she 'will not take care of herself – nor do anything to cure herself – so she is out of my good graces at present'.[18] On reflection Wordsworth also now worried she had not been herself for upwards of eighteen months.[19] By the time Aunt Dorothy arrived home, it was clear Dora was 'dangerously ill'. Even after the

---

* The whole affair became even more uncomfortable when, several years later, Emma married one of the men she had 'bewitched' in the neighbourhood, Reverend Tillbrooke. Tillbrooke had been a friend of those at Rydal, but after his marriage he had to choose between wife and the Wordsworths. Naturally he chose his wife. The Reverend Ayling died, unmarried, in 1853; having lost his mind, he starved himself to death.

sickness passed, she would not eat – her teeth were still too painful, she explained.

Dora ignored the concerns of her family but, having rejected marriage twice, she took her role of amanuensis to her father more seriously than ever. Wordsworth in turn grew more and more attached to his increasingly fragile and devoted daughter. Sara wrote later, 'Mr W. was not so fond of her in her middle childhood as when she was approaching her woman's height. Then he began to idolise her – to see in her genius and beauty, though all of a special sort.'[20] Dora was now twenty-two and the idolisation was mutual. Hartley Coleridge, a shrewd observer, thought Dora was 'as sweet a creature as ever breath'd' but had 'suspicions that she would be a healthier matron than she is a Virgin'.[21]

Hartley had not managed to maintain the teaching role at Mr Dawes' school and was now doing 'worse than nothing, viz getting drunk in low company, and running away from every engagement to skulk in pot houses'.[22] Drunk as he might be, he could see the conflict in Dora's situation more clearly than anyone else: 'strong indeed must be the love that could induce her to leave her father, whom she almost adores, and who quite doats upon her. I am afraid that there is little hope at present of another portion of the *Recluse*.'[23] Whether he connected these sentences deliberately or not, the two things were surely linked: Dora's desire to stay, and the unfinished state of *The Recluse*. Try as they might, neither Dora nor any of the other women of Rydal Mount could persuade Wordsworth to wrench the poem, which had for so long acquired the status of a holy text, from its 'hiding-place'.[24] To do so was Dora's greatest ambition. It also seemed to be slowly destroying her.

CHAPTER 9

BRIDESMAID AND BRIDE

1828–1829

'Dear Daddy'

Two years on, Dora remained firmly on her chosen path: she would be Wordsworth's 'living staff'. She had fallen into the habit of talking about his writing almost as though it were her own. At the start of 1828, Wordsworth signed a contract to write some poems for a popular journal, *The Keepsake*. Dora was resigned. Her father was to be well paid, but Dora felt, personally, it was 'degrading enough I confess'. *The Keepsake* was not a literary volume but a rather pretentious collection of sentimental stories and pictures. (In George Eliot's *Middlemarch*, Lydgate demonstrates his sophistication by asking a rival suitor, who has just admired it, 'which would turn out to be the silliest – the engravings or the writings'?)[1] Still Dora submitted to the shame, since 'we must pocket our pride sometimes and it is good for us'.[2]

The best of the poems Wordsworth contributed to *The Keepsake* was 'The Triad', which is about three girls: Edith Southey, Sara and Dora. Where Edith is admired for her 'rainbow's form divine' and Sara is portrayed with a book in her hand, Dora, in the longest and most complex picture, is a 'Mountain Girl'. She is 'to all but those who love her, shy'. Her insight is 'as keen as frosty star'; she would 'gladly vanish from a stranger's sight' and, most tellingly, she is 'submissive to the Might of Verse'.[3] It was as though she was permeating into Wordsworth and his vocation.

Dora was worried *The Keepsake* would drag Wordsworth, again, from *The Recluse*. Once he had finished, she hoped he would return to his 'great work'. Instead, in the summer of 1828, he asked Dora to accompany him and STC on a tour of the Continent. Mary thought her daughter's health was not good enough, but Dora accepted the invitation. In doing so she stepped firmly into the position once taken by her namesake, Aunt Dorothy. She would be a handmaiden and a secretary, carrying shawls, reading from books, worrying about whether it would rain and making travel arrangements. And, like her mother and aunts before her, she also resolved to keep a journal. Dora and Wordsworth spent a short time in London making preparations for the trip and, inevitably, keeping up the usual frenetic social life. 'The whirl has been so great that I am astonished I have any head left,' she wrote to tell her friend Maria Jane Jewsbury, ' – what with calling, and receiving calls, writing, and replying to notes – Dinners, breakfasts, Luncheons, routs – Operas, Theatre, Dioramas, exhibitions and last though not least *shopping* – we are overpowered not to speak of the *weight* of *talent & learning*, this is magazinish is it not?' When friends took her to 'fashionable resorts' she always felt inclined to shed tears. She stared with 'silent wonder' at their cheerful faces, but longed to be out of the city. It all reaffirmed her desire to remain a wren and not become an urban parrot. Her 'lot' with her father was 'one of the happiest in the world'.[4]

The threesome set off from Margate for the Rhine by way of Ostend on 21 June. The idea was poignant: the two ageing and stubborn poets, once such passionate friends and firebrands, reuniting for an adventure almost twenty years after their devastating row. They were an odd-looking trio. Dora, at twenty-four, was now so thin that, despite what Hartley described as the 'childishness that always hung upon her womanhood', she looked older than her age.[5] Sara thought she had 'lost bloom' and become 'liny'.[6] She also had a hint of the hunch she would one day develop in her back. But those who commented on her appearance also noted the sweetness of her expression and the youthful innocence of her quick smile and dark eyes. Dora's father – roughly dressed in a long brown overcoat, striped trousers and thick shoes and carrying an alpenstock – was lean, energetic and kindly. STC had been grey-haired and large in stature for years; now he was a massive man with snow-white hair. He puffed as he walked and he looked and sounded far older than his fifty-five years. His clothes were scruffy and his shoes almost worn through at the heel. He couldn't have made a greater contrast to Wordsworth, who still walked miles every day, whatever the weather. Where STC slouched, Wordsworth's back was ramrod straight and his clothes always neat and well made, if somewhat antiquated.

Thomas Grattan, a novelist they met on the way, was struck by Wordsworth's thick northern accent, and warmed to him in a way he could not to Coleridge. Wordsworth (whom Grattan thought resembled a mountain farmer) had a total absence of affectation or superiority, whereas STC was inclined to complain and never stopped talking: 'He seemed to breathe in words.' Wordsworth, who often didn't follow 'one syllable' of Coleridge's conversation, 'seemed satisfied to let his friend and fellow traveller take the lead, with a want of pretension rarely found in men of literary reputation far inferior to his'.* Grattan also noted with approval 'there was something unobtrusively amiable in his bearing towards his daughter'.[7] Dora liked Grattan. She wrote regularly to tell Sara all about the trip: Grattan was 'a most entertaining good humoured creature', and moreover, 'if he were not married her mother would run the chance of having for her son-in-law one of the ugliest men in the world'.[8]

Dora's diary of their tour is often extremely funny. Again and again she noted down the ridiculous and the absurd. On the coach to Waterloo, Wordsworth and STC were 'perched on the roof exactly like a pair of monkeys'. She painted a

---

* Grattan, reporting STC's conversation with more charity, said 'it would be pleasant to fall asleep to the gushing melody of his discourse, which was rich in information and suavity of thought. But there was something too dreamy, too vapour to rouse one to the close examination of what he said. Logic there was no doubt, but it was enveloped in clouds' (Grattan, II, p. 114).

typically self-deprecating picture of a scene on a boat: 'we stept into the boat – presently our ferryman begins to stamp and rave. I cast looks of enquiry upon my father to know what's the matter – he laughing so violently he cannot speak, then upon Mr Coleridge – more abroad if possible than myself – then I turn to the diligence – everyone dying with laughter then to a man in our own little boat against whom I fancied this fury was levelled – at last father contrived to say "sit down". The truth flashed upon me I was the culprit he wished me to be seated – but I could not understand. This scene must have been truly ridiculous – I innocently trying to discover with whom old Charon was so enraged – never for a moment dreaming it could be myself. Mr C. – more humble minded fancying he had seated himself in a wrong place and not knowing what to do rose – which movement increased the old man's passion, our dismay, – and the spectators laughter. But he was a perfect Fiend. He was paid more than his due yet not satisfied followed us storming into our very bed rooms and had not the gentlemen interposed would vi et armis – have entered mine and compelled me to give him something more."[9] It could all have been frightening but, for the journal at least, Dora made it comical.

Two more careless minders of a young woman it would be hard to imagine. During a long coach journey to Namur on 27 June, Dora was hassled by a young Dutchman while 'one of my guardians was below [Wordsworth?] and the other asleep or lost in his own meditations [Coleridge?]'. In Brussels she was once again left alone to be 'annoyed, not to say alarmed, by a young man who followed me from seat to seat – laughed but said nothing at all'. On top of this, Coleridge kept getting lost. Arriving late at night into Liège they found the city, with its narrow cobbled streets, dirty and depressing. There followed 'a weary walk to the inn' which was lengthened by STC wandering off when they were collecting their bags from the carriage. The Dutchman who had hassled Dora went in search of him 'but in vain. When we at last reached our inn, there we found him.' She laughed, but he tried her patience. When their new friend, Grattan, heard STC alone was accompanying

Dora to their hotel one evening, he prayed earnestly for her safe arrival.[10]

Both poets were exhausting. Even on trains, when she longed to sleep, 'father dears and pokes her all the time', demanding her constant attention. Despite her work, however, she experienced moments of pure happiness. In Bacharach she managed to find time to sketch. A small crowd gathered and, as she recorded, 'two boys remained by me the entire time never speaking, except when they saw a likeness of their church or castle on my paper or a tree springing up – they pointed to the real object with a gentle exclamation of real pleasure'. Sketching was one way of retreating into a world that was hers alone. More often than not, however, she was thwarted in her attempts to draw. In the Hague, she sat down to try, but 'soon a rabble was collected, my Father did his best to encourage me and disperse the crowd but it was all in vain and not having the nerve to bear the idea of positively blocking up the causeway I rose in a fluster'. So instead she sketched with words. She looked at the sites as a painter, and composed the subject accordingly: 'broken arches and breaches in the walls [make] exquisite frames or foregrounds to the landscape'.[11]

Dora's journal had three purposes. The first was an explicit attempt to do as Aunt Dorothy and her mother had done when they'd accompanied Wordsworth on his trip to France eight years before and kept diaries. Perhaps her detailed entries were an attempt to improve upon theirs, for they had omitted to write about great chunks of their time. Unknown to Dora, of course, that was the trip where they had met Annette and Caroline. So, inexplicably to her, Aunt Dorothy's journal had finished three weeks before the end of the tour with the words: 'Mr Eustace Baudouin met us at the door of our lodgings: – and here ends my Journal.'[12] Mary had not accounted at all for the same period.

Dora would keep a more meticulous account. Her second purpose was self-discipline: she wanted to remember everything she saw. Her final hope was to learn everything STC and Wordsworth could teach her. It did not occur to her to question them. At Heidelberg, they told her the paintings she liked were 'not good', so she made a careful note and accepted their opinions.

Reading these parts of her journal it is intriguing to compare Wordsworth and STC with Dora at the same age. At twenty-three, Wordsworth had just returned from living in France. His older French lover had given birth to his child and he was writing wild revolutionary poetry. STC was conjuring up his Susquehanna plans for a utopian, egalitarian commune. Dora, in contrast, was the epitome of middle-class feminine behaviour. She learned to listen to STC and Wordsworth's opinions about art and archi-tecture; she followed their itinerary, accompanied them on suitable excursions and assisted with practical arrangements. Yet she saw things that Wordsworth, for all his love of the common man, missed. One day, in Bruges, they came across a gypsy woman and her child. STC commented on the child's beauty to its mother. Not to be outdone, Wordsworth composed a poem ('A Jewish Family in a Small Valley Opposite St Goar, upon the Rhine') that described the beauty and concluded:

> Mysterious safeguard, that, in spite
> Of poverty and wrong,
> Doth here preserve a living light,
> From Hebrew fountains sprung;
> That gives this ragged group to cast
> Around the dell a gleam
> Of Palestine, of glory past,
> And proud Jerusalem!

Dora would never have criticised either of her father-figures, but she did write: 'I will not anticipate Father's poem by tran-scribing my thoughts and feelings; only one thing will I note. When Mr C told this Rachel how much he admired her child "Yes" said she, "she is beautiful (adding with a sigh) but see these rags and misery" pointing to its frock which was made up of a thousand patches.'[13]

The scene is blackly amusing: the two old poets grandly exclaiming and making poetry out of poverty, while Dora saw their misery. When STC saw children covered in dust, he saw 'a perfect vision'. Young girls, raking the field, looked like 'little saints'.[14] Dora saw children working. What the Romantic poets, and Wordsworth in particular, had done a generation ago had been new and important. Reactions to the early *Lyrical Ballads* verses like 'We Are Seven' or 'The Idiot Boy' had been explosive because writing poetry about ordinary people in simple language was astonishing – and therefore controversial. (As critic Duncan Wu writes in *Wordsworth, An Inner Life*, 2002 'A central aim of "The Idiot Boy" is to break through so as to demonstrate that the underclass of beggars, peasants and vagrants that throng the pages of *Lyrical Ballads* is no less sensitive than the higher orders.') By 1828 this way of writing was no longer new and Dora, who had grown up immersed in her father's philosophy, automatically saw what he still did not perhaps quite feel. For all that Wordsworth adopted a rural and simple life (which he did at least until he left Dove Cottage in 1808), the rural and simple folk never understood him – or he them. There is a delicious anecdotal account of Wordsworth from a local woman. 'Well,' said she, 'he sometimes goes booin' his pottery about t'roads an' t'fields an' takes na' nooatish o' neabody; but at udder times he'll say "Good Morning, Dolly", as sensible as oyder you or me.'*

Above all, Dora was a brilliant mediator. She would have made a great diplomat. Wordsworth thought he and STC got on 'famously' on holiday, even if STC had a tendency to 'fiddle-faddling'. Actually Coleridge thought all Wordsworth's faults – egotism, 'coarse concern about money' and commonplace talk – had increased astonishingly since early manhood. He confided in his notebook that 'the grandiose gigantic flowers of his

---

* Likewise a stone broker was once rather flustered on hearing 'ald Wudsworth's brocken loose again' – he was walking the hills and reciting poetry ('bummin away') which was regarded as a sign of insanity of a rather harmless sort. Dora, however, was a favourite amongst the people of Rydal (see Hardwicke Drummond Rawnsley, *Literary Associations of the English Lakes*, Glasgow: James MacLehose and Sons, 1894, II, p. 138.)

philosophical and poetic genius are faded and withered'.[15] But Dora's gentle humour ensured they never quarrelled.

Exhausted, but tanned and cheerful, Dora and Wordsworth arrived back at Rydal Mount on 27 August. Dora was pleased to be back on home territory: finally they could return to *The Recluse*. Southey asked Dora and her father to join them all on an expedition to the summit of Saddleback the following day: Sara's Henry had come to visit Greta. Dora was intrigued and wanted desperately to meet him, but Mary persuaded the travellers they needed at least a day to settle back into the nest. Dora and Aunt Dorothy turned their attention once again to *The Recluse*. 'He does intend to fall to the "Recluse" being seriously impressed with the faith that very soon it must be too late (His next Birth day will be his 60th),' Dorothy explained to her nephews John and Christopher. But it seemed that Wordsworth was once again to be distracted by other, less important, poems as he tried to get various small verses through the press. Dora felt frustrated: 'Till they are out of the way we feel convinced, his great work will never be touched,' she wrote with barely concealed exasperation to Edward, '& every day he finds something to alter or new stanzas to add . . .'[16] An entire year had passed – other lives were moving forward – and still *The Recluse* was unfinished.

'Launched on the Sea of Matrimony'

Henry's visit – his first to the north – was an important step in his courtship. Early the year before, to everyone's surprise, the Colonel had moved grudgingly towards giving his consent to the marriage. When and if his son's legal career and finances were established, the pair could wed. Henry arrived at Greta in August 1828 and stayed for several weeks. Southey marched him energetically up and down mountains and the young man wrote suitable poems in response. He gossiped with the aunts, talked politics, Portugal and poetry with Southey, and impressed Cuthbert, aged ten, with tales of the West Indies. Sara did not have a chance to introduce Henry to Dora, but he had passed muster at Greta. Southey took to him: he decided there was better metal than he had anticipated beneath Henry's Eton bronze. He would do.

All of which was good, of course, but Henry's visit meant Sara's marriage ceased to be an abstract idea – a love affair conducted in poetry – and became dauntingly real. Once Henry left, the question was not if, but when, they should be married. Soon after arriving back in London, Henry was offered a job with a regular salary by King's College, and the question became even more pressing. The more Sara thought about it, the more afraid she became. She would have to leave the Lakes. She would leave the Wordsworths, Dora, Uncle Southey, her Southey cousins, her mother. Suddenly 'all and everything here have become doubly dear and interesting to me since the prospect of leaving them has opened upon me'. Mrs STC openly hoped the wedding could be delayed. Sara secretly wished they could wait at least another year, writing hopefully to a friend: 'Many things may still prevent our union in August: we have a number of ailing relatives, whose serious illness or death may cause a delay.' But given the absence of an obliging dead aunt, Henry would not hear of postponement.[17]

In the late spring of the following year, 1829, Sara – still unmarried – and her mother went to stay at Rydal. Wordsworth was alone with his daughter. Though always cheerful, Dora was thinner than Sara ever remembered seeing her. She still claimed it was sore teeth that made eating difficult, but toothache was an affliction everyone had to deal with and most did not starve. She also had a cough which was so horrible that Sara noticed Wordsworth would leave the house rather than hear it. Wordsworth's eyes were inflamed and he could neither read, write nor compose. Blinded, he complained he was barely able to think. Despite her weakness, his daughter was therefore acting as both amanuensis and housekeeper.

Aunt Dorothy and Mary were away, and so the two young women fussed over and spoiled the ageing poet. He had recently had a nasty accident in the garden. Unable to see clearly, he had fallen from his terrace, landed on his face and split his nose open. Sara was pleased to report that both poet and nose seemed to have recovered from their ordeal; only his voice had altered: it was oddly husky. But Wordsworth was happy: 'Dora is my housekeeper, and did she not hold the pen it would run wild in her praises,' he boasted to Crabb Robinson. 'Sara Coleridge,' he continued, 'one of the loveliest and best of Creatures, is with me so that I am an enviable person.'[18]

Just before coming to Rydal, Sara learned that King's College had forced Henry to resign his position almost before he had begun – they'd run out of money. Sara still longed to marry him, but could barely disguise her relief that 'all prospects of our marriage which rested on the salary as a foundation have vanished, & we are now just where we were last year'.[19] Henry still hoped to be married in the autumn: 'His extreme eagerness for the wedded bliss rather I fear unsettles his mind,' Sara wrote, disloyally.[20] Henry spent half his leisure time writing his 'Eugenia' poems and the other half doing sums designed to persuade her they could still afford to marry at the end of the summer. Sara became worried about her housewifely abilities and terrified about restrictions to her intellectual life.

She began to rehearse arguments about how married women in general – and Sara Coleridge in particular – should spend their time. Her 'creed' was: 'domestic duties first and then literary recreation and improvement'. If the former were properly fulfilled then 'no one should quarrel with a woman devoting her leisure to literary pursuits instead of spending it in making knick knacks, or at the piano or with the pencil'. In any case, surely it was incumbent upon women to be as learned as possible in order to educate their children?[21]

Children were another subject altogether. She did not see how motherhood and a life of the mind could be combined. In fact, 'children are not always desirable and circumstances of health, wealth &c make the boon more or less to be prayed for'. Now that she thought about it, 'I must say I think any couple who suffers their cheerfulness to be impaired because it [child-bearing] is denied them are extremely blameworthy and unwise.'[22]

What most frightened Sara about the prospect of becoming a mother was the impact on her intellectual life. Like many a woman since, she tried to persuade herself nothing need change too much.

Dora held her own counsel, but one or two of Sara's friends ventured to challenge her. Louisa Powles worried she might be building 'airy castles' in her expectations of marriage. Had she considered a mother might 'lose her thirst for literary knowledge'? Sara responded brusquely. 'I can imagine that some part of it might be dormant,' she conceded, and that one might become less thorough in the use of a dictionary when studying new languages; but 'I cannot believe that where a pure taste for intellectual pleasures really exists it can ever be destroyed.' Far too many women in their rank of life claimed, she argued, to 'have no time for reading', yet 'if less worthy amusements were given up I believe almost every woman might devote some time to books'.[23] At the very least they should be reading 'during the alternate year of retirement from office' – that is to say, between babies.[24] Sara did not write about her views to Henry. Instead, she set out her position in long letters to female friends, who began slightly to weary of Ceruleanite Sara 'prosing' at them. Yet behind the prosing you can hear the real panic of someone who realises that the thing which gives her life meaning may be about to be ripped away from her. She worried about Henry's expectations regarding intellectual freedom, while the prospect of housekeeping made her feel sick.

On that front, Wordsworth was no help. His idea of a perfect wedding present to a literary-minded young woman was a set of scales for practising household economy.* Sara had no idea which way up to place the scales, let alone how to use them.[25] Taking the lead from her mother, she had always looked down on Dora's education. Suddenly her friend's ability to keep the

---

* When Felicia Hemans – probably the most famous female poet of the day – came to stay the following year, he extolled to her the virtue of knowledge of housewifery and explained why he thought scales the most suitable wedding present for a bride.

house so well in the absence of her aunts and mother seemed
a desirable skill. In fact, 'it is a privilege I think for any young
woman to have the opportunity of learning the arts of housekeeping while she is young and in her paternal abode; right glad
I should be to enjoy such an one before I become a wife with
so limited an income'.[26] Now Sara asked Dora's advice, wrote
to friends and relations for tips, and wished for 'a little more
opportunity of learning housekeeping before I am launched on
the sea of matrimony'.[27]

When she married Henry they would be on a tight budget.
There would be no room for her mother, there would be no
aunts, no Wilsy with her 'ladies of the kitchen' and none of
Greta's comfortable network of cobblers, gardeners and friendly
tradesmen. As soon as Sara returned to Keswick, she would
write to ask her long-suffering friend Louisa if she could
'conveniently when you come bring your account book for me
to look at and also your tongue to say how you order it . . . If
not perhaps you will be able to buy for me such an account
book as you think suitable for the present style of bookkeeping.'[28]
She asked another friend for the recipe for a very nice dish
she'd eaten at her table once: 'a small piece of beef shaped in
a particular manner', she wrote vaguely; 'You told me how it
was done, but I have forgotten.' In return for advice on 'needle
and thread' subjects, Sara offered help in writing love letters,
an art form she'd developed beautifully through the seven years
of engagement but which suddenly seemed less helpful than
the art of writing notes to the fishmonger. She felt the truth
of what she had once confessed to Derwent: 'how convinced I
am that I should have been much happier, with my tastes,
temper and habits, had I been of your sex instead of the helpless dependent being I am. The thing that would suit me best
in the world would be the life of a country clergyman – I should
delight in the studies necessary to the profession and I am sure
that I should not dislike nor shrink from the active duties of
it.' And though daydreaming was futile, she was full of 'regret
that I cannot make more use of this noble library while I still
have the advantage of it . . . there is so much I should like to

do and see and to copy and to transcribe before I lose the opportunity forever!'[29]

Sara would have liked to stay on indefinitely at Rydal, but she felt she ought to return to Cuthbert. After a month at home, however, she returned in July, unable to resist the chance to spend what little time was left with Wordsworth and Dora. The wedding was on again: as Hartley put it, Henry had 'prevail'd'.[30] A date had not been fixed, but Henry planned to travel north in August. Sara was living on borrowed time. Whenever the weather was fine, she accompanied Wordsworth on long walks. Sometimes Dora went; more often it was just Sara and her 'father-in-spirit'. Each of them carried a basket, a spade (for digging up the roots of interesting plants) and an umbrella, and they talked on every subject under the sun from botany and poetry to philosophy and politics.[31] The conversations carried on at dinnertime and then beside the fire in the drawing room. On botany and poetry Dora could more or less keep up; on politics and philosophy, she was usually out of her depth. It was the summer of 1829 and the whole of England was consumed by the question of Catholic Emancipation. In April, Parliament had finally passed the Catholic Relief Act, which removed many of the remaining restrictions on Roman Catholics in the United Kingdom: now Catholics could become MPs or take other public office. Wordsworth, like Southey, was firmly against the Act. To Dora's surprise, not only did Sara not agree, she also challenged Wordsworth's views vehemently. At Greta, when the conversation turned to the Emancipation question, Sara stayed silent, but at Rydal she 'talked much with W. who is equally strong against the measure, with Southey – but he will listen to another side with more tolerance'.[32] What was even more interesting to see was the way Wordsworth listened to Sara and engaged with her opinions. Sara was delighted. Southey tended to lecture; Wordsworth listened, and with admiration too, and gave her space to develop her thoughts.

Mrs STC, staying at Rydal with her daughter, was torn between thinking Sara talked too much about politics and pride in seeing her do so.[33] Mary, who had returned home by now, was unimpressed when Sara 'prosed away in learned matters all dinner time'.[34] Sara was quite oblivious to how she was seen. She claimed to believe women ought not to engage in political discussion: 'By nature and circumstances women', she argued, lack 'general and particular knowledge which can alone fit them to discuss political topics'. Therefore, 'their main argument generally resolves itself into "my papa or my husband says so and so"'. But over supper she went on to make it perfectly clear she approved of the Act before concluding, disingenuously, 'I am incapable of forming an opinion whether Catholic Emancipation will prove a blessing or a curse.'[35]

Eventually the time came for Sara to return to Keswick where she would be married. Before she left she made Dora promise to stand as chief bridesmaid and also to accompany her on her honeymoon. They selected a date: Thursday, 3 September; the banns were read, the vicar booked. At Greta, in the weeks leading up to the wedding, hatboxes and clothes-trunks clogged the passages. Like so many brides-to-be, Sara had declared she wanted a small wedding, but it was becoming a grander affair with each passing day. There was a great deal to do, the house would be full of guests, and lodgings needed to be booked for all the other friends and relatives who planned to attend. Edith Southey, as 'grand assistant', was in her element ordering dresses and stoles for bride and bridesmaids, and flowers and food for breakfasts and dinners. Sara let her enjoy it, but she herself was unable to summon the energy for all the things she supposed she ought to. She could not sleep or eat and as a result developed 'wells in my neck which I might drink a draught out of if I could only screw my mouth down to the brim'. Henry would have to 'console himself with the plumpness and loveliness' of her mind. When Edith got into a panic about Sara's wedding hat, the bride found it amusing. A misguided milliner had sent the bonnet from Bath in a wagon which had 'jolted my hapless finery into a miserable condition, it is all flattened and dropping & looks as languid and lackadaisical as its future wearer'.[36]

Sara's immediate family were less involved than her Southey cousins. STC did express his desire to come to the wedding, but everybody thought it would be a terrible idea. Fortunately, he decided his wedding gift, and its message, could make up for his absence. He gave Sara his copy of William Sotheby's *Georgica-Heptaglotta*, which, he said, 'was the most splendid way I can command, of marking my sense of the Talent and Industry, that have made her Mistress of the six languages comprised in the volume'.[37] Hartley promised to attend. He said he would walk 'all night, and all night again' if necessary (which it wouldn't have been from Ambleside), but on the day itself he didn't show up.[38] Derwent, recently married, was living in Cornwall so could not come, though he sent loving wishes.

The wedding day finally dawned. Southey, gloomy at the prospect of losing Sara, took on STC's role for a final time and prepared to give her away. Fulfilling the letter if not the spirit of his childhood promise, John Wordsworth – now the Reverend John Wordsworth – was to marry Sara to Henry. In the end he did not, as he had vowed twenty years before, need to carry her; Henry had borrowed a carriage. On the short drive to the service, Southey, searching for words, assured his niece that bright sunshine was a good omen. Crossthwaite church, beneath purple Skiddaw, glowed softly pink in the autumn light. Sara wore white silk brocade trimmed with white satin and the once-squashed hat more or less restored to life. Dora and the Southey girls wore pale blue-green satin and carried autumn roses as they followed her up the aisle. When the moment came to say the vows, Sara was in tears and trembling, but she 'spoke directly' and even, as she recorded with surprise, 'pronounced each syllable of the word obey without mental reservation whatever'. Henry's voice wobbled more than hers did.[39]

After the ceremony, they all returned to Greta for the wedding breakfast. The ladies of the kitchen, superintended by Edith, had done a wonderful job. They'd decked the table with fruit, decorated the cake with exotic red Mexican Tiger flowers and wreathed the sideboard and table with white lilies. Greta's dining room had never looked finer. That evening Southey threw a great party. But still Hartley did not appear. Mrs STC did not go down to the party either. She chose this moment to start her packing. With Sara married, she had no reason to stay at Keswick. She had decided, with resignation, to live with Derwent and his new wife in Cornwall, where he had been made master of a grammar school in Helston. She would rather have gone with Sara, who she feared was being 'transported from a too bustling family, to one of utter loneliness', but there was simply no room.[40] Disconsolate, she packed while the guests danced until the party broke up at four in the morning.

Leaving Greta was miserable. Southey reflected on his loss a week later: weddings were 'next to a funeral methinks the most melancholy of domestic events'. Sara's caused him real grief, more perhaps than he had anticipated. 'In this house she was born,' he wrote, 'it became mine before she was a year old; from that time it has been her home; and there is no likelihood of her returning to this place again . . . till at some indefinite distance of time when some of those she now leaves here will be removed, and others of us in the churchyard.'[41]

After a couple of days alone in Patterdale, the newlyweds made their way to Rydal to say a proper goodbye to their friends there. Aunt Dorothy described Henry and Sara as 'a very interesting pair'. She had seen Henry at Cambridge in 1820 'and thought him rather affected', she told her friend Jane Marshall, 'but that is worn off. He is clever and agreeable; and seems likely to make a very kind Husband.'[42] After they left, Wordsworth settled down to write a letter which echoed Southey's: 'My Dear Sara, I wish you were back in Cumberland – and take care that you keep your health, and the good looks of which I hear so much – farewell my very dear Friend.'[43] Sara and Henry left Rydal to complete their honeymoon on Coniston Water with Dora as their companion. Bringing a companion was not extraordinary for the time: mothers, best friends and sisters all regularly found themselves as the third member of a honeymoon party. But it cannot have been great fun for Dora. Sara and Henry travelled in a pony chaise while Dora had to ride her pony in their wake.[44]

Henry may have been 'agreeable' but he had been waiting to marry Sara for nearly seven years – and he was impatient.

During the courtship, he had not been shy in talking about his sexual desire for her as well as his spiritual love. 'If my passion for you, Sara, is not pure, then human love can never be so. There is appetite in it, it is the tongue of lambent flames which speaks to *Sex*, but the appetite is subordinate to reason to me . . . I am sick for complete union.'[45] Sara was more reticent by nature and, no doubt, more nervous of 'complete union'. Just days before her wedding she had written a final letter to Henry, which is telling about the way the long engagement had actually suited her: 'What an interesting, agitating yet consoling inter-change of letters we are now about to terminate,' she mused. 'I could almost weep to bid farewell to such a correspondence.' She reassured him she did want to marry, but warned him about the sadness she felt for the life she was leaving. 'You will not, I know, grudge a few tears.' After all, 'Does not Wordsworth point out to you how the most excursive bird can brood as long and fondly on the nest as any of the feathered race.'[46] If Sara, the parrot, felt sorrow and twinges of envy as she prepared for flight, one can only imagine what it must have been like for Dora – the wren – dining with the couple in the evening and making polite conversation while husband and wife navigated those first complex weeks of marriage and sex. She bore it all cheerfully, but acting as supportive bystander whilst others lived their lives was becoming a pattern. She had been in training for it most of her life.

CHAPTER 10

'SORROWS OF THE NIGHT'

1834

Five years later, during the hottest summer anyone could remember, Samuel Taylor Coleridge lay in his bed at Highgate trying to prepare for death.[1] Most days he was joined, for hours at a time, by his son-in-law and nephew, Henry, who sat patiently by his side, sometimes talking, sometimes simply holding his hand. On the other side of Hampstead Heath, Sara lay in her bed surrounded by letters and notebooks and writing furiously. Recently she had all but lost the will to live; only her 'scribblings' kept her afloat. If her father had allowed it she would have struggled into a carriage to see him one last time, but he refused to see her. Instead, she composed letters, notes and essays to fill her days.

On 16 July, Sara began to write to Dora, her oldest friend. She described in detail the miserable state of affairs in both the Coleridge households. Over several days, she added to the letter, writing in short and ever bleaker bursts. Her nurse was ill, her mother was ill, Sara herself was so ill she could not walk. Her father was getting worse. She apologised for sending nothing more cheerful, especially when she knew Dora was unwell too. 'I hope . . . before I finish it – I may have something akin to news – the poorest relation in the world even – to add to it. "It's bad" as the old whist player said, "to have na' trumps at aw."'[2]

But no news arrived, just more gloomy reports of her father. 'We have scarcely any hopes now. The pain does not abate except for a very short time. I know it is useless to go to Highgate – if there were the slightest chance of seeing him I would go . . . I have no better news to add my dear Dora.' On and on the letter went. Sara tried not to mind that her father only wanted to see Henry; tried to ignore the fact that she had never really entered his confidence or come to know him in the way she had once hoped. STC had placed her on a safely remote pedestal. He could not sing loudly enough of her virtue or intelligence, but it was nothing like his very real, and occasionally explosive relationship with Hartley. If anyone could understand how Sara felt it was Dora. Of all the people who had known STC, Dora's relationship had been the most like hers: a daughter, of sorts.

Perhaps Sara also hoped the letter might rekindle a relationship that had deteriorated in the years since they had last seen one another. The friendship was, as lifelong friendships sometimes are, at a low ebb. Both were ill and unhappy at opposite ends of the country. Their lives had become increasingly different. Sara, in literary London, now had two small children, a husband and a home. Dora in the Lake District had her ageing relatives and the poetic world of her father's generation. In her letter Sara was startlingly honest with Dora about what she was beginning to describe as her 'Invalid self'. Although she knew her 'nervousness' was real, it was also patently clear that it was different to physical illness, and she felt a terrible sense of guilt that her unhappiness was therefore of her own making.

Despite her pre-wedding nerves, married life had not always been like this. Initially, Sara was happier than she could have imagined. In those early days she could 'say with truth that both Henry and I have found marriage a state of far more unalloyed bliss than we had anticipated & we can see nothing that is likely to make us change our opinion'.[3] She might not have been a natural housekeeper, but she loved Henry and they muddled through perfectly well. They read *The Odyssey* together after tea and she reaped the benefits of his Eton classics masters. They lived a peripatetic existence, staying with first one friend and then another, while they tried to find a house they could afford. In early 1830, Sara realised she was pregnant and they were both excited.

In the run-up to Herbert's birth Sara was optimistic. They still didn't know where they were going to live, but Sara was surprisingly unfazed by the idea of a couple of weeks in one place, then borrowing a friend's house in Windsor for the actual birth and then 'about a month after my confinement I hope we may remove to Tavistock Hill'. As far as the pregnancy itself was concerned, she entertained some entirely sensible fears, but was essentially pragmatic. 'It being the fashion,' she wrote to Louisa Powles, 'I ought to talk about dying in the middle to end of September and never mention next winter without an "if I live so long".' But although 'it would be folly to deny that the event I look forward to is one door by which we ladies retire from this mortal stage . . . this is no reason', she went on in good humour, 'why expectant dames should tease and gloomify their friends with grumblings and presentiments for nine long months: if they escape – which they most probably will – all this misery will have been in vain; if they are to die who the deuce is to help it!' She'd taken against those women who became all 'presentimenty' during pregnancy and irritated those around them with visions of death and dying.[4]

If Mrs STC had not gone to live with them, Sara might not have managed so well, but, as it was, in the summer of 1830 Sara and Henry found a house big enough for both a new baby and Mrs STC. Sara was sad to leave Highgate for its proximity to her father but, without her mother, she struggled to manage the servants and the endless domestic decisions baffled her. The new house, 21 Downshire Hill, in Hampstead (which Sara always grandly called No. 1 Downshire Place), was perfect in every way except it was too far from Lincoln's Inn for Henry to commute to work each day. He therefore stayed in town during the week and returned home at the weekends. Downshire Hill had been newly developed less than fifteen years before. The house he returned to each Friday was a simple brick villa with a pretty iron grille above its front door.* Mrs. STC had left Derwent's

---

* In the twentieth century the house was lived in by Lee Miller and Roland Penrose.

Cornwall house and joined them in July, which, given the baby was due in October, was not a moment too soon. It had been a relief to be able to hand over a great deal of the running of the house.

When Herbert was born, Sara was taken aback not so much by the love she bore her son, but by how interested she was in his development. She began a diary to record how and when he ate, slept and drank, and she began to think seriously about his education. As he learned to talk, she started to write little poems – verses to comfort or amuse but also to instruct. She wrote them out onto cards and kept them carefully; some of them she sent on to friends and family with children of their own. They soon acquired a sort of fame within her circle and she continued to write and develop them as the children grew up. Each one displayed a sense of humour, aspiration, learnedness and a facility with words. This 'poemet' is typical, combining natural history and Latin vocabulary:

> The top of a tree *cacūmen* is called,
> And *umbra* is shade or shadow you see;
> To sit in the shade is pleasant enough;
> And Herbert shall climb to the top of the tree.[5]

Sara was skilled at gauging what was appropriate for a child of a particular age. The best known of her poems today – indeed, the only one which is generally known – is 'The Months': 'January brings the snow,/Makes our feet and fingers glow'. It went through several revisions, becoming increasingly complex as her children grew up.

Sara weaned Herbert in the late summer of 1831 and almost immediately realised she was pregnant again. She had no particular concerns beyond the ordinary at her confinement, and managed the pregnancy well. When well-meaning friends offered her interfering advice she gently rebuked them, showing a quiet confidence in her own ability as a mother: 'on no subject I think is there a greater diversity of opinions and practices than on that of the conduct of a nursery', she told one friend, 'and on no subject does female vanity shine forth more conspicuously than on that of children & the management of them: every mother thinks her way is the path in to which you should go & I am daily reminded of the arch fable of the old man, his son, & his ass & how necessary it is to come to the old man's conclusion that by our own judgement our own affairs ought to be regulated'.[6]

Edith was born on 2 July 1832 and for a month or two things seemed fine. Henry was delighted with the new addition to his family. Edith (or Edy), he wrote, was 'plump and fair of complexion, but not so comely methinks, as my sweet Herbert, who is a dear villain of a boy'.[7] Mrs STC was in her element, as she had been at Greta when all the children were small – and Sara was happy too. Her mother, who had initially worried about how her daughter would adapt to marriage and motherhood, had been pleasantly surprised. She added a note to Sara's letter to her friend Emily Trevenen: 'You cannot imagine how odd the change in Sara's habits appear to me – so different to those of her maiden days. Reading, writing, walking, teaching, dressing, mountaineering, and I may add, for the latter 10 years of that state – weeping – were her daily occupation with occasional visiting – Now, house orders, suckling, dress and undress – walking, sewing – morning visits and receiving – with very little study of Greek, Latin, and English – (no weeping!) make up . . . her busy day.'[8] STC was enchanted by his grandchildren. He was ill when Edy was born, but they planned her christening around his health and on 9 August he came to Hampstead for what Sara described as 'a golden opportunity of a most sunny season of my dear Father's health'.[9] STC was on great form that day, talking almost without drawing breath and making almost no sense at all. Henry tried to follow him but Sara and her mother were more preoccupied with getting the small children to church than following the flights of Coleridge's conversation. It was a good day.

From early September, however, the tone and content of Sara's diary about her children changed entirely. She continued to make entries about her babies' habits, but these were drowned out by the entries about her own health and happiness. Indeed, where she does write about a child the entry usually relates to its impact on her own health: Edy's suckling hurting her, for example, or Herbert's crying at night keeping her awake. Even now, to read the diary (carefully preserved at the Harry Ransom Centre in Texas) feels voyeuristic. The document, like the letter to Dora, is a long drawn-out cry of despair.

Sara had taken opium intermittently since her late teenage years: her mother recommended it as a cure for insomnia, travel sickness and a range of small illnesses. But now she began to feel dependent. Again and again comes the single word 'Alas!' Incomplete sentences are interrupted by the word, followed by a series of dots and then the next date written with a new pen. In desperation at not being able to sleep, she asked Mr Gillman (STC's landlord and doctor) – bitterest of ironies – to prescribe opium. Her own family doctor had told her early in January to stop taking the morphine as soon as she could. Instead she consulted another physician; again he could discover nothing physically wrong. Yet still her sleeplessness persisted, her mind 'inside out like a witches cauldron'.

It was not really the insomnia she found hardest to bear, but this 'inside-outness' which by Christmas 1832 she was calling hysteria.[10] Days in a row were 'gloomy and limited – at times despairing'. She had 'a nervous feeling at the back of the head' and found herself in 'wretched spirits' and irritable with the children; she spent hours at a time weeping. And then came the hysterical fits. There are many academic theories about precisely what hysteria was or is, but one thing is clear, to the sufferer it was real. This was not about swooning girls and smelling salts. It took doctors years to distinguish between hysteria and epilepsy and recent research has again blurred the boundaries. The physical symptoms of both hysterical fits and some types of epileptic seizure are similar – an inability to swallow or breathe, the sensation of a lump or obstruction in the throat, and uncontrollable muscle spasms.[11]

Hysteria was a psychosomatic illness in the strictest medical sense of the word. There are fascinating accounts of the way in which sufferers responded, or rather did not respond, to physical stimuli. In one study, blindfolded patients were prodded with needles while others had their feet plunged into ice. The feet did not change colour with the cold, nor did the needle victims so much as flinch with pain. In other cases, paralysis or extreme sensitivity to pain seemed to have no real physical cause. Some women suffered fits; others did not. Some women with 'real' physical illnesses were misdiagnosed as hysterics: the range of possible symptoms is bewildering. It has been suggested that hysteria has 'evolved' into anorexia and other eating disorders. Eating disorders are, it is argued, the current costume of the same disease or neurosis: both seem to have affected similar populations, and both seem to be almost 'catchable', or at the very least open to suggestion and imitation.[12] Somewhere between the end of the nineteenth century and the start of the twentieth, one illness seems to have metamorphosed into the other.

Sara had physical symptoms: irregular and painful bowel movements, sweaty palms, physical exhaustion, headaches, lack of appetite, furred tongue and dry mouth, and sickness. It's hard to gauge to what extent she realised that most, if not all, of these symptoms, plus the insomnia, were directly linked to her morphine intake. As is the way with any powerful addiction, the drug gave only temporary relief from the harm it caused, and she and it remained locked on a 'boisterous sea' from which she tried valiantly to swim to shore but with little success.[13] Physiologically speaking, Sara's drug use was closest to today's morphine and heroin addicts, but socially speaking it was closer to alcohol or painkiller addiction, or even an eating disorder. Dependency often goes unnoticed and is easily denied because there is nothing wrong or illegal about the day-to-day behaviour; the cumulative effect is what is dangerous. Today, low-calorie diets and painkillers are, of course, sanctioned and encouraged by doctors in the way that Sara's doctors had recommended opium.

Tangled up with all this misery, of which she kept a meticulous account, was an increasing anxiety about motherhood. The more ill she became, the more guilt she felt. 'This dreadful hysterical depression poisons everything. Alas!' she told her friend Sara Wardell, 'I seem to be mother and no mother.'[14] She told Henry after one episode, 'I shall endeavour in the future to prevent Herby's witnessing my bad fits. I will go to my own room when I can refrain no longer. He must not so often see "poor dear mama cryin".'[15] The image of a frightened little boy, less than three years old, worrying about his mother is pitiful. Equally pitiful, though, is Sara's anxiety – she knew too well the impact a disturbed parent can have on a child. She hated being a sick mother lying weeping and convulsing upon the sofa, a presence to be tiptoed around and worried about. The prospect of more children began to terrify her.

Soon after Herbert's birth, Sara began to note with an X in her diary the date of her period. After Edy was born she anticipated, recorded and analysed her menstrual cycles in agonising detail. At the end of April 1833 'the menses' came but she worried about the small amount of blood: did it count? May's diary begins simply 'Alas! Alas! May enters with grief for me. The m. quite stopped.' The reader of these journals, so many years later, turns the page with anxiety and feels relief on seeing Sara's 'X' on 30 May. The diary is a humbling reminder of what contraception and improved obstetrical healthcare have done for women's lives. You scan each page with concern – on 20 June (surely the very earliest she might have expected a period) – 'Alas no courses!' But it was as she feared: she was pregnant again. From that 'Alas' onwards she was more miserable than ever before. She couldn't sleep, was hysterical, and took ever greater doses of morphine.

Sara found herself utterly trapped, like her father before her, in a cycle of opium. She, more than anyone before or since (despite all that has been written on the subject), was in a position to understand the way STC had behaved in 1804 when he had left England and abandoned his wife and children for Malta. In 1833 Sara was thirty-one – exactly the age at which her father had fled the country – and, like him, she suffered from insomnia, headaches, chaotic mood swings, constipation and an overwhelming desire to escape domesticity and childcare: 'every thing, that forcibly awakes me to Person & Contingency, strikes fear into me, sinkings and misgivings, alienation from the Spirit of Hope, obscure withdrawings out of Life . . . a wish to retire into stoniness and to stir not, or to be diffused upon the winds and have no individual Existance'. STC's words, but they could just as well have been his daughter's.[16]

STC had acted upon his desires. In 1804, with three children under the age of seven, and shortly after Wordsworth had pledged to complete *The Recluse* on the mountain above Grasmere, he escaped. He set sail in the merchant ship *Speedwell* bound for Malta and stayed away for two years, leaving Sara, her mother and brothers at Greta Hall under the care of Robert Southey. Having gone, STC discovered he could not abandon the opium as easily as his family. He fought a daily battle against the drug and never fully returned to his children.

Opium has many unpleasant side effects; father and daughter both found severe constipation particularly distressing. For STC, 8 May 1804, when he was living on the *Speedwell*, was a particular 'day of horror': the ship's surgeon performed an enema, but the pains continued until finally 'Anguish took away all disgust, and I picked out the hardened matter and after a while was completely relieved. The poor mate who stood by me all this while had tears running down his face.'[17] Coleridge, in his shame, was acutely conscious of what Richard Holmes calls its 'grotesque symbolism of false birth and unproductivity', the mate watching like a midwife.[18] Coleridge later elaborated on the metaphor: 'To weep & sweat & moan & scream for parturience of an excrement with such pangs & such convulsions as a woman with an Infant heir of Immortality . . . O this is hard, hard, hard.'[19] He knew opium was largely to blame, and after this episode he tried, again, to stop taking it. But opiates cannot simply be left off and it would take him another twelve years and the help of the Gillmans to find a way of managing his addiction.

By 1833, Sara was taking the same combination of drugs as her father, often dispensed by the same doctor in Highgate, and recording, more delicately, many of the same symptoms as well as her own recourse to laxatives. An entry for 21 July 1833, soon after she had realised she was pregnant again, is typical: 'I had been very sick with the morphine in the morning and the pill (laxative) did not act.' Sara had not wanted to fall pregnant, but once she was expecting she developed a chronic fear of miscarriage, and to alleviate her anxiety she took yet more opiate. One wonders to what extent, if any, she questioned the effect morphine would have on her fertility and, when pregnant, on her unborn child. That October she wrote: 'dread of miscarriage. I took 60 drops of morphine.' It's a fragment of an entry, but the close juxtaposition of clauses suggests she knew, subconsciously at least, that her habit was dangerous to the foetus. As the pregnancy progressed Sara convinced herself she would die giving birth, and she almost began to long for it. 'My griefs are not to be expressed,' she told the unborn child in a poem:

> Affection's voice can charm no more:
> I ne'er shall find a steady rest,
> Till, torn from all I love the best,
> I seek the distant unknown shore.[20]

That active 'seek' suggests something more than fear of death. It would be best if she died and her children did not have to see her 'cares and fears'. Her mother grew terrified of the way Sara was constantly 'weeping and wishing to die'.[21]

Meanwhile Sara continued to make practical arrangements: she asked Wordsworth to stand as godfather; she sent Herby and Edy to the country and called the midwife. Then her mind and life turned inwards as the birth date approached. Her poorly handwritten diary entry for Sunday, 12 January is typical: 'Dreadful day. Strength almost gone. God be merciful to me. I am in the hands of a God of mercy and of wisdom.'[22] On 14 January, she gave birth to not one but two tiny, tiny babies. She named them Florence and Berkeley. Both were critically weak and two days later each 'gave up their feeble little lives . . . one in the morning the other in the evening'.[23]

Sara did not die as she had predicted, but she did fall to pieces after the death of her babies. Such as it is, her diary becomes an endless litany of the drugs she took, the tears she wept and an ever more obsessional record of every sort of vaginal discharge from 'the whites' through to the full-blown menses. She grew 'perfectly hopeless . . . as to her ultimate restoration'.[24] Her descriptions of the children's brief lives are raw and yet within the context of the diary in which she recorded them they are only part of an ongoing catalogue of anguish. It was left to Henry to write a poetic epitaph for his 'twin buds, too rathe to bear/ The winter's unkind air'. Touchingly, Hartley too composed a poem on the death of the niece and nephew he never met. Even before the twins' birth, Sara had been lost in a haze of depression and morphine dependency; after their death, the downward trajectory continued.

The only occupation she found any energy or enthusiasm for was composing short poems, mostly for children, usually written on the back of old calling cards for the children to learn to read from. Henry, at his wits' end as to what to do with or for his wife, bullied her into allowing him to collect these cards together and send them to J. W. Parker to publish. Sara was beyond caring and, as he told his brother, Henry needed to exert a certain amount of 'marital tyranny' to get her to comply.[25] It was all he could think to do – the volume was a 'child of grief' – but he hoped it might help. He also hoped it might bring in some money. Henry was struggling desperately to make ends meet while caring for his wife and father-in-law and attempting to shield both from his own financial woes. On top of long hours, he took on mountains of additional work in the form of exam marking. In the end, *Pretty Lessons in Verse for Good Children; with Some Lessons in Latin* was a commercial success. It went through five editions in as many years and many poems continued to be used in Latin primers for years to come. Parker was well rewarded for his fifty-guinea investment.

Sara, however, was always half-ashamed of the book and its publication certainly did not improve her spirits. Henry despaired. When Sara's old friend Louisa Powles invited them to her wedding, he turned down the invitation partly because his wife was in no state to attend, and partly because his heart would be 'out of tune with such a concert'. While writing his letter, it occurred to him quite how drastically things had changed since his own wedding day just five years earlier. 'Alas!' he exclaimed, 'it seems but yesterday that bright Thursday morning that I took Sara to Crosthwaite Church; old Skiddaw looked so calm & majestic upon us & the lake gleamed so many promises of joy! For two years the mute prophecy of nature was fulfilled and then the cloud set in, I fear forever.' Remembering himself – and the purpose of the letter – he insisted, 'I do not mention this to dash you up with bitters', but he could not lighten the tone and closed his letter: 'I say nothing now of my poor sufferer, but that for the last month she has been materially worse in all aspects and my hope of her recovery is gone. "In sickness and in health" – there is something very affecting in the priority of that second word sickness.'[26] Not the best letter to receive on a Monday morning if you are getting married on Thursday, but an indication of how desperate Henry was feeling. It says something impressive about him, and about nineteenth-century ideas of well-being, that he never once described Sara's state as anything other than an illness.

Spring 1834 slowly turned into summer and it was now apparent STC was dying. Sara grew more and more prone to fits of hysteria and nervousness. She worried she had invented her malady. Surely the poor did not suffer in this way; it was simply a result of being spoiled and having too much leisure time. Sensible, Ottery-like voices thundered in her head. Surely those who argued that good diet, exercise and determined cheerfulness would alleviate the spirits were correct. They were right to argue she should not take opiates to sleep; she should control herself better; she should take a firmer hold on herself. She tried again to leave off the laudanum, but failed again. She drank more wine than she had done before: it helped her to 'appear more bright and steady' when she had to meet friends. Her eating became more disordered: for months she ate practically nothing and then went through periods of binge eating where it seemed whatever she consumed 'were cast into a yawning gulf and did nothing toward contracting the gulf', while she felt 'stricken' at the thought of how she could possibly 'safely dispose of such a load of food'.[27] She began to write notes of her fears, and some of these made their way into the letter she was writing to Dora.

In her letter, which she wrote intermittently throughout July, Sara was not at all ashamed to describe her own misery or use of opium. She wanted Dora to know how she felt. She slipped in a copy of *Pretty Lessons* for Dora to see. Most of the poems in the book were nursery rhymes: inoffensive and useful in the schoolroom. But one or two were rather more. A poem called 'Poppies', for example, contrasted Sara's dependence on opium to Herby's enjoyment of poppy flowers; for her son, poppies are 'nothing more/than other brilliant weeds'. But he with his smiling face and 'eye and cheek so bright' can know nothing of 'that blossom's pow'r/Or sorrows of the night!' In its way, it was a small rebellion and assertion of independence. All this sorrow and horror was not especially pretty and Sara's family disapproved of her publishing the poem, but though she acknowledged their feelings, she was unrepentant.*

'Poppies' was Sara's way of defending and understanding her father's and her own dependency on the drug. Herby was lucky to see only pretty flowers; she and her father needed them.† STC in particular, and opium-taking in general, had come in for public criticism by the time of 'Poppies'. Though she probably did not see it this way at the time, the poem was her first

---

* Her brother Derwent thought the poppy poem would be detrimental to the family's reputation. Sara agreed: 'the Poppy poem in "Pretty Lessons" should have been left out and some other doggerel substituted – but I was poorly' (SC to Emily Trevenen, January 1835; HRC). However, as Dennis Low points out (*The Literary Protégées of the Lake Poets*, 2006, p. 128), Sara had many opportunities to remove the poem as the book went through at least four editions. Perhaps her position of having always felt an outsider made it easier to sully the family reputation.

† Coleridge believed to the end of his life – perhaps with justification – that an internal problem made opium necessary to him.

public defence of her father. She did not whitewash his portrait – she was too subtle and too honest for that – but she engaged seriously with him. It would be a couple of years before she did so publicly again, but it was an important first step.

CHAPTER 11

'WHAT IS TO COME OF ME?'

1834

Coleridge died on 25 July 1834. Sara had sent her news-less letter just days before and by the time it – and *Pretty Lessons* – arrived, Dora had received news of STC's death. Dora had already helped her father write a black-bordered letter of commiseration to Sara and Henry.[1] For the first time in a long while Wordsworth had written in his own hand rather than dictating to his wife or daughter. His words can hardly have brought much comfort to Downshire Hill. 'The last year has thinned off so many of my friends young and old, and brought with it so much anxiety, private and public,' he told Henry and Sara, in a letter which was really all about his own desolation: 'though . . . I have seen little of him for the last 20 years, his mind has been habitually present with me, with an accompanying feeling that he was still in the flesh. That frail tie', he continued relentlessly, 'is broken and I, and most of those nearest and dearest to me must prepare and endeavour to follow him.'[2]

Dora was not in a receptive mood when she opened Sara's package from Downshire Hill. She flicked through the anonymously published 'l'il book, not worth printing perhaps' without enthusiasm. Sara had warned her many of the poems were 'not really pottery' but verses written to amuse and instruct her children.[3] She knew Dora well enough to realise she would be shocked by the inclusion of the poppies poem, so when Dora reached that page she found a note addressed to her in Sara's neat handwriting. 'Some other of my Herby Cards should have been put for these rhymes – but there were mistakes in the arrangement of the small vol. at the press – lines crossed out left in & v.v. These however were retained through inattention on my part.'[4] This must have been disingenuous, for *Pretty Lessons* went through many more editions in Sara's lifetime and she cut out many other poems, but 'Poppies' stayed put. Sara defended the whole book, fearing Dora's disapproval: it had been 'Henry's fancy', she told Dora. 'He wished for a little record of some of my occupations during an illness which left so few in my power and in this point of view I dare say it may have some interest to you.'[5] The book did not 'interest' Dora – or at least not in the way Sara might have hoped.

Dora told Edward that Sara had 'done a daft thing and published a daft book – "Pretty stories for good Children" is its title I think in rhyme & really some of it is the most wretched doggerel I ever heard'. She was too honest, however, not to acknowledge to him there was perhaps a touch of envy or sour grapes in her attitude ('But you may well say "Old Maids and children" etc.') and so she determined to be silent.[6] Silence was Dora's response to unpleasant or uncomfortable situations. Unlike Sara, she preferred not to write about troubling feelings and we learn about her mostly through what others say about her illness and its symptoms. In her letters, she is bright and cheery but indistinct. Her life was a tight and painstaking routine. Small meals meticulously planned. Forced cheerfulness and scrupulous accuracy in copying work for her father. But she is fading out of her own story.

It was only in the years since Dora had last seen Sara that her wren's life had ceased to go according to plan. Four years before, at Christmas 1830, Dora had gone to London with her parents for the sake of her health. Their manner of travelling summed up Wordsworth at his eccentric, cheapskate and loving best. He was so keen Dora should have a horse once they arrived that he rode her pony, Billy, all the way from Lancaster to Cambridge, a total of 250 miles.[7] He completed the journey 'valiantly and economically', and, after calling on John, newly appointed a lecturer at Trinity Hall, Cambridge, Dora went to Sara's new house at Highgate. There she met Herbert, the newest member of the Coleridge clan. She had been overjoyed to see Sara and feel her marriage was 'cast in an angel light'. Her friend was loved by a man who admired her intellect and encouraged her scholarly pursuits. Sara had a much improved relationship with her father and enough domestic help in the form of both her servants and her mother to make it reasonable to expect she would adjust easily to married life and motherhood.

Dora was not envious, for though she had no Greek, and though no one had ever gasped at her beauty, she still had all that Sara had chosen to give up. Once she left London she would continue to help her father write. In the summer Rydal would once again be taken over by interesting guests (amongst them this time John Stuart Mill), and she and Wordsworth had plans to visit Sir Walter Scott together. She was learning German, discussing books she would read with her father, and, most important of all, she could still help him complete *The Recluse*. Dora was living the literary life to which they had both been born.

It is a measure of how low Dora's spirits had become that four years on her comments about *Pretty Lessons* were uncharacteristically mean-spirited. Perhaps she had also picked up on Sara's almost competitive attitude to their respective illnesses. Sara told her, 'Your stomach and my nerves, are the weak parts of our respective constitutions.'[8] She explained to a mutual friend that Dora's problem was 'an inflammation of the upper part of the spinious process – between the shoulders – not like mine a morbid state of the *nerves*: however her case is a slight one'.[9] Dora was in fact more unwell than either would admit. 'Dora, though in good spirits & uncomplaining looks ill & is thinner than almost anyone I ever saw,' wrote Aunt Sara to a friend in June 1834.[10] She resisted all 'accusations' of being ill as 'nonsense' and would go only so far as to say she lacked 'strength'. But her symptoms included a whole range of coughs, colds, gastric complaints and a bad back, and something underlying them all which caused her at this stage – and at others in her life – to lose weight and live (just) whilst painfully emaciated. It would be hard enough for any doctor to diagnose a patient he or she had not met. It is almost pointless to attempt to make diagnoses

in a subject dead for over one hundred and fifty years – almost
. . . but not quite.

According to her death certificate, Dora would eventually
die of 'pulmonary consumption' which usually meant tuberculosis. TB can lie dormant for many years and kill the patient
decades after being contracted. If Dora had caught TB some
time before 1834, perhaps even as early as the 1820s, it would
explain why she suffered so often from coughs, colds and general
weakness. It would explain her loss of weight and appetite.
However, the doctors consulted on her behalf struggled to
suggest what was wrong with her. We never hear reports of
Dora coughing blood – the most obvious identifying characteristic of common tuberculosis. This would lead one to assume
that if it was TB, then it was probably some rare form of extra-
pulmonary TB (where the bacteria are not located in the lung).

At some point in the 1820s, Dora had developed a hunch
or lump on her spine, and from then on she suffered intermittently from back pains. Pott's disease (TB of the spine) causes
a hump to develop (the hunchback of Notre-Dame is thought
to have had Pott's disease): like pulmonary TB, it would also
explain Dora's loss of appetite and general 'unwellness'. Another
explanation might be abdominal TB, which could explain her
cough and regular bouts of diarrhoea and 'deranged' bowels –
but not her curvature of the spine. Another possibility is kidney
disease, which might explain occasional references to her sallow
or yellow skin tone. None of the diagnoses is perfect, and many
others can be made to fit, including Addison's disease, lupus,
kidney failure or simply an unrelated series of unpleasant bugs
and viruses, perhaps combined with one of the diseases
mentioned, perhaps not. Of all these diseases, kidney disease,
which could explain both her weight loss and her intermittently
jaundiced appearance, is perhaps the most likely.

However, in her family's letters it becomes apparent that,
perhaps unfairly, they believed that she herself, rather than an
illness, was responsible for her weight loss. In the absence of
other evidence, some credibility at least must be given to their
views. Aunt Sara was wise, and she was convinced Dora needed

to be persuaded to eat more. Her approach to Dora's illness suggests there was a psychological dimension to Dora's ill-health. The term anorexia brings with it a whole raft of associations and assumptions, social and psychological, some of them helpful, many not. But, with caution, some of our contemporary thinking about the disorder may be applied to Dora in 1834. Anorexia is often understood as a way of controlling the uncontrollable. It classically affects 'good' children from close families. In 1834, Dora could hardly have had less control over her life, and she could hardly have been more loved – or more trapped. The diagnosis is anachronistic, in that the term was not coined until 1868, but it fits the symptoms at least as neatly as Pott's disease. Dora's hunched back might then be attributable to osteoporosis, from which chronic anorexics suffer: osteoporosis can cause 'Dowager's Hump' (kyphosis). This syndrome in itself causes difficulty in breathing, neck and shoulder pain and fatigue.

Whether Dora's illness had one underlying cause or many, and whether its origin was predominantly mental or physical, one thing is clear: the extent to which it became a part of her character and gave her life purpose. Whatever their cause, every small change in Dora's health caused a great deal of analysis and a flurry of letters. Recording and reporting her symptoms became a daily activity for her relatives. Rejecting their concerns and ministrations became a part of who Dora was. It came to define her relationship with her father. He worried about her, and protected her more rather than less as she grew older.

The one person who asked Dora for help, rather than only offering her advice, was Edward Quillinan. Since his wife's death ten years earlier, Edward had lived a footloose life with his two daughters. He moved back and forth between London and Portugal, Canterbury and Paris, never quite making it as either a businessman or a poet. For his children, Rydal Mount, under Dora's care, was a place of security and they had grown used to spending school holidays there. Edward's girls were the only people who needed Dora's protection. In 1831 Edward left Rotha, who turned ten that October, to be taught by Dora for a few weeks while he took Jemima to France. He didn't collect his daughter for seven months. It says much of his relationship with the Rydalians that he felt he could impose on them and entrust his daughter to them. In the seven months, Dora became almost a mother to the motherless little girl. When Rotha eventually returned to her father, her teachers were astounded at the progress she had made. They reported she was well ahead of the boarding school-educated Jemima (two years her senior). While Dora's friends were busily getting married, Rotha's love of Rydal made Dora happy, and she told Edward she would always think of his daughter 'with a Mother's anxiety and love'.[11] Looking back, one can detect – or perhaps imagine – romantic undercurrents in the relationship. Edward had always flirted outrageously and safely with his 'lover', the older Aunt Sara Hutchinson ('My Hutton'), but now his relationship with Dora was increasingly important to him.

A year later Edward wrote secretly to Dora asking her to become the guardian of his children – as though he were testing, very cautiously, a path. This time his request was not so well received. Dora showed her father the letter. Wordsworth sat her down and dictated a stern reply. So, a few days later, Edward read Wordsworth's words written in Dora's neat hand: 'Dora reads me that part of your letter marked private . . . I doubt not she would be happy doing all that could be done for your children.'[12] But it was out of the question. Not only would Dora not understand (trusts are complicated things) but Edward was taking advantage of Dora's kind nature and risking her health: 'the ardent and anxious temperament of my Daughter in conjunction with her weak frame disqualifies her from such an offer'.[13] Wordsworth's polite message was clear: do not presume to write to my daughter behind my back and, if you do, she will not keep secrets from me. He went on to imply that as well as imposing on Dora, Edward was neglecting his duty to his own daughters; for their sake he should find 'a man of experience, integrity and ability'.[14] He recommended Henry Nelson Coleridge. Wordsworth knew Edward's family was mired in a legally complicated financial dispute: a man of experience might be useful. He did not say, but almost certainly feared, that standing 'guardian' would mean being financially responsible. And since Dora was unmarried, this would actually mean *he* was responsible. The Stamp Distributor of Westmoreland was not a man to take on financial burdens lightly.

Dora herself had capitulated with a 'no' but one which revealed her desire to please both men: 'Father has answered the main points of your very kind letter but you must now allow me to assure you . . . of what I have so long and often thought and felt – that as long as life is given to me your Darlings will have one friend . . . whose only regret will be or rather is that her power of serving them falls so far short of her desire to serve.' [15] It was the first of many tug-of-war battles between the two men over Dora. Rebuked by Wordsworth, Edward had disappeared back to Portugal and elsewhere and was not seen in the Lakes for several years.

So another reason, apart from ill-health, for Dora being downcast when she received Sara's *Pretty Lessons* was a recent disappointing letter from Edward. Early in 1834 he arrived back in England; they all hoped he might visit, but in June he wrote to Rydal to say he was off to Portugal again. Would they, he asked, allow him to send Rotha to them for the summer? Jemima was being educated in France but perhaps he might leave Rotha under Dora's care again? Wordsworth sent him a thunderer of a reply. With some justification, he thought Edward was wrong to leave the country again and told him so. 'You are silent on the cause which made you think of going to Portugal – You must remain in England as a duty to your Children and those who have a common interest in the remains of what will probably be their inheritance.' He was not keen to have Rotha; he felt it showed a scant disregard for Dora's health that Edward had even asked. She *could* come, he said, if Edward had 'no objection to Rotha running wild at Rydal for a couple of months . . . though we cannot receive her for 6'. His real point was about Dora: 'you must understand what I mean by "running wild" – it is going without tuition. Dora's health and thoughts are too much deranged and occupied to allow her making the least exertion in this way and indeed she is unequal to it.'[16] If all this was understood then he would with 'pleasure' have Rotha to stay. Edward responded by taking Rotha with him to France. He gave no indication of when he would return, and Dora was left feeling more isolated than ever.

As Dora's symptoms worsened, her characteristic stoicism altered her relationship with a number of people but especially with Edward. Aunt Sara knew how much Dora had always looked up to Edward. Now she adopted a new tactic in her campaign to restore her niece's health – she recruited Edward. In every letter to him, she described Dora's refusal to eat. Aunt Sara knew Edward would write to Dora, and hoped his words would have a greater impact than her own. Her ruse worked: in the autumn of 1834, Edward wrote Dora the first of a series of regular and strongly worded letters on her 'wicked habit of starving herself'.[17]

Aunt Sara encouraged him, but at the start of 1835 she told Edward no progress had been made: you 'will be grieved to hear that . . . her appetite is as bad as ever – she persists in living on *prison fare* – bread & water ie Tea as weak as water – though the medical men are of the opinion that this spare diet is the cause, in her case, of the complaint and cannot therefore be the remedy also!'[18] Edward sharpened his tone to Dora: 'I have received a very disquieting account of your health, of which you tell me so little. I, long, long ago, perceived that you were destroying your health by that pernicious system of starvation: but you were always so wilful on the subject that I could not presume to venture on anything like repeated remonstrance, which indeed could have produced no effect but irritation . . . But at this distance, when I learn that you are reduced to serious illness, and that you still persist in your determination to be unable to eat (for that is my construction of the fact) I do take upon myself to implore you to be persuaded as to the duty of habituating yourself to a more generous diet . . . If you continue obstinate I shall still think of you fifty times a day but it will always be as Dora Wordsworth the Wilful.'[19] She wrote crossly to defend herself from his accusation, but she did acknowledge she was flattered by his attention and concern. Edward in his turn found himself drawn into his role (as cast by Aunt Sara) of protector to this damsel in distress.

And Dora *was* distressed, even if she denied it. Her father's spirits had been so low for the past couple of years that Rydal Mount was under a perpetual shadow. Aunt Dorothy had tried to persuade Dora to go to Leamington Spa for the sake of her health. This Dora declared she could not do, explaining to her aunt how 'she should be so very wretched at a distance from her Father, till his eyesight is more strengthened and secure'.[20] Dora could not bear to see her father unhappy. The sadder – and blinder – he grew, the greater she felt her responsibility. She would not contemplate leaving his side for a moment. Aunt Dorothy's only hope was that father and daughter might travel somewhere together. But even if Dora wanted to travel, her health would have made it difficult.

Dora's world was becoming increasingly strange. For though Wordsworth wrote less and less of merit, his fame continued to grow. Rydal Mount became a focal point not only for their friends and acquaintances, but also for complete strangers. In the summer of 1832, 267 'authorised' visitors came to see Wordsworth, and carriage-loads more unauthorised. 'Father's popularity is amazingly on the increase if we may judge from the odd and queer indeed impertinent, I had almost said expedients, that have been resorted to this summer by strangers high and low to have sight of him or his dwellings,' mused Dora. One day a carriage drove right up to the door to allow its occupants to have a better look. 'One man sent in a note, well written, with some needles to sell price 3d – "as a Lover of poetry, the Author of the Excursion would confer an additional great obligation by paying the bearer in person . . ." We have had two or three others quite as funny.'[21] Dora was a private person – more so than Sara – and however hard she tried to deflect it with humour, living with this level of public scrutiny was uncomfortable. Wordsworth was charming to those visitors he wanted, furious with those he did not, and frustratingly low when the family was alone.

It is hard to live with someone who veers about so chaotically but cannot disguise his gloom from those who love him most. Dora remained determined to cheer her father but it wasn't easy. Since 1830 Aunt Dorothy's health had also been deteriorating, and by 1834 Dora, Mary, Aunt Sara and Aunt Dorothy herself had begun to prepare themselves for her death in the not-too-distant future. 'Alas! My dear friend I fear she will not be long with us,' Aunt Sara told Mrs STC as early as February 1833, 'her weakness & languor are truly deplorable – indeed without the help of stimulants you could barely believe her alive.'[22] The doctor, Mr Carr, had told the women that Aunt Dorothy didn't have long, and they did their best to protect Wordsworth from the knowledge. Deep down, Aunt Sara thought, he probably knew. The love between the two siblings was famously strong. Orphaned at a young age, Wordsworth had rescued his sister from an unhappy childhood to set up their unorthodox mountain home together. She was the subject of many of his greatest poems, his first muse, confidante and amanuensis. The idea of Dorothy's death was almost too much for Wordsworth to bear.

By November 1834 Wordsworth was losing his sight again. Previously, the infections in his eyelids had made seeing difficult, but this had not terrified him. Now the infection was in the eye itself and he began to fear – as the newspapers were reporting – that he was going permanently blind. Unsurprisingly he became more and more dejected. For the past four years, since November 1830 in fact, Wordsworth's temper had been clouded by grave fears about the nation's moral health. All his life the Tories had been the dominant force in the House of Commons but that November Earl Grey led the Whig Party to election victory. Grey was determined to make Parliament more representative of the people in the country and to this end, he introduced the Reform Bill in 1831. After a period of turmoil, including a brief return of a Tory government, the Bill was made law as the Great Reform Act of 1832. Wordsworth was sure the extended franchise would destroy England altogether. He had semi-suicidal thoughts: 'They are to be envied, I think,' he wrote bathetically to his brother Christopher, 'who, from age or infirmity, are likely to be removed from the afflictions which God is preparing for this sinful nation.'[23] When Dora's friend Maria Jewsbury wrote to tell Dora she was leaving the country to follow her husband to India, Dora responded with a letter of such devastating misery that it was (as she knew) comical: 'my regrets I know are selfish for England I know has nothing now to offer but fire, sword & pestilence & happy are they whose destiny leads them far from her happy shores – at least so Father thinks & of course I think like him'.[24] (Her 'of course' suggests a great deal.)

It might seem odd that the prospect of reform so depressed Wordsworth, a man who had after all been a passionate supporter of the French Revolution. Actually it was his very experience of France in the 1790s which made him so frightened by the prospect of reform in England. 'In my youth,' he explained to a friend, 'I witnessed in France the calamities bought upon all classes and especially the poor, by a Revolution, so that my heart aches at the thought of what we are now threatened with.'[25] His political view was perhaps hypocritical, but there is no doubt Wordsworth's heart ached. On top of his unhappiness about the political situation he bemoaned not only the state of his own poetry, but of all poetry, and indeed art. Wordsworth was sixty-four and feeling every year of his age. Church and monarch seemed under threat; poetry was in the doldrums; he was blind; everyone was ill and life was bleak.

Mary, Aunt Sara and Dora had not only to run the house, read to him and help with what poetry he attempted, but also to take down dictations of his long and melancholy letters. Occasionally one of them would snap, as Mary did in November 1833 after half an hour or so of transcribing Wordsworth's thoughts for Henry Crabb Robinson. The letter roared fury: 'My opinion is, that the people are bent upon the destruction of their ancient institutions . . . nothing since . . . the broaching of the Reform Bill could, or can prevent it . . . the march toward destruction . . . they are more blind than bats or mole . . . overthrow of social order . . .' – and on and on he went: you can practically hear him pacing across the drawing room of Rydal Mount as he spoke. 'As to France and your *juste milieu* it is not worth talking about' – but here Mary finally refused to cooperate: 'And I MW *will not* write another word on this subject.' Wordsworth changed tack, slightly. 'My eye has had another relapse', he wrote – and so he continued.[26]

Dora was not as bold as her mother, however. It was more in her line to tease 'trumpery old Daddy', but she too grew weary of the demands he made.[27] Wordsworth found the long evenings 'distressing and tiresome' and demanded that Dora or Mary read to him, a task both women hated. Dora found it tiring and frustrating since 'at best one gets on so slowly'.[28] Mostly Wordsworth would fall asleep halfway through, then demand the reader backtrack to where he thought he had last been awake. He was surer than ever he was going blind, and Dora could do nothing to jolly him out of that. Worst of all, Dora was beginning to believe he would never write *The Recluse*, which had been for years as much her *raison d'être* as his. She spent her life 'wishing for impossibilities'.[29]

So by the time Dora received Sara's letter in the summer of 1834, when she was about to turn thirty, she felt doomed to life as a spinster aunt. Her life revolved more than ever around her ageing family. The year before, Maria Jane Jewsbury, had travelled to India with her new husband and had died of cholera in Pune. Just a few months after that blow, during a brief respite from ill health, Dora had gone to Keswick to spend 'a few last days' with Edith Southey before Edith's wedding. Edith was 'the last of her unmarried friends of an age agreeing with her own'. As Aunt Dorothy had said: 'of course Dora is happy in anticipation of her Friend's happiness; but she so dreads the loss of her, and knows well what a chasm will be left in her parents' house'.[30] Dora had been fearing this with gloomy inevitability for years. 'What is to come of me when all that are dear to me are gone,' she had asked in 1832; 'with Edith married – Sara married – And everybody married that [and here her writing becomes illegible for a couple of words] care about – but if they are made happy I must be made happy too – but I find it very hard to live on the happiness of others.'[31] By 1834, when Dora received Sara's letter, there was very little happiness to be lived on at home.

INTERLUDE
1834–1835

At about this point the fire we call the Romantic Period flickered
and died. In fine art, Romanticism stiffened into realism, the
painstaking recording of what was there. Ruskinian emphasis on
close observation would lead eventually to the work of the
Pre-Raphaelites with their exacting eye for the shape of every
leaf and cloud, or fold of a medieval temptress's dress. The novel
replaced poetry as the highest literary form; evangelical
Christianity replaced the more relaxed approach to orthodoxy
that had characterised the preceding generation. And although
Victoria was not yet on the throne, 1834 seems to mark the end
of the Georgian era and the start of the 'Victorian'. Princess
Victoria's frail uncle, King William IV, was determined not to
die for another three years until his niece turned eighteen and
could rule without a Regency. The date is as good as any other
with which to mark the moment at which Dora and Sara, whose
fathers had defined the prevailing culture of the previous era,
each began to step out of that blinding light and take control
of their own identities.

The year was also a turning point for England. A new chapter
of economic, cultural and political history was beginning. Three
symbolic events marked it out as a caesura in time: two deaths
and a fire. The first death was Coleridge's. He joined a host of
other dead poets and Romantic writers: Scott, Shelley, Keats,
Blake, Byron, Hazlitt and Lamb were all in their graves.
Wordsworth said a light had gone out in the world. And though
the old Bard himself lived on, most people saw his old age as

an unproductive one. The one-time firebrand of revolutionary literature was turned Tory sage and tax collector. The second death of equal symbolic significance was the Reverend Thomas Malthus's. Malthus's prophecies of doom – namely that over-consumption of finite resources by a booming population would lead to inevitable ruin – had largely been accepted since 1798, when he had published *An Essay on the Principle of Population*. But now his ideas were being challenged. A new kind of thinking, based on expansion, prosperity, technology, capitalism and – eventually – Empire, was underway. Malthus had not foreseen that 'Britain' would expand around the world, meaning that the supply and demand on which he had based his apocalyptic prediction did not actually apply – at least not yet. This was Britain's century, and her phenomenal economic growth was supported by, and even demanded, a growing population.

Then came the fire. Joseph Mallord William Turner was among the many who watched the destruction of the ancient Houses of Parliament on the night of 16 October 1834. His paintings of that night are testament to the sense of apocalyptic splendour. Rosemary Hill described the fire as the 'last great show of Georgian Britain'.[1] The building that replaced the old Palace of Westminster – Charles Barry's Gothic masterpiece we see today – was built for an increasingly democratic Britain. Already Catholic Emancipation (1829) and the passing of the Reform Bill (1832) had convulsed the country. As George Eliot's *Middlemarch* chronicles so vividly, disputes reached out from Westminster to touch every community in the land. In 1834 the government passed bills for the New Poor Law. The Act abolishing slavery in the British Empire the year before was coming into effect, and the impact of the Great Reform Act was beginning to be felt as rotten boroughs crumbled. Corruption and the aristocratic domination of politics waned. In November 1834 the King dismissed the Prime Minister, Melbourne, and replaced him with his favourite, the Duke of Wellington. But even the Duke's star was fading, and the following year a general election returned Melbourne to power. Melbourne was the last Prime Minister to be sacked by a monarch, and the first to be elected by the people against the will of the monarch.

For Dora and Sara, change was precipitated not by fire but by an article about Coleridge published in September 1834 by their old friend Thomas de Quincey. It made Sara so angry she took up her pen and started to write letters. But it's awkward to write letters lying down in bed. As her pen covered the pages, she graduated from lying to sitting. By October she was walking downstairs where she could write more easily in the drawing room of her Hampstead home. 'De Quincey's article in Tait's Edinburgh Magazine makes me despise him,' she told her husband on 7 September. 'He is now utterly reckless, sensitive only where vanity is concerned, and ready to stoop to the readiest mode of supplying his pressing necessities.'

De Quincey had taken advantage of a resurgence of interest in STC to publish a series of essays in *Tait's Edinburgh Magazine* amounting to a short – and devastating – biography. De Quincey criticised STC's writing, his lifestyle and his morals. Almost worst of all he implied that STC had been guilty of plagiarising the German philosopher, Schelling. Nor was de Quincey alone in publishing articles about the late poet, and many of the others were as bad, if not worse. Somebody wrote an anonymous article in *Blackwood's Magazine* in which he concluded that Wordsworth was more important than Coleridge. (Sara correctly believed the author to be John Wilson, another old friend of the Wordsworths: the man who had looked after Dora during the whooping cough.) Sara was maddened: 'He is a fool to speak of my father's *master* . . . Wordsworth the master of Coleridge indeed! This is gross flattery of the living Bard . . . He may say the one is a greater poet than the other if he will, but this, methinks, is an incorrect way of expressing the opinion.'[2] J. A. Heraud wrote an essay in *Fraser's Magazine* which Sara condemned as 'stupid'.[3] She took particular exception to Heraud's spiteful expression of surprise that Coleridge had anything to leave in a will, living, as the author claimed he did, 'on benevolence'.[4] 'What', asked Sara, 'can be the delicacy of the man who pens such stuff of one who has children living?'[5]

By the end of the month she was sleeping without the aid of opium. Her hysteria and grief were temporarily blasted aside by anger and a sense of betrayal as she took up her pen and wrote. On a visit to London, Aunt Sara saw Sara Coleridge's looks and health were much improved. She attributed the change to two causes, the first of which was quite correct: 'Her father's death rouzed her – but before that she had profited by my advice & plain speech . . . & now she seems determined to be well.'[6] Sara now began to regain some of the lustre that had made her a famous beauty. Anger suited her.

Two hundred miles away in the Lake District, Dora was equally angry at de Quincey's betrayal. Dora could not have anticipated the fury she would feel on reading the devastating biographical articles. When the anger came, she felt herself drawn to Sara. On 1 October 1834, she wrote an uncharacter-istically violent letter about the 'atrocious article by the opium eater' to Edward: 'Hartley says he "will give it him" & I hope he will – for such unprincipled wretches do deserve to be shewn up & without mercy – Aunt Sarah burns with indignation against the little monster – whom she never liked over well.'[7] Like Sara, Dora had abandoned her sickbed to write. She was emaciated, weak and in pain, but still she wrote great long passionate letters concerning the betrayal. Like Sara, she was regaining her former vim and vigour. The relationship between the two women, which had drifted since Sara's marriage, became important once more. In the first place, STC's death united them in grief, and then the ghastly fall-out from the de Quincey episode cemented their tie. Dora wrote, sympathetically now, to Sara about the little monster de Quincey. Dora wrote to Edward, and she began to wonder about going herself to London to see Sara and other friends. It was a temporary but important relief from ill-health. Anger seemed to suit her too.

Immediately after STC's death, Henry had begun work on a volume entitled *Specimens of the Table Talk of Samuel Taylor Coleridge*, which would be a record of STC's conversations and opinions as remembered and transcribed by his son-in-law.

Henry's purposes were simple. He wanted the book to act as a good Victorian memorial, and he wanted to reposition Coleridge's political views in the mind of the public. His uncle had been much misrepresented: Henry wanted the book's readers to 'gain a clearer insight into the deep and pregnant principles, in the light of which Mr Coleridge was accustomed to regard God and the World'.[8] He longed for Sara to help him. When trying to make sense of some of Coleridge's thoughts on the Bible, for example, he implored her: 'Beloved Wife – counsel me – you are deeply interested and will neither err from timidity or foolish recklessness. I shall abide ultimately by what you advise.'[9] But Sara did not counsel him, even after repeated pleas. Despite Henry's free acknowledgement that 'all your remarks & alter- ations on my poor proofs are just . . . you are superior to me in fineness of feeling & discrimination', she lacked confidence in her own understanding of her father.[10] After all, as she told her friend Mrs Plummer, 'Henry could sometimes bring him down to narrower topics, but when alone with me he was almost always on the star paved road, taking in the whole heavens in his circuit.'[11]

Instead, while thinking about her father, Sara was inspired to write a meditation on her own mind. She did have another self, a 'Good Genius' who could be pitched against her 'Invalid Self', and she began to write an essay, tentatively entitled 'On Nervousness'. It allowed her to challenge the views of well- intentioned friends who advised that 'reasoning and perseverance alone' could conquer an afflicted mind. After all, these sensible voices argued, the poor did not suffer in this way. But now Sara wondered whether reasoning powers alone might be as useless 'as if we tried to curb the wind with a bit & bridle or to pierce a shadow with fire and shot; we fail and the failure [means] . . . the sufferer's heavy burden is rendered more galling than before'.[12] The children's nurse, Ann Parrott, known as Nuck, gave her the confidence to believe otherwise. For some years now, Ann had herself been struck by hysterical fits. As Sara tried to comfort the older woman it occurred to her that people who argued the poor did not suffer as Sara suffered had themselves nothing but 'a superficial acquaintance' with the working classes. Warming to her theme, Sara set out an alternative way of viewing the whole subject of what we would today call mental illness. She had heard of a person, for example, who believed his leg was made of glass. Did such a delusion (akin surely to her own hysteria) mean he was insane? No, she reasoned, she could well imagine a man might be unable 'to bear to treat his leg as if it were not of glass because the imagination of breaking a glass leg lies like a horrid incubus upon his spirits'. But, she realised, there was a distinction between this and madness. The man would only be mad 'the moment he believes his leg to be really made of glass'.[13] Sara's analytical powers, turned on her own unhappiness, were acute. She did not become happier, but a modern therapist might argue that her enlightened opinions on the 'mystery' of the human mind and body, and the parallels between a physical 'wound' and a mental one, could be helpful. She wrote the essay as a dialogue between her Good Genius and her Invalid Self and in doing so invented her own talking therapy.

Only when Henry's book was about to be published, in the spring of 1835, did Sara finally turn her attention towards a defence of Coleridge for the introduction. It was not an easy task. The multiple charges against her father ranged from plagiarism and religious impropriety to marital infidelity, financial mismanagement and poor parenting. All the accusations had some element of truth, and a simple denial would not suffice. Any analysis had to be subtle, sensitive and well informed. The various attacks needed to be read carefully, and in doing so Sara began to engage honestly with the real Coleridge. Re-presenting her father properly was too great a task for the introduction to *Table Talk*, but it set her thinking and, amongst other things, she came to see that though much of what de Quincey had written was offensive, much of it was well done. De Quincey had described her father's genius and mode of discourse with 'eloquence and discrimination'; and justice.[14] She saw Coleridge had been 'singularly regardless of his literary reputation as well as his worldly interests' and her mind turned inevitably to the question of what exactly had been the nature and ambition of that genius.[15] She was too ill to do anything about it at that time, but an idea was born.

Sara and Henry made a plan that they ought to collect and reissue as many of Coleridge's works as possible. William Pickering, STC's publisher since 1828, agreed to publish *The Literary Remains of Samuel Taylor Coleridge*. These four volumes would comprise an assortment of notes, letters and other writing, much of which had not been published before. The volumes would appear at regular intervals between 1836 and 1839, and Sara would help if she could.

It was when grief was added to anger that Dora began to heal. In the summer of 1835, both Dora and her Aunt Dorothy were ill and confined to bed. They were all sure Aunt Dorothy's was her deathbed: her mind was wandering, and she was sick and weak. Although Dora herself was barely strong enough to stand, and her throat raw with months of coughing, she tried to keep everyone's morale up. Her mother wrote that her 'spirits were as buoyant as ever' and her 'enjoyment of a hearty laugh no less than it used to be despite the painful consequences'.[16] Aunt Sara, however, was not deceived, and upped her campaign of writing letters seeking Edward's help. Dora's diet was 'as bad as ever' she had told him in January – 'you may guess my dear friend how great our anxiety is & has been'.[17] In April, she had tried Sara Coleridge: hoping Dora's old friend might have some influence she wrote and told her Dora was over-fatigued from waiting on others. But Dora deflected all their worry with concern for Aunt Dorothy – and Wordsworth. She explained to Sara that she merely found it frustrating to be confined to a sofa since she was 'the only person in the house who understands how to manage father's eyes'.[18]

At the start of June the Wordsworths prepared for Aunt Dorothy's death. They were not helped by the fact that now Aunt Sara was also set back by a rheumatic illness. As soon as Sara heard the news about Aunt Dorothy, she wrote to Dora: 'I feel assured that her last days and hours on earth will be as full of quiet joy and humble yet exalted hopefulness as her blest and blessing life has ever been. Will you give my sincere and grateful love to her: it is nothing to say that I shall never forget her face and voice, and the many happy occasions on which I have seen and heard them; may they be frequently present with me for useful influences – to support, to soothe, & to elevate!' Eight days later, while all the attention was focused on Aunt Dorothy, Aunt Sara silently, and unostentatiously, died. Her death was characteristic of the way she lived: even weeks before the end she appeared perfectly well, and was busy being kind and worrying about Dora's continuing weight loss. It was only at the last minute, literally hours before her death, that the doctor was summoned. Dora rose from her sickbed to tend to her aunt. Dr Carr pronounced the case was hopeless. Stunned, Dora begged him to take away any pain. Aunt Sara opened her eyes and said in a strong voice, 'I am quite, I am perfectly comfortable.'[19] They were her last words before she slipped out of the world without fuss. Shocked letters were dispatched around the country. Henry Crabb Robinson went to tell Henry in his chambers in London, and he broke the news to his wife.[20]

Henry wanted to write to Wordsworth himself, but Sara was not having it. Dora was her friend, and she wrote immediately: 'alarmed as I have been for dear Miss Hutchinson – the probability of her being called away this time never once crossed my mind . . . When your dear Aunt was here we were quite gladdened by her looks and manner – she was so little worsened in appearance from what we ever remembered her . . . Everything seemed to promise prolonged life for her, and an old age of more than common enjoyment and usefulness . . . many friends will feel not only the pain which is unavoidable when old ties are broken, but a deep regret at the thought that they can never more have the pleasure and benefit of her society. She was an excellent kind hearted creature, and possessed a fine clear understanding, which was never put to any but good purposes and was always ready when wanted.'[21] The letter was thoughtful and heartfelt. The friends were bound together by grief: first for STC and then for Aunt Sara and soon, in all probability, Aunt

Dorothy. 'Dear Dora,' Sara ended, 'I pray that you may bless your parents yet with recovered health.'

Dora's little family was now so tightly coiled that even a wren had barely any room for manoeuvre. Aunt Dorothy did not, in fact, die, but after Aunt Sara's death she suffered a shock from which she never truly recovered. As Wordsworth explained to a friend, 'her mind since Sarah's departure has been so confused as to passing events, that we have no distinct knowledge of what she may actually have to support in the way of bodily pain'.[22] Physically she regained strength, but her mental faculties were severely impaired. At the age of sixty-four she had begun a descent into what the Wordsworths could only assume was some kind of 'Premature Dotage', which we might today describe as Alzheimer's.* Dora's own health also worsened, and, as she told Edward, 'whether Dora Wordsworth the Wilful will gain the battle against the World is yet to be proved'.[23]

---

* Historians argue about this diagnosis for Aunt Dorothy. She had intermittent moments of perfect lucidity that have led some to suggest that her illness cannot have been Alzheimer's. Most recently Frances Wilson has suggested the illness was depressive pseudodementia (see *The Ballad of Dorothy Wordsworth*, p. 247).

PART THREE

CHAPTER 12

A MOMENT'S BLAZE ACROSS THE DARKNESS

1836

In the summer of 1836, a year after Aunt Sara's death, Dora and her mother were at Rydal and on tenterhooks. Every post brought a letter from Wordsworth in London. Dora and Mary were hoping to hear he had decided to go on holiday to Italy with his old friend Henry Crabb Robinson. Instead, Wordsworth was threatening to come home. If her unhappy – and therefore crotchety – father returned, Dora knew she would be plunged back into another round of thankless revising and copying. He would drive her hard as a scribe, and drive her mad with fretting and panicking over her health. Every cough, every ache, every yawn and every lost ounce would be analysed and his own mood would shift accordingly.

Wordsworth had gone to London to talk to Thomas Longman, who had published his poetry for almost forty years, but with whom he was growing increasingly dissatisfied. Without properly explaining the implications, the publisher had changed the process he used for printing Wordsworth's books and begun to print in stereotype. This was a new money-saving method, which not only made it hard for Wordsworth to make his customary last-minute changes, but produced an inferior quality of book. Longman's paper was cheap, the new editions would not match the old, and altogether the man was too driven by profit. Wordsworth was a perfectionist about the physical quality of his books, and his publisher's tight-fisted attitude (not so very dissimilar to his own) upset him. Besides which, he thought his own cut of the profit was too small.

His wife and daughter had heard a great deal about his feelings on the subject and by the summer of 1836 they had decided Wordsworth should go to London to stand up for his 'own legitimate interest' and, in doing so, possibly find another publisher.[1] Wordsworth left at the start of May during a temporary improvement in Dora's health. Even before he was out of the house, Mary and Dora set to work on their desperate campaign to persuade him to go on his holiday. Dora wrote to Crabb Robinson and begged him to 'embark with father for any part of the Continent where travel won't be more fatiguing than a man in his 67th year with "all diseases that the spittals know" (in his fancy at least) ought to undertake'.[2] Wife and daughter were convinced that Wordsworth needed to get away after a cheerless year at Rydal.

Since Aunt Sara's death, Aunt Dorothy's moments of lucidity had been few and far between. Instead, she had shocking episodes of rage during which she would hurl abuse at Dora, Mary, Wordsworth and all who tried to care for her. They gave her opium, which helped, but did not halt her decline. On good days she played, childlike, with water in a bowl or sat on the stairs beneath the cuckoo clock waiting with excitement to hear it chime. After a lifetime of abstemious living she was visited by an astonishing appetite and took to raiding the larder at night until, eventually, food had to be kept under lock and key. She ate whole roast chickens, cakes and pats of butter and, when sent a present of a turkey and two white chickens, she nursed the dead birds on her lap with greedy delight.[3] She told her brother she was 'never happy but when she was eating'.[4] The porridge of Town End Cottage returned to haunt her, and she lived under a 'great craving for oatmeal porridge principal[ly] for the sake of the butter that she eats along with it'. The entire family were forced to be vigilant in 'refusing her things that would be improper for her'.[5] As Aunt Dorothy's body grew, Dora's, as though in reaction, shrank.

What Dora and Mary did not explicitly say to Crabb

Robinson, when they tried to persuade him to take Wordsworth away, was that they needed a break from the poet's constant and exhausting melancholy. Wordsworth was infuriatingly reluctant to leave, despite the fact he and Crabb Robinson had been planning an expedition to Italy together for years. 'I like the idea less and less every day, I so long to see you, and I feel fevered,' he wrote pitifully from London.[6] Stony-hearted wife and daughter continued to bully him, but 'I sicken at the scheme as I draw near to the appointed time', he told them plaintively. 'Do not scold me.'[7] They must see that until he could assure himself Dora was 'recovering the flesh I am sure she has lost', he did not want to leave.[8] No matter how much they proclaimed her vastly improved health, he worked himself up into a fever of anxiety.

Wordsworth knew Dora was being bled, which was standard practice. On 25 June, however, he wrote in a great state because he had just met someone called Clara Graves and 'almost the first word Miss Graves spoke, when she had enquired after you was a dagger to me. She said her Brother told her bleeding in spinal cases was quite exploded, it had harried the patient so much.' Wordsworth panicked and urged Dora to 'take more and more care'.[9] Mary would begin her letters with positive reports of Dora's health but Wordsworth was having none of it. To one such letter, he responded crossly: 'My dearest Mary . . . I rejoice that Dora is in your opinion "now really improving" – and grieve much that my letters have made you unhappy. All I have to say is . . .' that he didn't believe her and wanted to come home. He would linger, he explained bitterly, only to meet Dr Holland to whom he would present Dora's symptoms 'whether real or imaginary' (presumably one of the doctor's trickier consultations).[10] He claimed he did not want to cancel, just to postpone his trip: 'Dearest Dora, get well,' he pleaded, 'and we will go to Italy together.'[11]

In London Wordsworth conferred with the best doctors who all, apparently, agreed it would be best for Dora if he went home. In any case he was himself 'heartsick and homesick' and making himself ill with worry not only about Dora but also

Aunt Dorothy.[12] Eventually Mary took pity on him and gave him permission to return. In any case, she had learned to her dismay that rumours were circulating in London that she was deceiving her husband about the state of his sister's health. On Monday, 27 June, Wordsworth told Dora and Mary: 'Mr Robinson with his usual goodness (though disappointed) cheerfully lets me off, and in consequence, God Willing, I shall be home on Thursday evening.'[13] Mary did suggest he might stay a little longer in London if he was really not going to Italy – but Wordsworth rejected the idea. He was ill, he said, perspiring terribly in the night: he had to get back.[14] He told them it was 'not impossible' he might bring Edward with him to help scribe and revise. He had asked, and Edward was considering the invitation. This was tantalising. Dora knew if Edward came, everything would be easier.

While waiting for an answer from Edward, Wordsworth had dinner with Sara and Henry. He wrote a long melancholy letter afterwards, saying Sara looked 'neither well nor strong' and he himself would probably be dead soon.[15] Yet despite the tone of the letter, now that he was homeward bound, Wordsworth was feeling more optimistic than for some time. After a difficult series of negotiations, he and Longman had decided to part company. The final straw for Wordsworth came on his arrival in London: Longman had sent a cursory note cancelling their appointment. It confirmed Wordsworth's opinion that the publisher did not show him due respect. Instead, Wordsworth struck a more lucrative deal with Edward Moxon. As part of the new contract, Moxon persuaded him to prepare a second edition of *The Excursion* and a new six-volume selection of verses. The amount of work would be tremendous. Wordsworth redoubled his efforts to get Edward to come and stay; there was no one who could be more useful. A week or so later, Wordsworth triumphantly informed his family that Edward had agreed. He cunningly committed Edward to fulfilling his promise by finding two young ladies who needed an escort north, and assuring their mother Edward would accompany them soon.[16] Wordsworth left on the afternoon Edward agreed; Mary and Dora's brief holiday was at an end.

Wordsworth had done well from the negotiations with Moxon. He was to be paid £1000 for the poems, meaning his profit that year would be 'scarcely less than 500£ which may be reckoned as a sort of Godsend'.[17] It's almost impossible to make meaningful statements about how much historical currency is worth today, but in terms of household goods £500 would have been equivalent to about £36,000 in 2013.* Wordsworth now had his work cut out to produce the new volumes. The revising began straight away and he worked his assistants like slaves: no matter they were his wife and sick daughter. A year later he would apologise to Mary for 'how harshly I often demeaned myself to you, my inestimable fellow-labourer, while correcting the last edition of my poems, I often pray to God that He would grant us both life that I may make amends to you'. Attempting to excuse his behaviour, he continued: 'But you know what an irritable state this timed and overstrained labour often put my nerves. My patience was ungovernable as I thought then but now I feel that it ought to have been governed.' At least Mary received an apology. To Dora he would simply say: 'I say nothing of this to you dear Dora, though you also have had some reason to complain.'[18]

Dora missed Aunt Sara desperately. Aunt Dorothy needed constant care and Dora spent hours wheeling her around the garden in a bathchair and reading aloud. Her aunt's madness hung heavily on them all. Wordsworth, Mary and Dora formed an almost impossibly stifling triangle. Southey compared the miserable situations at Greta and Rydal. His wife, who had never recovered from the grief of losing four of her eight children, had entered a lunatic asylum at York in October 1834. He had

* The best guidance on this topic comes from the website www.measuring worth.com which has a number of different calculators to give an indication both of relative worth and spending power. An indication of how confusing the subject is lies in the fact that in 1836, £500 was worth approximately £36,000 as a 'real price', i.e. using a bundle of goods bought by a typical household, but about £1.4 million as a figure which described 'economic power'. This latter figure is the value of the sum relative to the overall income in the country in 1836.

lost her to something 'worse than death', yet despite this he felt 'at this time Wordsworth's is a more afflicted house than my own. They used', he reflected sadly, 'to be two of the happiest in the country.'[19] In Aunt Sara, Dora had lost a much-needed champion. Her health grew worse, but despite eating 'nothing' and being 'deplorably reduced in flesh', she tried to pretend she was fine.

Edward arrived at Rydal at the end of July; he had barely greeted Dora and Mary before being set to work. Despite this, however, August was the happiest month at Rydal Mount anyone could remember for a long time. In August, Willy and John and other relations came to stay. Hartley Coleridge paid regular visits, and the house was a magnet for friends, including Thomas Arnold and the esteemed London physician, Sir Benjamin Brodie. Crabb Robinson, cheated of his holiday in Italy, came to Rydal for a week or so instead. Mary thought Edward was a 'Godsend'.[20] He could deal with Wordsworth, he believed in him and admired him and he was happy to bear the brunt of the work. Edward made notes of Wordsworth's conversation on an almost daily basis as the bard held forth on topics ranging from humour amongst the Ancients to French literature.[21] He was genuinely pleased to be of use to the poet he admired above all other men. Wordsworth and Mary noted, in jest, that Edward had supplanted their place in the household, and quite thrown them 'into the shade. However the poet is obliged to be thankful for his old helpmate.'[22] The hint of jealousy in the joke was justified.

Edward managed to make time for brief conversations, trips and visits with Mary and, more interestingly, with Dora. He was a trusted member of the household and therefore free to escort her when and where they liked. Dora and Edward shared a similar intensity of love for Wordsworth and worked as hard as each other revising his poems. He grieved for Aunt Sara, 'his lover', almost as much as Dora did, and he believed he knew what was good for Dora's health. Dora loved Edward's children; Edward loved Dora's father. And Dora had grown up since he had last seen her. She viewed Wordsworth more clearly. She knew *The Recluse* was almost certainly never going to be finished. She had lost one aunt to death and the other to insanity, and lost as well the companionship and sanctuary of Greta Hall. Edward could only admire her forced cheerfulness, which was quietly heroic.

Hartley, meanwhile, saw Dora's dilemma more clearly than anyone else: 'Dora, dear creature,' he told his sister and mother, 'too manifestly tries to seem as well as she can, without much success. Mr Quillinan' is there.[23] Hartley connected Dora's subterfuge with Edward's presence. What Wordsworth and Mary did not see was that Edward's presence was both the best and the worst thing in the world for Dora. Between the couple who were more equal now than they had ever been, childish flirtation had mutated into sexual tension.

And then there is a maddening gap in the record: a biographer must retreat just at the point where a novelist would advance. We have a few facts. On 13 September, Mary and Wordsworth went out for a drive. That same day, Edward took Dora out for a ride on Davy, Aunt Sara's old pony. At some point during the day he asked Dora a 'startling question'. Dora responded 'favourably'. On hearing her answer, he told her he had 'in my heart of hearts held you dearest of all for years too'.[24] The rest is guesswork.

Perhaps it was like this. While William and Mary were driving, Edward led Dora on Davy.[25] They were silent, each thinking of the other, thinking of the weeks gone by and of the fact that Edward was due to leave in a day or two. There had been moments: a walk to the falls above Ambleside, running an errand together in Grasmere village. There had been long hours, long glances over Wordsworth's poetry. She had brushed his hand as they worked in a way that may or may not have been deliberate. He had laughed at her jokes, but none of it added up to anything. It was one of those perfect late summer days and the view across Rydal Water sparkled with possibilities. Old Davy twitched his ears at flies. Edward opened his mouth to say something about the view and heard himself tell Dora he loved her. Above the lake an osprey hovered, silent. The pony, sensing no one would notice if he took this moment to gorge himself on the long grass at the side of the lane, stopped. Dora said nothing. Edward looked up into her grey eyes with the same slightly worried expression he'd had when he had first come knocking at the door all those years ago. Dora flushed red, but took the hand he offered and slipped down from the saddle. And this time, when she reached up for the bridle, the touch of her hands on his was deliberate. They didn't kiss, not then, not yet. The osprey whistled and yewked. Edward and Dora, and Davy, walked slowly back to the house; they barely noticed it had begun to rain.

However it actually happened, Edward and Dora declared their love for one another and nothing could be the same again. Dora might love and live a different life. But. She would have to tell her parents; she would have to tell her father. Dora was Protestant, Edward was a Catholic. Edward had no money. He was too old for her. Dora was ill. So she would stay silent. She would keep a secret from her father. Wordsworth was not informed of anything and on 16 September Edward left Rydal bound for London via Keswick and 'this meant Farewell to Rydal + Dora W.'.[26]

Shortly after Edward arrived back in London, he wrote to Rydal to announce he was setting sail for Oporto. He addressed his letter, quite properly, to Mary, but knew Dora would read his words as well. His departure was a sudden and unexpected shock. 'I myself see nothing agreeable to my feelings,' he said of his journey 'But if one cannot have the society one most prizes, it matters little whether one is at ten or ten hundred miles from it.'[27] Why did he leave? Perhaps he and Dora, having acknowledged their love, had decided they could not act on it. Perhaps Dora alone had rejected marriage as impossible and this was Edward's response. Either way, in his letters from this point onwards, it is easy to read (or imagine?) coded messages to Dora. In this first letter, he said that he had asked Jemima 'Why is it that I feel a sort of awkwardness in telling the Wordsworths (and with no others do I feel it) that we are suddenly going to Portugal?' Her response, he claimed, was 'because it is a sudden change of mind; and you think more of their good opinion than of anybody else's'. It was as close as he could get to telling Dora he was sorry.

Two weeks later Edward wrote again, and this time his letter frightened Dora. He described how he and eighteen-year-old Jemima had been caught in a storm in the Bay of Biscay on their way to Portugal. He wrote of the 'breakers & rocks . . . the flashes of lightening that struck a moment's blaze now & then across the darkness'. Dora read that Edward had woken Jemima to tell her of their impending death: 'Her eyes dilated fearfully as they searched mine. She saw that I was in earnest; considered for half a minute, & then said: "Papa, I will bear it." I then told her plainly that there seemed little hope of escape, and as I could not possibly save her in such a night and on such a coast, she might depend on my not deserting her for a moment till we perished together . . .'[28] Perhaps the whole trip to Portugal was a 'punishment' devised to spur Dora into action. Perhaps Edward's account of the wreck (though an historical fact) was skilfully written to the same end. Another letter followed a few days later giving more details. The storm – and the letter – shifted things. Now particular passages in his letters seem to leap out to the reader in the know. 'Take care of yourself for God's sake and for many sakes,' he implored her.

But Dora's health did not alter. She had made some significant improvements in the autumn, even gaining a little weight; now, with great control, she more or less maintained that state. Yet, as Wordsworth said, it was fragile: 'She takes a great deal of pains to be well, and strictly follows Sir B Brodie's advice – but the pain in the side and about the heart is not removed – and the least possible addition to the small portion of animal food she takes, or a sip almost of wine puts the heart wrong immediately.'[29] Unwittingly, Wordsworth had recognised Dora had a new reason to refuse food: it no longer 'deranged' her stomach, but her heart. She had a choice to make. An alternative future had presented itself to her.

CHAPTER 13

'THIS FILIAL LIKENESS'

1836

Then hail the twilight cave, the silent dell,
That boast no beams, no music of their own;
Bright pictures of the past around me dwell,
Where nothing whispers that the past is flown.
                                        Phantasmion

While Edward was being tossed about in the Bay of Biscay in November 1836, Sara, wearing a grey dressing-gown in the middle of the day, was lying in a room at the Castle Inn, Ilchester, a small and declining coaching town in Somerset. From her bed by the window, she could see a neglected garden. Mice scuttled under the floorboards and the noise from the bar downstairs precluded sleep. But she could not move. Sara had taken a room at the Castle Inn for one night to break a long coach journey, and in the morning she found she could not leave it. Through a cloud of hysterical depression, her despair was almost comical. 'My love, my life is blighted,' she informed poor baffled Henry, 'I can never bear the motion of a carriage again. I shall never see Hampstead more. I must live', she concluded dramatically, 'separated from my husband and children.'[1] She did, in fact, see Hampstead again, but not for more than a month.

Sara was trying to return home with her children from a visit to Henry's cousins, 'the Ottery Coleridges', in Devon. Going to stay at Ottery in August 1836 was a duty she had performed only with the greatest reluctance. Henry had been pressing her to make the journey for months, while promising the relatives the visit was imminent. After a summer of reasonable health, Sara finally ran out of excuses and set off with the children and Nuck. Henry travelled down with her but only stayed a little while before heading back to work. As a revising barrister, he was obliged to spend several months of each year travelling around the west of England hearing cases in local courts. So, while Henry traipsed the length and breadth of Devon from Cullompton to Barnstaple via South Molton and Tiverton, Sara stayed at Ottery for two disastrous months. She barely left her room, and ate most of her meals alone. Little Herby told her she had 'come for nothing', since she only once went so far as the flower garden and was therefore 'a poor dull woman who can have no enjoyment'.[2] Her son's criticism stung. He had gone – as six-year-olds will – straight to the point. Fearing she was a bad mother only made things worse. Once again she worried that the sensible, orthodox Ottery adults would believe her problem was 'childish weakness and self indulgence'.[3] As per her 'Good Genius' essay, she tried to believe that the 'harshness & the indelicacy' they showed her was in fact a result of her own tendency to 'magnify such evilmindedness in others'.[4] But it was hard advice to heed, especially in the worst throes of paranoid hysteria. Holed away in her room, she read and wrote long letters to those friends whom she hoped would be more sympathetic than the Coleridge clan. Slowly the days dribbled past and eventually the time came to return home.

On 14 October she set off for the first coaching inn with Herbert, Edith and Nuck, accompanied by a Mrs Boydell, who had also been staying at Ottery. Two days later, between three and four in the afternoon, they reached Ilchester and made for the largest inn, The Castle, run by a couple called Braine. They still had another three days' travel and 130 miles to go, but Sara's 'nervous anticipation', which had been building during the entire Ottery trip, reached breaking point. She did not sleep at all that night and decided in the morning that she simply 'could not proceed'.[5] She sent Mrs Boydell back to Ottery with the children. Nuck was kept in attendance on her mistress. Sara lived in terror that Henry would summon her home – or even come himself to fetch her. Within a couple of days she had sent him a stream of bleak letters explaining why it was utterly impossible for her ever to move from where she was.

Henry responded with concern and, reasonably enough, suggestions about how she might best be transported home. Sara worked herself up into a great anger as she fought to stay put. 'It still agitates me', she told him five days after arriving, 'to see that you have yet no notion of my weakness, and still fancy I can travel in ten days. No more than I can drag the carriage myself to Ottery.'[6] Other kindly meant suggestions equally infuriated her: 'Mrs Boydell's proposal about driving drove me almost wild,' she reported to her diary.[7] Despite the mice and the noise, she wanted not just to stay at the Castle Inn, but also to live there for some considerable time. In desperation, she persuaded Nuck to write to Henry. Her nurse obediently wrote a neat letter. 'My mistress thinks that you are quite in the dark as to the state of her weakness,' she told Henry. He was indeed in the dark, and desperately worried. Sorry as she was about the expense, Sara refused to countenance the thought of going to stay with nearby friends. Indeed, she explained, she could barely walk from her bed to Nuck's on the other side of the little room and certainly could not dress herself.[8] She thought she would need to stay until Christmas at least. On 22 October, she finally received the letter she had been hoping for in which Henry gave his uneasy consent to her decision to stay put. 'God Bless you a thousand times,' she responded. He had apologised for not being able to come to her. 'Of course you could not leave,' she soothed him: it would be far too expensive. 'I am quite cheered by your letter,' she informed her anxious husband.[9] Now she was able to relax and, though her symptoms continued, she reported a slight improvement in her sleep and in her appetite. She took up her pen and set to work.

She had multiple projects, but the one that most allowed her to escape the confines of the room was a fantastical story she had begun writing the previous autumn while Henry was away for several weeks. She had been ill and hysterical then, but the project had done her good. Five days after starting she had found to her surprise, 'my spirits are quite re-established'. She slept better, took less laudanum, and could 'walk in the garden for seven or eight minutes at a time, and sit up, uneasily – for nearly an hour'.[10] She had put 'The Tale' aside when Henry returned but after a few weeks she took it out again to show him. Henry was encouraging and so, between her duties as a wife and mother and her work helping Henry edit her father's works, she had found pockets of time to spin an increasingly elaborate narrative.

Before Ottery, she had thought her tale nearly finished, but she was not quite satisfied. Chapter eleven needed work, and she wanted to write some more verses for Zelneth, her beautiful, complex protagonist. She took the manuscript out at Ilchester and set to making cuts and editing Zelneth's voice to be sure it was distinct from the fairies. The fairy-tale allowed Sara to escape her sickroom. As she wrote, she 'had out-of-door scenes before me in a lightsome, agreeable shape, at a time when I was almost wholly confined to the house, and could view the face of nature only by very short glimpses'.[11] The landscape is recognisably that of the Lake District, and Sara enjoyed revisiting it in her imagination. She read and reread the adventures of her hero Prince Phantasmion.* 'Dark and cold was the place in which Phantasmion was confined, and such as might have chilled a less ardent temper than his; but he paced the stone floor, like a leopard in a cage, devising plans of escape, and nursing hopes of vengeance. He had now leisure to review the events of the morning.'[12] As she edited she had time to think about what she was writing and why.

Initially, Sara had been despondent about the notion of a fairy-tale. She feared it was 'the very way to be *not read*' – the genre belonged to an oversaturated market and her particular story was (unlike her nursery poems) unfashionably long.[13] Worst of all, and again unlike most of her children's poems, it lacked

* For a summary of the plot of *Phantasmion*, see Dennis Low, *The Literary Protégées of the Lake Poets* (2006), pp. 137–9.

a good Victorian moral. Today we might describe *Phantasmion* as a fantasy novel for young adults, an early precursor to *The Lord of the Rings* or *Northern Lights*.[14] Prince Phantasmion is granted various special powers: an invisibility cloak, the ability to walk at the bottom of the sea, butterfly wings and fly-sucker feet to jump across cliffs and mountains. The book is peopled with an 'evil fishy woman', queens and kings, fairies and pirates, but it does not teach children how to behave. The prose is beautiful, but dense, and it's hard to imagine many children ploughing their way through its 350 pages. At Ilchester, Sara also reread her father's books: his words helped her form a defence of her own writing.

Rereading Coleridge was an important step. It was what Henry had been trying to make her do ever since he had started work on *Table Talk*, two years before. Today we primarily think of STC as a poet, yet in the second half of his life he was at least as well known as a philosopher, theologian and critic. Richard Holmes has called him a 'hero for a self-questioning age' and he was one of the greatest minds of his, or any, generation.[15] At the time of his death, however, his reputation was, at best, mixed. Sara and Henry's hope, with the *Literary Remains*, was to elevate him in the eyes of the public. Sara hoped to do so in a subtler yet more persuasive way than in Henry's *Table Talk*, which had generally been regarded as a disappointment. Capturing Coleridge through his notoriously complex, even baffling, conversation was an almost impossible task.* When this was combined with Henry's determination to portray him as a good upstanding Anglican Tory, the result was a text which oversimplified Coleridge and made him less than he was.

Hartley's criticism of *Table Talk* was the most astute, but also the hardest for Sara to hear. Their father, Hartley argued, had seen the need for political change but not 'in servile compliance

---

* *Table Talk* was, according to Earl Leslie Griggs (Coleridge's great twentieth-century editor; see *Coleridge Fille*, p. 100), 'the only editorial work in which Henry may have misinterpreted Coleridge'. It was also the only book in which Henry was not assisted by Sara.

with the spirit of the age' as Henry's book suggested.*[16] Wordsworth was equally unimpressed, and though Sara defended her husband's work, she recognised its limitations. Henry was a lawyer and a critic and produced logical arguments for a living. Henry once told her: '*Your characteristic fault* (pardon me) is diffusion – splintering your thought into many bright fragments.'[17] It might have been a fault, but both recognised that Sara's 'heaven haunting' mind was closer to Coleridge's.[18]

It is hard to tell precisely how involved Sara was in the process of putting *The Literary Remains* together, but by 1836 the first volume was ready and Henry sent it to Ilchester. Sara was delighted to see the fruits of their labour. In the inn she immersed herself in her father's words and philosophy again. 'How delightful are the *Remains*,' she wrote to Henry. 'I quite grieve to find the pages on my left hand such a thick handful.'[19]

Alongside the *Remains*, Sara also reread STC's 1825 book, *Aids to Reflection*. When *Aids to Reflection* had first been published Sara was twenty-three and waiting at Greta for Henry to return from the West Indies. She did her best with it, but admitted quite cheerfully that most of it was beyond her comprehension. She had told Derwent she was 'delighted with all I can understand, but much of it is worse than Greek to me'.[20] Sara thought Derwent would be able to make sense of it if anyone could.[21] She had not quite finished before Wordsworth asked to borrow the Keswick copy. Now she read it again and, aged thirty-four, understood it and the true nature of her father's genius.

The key point regarding Coleridge's book about religion is that it instructs people not *what* to believe and think but *how*. He followed Kant in placing reason above blind faith. Coleridge argued that the 'noblest object of reflection is the mind itself'; if readers could maintain the connection between their intellect and morality and their sensual feelings, then

---

* Henry was offended by Hartley's criticism. Hartley assured him that 'nothing could be more remote from my intention than to accuse you of misrepresentation . . .' He went on, however, to give several pages of corrections (Hartley Coleridge to HNC, 8 May 1836; HCL, pp. 188–93).

'*false doctrine, blindness of heart, and contempt of the world*' could
be overcome. As Alan Vardy has argued in *The Unknown
Coleridge*, *Aids to Reflection* carried Sara through her emotional
crisis, exactly as Coleridge had hoped it might guide
humanity.* [22]

So, despite the hysteria and drug-taking, the way in which
Sara thought underwent a major change in Ilchester. Informed
by *Aids to Reflection*, *The Literary Remains* and *Table Talk*, she
grew more confident about what she was doing. Rereading *Table
Talk*, Sara was reminded that Coleridge had written of his
admiration for *Peter Wilkins* and *Robinson Crusoe*. She realised
she need not worry about *Phantasmion's* lack of moral. It should
not be compared to books like *The Pilgrim's Progress* in which
'the character and descriptions are all for the sake of an allegory', but 'to that class of fictions of which *Robinson Crusoe*,
Peter Wilkins, *Faust*, *Undine*, *Peter Schlemil* and the *Magic Ring*
or the *White Cat*, and many other fairy tales . . . are instances:
where the ostensible moral, <u>even if there be one</u>, is not the
author's chief end and aim, which rather consists in cultivating
the imagination'.[23] Sara was engaged in an intellectual inter-
rogation of her father, and *Phantasmion* was what we might,
awkwardly, call 'research by practice'. It has also been described
as 'an act of Preservation' because it was Sara's attempt to do
what Coleridge had never managed: to write a 'phantasmagoric
allegory'.[24] He had said: 'the prominent characters of the
phantasmagoric Allegory are its breadth, or amplitude, and
its rapid Auroraborealis-like shifting & thorough flashing of its
cones and Pyramids – yet still within a predetermined Sphere'.[25]
By writing her book Sara was doing something Coleridge would
have approved of – but it was also something he berated himself
for never having achieved. *Phantasmion* was part hagiography
of, and part victory over, her father.

---

* Interestingly the book had done something very similar for Derwent when
he was undergoing a crisis of faith, after leaving university. Indeed, it was
largely to help his spiritually lost son that Coleridge had been inspired to
write it.

The spell at the Castle Inn marked a shift. Since Coleridge's death, Sara had spent most of her time not only unhappy and unwell, but also, somehow, directionless. Afterwards, though often unhappy and unwell, she was never again without purpose. She felt, more than ever, that she could identify with STC: 'I never try to imitate my father – but when I have finished a sentence I often laugh inwardly at this filial likeness of manner and aim – though the execution and degree of force of thought are so different.'[26]

It was not only intellectually that Sara resembled her father. Like STC, she was always fascinated by the mind. She observed her own with a clinical eye, even as it let her down. She tried to imagine why she suffered as she did. Like her father before her, and psychologists since, she suspected it was down to the impact of childhood experiences. She found the connections between past and present selves fascinating. Writing to Henry, she wondered if her own illness might have originated when, as a child, she attempted too rapid an ascent of Helvellyn. Or could it have been because she had fallen in the stream at Greta and nearly drowned when she was two years old? Consciously or not, she was putting herself into the same place in family myth as the one STC inhabited: one cold October night, after a quarrel with his brother Frank, seven-year-old Samuel Taylor ran away. The story of how he stayed out all night and almost froze to death has become famous, and STC used it to fashion his own image of himself. He later attributed ill-health and 'ague' to the incident.

Also like STC, Sara was plagued by nightmares and bleak visions. For as much as *Phantasmion* was an escapist story, its often frightening language and images bled into Sara's daily thinking at Ilchester. She tried to describe how she felt to Henry: 'O this Devonshire visit has been a black vulture which for two successive summers came every now & then as I sate in the sun, to cast his grim shadow over me, & give me sight of his beak and claws. Now he holds me down upon the ground in his horrid gripe: I am even yet struggling for breath & liberty: if I ever get out alive of his clutches I will drive the monster away and when he comes near me again he shall be received on the prongs of a pitchfork.'[27] Writing *Phantasmion* was a means of controlling the monster – an alternative to hysteria. When her hero, Prince Phantasmion, was attacked by vultures, he 'thrust among them with his drawn sword, and pushed onward, leaving a cloud of his delicate plumelets fluttering in the air'.[28]

A couple of weeks into her stay, Henry came to visit. He arrived on Saturday, 29 October, and left the following Monday morning. He evidently thought Sara was perfectly capable of leaving and, as soon as he arrived home, wrote to tell her so. She worked herself up into a great state with all the fury of a cornered animal. 'Your letter has thrown me into a state of agitation which I will not describe,' she told him, since 'it would make no alteration in your opinions, and Heaven is my witness that I make no complaints which give pain to you for the mere sake of complaining. I reject all those burning expressions which suggest themselves to my mind in crowds and will endeavour to write only at the direction of that highest mind . . .' With brutal honesty, she asked him, 'O who will deliver me from this body of death!' and told him, 'Now indeed do I intensely long, like my poor father, to have my imprisoned spirit released from this tabernacle of weakness and misery.' She ended furiously by asking, 'If I reach Hampstead paralysed or dead what will it signify that mother, husband and children are there – what good will my return do them?'[29] She suffered agonies waiting for a response.

What Henry had not fully appreciated was how closely Sara's nervousness was linked to her womb – if not quite in the way that medical men of the nineteenth century tended to suggest. This was a concern her father never had to face: he was able to skip in and out of the lives of his wife and children. Sara was menstruating in the first week of her stay at the Castle Inn, but during Henry's visit, despite her state, he exercised his conjugal rights. Afterwards she panicked: she might be pregnant again. Sara was vexed because she had 'the whites' (increased vaginal discharge is often an early symptom of pregnancy). Her cycle was normally extremely regular and her next period should therefore have come by around 12 or 13 November. On the 13th, when it still had not, her hysteria and nervousness increased. She was constipated, sleeping badly, taking too much opium. She tried to explain to Henry what it all felt like, and concluded that he sympathised 'as much as a dear intellect, a tender heart, and tried affection for me can make you do' – but he did not really understand. After all, when bystanders like Henry 'talk of nervous agitation and prostration they do not represent to themselves the misery by any means so vividly as when they speak of a broken leg an amputated limb or any other kind of severe pain'.[30] Sara tried to take the advice she had given herself in the dialogue between her Invalid and Good Genius selves:

> **Invalid**: Under the most favourable circumstances, derangement of the nervous system must be a heavy trial, but how greatly is it aggravated by our own experience and that of others!
> **Good Genius**: Nervous derangement is in many ways most trying both to those who undergo and them who witness it: those who suffer have to allow for the ignorance in others of what can be recognised by so few outward signs, and those around have great need of charity and candour to put faith in our report, and shew pity for ills with which they cannot sympathize.[31]

But whatever she told herself, Henry's attitude still felt harsh and indelicate. Sara, obdurate, told him that, on the advice of the doctor, she would come home as soon as her period had been and gone.

That same evening, in a complete state by now, Sara took an anodyne of some sort (probably opiate-based), combined with a pill to promote her 'courses'. Emmenagogues, as the latter treatments were called, were a common part of nineteenth-century medicine. They provide a fascinating insight into the lives of nineteenth-century women. There was a firm and long-held belief – endorsed by men and women – that it was critically important for menstrual cycles to be regular. Various ills would ensue if they were not and hysteria and nervousness were considered chief amongst the symptoms of uterine 'blockage'. Blood flowed in the wrong direction and upset the nervous system. To maintain regularity, there were a plethora of pills, potions and practices, including emmenagogues. There is a complicated ambiguity about such treatments; if Sara hoped to bring on her period to improve her health that was well and good, but it was perfectly obvious the drugs could also be used as abortificants. The advertisements warned against use during pregnancy, thus broadcasting their alternative property. (The more coy warned against use by 'married ladies'.)

Emmenagogues varied in type: some were harmless, but many contained ergot, aloes, savin, lead or arsenic, all of which could induce an abortion.[32] In the nineteenth century a researcher named Van der Warkle made systematic observations of emmenagogues by testing samples on himself and his dog. His description of the effect of savin is particularly vivid: 'A violent pain in the abdomen, vomiting and powerful cathartic action, with tenesmus, strangury, heat and burning in the stomach, bowels, rectum and anal region, intoxication, flushed face, severe headache . . . salivation is often present.'[33] On the morning after taking the drug to induce menstruation, Sara experienced a total setback. Once again she told Henry all thoughts of the return home must be postponed because of the effects of the anodyne. She did not mention the other pills to him. Three days later she was still 'very weak and tremulous – my thighs back and limbs sensitive and uneasy'.[34] Nonetheless that night her period had come and she was ready to return home. She did not wish to wait, as the doctors had suggested, until she had finished menstruating. She left on the 17th and, taking the journey in small sections in the invalid carriage, she arrived home at Downshire Hill on 23 November and went to sleep in her mother's bed.

CHAPTER 14

SAUDADES AND THE DREAD VOICE
THAT SPEAKS FROM OUT THE SEA

1837–1838

The small carriage reached the Market Cross in Ambleside, rattled over the river, past Smithy Brow, and made an unsteady progress along the Rydal Road. Jackson of the Low Wood, under instruction from Wordsworth, drove a reluctant horse as fast as he could. Rain battered against the windows and the occupants could hardly see or be seen. Inside sat an uncomfortable and exhausted Dora with Miss Fenwick. Perhaps as they bumped along the two women talked of the events of the past year, events in which Miss Fenwick had played such an important role. Perhaps, as the horse strained at the bit to pull through the mud, Dora expressed her extreme anxiety about seeing her father. Perhaps Miss Fenwick gave her younger companion a last few words of advice. Most probably Dora was silent: 'to you my dearest Miss Fenwick I say nothing because my feelings be too deep for words'.[1] It was June 1838 and Dora was returning to Rydal for the first time in over a year.

Fifteen months before, in the spring following Edward's sudden departure for Oporto, Dora had travelled to London and Hendon for the summer. She planned to see friends and relations, including, of course, Sara Coleridge. Wordsworth had finally agreed (not without a certain amount of bullying from Crabb Robinson) to go on the postponed trip to Italy: when he

arrived back at the end of the summer he would collect Dora
and the pair would travel home together. Until then she could
enjoy her freedom.

As soon as Dora reached London – and later Hendon –
Edward took advantage of her relative privacy to write increasingly
unguarded letters. He tried to persuade Dora to come and visit
him in Portugal. She refused. He was cross. 'So you are not
only not coming, but you would not if you could! – I score that
down with three black crosses. – Then you add that I shall like
you the better for such a resolution: now there you are mistaken:
I could not have liked you better than I did, but I do like you
a little less for this confession of yours. Never mind. I shall be
hard enough in time (it is high time I should petrify) and I feel
a new layer of thick crust already lightly fitting itself around
that turbulent self-tormentor which the sight of your letter put
into a gallop and the reading of it pulled up into a walk.' She
had told him it would be for the best if she did not visit. He
disagreed, and in telling her so, mixed his metaphors most
perplexingly. 'Nothing can be more execrable than this style,
which is neither correct in metaphor nor plain in meaning, but
I dare not trust my manners to the care of plain language in my
present temper. – But whatsoever is is best: so, Dora, my best
of Optimists, let that be my creed, as well as yours for the future.
It is best that you should be a Nun at large and your own Lady
Abbess, and it is best that I a widower of 45, not inexperienced
in troubles, should at last look out for a rich widow or a maiden
heiress after having dreamed for more than fourteen years of a
Rachel of my own (mute) fancy without consoling myself with
a Leah in the interval! It is best that it should be so. I have
already', he continued cruelly, 'a widow or two in my eye and
some half dozen of fortuned misses.'[2] It is hard to know how
seriously to take either his anger or his flirtation: the barb of
each is blunted with humour.

Dora spent the summer of 1837 in a state of confusion. She
couldn't quite trust or believe Edward really loved her – she had
her suspicions that he loved her at Rydal, where she was
Wordsworth's daughter, but not when she was away from home.

This Edward denied: 'Who told you that I ever found you stupid or uninteresting when removed from Rydal? that is indeed a puzzle to me; and whoever was your informant has wronged both you and me.'[3] Whatever the truth, he had a very busy social life which in all likelihood did include several glamorous heiresses. How could Dora compete?

During the summer, Dora visited Sara several times. She explained Edward was due to arrive back in England at about the same time as Wordsworth. When Wordsworth arrived, he and Dora would travel home to Rydal with a visit on the way either to relatives in Bath or relatives in Herefordshire. There then comes another of those maddening gaps in the record. We know what happened, but not why it happened, nor who was behind the various alterations in the plans. It's just possible Sara helped Dora devise a plot. How would it be if Dora engineered her father's travel plans to ensure an encounter with Edward on the way home? The obvious location was Brinsop Court, in Herefordshire. Brinsop was the home of Dora's uncle, Thomas Hutchinson, and his family. Wordsworth had introduced Edward to the Hutchinsons years before, and Thomas and his family had become great friends with Edward and his girls. The Quillinans had an open invitation any time they chose. As it happened, Tom Hutchinson was unwell – surely this would persuade Wordsworth to visit Brinsop rather than relatives in Bath? Once all together, Dora and Edward could find an opportunity to be alone. If events proceeded as Sara suspected they would, then Edward could talk to Wordsworth and the whole thing might be resolved to everyone's satisfaction – or at least laid out in the open, which would be preferable to all the secrecy and second-guessing.

By the time he landed in England, Wordsworth had agreed that, for the sake of Thomas Hutchinson's ill-health, he and Dora should visit Brinsop.[4] He reached the Customs House on 7 August and, after a tussle over his luggage, he made for Edward Moxon's house in London where he was to stay. The first thing he did was send for Dora.[5] As he held her thin body in a tight embrace, all Wordsworth's anxiety about his daughter returned.

Dora claimed her appetite was good, but even she had to admit she did 'not gather strength as I expected'.[6] Her father took her off to visit two of London's most expensive doctors: the eminent surgeon, Sir Benjamin Brodie, and Dr Davy. Both doctors' verdicts were quite clear: Dora must not return to the north; she needed sea air and a mild winter.

As soon as the medical men suggested staying in the south for winter, a new ally and confidante of Dora's, Miss Isabella Fenwick, offered to have Dora to stay. Unbeknownst to Wordsworth, Miss Fenwick was fully up to date with the details of the abortive affair, and was firmly on the side of love. She told Wordsworth she would be happy to seek out a suitable cottage somewhere on the coast, probably Dover. The family changed its plans: although Dora would accompany her father west to Brinsop, she would then retrace her steps to spend the winter in the south for her health. Wordsworth would return alone to Rydal.

Crabb Robinson travelled with Dora and Wordsworth to Brinsop because he and Wordsworth had decided to take a 'supplementary' tour in England. Once they had settled on Brinsop, the nearby Wye Valley became the obvious place for their excursion.* Dora was excited about the prospect of seeing the place where her father had written some of his most famous poetry. It would be a good way to pass the time while waiting for Edward. But, after several weeks at Brinsop, there was still no news from him. Initially Wordsworth was happy enough to stay put with the Hutchinsons. The weather was miserable, and both he and Robinson preferred to wait until it improved before they braved the Wye Valley. As the weeks passed, however, and the weather remained as grisly as ever, the poet grew impatient to get back to Rydal. On 20 September, the very day they heard

---

* Wordsworth had not much enjoyed his continental tour, partly because he was worried about Dora's health and partly because he and Robinson had not got on terribly well. When they returned to London they resolved to embark on the 'supplementary tour' in order to put an end to the rumours that they had quarrelled.

Edward had reached British shores, Wordsworth dictated a letter for Dora to send Edward. He explained that though he had hoped to see him in Brinsop, an infection in his eye meant he had asked Dora (his living staff) to accompany him home: 'Our places are taken in to-morrow morning's coach for Liverpool, so that therefore we must be disappointed in seeing you and Jemima here at Brinsop.'[7] Looking at her handwriting in the letter, one wonders if she were somehow trying to impart a message, but the letters are neat, regular and inscrutable.

As Wordsworth saw it, 'Dora could not bear to let me come home in that helpless state by myself, and to say the truth it was a great consolation to me to know that she would have this opportunity of seeing her Mother and Aunt before her winter campaign in the South.'[8] Sara heard from Mary that 'Mr Wordsworth's eyes had become so bad that he was forced to proceed home hastily <u>with</u> Dora whose companionship he could not do without.'[9] What did Sara make of that underlined 'with'? Had Dora run out of courage or had Wordsworth's eyes truly grown so very much worse? Was it possible the poet had an inkling of what was happening?

Edward was cross and wrote to Wordsworth: 'But it has all turned out as it began, badly, so far as <u>my</u> hopes were concerned. First, having vowed to go at least 100 miles out of my way to see Dora & you, wherever you might be, I lay out my route at Oporto so as to be sure of catching you at Brinsop. I land with all the sorrows of much luggage at Falmouth for that purpose, instead of proceeding first to London. An hour after landing, I find your letter & Dora's, telling me that you are off for the north.' Edward's next hope was to catch Dora on her way back south – at Leeds, or Birmingham – but it was not to be. Willy was accompanying his sister and Edward only learned they reached each city once they had left. Eventually he gave up. He would make 'no more plans for overtaking or intercepting such Willy-o-wisps as Willy & his sister'. He concluded his letter: 'As to you dear detestable Dora. I hate you almost as much as if you had really dreamt up all these contretemps.'[10]

If Sara had been plotting then she would have been

disappointed in Dora. However, since Dora had not abandoned her plan to winter in the south, Miss Fenwick's scheme still stood a chance. When Edward heard Dora planned to be in Dover, his own plans just happened to change too. As he explained to Wordsworth: 'if the most sagacious foresight had been devising to throw me out, Dora's escape from me could not have been more cleverly contrived . . . But patience, I shall still see her at Dover, I suppose, as Canterbury', he continued blithely, 'is one of the places to which I must go, as that is the neighbourhood in which Mrs Holmes has long been looking out for a residence for me, though I am by no means certain that I shall make up my mind to live there.' Mrs Holmes, his first wife's sister, had indeed been encouraging Edward to settle down. This was the first time he seems to have taken her suggestion on board. On 25 October, Edward noted in his diary, 'DW leaves Rydal on Monday October 30th – arrives at Birmingham by the mail train at ½ past 7, Tuesday evening sleeps at the Swan and leaves for London at 9am on Wednesday morning.'[11] His quarry was returning into sight. When Dora and Willy reached London, Edward was waiting to escort Dora on to Dover. The offer could not be turned down. In London, Dora paid a flying visit to Sara, promised a longer one in the spring and prepared for her journey.

Edward and Dora met just after sunrise on Tuesday, 9 November, in the fog and damp of London Bridge. They had not seen one another's faces since Edward's stay at Rydal when he had declared his love for her. In the intervening fourteen months, they had written countless letters and said almost nothing at all. At London Bridge, in the confusion, noise and chaos of the busy port, they missed their steamer to Herne Hill and were forced to travel by coach instead.* Edward sat on a cheap outside seat while Dora paid twice as much for an inside one.[12] She did not complain, but was sad he had not paid to talk to her during the long journey. Edward left the carriage at Canterbury for Mrs Holmes' house, and Dora travelled on alone to Dover. It was

---

* Steamer travel was considerably cheaper and more reliable.

late, and she was exhausted when she finally reached Miss Fenwick's little brick cottage in Clarence Place.

Miss Fenwick had been introduced to the Wordsworths in 1834. By 1837 she was a young-looking fifty-five, with the kind of face that 'might have been called handsome, but that it was too noble and distinguished to be disposed of by that appellative'.[13] She had dark hair, large intelligent eyes, a delicate mouth, and everyone considered her 'one of the finest old women ever discovered'.[14] She was a shrewd observer and a good listener, and had become an intimate of the Wordsworth family, staying with them at Rydal and seeing them in London. Initially she was Wordsworth's friend. He quickly came to trust her utterly and depend upon her judgement in almost every aspect of his life and poetry. What he did not realise was the extent to which his daughter had done the same, on the subject of Mr Edward Quillinan. Dora had started to refer to Miss Fenwick as her 'Guardian Angel'.[15]

The day after their arrival, Edward saddled Mrs Holmes' horse and rode to Dover to call on Dora. Miss Fenwick greeted him kindly; she encouraged Dora to accept an invitation to Mrs Holmes' in Canterbury and in return asked Edward to stay with her in a few days' time. Throughout November, almost daily, Edward rode and sometimes walked the cold miles between Canterbury and Dover. He and Dora walked and talked with exhilarating freedom along the newly completed esplanade. At the bustling harbour, they watched as reluctant horses were swung from steamers by gigantic cranes, and spotted turbaned Moroccan merchants coming ashore.[16] From Shakespeare's Cliff they saw fishermen as small as mice on the beach below; they watched shorelarks shuffling in the shingle and looked out towards France. Later, Edward wrote a poem in which the waves 'kiss the feet of that immaculate cliff'.* Once Dora went to

---

* For the poem 'The Shakespeare Cliff', see EQ to Dora, 20 March 1837 (Dove Cottage, WLL/Quillinan, Edward/1/78). Dora and Edward had visited the cliff (known as Shakespeare's because it appears in *King Lear*) before Christmas. Dora wrote to tell her father about it and Wordsworth replied, 'I rejoice that you have stood on Shakespeare's Cliff' (MW and WW to Dora,

Canterbury; they visited the cathedral with Mrs Holmes, while David's Psalm 'Plead Thou My Cause' thundered ironically from the organ.[17]

Edward declared his love again and again. Dora tried to tell him that since he was like a son to Wordsworth, he could only ever be a brother to her. But within days, she relented. She did love him. One imagines her reporting back to an increasingly well-pleased Miss Fenwick each evening. After three weeks, which were as romantic as they were terrifying, Edward left. He had been summoned to Rydal where Wordsworth wanted him to help revise some poems. Dora stayed behind at Dover while Edward (acting like a dutiful son-in-law) made his way obediently to Rydal. They vowed to write, and their words flew back and forth the length of the country.

Dora and Edward pored over one another's letters and answered questions directly and methodically, so reading them is spine-tinglingly close to eavesdropping on a deeply intimate and heart-rending conversation. Not all the letters survive, but Edward had a habit of quoting the part of Dora's letter to which he referred, so it is possible to piece together their highly charged relationship. The closer Edward got to Grasmere, the more sure he became of his feelings. For Dora, the reverse happened. The thought of Edward with her father frightened her, and as he approached Rydal, she panicked and changed her mind again.

Edward: 'I stole away with my letters into my room, + eagerly opened up the letter of DW . . .'

Dora: 'My love for you is spiritual Platonism such as man might feel for man or woman for woman . . . I wish for your sake you were fairly married to someone else.'

Edward: 'I ought to have been glad that I was loved on any terms, but I was sad and a voice from the paper seemed to say; "Thrice the icy spell was broken, / And the third time his heart was broken" and I read no more that evening.'

---

23 November 1837; *WW LLY*, III, p. 81). He might not have rejoiced so much had he known the context of her visit.

That night Edward had a dream about Dora. He wrote to describe it to her in a strange and vivid prose poem. 'I sat on a black rock near Oporto,' he told her, and 'I said to the star Venus "Star what are you?" & the star answered, "I am her heart."' So Edward asked '"Star, where is she?" and was told "In the Palace of Frozen Tears . . . Follow me!"' Edward tried to follow but 'was wrecked and cast upon an iceberg . . . the North wind said to me, with a voice like a scythe "Mount I will be your horse" it carried me away over seas and frozen regions following the star . . . into a Palace illuminated by Northern lights'. In the Palace of Frozen Tears, Dora 'sat – alone – & on her head the crescent moon – & the star glided into her bosom, through which I saw it glittering . . . "Star" said I, "what are you doing there in the place of a heart?" Venus replied. "I am <u>her</u> heart I am a frozen star."'[18] By the end of his letter, written at Rydal, Edward's writing becomes uncharacteristically messy. 'I have not half done' – the hand-writing quick and large – 'but here comes Mrs Wordsworth and says I <u>must</u> have your letter now or never. [the writing increasingly illegible and loopy] Do not be alarmed: I am not mad.' And then a final afterthought: 'To be burned when read on honor[*sic*].'

Dora had not known how to reply to that letter and so had not written a word. Two days later, she had received another letter, written while Edward was sitting by the fire at Rydal Mount. In it he described how Mary had entered the drawing room, seen Edward reading Dora's letter and asked: 'That is Dora's letter is it not?' Mary wanted to see it and Edward had to lie about its content to dissuade her. But, he confessed to Dora:

Edward: 'I felt ashamed as if I were guilty of some, I do not know
          what to call it, for it is not disingenuousness in its culpable
          sense – my regard for you is not, cannot be a secret in this
          house – but it is exactly in this house and to its owners
          that I could not own a syllable about it . . .'

And so their conversation continued.

Dora: 'In all truth and soberness . . . you ought to marry – and not me . . .'

Edward: 'you would provoke a saint. – It *sounds* so heartless. I *know*, my dear Dora, that it is not so; but it sounds so, and it feels so, & it tastes so: it is a woodpecker's tap on a hollow tree in my ears; it is a squirt of lemon-juice in my eyes, and it is gall and wormwood on my tongue. – But you are right and I will follow your advice: I give you my word of honor [*sic*] I will, when you have shewn me the example.'[19]

Dora: 'I have been much perplexed . . .'

Edward: 'I have been "much perplexed".'[20] . . . 'for the greater part of sixteen years you so skilfully mystified me'.[21]

Dora: 'concealment . . .'

Edward: 'I never had, or wished to have, a concealment, except as a guard to self-respect so long as we were in mutual ignorance, and had a separate secret – we were too long mutually deceived . . .'

Dora: 'You have had flirtations and fancies . . .'

Edward: 'True: a thousand. How many have you had? Not many: then you are the true lover: no: – oh, I could tell you strange things: and when I had told them all you would believe that you have *some hold on my affections*.'[22]

Dora: 'You are not spiritualised enough . . .'[23]

Edward: 'But in society or alone, gay or miserable I have never for a moment forgotten you . . . and whenever I have been on the verge of a new world of hope and passions (how shall I express this for I cannot be explicit), whenever I have been about to surrender myself in desperation irrevocably to some other influence, up sprung the image of the mountain Maiden, and I felt it was impossible. – There you have as much of the secret of my heart-and-hand loneliness for the last eleven or twelve years as I can venture to expose to you just now.'[24]

Dora: 'You sat on the outside of the Dover Coach . . . You have shown coldness of feeling . . .'[25]

Edward: 'There never was any coldness of feeling . . . inside or *out*side of a Dover Coach, or anywhere else.'

Dora: 'I have burned your early letters.'[26]

Edward: 'There is not, I believe, a scrap of your writing to me
. . . that I have not preserved from the very beginning
of our acquaintance: from "you man of the Moon who
were once a Dragoon" to your last letter . . . rec'd by
me 2 days since . . . My love for you Dora is not only a
man's love but (breath it not in Ascalon!)* a poet's love
. . . Saudades.'[27]

'*Saudades*' was the Portuguese word Edward had taught Dora,
which meant longing and love and yearning.

Dora: 'I am a scourge to your happiness . . .'

Edward: 'Why, you have been my pioneer through a thousand woods
of thorns. My love for you has certainly, in one sense, not
been a happy one; but without it I should have been dead
long since.'

Dora: 'Would that I were on a footstool and you a chair and we
could talk.'

Edward: 'the relative positions should be reversed, and I would listen
to you and not interrupt you, unless with 1000 kisses or
so, until you had done . . .'

Dora: 'All objects are coloured to my eyes and thoughts by one
person . . .'

Edward: 'What *you* say about having all objects coloured to your
eyes . . . is what I have experienced for years, for years.'[28]

Before Christmas, Dora went to London. She visited Sara in her
smart new house near Regent's Park and, shortly afterwards (on
Sara's advice perhaps?), wrote to Wordsworth to tell him she loved

---

* A reference to David's wonderful lamentation over Jonathan in 2 Samuel
1:19: 'The beauty of Israel is slain upon thy high places: how are the mighty
fallen!/Tell it not in Gath, publish it not in the streets of Askelon.' Ascalon
was one of the primary cities of the Philistines who were considered by the
Victorians to epitomise anti-intellectual and unenlightened existence. It was
also a city which, throughout history, has been associated with warfare and
violence – a very different kind of manliness to Edward's poetic love.

Edward. It was an act of terrific courage and though one wishes her letter still existed, its disappearance is surely not coincidental. It is easy to imagine the poet, white-faced with rage, ripping it into shreds or thrusting it into the fireplace at Rydal. Dora was terrified of what her father would say. While waiting for a response, she wrote to ask Edward (now back in London too) if she had done the right thing. He replied on 19 January 1838: '[You] are right to be candid on the first opportunity you have found, and having done right you have done wisely.'[29]

While still waiting to hear from Rydal, Edward and Dora, this time accompanied by Rotha and Jemima, returned to Canterbury – looking for all the world like a family. They took the express coach from the Golden Cross Pub in Charing Cross at ten in the morning on Thursday, 25 January. Nearly nine hours later they drove under Canterbury's postern arch of West Gate. Dora stayed with Mrs Holmes and the girls while Edward spent the night at nearby lodgings. The following day he took her to Miss Fenwick's at Dover and stayed the night in the York Hotel. All of them were anxious about what Wordsworth might say.

When Wordsworth's response came, on 29 January, it was a letter explosive with fury and far worse than Dora could have imagined.[30] Edward came rushing over to see her and read the letter, but Dora was plunged into an agony of doubt and anxiety. How could she have so hurt her father? What was she to do? Edward wrote to Rydal, but his letter was ignored. For nearly three weeks they heard nothing. Eventually Mary ordered her husband to write their daughter a 'peace offering'. So, on 8 February, he sent a sonnet* 'at your dear mother's earnest request'. The poem 'At Dover' begins:

> From the Pier's head, long time and with encrease
> Of wonder had I watched this seaside town,

---

* Wordsworth published the sonnet, in revised form, in *The Sonnets of William Wordsworth*, 1838. Later he made further alterations and included it in *Memorials of a Tour on the Continent, 1820* in 1845.

The speaker's 'turmoil' is quelled, more or less, by the ocean. The waters have their work cut out, however, against

> . . . the dread voice that speaks from out the sea
> Of God's eternal word, the voice of Time
> Deadens, – the shocks of faction, shrieks of crime,
> The Shouts of folly, and the groans of sin.[31]

Conjuring up, as it does, a watchful and vengeful father, the poem is not everyone's idea of a peace offering.

Meanwhile Dora and Edward stayed put. They knew they were living on borrowed time. They went sightseeing, listened to concerts, visited Dover Castle in a fly. The little imitation family scrambled about with Mima and Rotha over the fort, looking at Dane John Gardens and walking the walls of Canterbury's Norman motte and bailey. From the western battlements of Dover Castle, where King Arthur held his court, they looked down on to fertile valleys and the London Road. Days sped past, but as winter ended, so did their time together. Miss Fenwick was leaving Dover, and so Dora headed towards London, leaving Edward behind.

Dora: 'When writing to you I never know how to stop, for a stopping is like a parting.'
Edward: 'It is just what I have always felt in writing to you . . . Saudades . . . a sign and symbol between you and me.'[32]

At the start of March, Sara asked Dora to visit and she accepted with alacrity. She longed to see and talk to her old friend, but on the very day she was due to arrive – 8 March – Sara gave birth to a stillborn child, dead for two weeks. Instead, Dora visited other friends and hoped her father would refer to Edward again. He did not, but he was in touch regularly, asking her advice about and support for a new edition of poetry he was to bring out. Putting aside her worries, she responded as best she could to his demands. On 20 March she received another cold letter. It was clear Wordsworth was set against the match. She wrote to Edward and he marked the day in his diary with two black crosses and the words: 'a disastrous day letter from ww and from dw'.[33]

A week later Edward followed Dora to London. Once there, the star-crossed pair met when they could. They spent long afternoons together – slow carriage journeys and intimate conversations. During one such journey in April, Edward proposed and gave Dora a ring with 'Saudades' engraved into it. Dora panicked. She could not consider herself formally engaged without the consent of her father. She wrote again to Rydal.

Wordsworth chose to reply with a long letter about a parallel drama which was playing out for a friend of his, the playwright Sir Henry Taylor. Taylor was a cousin of Miss Fenwick's; in fact, it was he who had first introduced her to the Wordsworths. Taylor at thirty-six had just proposed to a seventeen-year-old girl. Wordsworth thought the whole thing deeply inappropriate. The girl's father had, quite rightly thought Wordsworth, turned Taylor down. Wordsworth described his approval to Dora: 'If men and women will form engagements so little in accordance with nature and reason,' he concluded, 'they have no <u>right</u> to expect better treatment.'* He felt pity for Miss Fenwick, who he knew was upset – but he didn't realise that Miss Fenwick was firmly on Taylor's side and that was the cause of her upset.[34] Wordsworth did not make direct reference to Dora's message about Edward. It seemed obvious to him that the combination of Edward's age, religion and lack of career put him beyond the pale. Perhaps, too, he could not bear the idea of losing his helpmeet. His letter ended simply: 'I take no notice of the conclusion of your Letter; indeed part of it I could not make

---

* Wordsworth used the example not only because of the disparate ages of the couple, but because they were of different religions. The seventeen-year-old's father had broken the engagement. It shows clearly how Wordsworth thought of his thirty-four-year-old daughter. The comparison was additionally unfortunate since when the pair did eventually marry, it was an exceptionally long and happy union. (She was Theodosia Alise Spring Rice, daughter of Thomas Rice, the Secretary for War and Colonies in Melbourne's final government.)

out. It turns upon a subject which I shall never touch more either by pen or voice. Whether I look back or forward it is depressing and distressing to me, and so will for the remainder of my life, continue to be so.'[35]

It mortified Dora to think that her father was not only upset about her future, but by the fact that he now regretted his history of friendship with Edward and feared he had lost trust in his daughter. She decided to go home and face her parents. Edward pleaded with her to stay in the south. 'I wonder if you and I shall ever be in heaven together! and whether we shall know and love each other as we do now and have done these fourteen years . . .'[36] But Dora's mind was made up. She wrote a 'bold speaking out letter' to her father and prepared for the long journey.

Miss Fenwick, perhaps to buy Dora thinking time, offered to pay for her to visit Tintern Abbey and the Wye Valley on the way home. The valley was, and had been for the past thirty years, an essential part of the nineteenth-century sightseeing tour of Britain. With the help of Miss Fenwick's servant James, Dora took herself to Brinsop, from where a small party of tourists was departing for the Wye. They left in two carriages during torrential rain on a grey April morning. Dora was cold, damp and uncomfortable. Every rut in the ground sent jolts of pain through her thin body. Sitting was acutely uncomfortable and she had a chill deep within her bones. She did not know the rest of the group well and their grand expedition was so far not much fun. The others – a collection of distant cousins and their friends – were a cheerful bunch, considerably younger than her, and mostly well known to one another. She felt rather fragile as they clattered along.

Wordsworth's 1798 'Lines Composed Above Tintern Abbey' was, and has remained, amongst the most celebrated of his poems. The poem was bound up with Wordsworth's public identity, and hence with Dora's sense of herself. Dora had been particularly looking forward, therefore, to their first stop – Wyndcliff – a famous viewpoint from which she knew her father had drawn inspiration. Coleridge once described it as a vantage point from where you could see 'the whole world imag'd in its vast circumference'.[37] A contemporary, visiting the same spot, said: 'The river forms almost a circle, the rocks a richly wooded amphitheatre and the fields fade into the Severn.'[38] For Dora's father the valley had been a place of ecstasy, beauty and pleasure. But on that morning Dora, glimpsing it through rain-streaked, fogged-up windows, did not feel ecstatic. As the carriage reached the summit of Wyndcliff, the sun came out, to the delight of the others, and they all clambered out. Even then, Dora could not quite feel the joy for which she had hoped.

The weather continued to behave dramatically. One minute the sky was light, the next dark: 'flashes of sunshine & shadows of clouds' lit up the meadows and down to the sea beyond, but, heavy-hearted, she could not enjoy any of it. She was fully aware of the irony: 'Lines Composed a Few Miles Above Tintern Abbey, on Revisiting the Banks of the Wye During a Tour, July 13, 1798' is not actually about the abbey at all, but the landscape in which it lies and the poet's feelings about returning to a beloved place. The memory of this view had sustained him through five difficult years 'in lonely rooms, and 'mid the din/ Of towns and cities' but Dora felt 'this beauty was over-powering'. She 'could only weep and wish myself more worthy of such privilege'. She wandered about for a couple of hours, exploring nooks and pathways in the cliff. Deliberately misquoting her father she later wrote: 'I felt it was all to me as is a landscape to a blind man's eye.'* No sooner had the group returned to the carriage than it began to hail. It did not stop as they made their way down the hill and a couple of miles on to Tintern Abbey. Again they could see nothing as they drove, and on arrival were forced to shelter in an inn until the sun returned.

Dora found the sadness and desolation of the ruins more in harmony with her feelings. Leaving her cousins, she disappeared

---

* Wordsworth had written: 'These beauteous forms,/Through a long absence, have not been to me/ As is a landscape to a blind man's eye.'

off 'into the Abbey and up to the topmost of its walls'. These she 'ran round like a cat & gathered some fern & some wild rose in full leaf'. Despite the wind and the cold she was reluctant to leave and lingered as long as she could, drinking in the land-scape and committing it to memory until it was time for the carriage to complete its final leg of the day – to Monmouth where the travellers would spend the night.

By the time they reached the inn, Dora was 'positively stiff with cold' and exhausted by the whole expedition. Everyone else went energetically off for an evening walk on the heights above Monmouth; she stayed behind alone and 'dreamed away the time upon the sofa'. She had done the same thing the night before, at Chepstow, when the others had gone off to look at the castle. While they explored, she returned, cold and unhappy, to her 'sad & lonely thoughts on the sofa'.[39]

Dora returned to her Hutchinson relatives at Brinsop with relief. While Mary wrote regular chatty letters telling her how much she and Wordsworth wanted their daughter home, Dora barely wrote to her parents at all. As usual, Miss Fenwick came to the rescue – she had decided to take a house in Ambleside and asked Dora to accompany her there. So it was that Dora came to be sitting in the carriage next to Miss Fenwick, with rising anxiety about reaching home. Doubtless her older friend now reminded her she had received a tender 'home-welcoming letter' from Wordsworth. Dora may also have remembered the advice Edward had given her in his last letter on what she should do when she returned home again: 'Nothing at all: be quiet, my dear Dora, and do not attempt to argue the point. Dutiful to Him I know you will be, and dutiful to Her I pray you to be . . . She has not been very kind to me, but I am sure that she has many a heartache about you.'[40]

In a few minutes the house would come into view, but there was a problem. The half-drowned horse was refusing to climb the hill, and Jackson was unloading all the luggage in the hope the wretched animal might be persuaded to keep going with a lighter load. It was no good: the horse refused to move another step, so Dora and Miss Fenwick were forced to climb out and walk uphill. Somewhere, in one of the trunks, lay all of Edward's letters.

> How much better, dear Dora, do I know you than your father does . . . I never in any way played them false.[41]

> . . . for the greater part of sixteen years you so skilfully mystified me.[42]

> You became anxious and lost your health . . . I lost my money and peace of mind.[43]

When Miss Fenwick and Dora finally reached the front gate of Rydal Mount their hair clung to the sides of their faces, they were wet through to the skin and shivering. Wordsworth was furious; berating Jackson for using a horse that had never before been in harness. Mary and the servants bustled to get the two women inside and warmed up.

Astonishingly quickly, Dora settled back into her usual life at Rydal: 'all sights & sounds are so familiar to me that there are moments when I can hardly understand that I have ever been separated from them', she wrote to Rotha.[44] Wordsworth reclaimed Miss Fenwick as his friend and took her off for walks and visits which Dora was not considered strong enough to make. Her time with Edward might have been a dream. Her doves still cooed, Aunt Dorothy was much the same, and Dora was plunged straight back into her usual role of amanuensis to her father.

Wordsworth's latest project was a single volume containing all his sonnets, and Dora was soon immersed in proofreading. She was also expected to get as exercised as Wordsworth – or at least calm him – in a debate about a copyright bill.[45] These were the subjects of importance at Rydal. Her father was, once again, all loving tenderness and concern, but on the subject of Edward Quillinan nothing was said. Wordsworth did not mention that Edward had a legal dispute hanging over his head, one with huge implications for his future financial security. He did not bring up the subject of Edward's religion. Dora, in her thirty-fourth year, did not need her father's permission, legally speaking. Emotionally speaking, however, both knew she could not marry without it. Within a couple of months, Dora – thin and weak – was confined to the sofa again. The reunion she had so feared had proved an anti-climax.

CHAPTER 15

'HOPES & FEARS'

1838–1840

'Every Other Thinking Mind'

In September 1838, while Dora faded on the sofa at Rydal, Sara declared herself prepared to abandon her oldest friendship. Dora had offended her seriously by not replying to her last letter. Sara had been loyal and had done her best to counsel her friend about Edward, and so 'If Mr W's daughter could have been among my partial cordial friends I should have been gratified. But as it is not to be I am content to be on the terms assigned me and to constitute other friendships.' Sara felt jealousy towards the Southey girls, whom she thought Dora preferred. 'If it were not for <u>Auld lang syne</u>,' she told her mother, 'I should whistle it all off very easily: which in time I shall do so and it <u>is</u> – for I have plenty of friends, and plenty of kind relations, a good mother and sweet children and a husband who, to my seeming, is not to be matched in the wide world.'[1] Sara, who had no idea how hard things were for Dora, determined to ignore her. Her life, apart from that, was bright. Her children were well, her health much improved and her new house beautiful. She and Henry had moved to their larger house the year before. From here, Henry could commute daily to Lincoln's Inn, and Sara had more space and quiet in which to work. Number 10 Chester Place, built by John Nash in 1811, was a considerable step up from Downshire Hill. The whole terrace is a 900-foot sweep of neoclassical-style cream stucco, with Corinthian pillars at each end. The houses all had wide entrance halls, enormous windows and sweeping staircases. The girl who had once been resigned to life as a governess was now mistress of Number 10.

Sara had just begun working on an essay about religion – inspired by two things. The first was a new edition of her father's *Aids to Reflection*, the book which had meant so much to her in Ilchester; she had been helping Henry with the proof sheets. The second was the religious debates which had gripped England for the past decade or so. Briefly, the Church had been riven with disagreements between Low Church evangelicals and High Church Tractarians. The warring factions were fuelled by the Victorian revival of religiosity after years of apparent decline during the Romantic period. The emancipation of the Catholics in 1829 had been a traumatic event for English Protestants (and even more so for Irish Protestants) and, in the years following it, the Anglican Church (which was riddled with corruption and in need of serious reform) was thrown into crisis. In the nineteenth century, religion mattered in a way that can be hard to imagine. Nothing divides and excites public attention today to the extent that the Victorians worried about the whole business of salvation and how to get to heaven.

Debate continues as to whether division and dissent within the Church was an indication of strength or weakness, but it's clear there was a huge flowering of disparate and passionately opposed sects and groups. At one end of the spectrum – the 'catholic' end – were the high churchmen behind the Oxford Movement (many of whom, like John Henry Newman, would eventually convert to Roman Catholicism); at the other were the Evangelicals of various persuasions.* Beside and between these was the broad church social movement. At the same time, a full range of alternative traditions from Unitarianism to

---

* Sara gave the best account that exists of how the Oxford Movement functioned. 'No sooner has Newman blown the Gospel blast, than it is repeated by Pusey, and Pusey is re-echoed from Leeds. Keble privately persuades Froude, Froude spouts the doctrine of Keble to Newman, and Newman publishes them as "Froude's Remains." Now it seems to me that under these circumstances truth has not quite a fair chance' (*Memoir*, I, pp. 224–5).

Spiritualism, by way of Methodism, flourished and in the turbu-
lence a growing number of people like Thomas Carlyle began
to abandon religion altogether. As she wrote her essay, Sara read
more and more theology and less and less fiction: 'I . . . grudge
to bestow time on the literature of the day.' She noticed she
had begun to think like a writer and editor rather than a reader:
'What a strange, superficial thing is the ordinary way of reading
a book,' she mused to Henry.[2] As she thought and read more
widely about religion, she reasoned her way to a position of
intelligent, yet respectably conservative Protestantism. She was
sympathetic to the arguments of Newman and his high
churchmen, but opposed to the 'unspiritual and unreasonable'
lengths to which he and his fellow Apostolicals might go. He
would, she argued, 'overthrow the foundations of all religion'.[3]
Her religious essay became an extended thesis and, in her letters,
one can see her theological opinions growing in complexity and
confidence.

All the different factions could, and often did, use Coleridge
as a source of inspiration. Over time, Sara's essay became as
much about STC as about religion. She was driven by anxiety
about the way his name was being used. She thought he was
being horribly misrepresented, and not just in the field of religion. That very year, Gillman, who was a doctor and not a
philosopher or poet, had the audacity to publish a biography of
her father. Sara would never be anything but grateful to Gillman
for what he had done for her father's health, but really the book
was intolerable. It was 'an absurd hodge podge of stale and vapid
ingredients'. All it proved was 'how long an unwise man may
live with a wise one without catching any of his wisdom'.[4]
Maddeningly, people would probably read it; after all, it was
well known that STC had lived with Gillman for the best part
of two decades.

Even more upsettingly, as she read, thought and learned,
it became increasingly obvious to her that much of what Henry
had written about STC was inaccurate. His last project,
completed while she was still in the depths of opium-filled
despair, had been a new edition of STC's journal *The Friend*.

Reading it now she was disappointed: 'I rather wish', she told him, 'that you had not used that vague High Church cant phrase of abuse *rationalised*.' Her father talked about the *rational* which was a 'definite phrase' while 'rationalised' was not[5].* It was the kind of subtlety, she was beginning to notice, that Henry did not really understand. Yet Henry was the self-appointed editor of STC and her father's reputation depended on him. It was worrying. Sara assisted Henry as much as she could in preparing the new STC editions, and felt 'my knowledge of STC's mind and inclusivity of every other thinking mind, increases in depth'.[6]

Over the next year or so, Sara gave as much time as she could to her religious essay, but she was frequently interrupted by the gruelling and often tragic realities of being a woman in Victorian England. In the spring of 1839 she suffered a late miscarriage. It was a brutal reminder of the little boy who had been stillborn on the day Dora was meant to come and see her the year before. In the winter of 1839 she realised she was pregnant again. It was her seventh pregnancy in ten years and she also had Herbert and Edy to worry about. Until this point, Sara had been primarily responsible for their education. She had to stand up for the intense way she taught her children just as her own mother had been forced to defend Sara's education. Sara was outraged when a physician once deigned to suggest she was over-exercising four-year-old Herbert's intellect. She taught her children rigorously, but with a good dash of Southey's fun. 'Jog-free' was taught from maps, reading from fairy-tales, and history and Latin in rhymes:

> In words of declension the first –
> Attend, little scholar to me –
> The singular genitive case
> Doth constantly end in an æ[7]

* She was referring to HNC's 1837 edition of *The Friend* in which he had attempted to give a breakdown of the contents. The expression Sara objected to was in this 'synoptical table'.

Herbert and Edy chanted their way through a 1066-and-all-that approach to history:

> One thousand five hundred and fifty-three
> Began Queen Mary's fiery reign;
> The worst of counsellors had she,
> And an evil spouse in Philip of Spain.[8]

It was thorough, if partisan, and the bulk of Sara's days had been spent teaching, but that year, 1839, they had sent their nine-year-old son to school for the first time. Doing so bought Sara a little more time for editorial work, but a great deal more anxiety. Herbert, more than Edy, had inherited his mother's native intelligence, but Sara was shocked by his school in St John's Wood. The teachers simply demanded the students be busy, so Herbert would do his sums and rub them out to do again, in case he got into trouble: 'the system of instruction needs thorough reform', Sara concluded.[9] It broke her heart to see him 'stumping off to his uncomfortable Preparatory School with large teardrops in his large bright eyes, but never lingering for a moment'.[10]

Through all this, however, she did not stop trying to help Henry revise and republish Coleridge's works. Henry's new edition of *Aids to Reflection* was finished in 1839. It is hard to ascertain how closely involved Sara had been – she was not acknowledged on the title page – but she had certainly helped Henry iron out editorial inaccuracies in the previous edition of 1830. *Aids to Reflection* was released at a time when the country was absorbed in religious debates, and it sold well. Sara began to wonder if she could do more with the volume; whether in fact, with a slightly different introduction, her father could help Britain navigate its way through the turmoil associated with the Oxford Movement.

At the start of 1840 Dora, whom Sara feared she had lost as a friend, wrote to ask if she could come and stay with her in London for a couple of weeks. Sara was delighted: Dora wanted to make an effort after all. Sara had never wanted to give Dora

up, and so now she set about making plans with enthusiasm.
Dora had seen Chester Place once or twice, but it would be her
first extended stay and Sara knew Dora, of all people, would
understand why she loved the house. Sara would show her the
park – newly opened to the public – 'with its acres of green turf,
and flocks of country looking (and sounding) sheep . . .'[11] She
arranged for tickets to see the Picture Gallery at Grosvenor
House: not easy to get hold of, but she wrote to Edward
Quillinan, who had returned to his London lodgings near Baker
Street, to ask for help. Both Sara and Mrs STC looked forward
to Dora's visit. They wanted to hear about the Lakelands, the
places that, to Sara's mind, always seemed 'more substantial more
bright'.[12] They wanted to hear the news from Hartley and all
at Rydal and Greta: there had been a terrible quarrel in the
Southey household. And Sara wanted to know how Dora's love
affair was progressing.

'Do You Dare?'

On a cold February afternoon in 1840, as pale winter sunlight
streamed through the wide first-floor windows of Number 10,
Chester Place, Dora and Sara sat talking. The drawing room
was filled with watercolours, including views of the Lakelands
and Rydal. At thirty-eight, Sara, fair and elegant, was still
strikingly beautiful. Her centrally parted hair was scooped up
at the nape of her neck as was both fashionable and respectable. She was fine-boned and still retained that 'fairy' quality
so often remarked upon in her youth. Her enormous blue eyes
were fixed on the dark-haired and gaunt Dora. Where Sara
was willowy, Dora was disturbingly thin and, though younger
than her friend, looked considerably older. It was a delight,
however, for Sara to see Dora's same 'overflowing lips and
width of mouth' which had always, somehow, reminded her of
the ocean.[13] Sara, like Wordsworth, thought that Dora looked
like the colossal statue of Memnon in the British Museum. It
was not an entirely flattering comparison, but what she loved

in Dora's eyes was their calm grace, even when talking about difficult topics.

Dora's affair was barely progressing. Since she had returned to Rydal in the summer of 1838 – after Tintern Abbey and the proposal – life had consisted of a series of skirmishes between father and lover. At the start of 1839 they reached a new pitch. By then the whole situation was being gossiped about by mutual friends, a fact Dora found hard to bear. Most were against the idea of marriage, for much the same reasons as Wordsworth. Dora's friends and relations were not afraid to tell Edward that he 'was the cause of much evil' to her and was 'not using her well'. Sara was one of the few who thought they *should* marry, but she agreed with Edward when he said: 'things ought not to be allowed to go on between us any longer as they had done'. Sara approved when Edward told Dora it was 'high time indeed for your sake, as well as for my own honor, that the matter should be terminated one way or other'.[14]

To try and reach a decision, in February 1839 Edward had written to Dora at Rydal pressing her for an answer to his proposal. Dora did not reply – or at least she did not 'answer the point' – but she did talk to Miss Fenwick. The upshot was Miss Fenwick invited Edward to come and stay with her at Ambleside. Before Edward would accept, he wanted reassurance from Wordsworth that he would not be an 'imposition' in the neighbourhood. In early February the poet dictated a short message for Mary to send, assuring him he had not 'forfeited my friendship' and that he would be pleased to see him at Rydal. Mary gave him further encouragement by adding a postscript, which her husband could not have read since his eyes were bad: 'Dora is looking ill', 'and has lately lost her appetite which you know was never to boast of'.[15] So Edward went. He stayed a week, and nobody said a word about anything.

What Edward should have done was speak to Dora, brave Wordsworth and Mary and force everything into the open. Only once, when alone with Dora, did he bring the topic up, saying: 'Dora, you have not answered my letter!'[16] She did not have a ready answer, because she was not absolutely certain what he was trying to say or what he felt. And so Edward made no further reference to the subject. Afterwards he claimed he had not pressed her further 'because I would not like anything like an undue advantage of my visit at Rydal under the circumstances' – whatever he meant by that. Throughout the visit, Dora and her health suffered (as Edward saw) 'under a conflict of hopes & fears & duties & disappointments'.[17] Meanwhile, Wordsworth thought they were all 'at ease with each another'.[18] He assumed the ridiculous marriage business had been forgotten; Edward took this as a sign that the poet was coming round to the idea. Edward told Dora the visit had 'removed the ill-omened gloom that darkened your house to me'.[19] He lived in 'trust' that the hoped-for attachment would no longer be delayed. Wordsworth wrote cheerfully to Southey, 'I had no private conversation with him [Edward] – but thro' Dora he understands what my judgements and feelings are.'[20] As far as Wordsworth was concerned, the affair was at an end. But it was only the lull before the storm.

Most of this Sara already knew from talking to Edward. On leaving Rydal, he had written to tell her he was frightened by what he had seen of Dora's behaviour: she had lost even more weight and was now 'grievously thin'. He'd written to Dora, begging her to 'acquire the habit of taking more food. It is quite evident to me that you are absolutely wasting away for want of sustenance which seems . . . to be neither more nor less than sure though not as speedy a suicidal process as any other . . . you are actually starving your frame down to debility and death.'[21] Looking at her wasted malnourished friend, Sara could see, his words had not had much effect. What Dora had needed was a reiteration that he still wanted to marry her. What she received was a strange half-serious letter, which alluded to love and marriage but gave her room for doubt. She waited several weeks, thinking about how to reply, before telling him she 'could not read his riddle'. Instead of making himself more clear, Edward decided Dora's reaction was 'a voluntary puzzle on your part to your fear of encountering a denial from your Father'. It seemed quite possible they could dance around one another for years to come.

What happened next made everything even worse. Edward wrote again to Dora, in April 1839. One imagines Dora taking a crumpled and much-read letter and showing it to Sara in the drawing room of Chester Place. This time Edward offered her an ultimatum. He wanted either 'marriage or a final under-standing that there would be no marriage'. He wanted to 'urge more forcibly . . . the necessity of ascertaining on your part whether you had any influence with your father'.[22] In short, would she, he asked, take a 'rough chance' and marry him?[23] The problem was that by the time Dora received the letter she was – to all intents and purposes – alone at Rydal Mount. Wordsworth and Mary had taken Willy to Bath because he was unwell. Dora remained at home with only mad Aunt Dorothy and a young cousin. Dora was living in her father's orbit, however; she was transcribing reams of poetry which both still hoped would form a part of *The Recluse*. Not only was she inhabiting his mind, she had been re-inspired by his vision and the ambition of what *The Recluse* could do for the world. She panicked, and her response was to write not to Edward but to her father, quoting liberally from Edward's letter.

Sara could easily have imagined Wordsworth's fury as he read what Edward had said to Dora. 'Do you trust? Do you dare? Have you influence enough with your father, and if so will you exert it.' It was a foolish letter of Edward's – but by copying such inflammatory parts to her father, Dora did nothing but provoke him. Wordsworth felt Edward had deliberately tried to take advantage of his absence. 'It was an ill-judged proceeding – a cowardly attempt to work upon you & induce you to do wrong when you were deprived of the shield of their presence.' Edward was mortified: 'no parent friendly to me, or even tolerant, could have put such a construction on any sentence I ever penned'.[24]

The row was miserable. Mary was furious and wrote to Dora: 'neither you nor Mr Q. do your Father's feelings justice or shew him proper *respect even* . . . All the feelings for your sake, that he has extinguished – should not indeed . . . have been met in this spirit – by either of you.'[25] Her father did not send his love. Edward wrote several times more trying to justify his actions, but also, apparently, giving up hope. 'You have had too painful a conflict between your love for your father and your kindness for me & now that the hopelessness of the case is manifest, I believe in my soul and conscience that you will be the less unhappy for having arrived at the conviction of its hopelessness.' [26] Dora, more ill than ever before, didn't know how to reply. Edward grew more angry and melodramatic in London. On 5 June 1839, he wrote: 'I have not heard from you since the 24th May . . . as my hopes, "long subdued & cherished long", seem to approach their crisis I am in a fever of impatience about you, and am sure you will slip out of my hands. All your people too seem rebellious or sullen: I do not hear one word or intimation from any of them that they know I am alive . . . – if they have seen my letter & not thought proper to answer it I shall think them all a parcel of churls, and never care two three pences more for any of them: – but that makes no difference as to you: none but yourself can make me otherwise than I am to you, your true & faithful lover & your husband when you please, if you are not afraid of being pleased.' As ever, he was 'writing to you half in melancholy fun & half in affectionate & hopeful earnesty'.[27]

In her sympathy for Dora, any doubts which Sara had harboured about their friendship dissolved. Dora's story continued. Just days after the 'melancholy fun' letter, Edward had met Wordsworth in London. There followed several rounds of uncomfortable negotiations. After each bruising session, both men would write wildly different accounts of the interview to send to Dora sitting at home at Rydal. To Edward it seemed obvious the problem was that Wordsworth continued only to think in 'L-s-D' [pounds, shilling and pence] and he told him so.[28] To Wordsworth it was clear Edward had no regard for his responsibilities to Dora as a husband; he had sympathy for Edward, whom he saw was wretched, but he could not approve the match. Despite this, they eventually reached a conclusion of sorts. On 9 June, Wordsworth had told Dora: 'The sum is:

I make no opposition to this marriage. I have no resentment connected with it towards anyone: you know how much friendship I have always felt towards Mr Q, and how much I respect him. I do not doubt the strength of his love and affection towards you; this, as far as I am concerned, is the fair side of the case. On the other hand, I cannot think of parting with you with that complacency, that satisfaction, that hopefulness which I could wish to feel; there is too much of necessity in the case for my wishes. But I must submit, and do submit; and God Almighty bless you, my dear child, and him who is the object of your long-tried preference and choice.'[29] The deal was on, Wordsworth told them, and the treaty could be concluded 'subject to prudential considerations'.[30] When Edward made some money, Wordsworth would remove his opposition and give his blessing.

Edward wrote to Dora at once: 'How delighted you will be . . . if you are really my own Dora, at what I have to tell you.' Edward cannot have known Dora as well as he claimed to if he really thought she would be wholly delighted. When Dora did not reply with the enthusiasm he expected, he accused her of 'reluctance to conclude our treaty'. Desperately anxious about hurting her father and apprehensive about leaving Rydal for an uncertain lifestyle, she suggested to Edward that perhaps she was 'too old to be transplanted'.[31] It is hardly surprising that when Wordsworth came home again, in the middle of June 1839, he found Dora 'as thin as a Ghost and almost as sallow as an autumnal leaf'.[32] She saw she would have, at some point, to betray the love of one of the two men who mattered most to her. It was also perfectly obvious that negotiations had, in fact, reached a deadlock rather than a conclusion. Edward showed no signs of making any money. Indeed, details were emerging of a financial lawsuit, to do with his wife Jemima's family, which threatened to make him even poorer. Yet Edward was optimistic: he had hopes of becoming a secretary of a new joint-stock bank. It was a speculative and uncertain venture, which did not in the event come off.

'Poor dear Dora's affairs are as miserable as ever,' Sara had told Mary Stanger* in December, '. . . nothing has been settled. What <u>could</u> they settle unless they could coin a little money?' She found it quite 'grievous to think how the whole family suffered in their old age by this unfortunate affair'.[33] Sara was not unequivocally on Edward's side now. She thought the fact he was a Catholic a real problem, and had no doubt Dora felt the same. Still, he had at least brought his girls up to be Protestant. Of course it would have helped if he'd had a little money, but sympathetic as she was to Wordsworth's point of view, she had no doubt Dora should marry. The question of Dora's weak health did not seem to her an impediment at all. People had always raised that question throughout her own long engagement, and she was certain separation would only make Dora's health worse.

So when Dora came to stay in February 1840, it had occurred to Sara that she might be able to help, rather than sit idly by and watch Dora starve to death. She wrote to Edward asking him to dinner. Bravely, she turned the occasion into a statement. Other than Edward, she invited no one but Henry Crabb Robinson; the latter quite correctly took this as 'a sort of public annunciation of the connection intended to be consummated between them'. Crabb Robinson predicted in his diary that the course of true love would not run smoothly for the pair.[34]

Sara enjoyed Dora's company for several weeks, and if nothing had been done to speed up the wedding, the women had at least gone some way to restoring their own relationship. Perhaps Sara also told Dora she was pregnant – perhaps Dora guessed. Certainly, when Dora left at the start of March the friendship was stronger than it had been for years. Sara thought Dora 'sweeter than ever'.[35] Sara had done all she could for Dora, so returned to her religious essay while preparing with genuine excitement for the birth of another child. She thought she might ask Hartley to stand as godfather.

* Mary Stanger, née Calvert, the childhood friend she and Dora had played with at Keswick.

As the months passed safely by, it seemed she and Henry might finally have another healthy baby. They were filled with hope about this child who would be 'our darling – a third joy of our middle life and a comfort of our decline'.[36] Sara had regained her youthful optimism about pregnancy. She did no 'gloomifying' during this pregnancy, and much in the way of making practical arrangements. Her calm was shattered, to some extent, when she read a devastating article in *Blackwoods Magazine* in which the critic J. F. Ferrier accused STC of plagiarism.[37] He claimed STC had copied whole sections from Schelling and other German authors verbatim, taking advantage of the fact that no English translations existed. 'Something should be done,' pleaded a devastated Hartley.[38] Sara could do nothing before her child was born, but the criticism of her father stung bitterly.

Sara wasn't worried about herself or her child, but she did fret about Henry; his health was not good and she began to think of getting him out of London once the baby was born. By July she was almost at term and the final arrangements were made. She sent the children to Ramsgate with Nuck, and her midwife, Mrs Sherbourne, was once again installed in Chester Place. On 13 July 1840, Sara gave birth to a baby girl. She and Henry named her Bertha Fanny. They decided Bertha, more than any of the other children, looked like her mother. In particular, she was like the picture of Sara Coleridge by Matilda Betham with 'the same small cheeks little roundish nose narrow regular features and large full eyes'. Bertha was a couple of weeks early, and both mother and child were very unwell for the first five days. As Sara recovered, Bertha grew worse. Sara called Henry back from Lincoln's Inn and sent for the clergyman to baptise the baby.

On the eleventh day Henry, sunken-eyed and exhausted from watching over Bertha all night, came into Sara's room. 'She is gone,' he told her. Mrs Sherbourne followed him and placed the dead child into her mother's arms. At that moment, Bertha 'opened, or half opened her eyes'. Though pale and blue, the little girl was clinging to life. Her mother was mesmerised by those eyes which were 'large, bright and dark – of indeterminate

Sara Coleridge aged six, by Matilda Betham, 1809. Sara was wearing the lace cap her father so disliked. (Sara later wrote: 'I appear in a cap, playing with a doll, in a little miniature taken of me at that age by the sister of Sir William Bentham, who also made portraits in the same style of my Uncle and Aunt Southey, my mother, Aunt Lovell, and cousins Edith and Herbert.')

Aunt Sara – Sara Hutchinson – by an unknown artist. Itinerant silhouette cutters would travel the country 'taking shades' as the most affordable means of capturing a person's likeness. They were eventually put out of business by the rise of photography.

Mrs STC – Sarah Coleridge (neé Fricker) Sara's mother, by Matilda Betham, 1809. Betham took Mrs STC's portrait at the same time as the one she did of little Sara. By this stage in her life Mrs STC wore a wig.

Rydal Mount by Dora, who sketched the picture sometime between 1820 and 1830.

Sara Coleridge by William Collins, 1818. Collins exhibited the painting at the Royal Academy as 'The Highland Girl'. He was perhaps referring to Wordsworth's poem 'To the Highland Girl of Inversnaid'

STC, by George Dawe, c.1812 – the last year in which Sara saw her father until she was an adult.

Dora Wordsworth as a bridesmaid
to Sara Coleridge in 1829,
by Miss Rainbeck.

Statue of Rameses II, in the
British Museum, which was originally
thought to be the Younger Memnon –
the face reminded both Wordsworth
and Sara of Dora.

Isabella Fenwick by Margaret Gillies.

Edward Quillinan,
the only known portrait
by an unknown artist.

St James' Church, Bath. The church was destroyed by bombing during the Second World War.

Sara Coleridge, print from the portrait by George Richmond, 1845. This was the painting commissioned by her brother-in-law Edward before she descended 'into the vale of a certain age'.

Wordsworth's profile on a silver medallion by Leonard Wyon. The coin was cast in 1848 from a drawing made in April 1847.

Caroline Vallon,
Wordsworth's illegitimate daughter,
as an old lady, by an unknown artist.

Dora Wordsworth by
Margaret Gillies, 1839.
The painting was
altered twice. The first
time Gillies reduced
the size of Dora's nose.
Quillinan took the
portrait with him wherever
he went. After Dora's
death, he sent the miniature
back to Gillies asking her
to make it more spiritual
and holy. She agreed saying
holiness was what she
had wished to convey.

William Wordsworth and Mary Wordsworth by Margaret Gillies, 1839.
The painting shows Mary taking dictation for William in the drawing room
at Rydal Mount. Dora referred to it as their Darby and Joan portrait.

William Wordsworth by
Benjamin Robert Haydon, 1842.
The portrait shows Wordsworth
on Helvellyn as he composed a
sonnet inspired by Haydon's
painting of the Duke of Wellington.
In fact Wordsworth sat for the
picture at a studio in London.

Left: Robert Southey by Peter Lightfoot, after Sir Thomas Lawrence, line engraving,
published 1845. Right: Greta Hall ('The Aunt-Hill'), where Sara was brought up
along with Southey's children.

dark colour a greenish grayish tint presenting in them more than brown but when wide open they seemed rich and dark and purplish'.[39] The astonished Mrs Sherbourne returned the child to its crib and Sara remained in bed as the day dragged on. Henry came and went between his wife and daughter. Bertha did not gain strength and at about 8 p.m. Sara heard Henry sobbing aloud. This time Bertha had died. She was ten days and sixteen hours old.

Sara held the child's body. As she looked at the now closed eyes, delicate tapered fingers and grey face, a vision overwhelmed her of Bertha's 'future face – expanded and enriched with red and white and lighted up like a lamp'. The memory of the baby's eyes would haunt Sara. She returned to her diary months after the death, still struggling to describe them: 'like purple violets with dew on them in the sunshine'. The pathetic little funeral took place on 30 July, but Sara did not attend. Bertha's body, in a net cap and long-sleeved dress made by Mrs STC, was buried in a white coffin beside her twin siblings Florence and Berkeley.

At home, Sara tried to rationalise her grief through religion and was in some ways more successful in doing so than Henry. He had watched Bertha die 'like a breeze: growing fainter and fainter without a struggle and so thus, faintly, faintly tied to earth – she was set free'. He could not – as Sara tried to – visualise his child as a 'glowing white winged angel, basking and sporting in bright hazy sunshine over banks of radiant blossoms whence heavenly fragrance diffuses itself around'. Looking at the body, Sara was 'not shocked or saddened to see how cold how <u>dead</u> – how void of living brightness and glory her little tabernacle now shows'. Henry found the grief harder to bear, and Sara was almost critical of him for the way he had watched Bertha 'so closely when it was plain to see the little darling was not for this world', though she felt guilt that she had somehow coped more successfully with her grief. Bertha's death was a tragedy that Sara survived without disintegrating. By the summer, she was up and about.

Through the autumn and winter of 1840–41, Sara worked at her STC projects with Henry. He was beginning to think

about a new edition of STC's *Biographia Literaria*, the book
which had borne the bulk of Ferrier's plagiarism claims. Sara
and Dora also wrote regularly to one another. Most of their
conversation was about the Great Quarrel at Greta Hall.
Southey's wife Edith had died in November 1837. She had been
committed to an asylum in 1834, where she spent a year, but
when she returned to Greta her mental health was worse than
ever. Southey could hardly bear to be at home and for two and
a half long years Bertha and Kate nursed their mother in
increasing isolation, since none of them could abide guests. After
Edith's death, Southey had surprised everyone by marrying, very
quickly, the author Caroline Bowles. Kate, the only one of
Southey's daughters still living at Greta, had fallen out with her
new stepmother. She feared Southey was losing his mental faculties (which it soon became clear he was) and Caroline was taking
advantage of him. Caroline refused to allow Kate access to her
father for more than a few minutes at a time, and Edith, in the
south, supported her stepmother against her sister. The whole
thing was deeply upsetting. Although it was a source of sorrow
to them both, the Greta quarrel solidified Dora and Sara's friendship and they wrote long letters full of the people and places of
their shared history. What each wanted, though, was another
good talk: plenty was happening which could not be trusted to
a letter.

CHAPTER 16

'A NEW HAT WITH AN OLD LINING'

1841

'A Bright Spark Out of Two Flints'

The Quillinan–Wordsworth truce forged in June 1839 held for eighteen months or so. In the intervening time Edward came to stay several times at Rydal. Initially he seemed cheerfully oblivious to the fact he was no closer to marriage. In the summer of 1840 he took Jemima to stay there, pleased to be back in Wordsworth's favour. One bright August day all the Wordsworths and various visiting friends and relations decided to climb Helvellyn. Wordsworth, leading Dora on her pony, set the pace. Edward and the others followed. It was a tough walk, 'very steep, very hot work, very craggy at times and in some places worse from being wet & spongy'. Wordsworth muttered to himself all the way, composing a sonnet as he trudged. He was followed by a great train of fans eager to see him in action.

Edward wrote afterwards to Rotha: 'I wish you could have seen the Old Poet, seated from time to time, as we paused for breath, on a rock writing down his Waterloo Sonnet* . . . It

---

* The sonnet was inspired by Benjamin Haydon's painting of Waterloo and addressed to the artist. It is a wonderful piece of poetry in which Wordsworth expresses his idea that all art, be it poetry or painting, is the same and stems from the same place. It begins:

> HIGH is our calling, Friend! – Creative Art
> (Whether the instrument of words she use,
> Or pencil pregnant with ethereal hues,)
> Demands the service of a mind and heart,

is a curious fact that even on that great steep mountain the Poet was followed by strangers – rather a bore, yet evidence of the reverence he is held in. – Nobody that is not here can have the least idea how he is hunted, flattered, puffed, carest, &c&c. It is enough to spoil any human being.'[1] The letter reveals Edward's pent-up fury at the arrogant old man – but also his pride in being part of the inner circle.[2] Edward stayed for six weeks, was charming to some visiting African princes, courteous to Queen Adelaide who came to call on Wordsworth, and amusing to everyone else – but still he did nothing at all to earn any money. Unsurprisingly, Wordsworth did not alter his position and Edward's frustration grew.

In the end, Dora broke the deadlock herself, silently. By the winter of 1840–41 it was clear, at least to Miss Fenwick, that Edward and Wordsworth's arguments would soon be academic. Caught in an impossible position between the two men she loved, Dora was slowly dying of malnutrition. It was all very well for Edward, in London, to make bitter attacks about the 'Rydal Ravens and other birds of ill omen' who did not want the match.[3] It was fine for him to suggest Dora might have to rely on the 'blessing of your Father who is in heaven for that anxious aspiration of filial piety towards your parents on earth'.[4] And it was easy enough for him to flatter her with a sideswipe at her parents: 'you are the best poetry he ever produced: a bright spark out of two flints', but it had only made her long winter nights at Rydal harder to bear.[5]

Eventually, Dora's spiralling weight loss forced a resolution. By the end of February 1841, Wordsworth could see his daughter was 'emaciated to a degree which it gives me pain to look upon'.[6] Encouraged by Miss Fenwick, Wordsworth finally told Dora that, despite Edward's finances being ropey as ever, he would allow a settlement to be drawn up: he was withdrawing his

---

It makes sense that this poem to the 'high' calling should have been written whilst ascending a mountain. Wordsworth was quite literally 'strenuous for the bright reward' and needing to believe that 'Great is the glory, for the strife is hard!'

opposition. Even Miss Fenwick could not get him to give his blessing. In addition, Wordsworth had his terms: the small amount of money he planned to settle on Dora must remain hers after marriage. Edward was infuriated: this was what he had agreed to – indeed, insisted upon – from the start.* Still, a settlement was agreed: if Edward outlived Dora, the money would revert to the Wordsworth family. But it did not make Dora more contented. Her father was evidently deeply unhappy about the marriage. She explained to Edward, 'I feel as if I could never be a blessing to your home unless I took with me a parent's blessing, sealed with a kiss.'⁷ She would clearly never have either. On the other hand, Edward, now in London, was confident their wedding was imminent. He told Dora with delight that he had been out to dinner and confused his friends who had 'not the least idea we are so near the brink of eternity – of love'.⁸ For the past couple of years, Edward had been writing a romance novel, *The Conspirators*. It had just been published, and he thought it would make his fortune – but that has never been a sensible way to try and get rich.†

With Dora growing weaker by the day, Miss Fenwick more or less insisted on taking her away from Rydal. She was firm with Wordsworth and told him his daughter needed to go to

---

* Two years before, he had written to Dora explaining that he would only marry her if any money settled on her by Wordsworth should be settled 'absolutely' and that 'every other farthing that you may have . . . may be absolutely out of reach of any misfortunes that may occur to me which God at all events averts for your sake' (EQ to Dora, 10 June 1839; Dove Cottage, WLL/Quillinan, Edward/2/88).

† Edward Quillinan, *The Conspirators, or a Romance of Military Life*, 3 volumes (London: Henry Colburn, 1841). It is tempting to paint parallels between his fiction and his life. In Edward's novel a hero, Stanisford, is in love with Dona Francisca, the daughter of a friend. He is confused by her behaviour and, on one occasion, the very day he arrives at her house, 'away went the lady back to her own home among some unknown mountains'. Meanwhile, Portuguese Francisca loves a Frenchman – intolerable during the Pensinular wars. When she fears he is dead, she grows 'silent and spiritless'. Her family do not notice that 'the excuse of illness and nervousness, which indeed was hardly a pretext, served to silence inquiry'.

the south for a gentler climate. Besides, she wanted to go to London herself, and needed a travelling companion. Dora wrote to tell Sara she was coming to London – could she stay at Chester Place? And, 'if I do how much I shall have to tell you'.[9] Sara could not have been happier. Dora and Miss Fenwick left Rydal on 4 March, staying with various friends en route before arriving at Chester Place towards the end of the month.[10]

Sara took Dora to see the baby tigers that had just been born in the zoo. Both were enchanted: 'they were worth going 5 miles to see', Sara told Mary Stanger with excitement.[11] Sara was delighted to find her old friend as 'thoroughly warm-hearted' as ever.[12] She still worried Dora might sacrifice her love of Edward for the sake of her father and *The Recluse*. In Sara's opinion, Dora was, and always had been, 'all tenderness to others and self-postponement'.[13] So while Dora was staying, Sara invited Edward to dinner again. He talked about the wedding as though it was a foregone conclusion. For Dora the crucial question was whether Wordsworth would attend; she needed some gesture to indicate that she had not broken his heart.* Over supper the conversation was all about where the wedding should take place. Edward wanted it at Rydal so the world might see he had Wordsworth's support. Furiously, however, he showed Dora and Sara a letter from Wordsworth in which he'd said he could not attend the wedding, for 'he will not be put out of his way and his way was & is to be in London about the time fixed for the marriage'.[14] Sara did not try to disguise her shock; she thought this quite wrong: 'he ought to bend his way for once . . . to the accommodation of others on such an important occasion'.[15]

Sara was not Dora's only ally: Miss Fenwick had been working hard behind the scenes. First she brought the marriage date forward to give the poet less time to stew. Next she suggested Bath as a neutral location for the wedding. As an incentive for Wordsworth to travel to Bath, she built into the plans a trip

---

* Once she arrived in London Dora wrote (perhaps on Sara and Henry's recommendation) to persuade the Trustees to add in a clause to let Edward keep the settlement money during his lifetime, should she predecease him.

down memory lane: they would all visit the Wye Valley on the way.[16] The ruse worked, and Miss Fenwick scooped Dora up and took her to meet her parents at Tintern Abbey. They were reunited on Tuesday, 13 April, and, after seeing the ruin once again, they all went on to Bath by train. Sara would not attend the wedding herself. She continued to struggle with long journeys and weddings tended, in any case, to be more intimate, less social events than they are today. But, like Miss Fenwick and Dora, Sara desperately hoped Dora would finally be married from Bath.

On 6 May 1841, Miss Fenwick, practically crossing her fingers as she wrote, told her cousin Henry Taylor: 'our marriage still stands for the 11th, and I do sincerely trust that nothing will interfere with its taking place on that day. Mr Wordsworth behaves beautifully.'[17] Wordsworth's closest family still did not believe he had withdrawn his opposition and he signed the settlement only the day before the wedding. And it was only then that Christopher Wordsworth, Wordsworth's brother, wrote to say he would like to give £1000 to Dora. Even at that late date, Christopher was uncertain how Wordsworth would react and wrote in confidence, acknowledging he might want to 'keep the matter entirely to yourself'.[18] Wordsworth responded with gratitude that Christopher had not made the offer 'previous to my opposition' being withdrawn.[19] He did at least accept.

Tuesday, 11 May dawned bright and clear, if windy. At 12 North Parade, Bath, servants bustled to brew hot drinks. One by one the party came downstairs: Dora's mother, her brothers John and Willy, and her cousin Ebba Hutchinson were all staying in the house Miss Fenwick had taken. That morning they were joined by various other friends, relations and bridesmaids. Edward's half-brother, John Quillinan, had come from Portugal (he had insisted on choosing and buying Dora's wedding ring 'for luck') and Miss Fenwick's nieces were to serve as bridesmaids. Mary was fraught and tense, and Wordsworth nowhere to be seen. Shortly before nine o'clock, Edward arrived and admired Miss Fenwick's and Mary's fine new 'gravely grey' dresses, which were 'just as they ought to have been'.[20] Dora, obeying convention, did not appear.

Upstairs, Wordsworth was bidding farewell to his daughter. The conversation itself is another frustrating silence. One might imagine Wordsworth in smart new clothes and Dora in white sitting on a bed. They are surrounded by hat boxes and discarded clothes, in tears and unable to comfort one another. Wordsworth is kissing his daughter's forehead, Dora whispering in his ear as he holds her; telling him he doesn't have to come to the wedding, but hoping he will.

When Wordsworth came downstairs he found Edward with a cup of coffee in his hand about to depart for the church. He pulled Edward aside: 'this interview with my child has so upset me that I think I can hardly bear it'.[21] Edward 'begged' Wordsworth not to attend, and minutes later left for the church with Dora's brother John, who was to conduct the ceremony.[21] The two men walked together the short distance from North Parade to St James' Church. At half past nine, two carriages arrived for the ladies. In a flurry of silk, lace and flowers Mary, Miss Fenwick, the bridesmaids and the bride herself piled in. The remaining men – John Quillinan and the husbands and fathers of the bridesmaids – set off after them on foot.

The Vicar of St James' was having a busy morning. By 9.30 a.m. he'd already conducted one wedding and then in a moment of inspired entrepreneurship – not necessarily to be expected in a man of the cloth – had charged this first wedding party a guinea a head to sit in the gallery for the next. It was not every day one had the chance to see the poet Wordsworth and watch his daughter get married. The audience peered over the gallery above the altar, waiting for a glimpse of the bride. There was a delay. Men huddled in the vestry, but no women – no bride. Minutes passed and then a stir of activity. Dora Wordsworth had arrived. As the onlookers strained to hear, the ladies accused the gentlemen of not having been in the correct place to meet their carriage.[22] Once the women had collected themselves, and the men apologised, whispers and the full cast lined up. Everybody held bouquets. Dora's bridesmaids carried pink flowers and wore matching white silk bonnets, pink scarves and lilac-coloured dresses. The bride herself was in a dress of white poplin with lace collars and ruffs. Dora described her appearance as 'simple', but it was, in fact, surprisingly fashionable. It was not (yet) traditional for brides to wear white but the year before Queen Victoria had worn white satin and lace to marry Albert and in doing so had started a trend which soon became a tradition and which continues, against the odds, to this day. But the spectators who had hoped for a glimpse of Wordsworth were disappointed. Instead, they watched Dora follow her brother John, and the industrious clergyman, down the aisle on Willy's arm.

Brother and sister proceeded slowly and painfully towards the altar; several times Dora stumbled. Her face was 'as white as her dress' and strained. It was only in the porch that Dora had realised her father was really not coming. Even when she reached Edward's side she continued to totter and sway, so much so that Edward thought she might fall over. 'Dearly Beloved', the vicar began but Dora still didn't relax. 'We are gathered here in the sight of God . . .' The words echoed through the cold church. '. . . this man and this woman . . .' Dora was swaying. '. . . mystical union . . . nor taken in hand, unadvisedly, lightly or wantonly . . . let him now speak, or else hereafter forever hold his peace'. In contrast to Dora, Edward looked utterly relaxed in 'an old pair of boots [and] an old pair of white trousers'. It is hard to align this cool figure with the man who had expressed such desperation in his love, even if he had at least bought 'a new blue frock coat with a velvet collar'.[23] Dora's voice was so weak that Edward worried she would not make it to the final 'Amen', but by 11 a.m. Dora Wordsworth had at last become Mrs Edward Quillinan. She would turn thirty-eight that summer, he fifty. It had been a long courtship.

As the church bells pealed, the crowd watched Dora walk back down the aisle on the arm of her husband. The party returned to North Parade to find Wordsworth and their wedding breakfast – a large Carlyle cake in the middle of a table decked with early summer flowers.[24] The waiting poet had fallen into a strange sense of déjà vu. Nearly forty years earlier, on 4 October 1802, William Wordsworth had married Mary Hutchinson. His sister Dorothy (with whom he had lived for the previous seven years) remained at home, distraught, desperately trying to keep busy. When she received word the ceremony was over, she threw herself on the bed unable to bear it any longer. The night before, she and her brother, in a strange parody of the wedding ceremony, had kissed and exchanged wedding rings. Dorothy wrote a meticulous record of her actions in her famous journal. Somebody later scored out these sections. Yet since the lines were revealed by infra-red light in 1958, it is this scene – and what it seems to show about the relationship between Wordsworth and his sister – which has most intrigued and disturbed people about the poet's life. Now a marriage with peculiar parallels had taken place in Bath. This time it was Wordsworth who had waited at home to hear that it was all over. Before the wedding breakfast the poet, according to Edward, 'gave us his blessing'. It reads almost like a statement of victory. Poor crushed Wordsworth stays behind; Edward in a 'new hat with an old lining' takes the prize, and Dora staggers down the aisle.[25]

'In Passion, Life and Movement'

Once Sara heard Dora was safely married, she turned her attention to worrying about Henry. He'd not been himself for the best part of a year. It had begun with periods of 'languor' and exhaustion which made his working life hard. Over the summer of 1841 he was decidedly unwell. For the first time in their married life, she was more worried about him than he about her. In the autumn she finally managed to persuade him to get out of London for the sake of his health. She had been campaigning for the seaside but in the end managed considerably better than that: he agreed to visit Belgium. Sara put aside her theological essay and her fears about travelling, and had a most wonderful time. For her, the focus of the holiday was art, for which she had a keen academic interest. (She credited this to her 'spiritual father', Wordsworth: he 'first put my thoughts in to a right direction' about painting and architecture.) In Antwerp she experienced the most joyful visual experience of her life: the discovery of Rubens' religious paintings.

Sara stood before the altar of Antwerp Cathedral for an age, and gazed up at the great *Descent From the Cross* triptych. She thought it was 'the most beautiful painting I have ever seen'. She admired the painting's '*abandon*' and it made her glad she had seen 'sedate' works by artists such as Van Dyck and Memling first. In Antwerp's museum, she had an even greater shock; she saw Rubens' *Crucifixion*. No painting had ever affected her so strongly. She thought it 'a tremendous picture; in the expression of vehement emotion, in passion, life and movement'. 'How tame + over-fine Vandyck shews beside Rubens!' she exclaimed in a letter to Emily Trevenen. Thirteen years later, George Eliot responded in almost exactly the same way.* In Antwerp, Henry and Sara decided to attend a Catholic Mass in the cathedral and Sara found the experience both wonderful and worrying. She recognised a split between her long-active intellectual self and her waking sensual self. She was aware of the way these two sides disagreed in their response to Rubens. His paintings, like the Catholic service, though religious in subject matter, did not 'satisfy a religious mood of mind. The Rubens' are somewhat over-bold; they almost unhallow the subject by bringing it so home, and exciting such strong earthly passion in connection with it.'[26] Likewise, during the Mass she was overwhelmed by the beauty and power of the architecture and ritual. Afterwards, however, she was led to 'many serious reflections . . . on the defects of such unintellectual worship, which has all the outward-ness of Jewish religion without its inwardness and meaning'.[27]

---

* On 20 July 1854, the picture impressed George Eliot with 'the miserable lack of breadth and grandeur in the conceptions of our living artists. The reverence for the old masters is not all humbug and superstition' (*Journals of George Eliot*, edited by Margaret Harris and Judith Johnston, Cambridge: Cambridge University Press, 1998, p. 15).

It wasn't just paintings and Catholicism which electrified Sara on her tour, but also architecture. She thought Bruges 'the most perfect gem of a town' and found Ghent's cathedral equally awe-inspiring.[28] Everywhere she went, she was making comparisons and connections. Bruges she saw through the eyes of Southey's poem 'The Poet's Pilgrimage to Waterloo'; Rubens' paintings she compared to Sebastiano del Piombo and Michelangelo. The images and buildings fed into her thinking about her religious essay. The essay itself was becoming dense and complex. She kept finding herself adding footnotes to footnotes. Nonetheless, as she studied her father's writing, her own theological thoughts were developing in a fashion more impressive and comprehensive than most men's.

When she and Henry returned from Belgium, full of news and excitement about what they had seen and done, Sara was pregnant again. In December she miscarried, but at a relatively early stage, and though she mourned, she did not return to the low spirits which she had previously experienced. In fact, as she told Mary Stanger matter-of-factly, 'My hopes were so light of having a living child, much less one likely to live long, that I can hardly call the termination of my expectations a disappointment.' She went to see Dora whom she rather hoped might be pregnant herself and was disappointed to hear this was not the case.[29] Instead Sara focused her energy on reworking her religious essay. Her arguments were informed by STC's thoughts on faith and rational thought, and she read Kant's *Critique of Pure Reason* in the original. Kant was the guiding light behind her interpretation of her father, and her reflections in Bruges and Ghent on the 'weakness of human nature and its aptness to elude every form of religion devised to entice it into heart and soul worship' influenced her understanding of both philosophers.[30] She began to consider appending her essay to a new edition of *Aids to Reflection*. Meanwhile, she helped Henry with the latest edition of *The Literary Remains*. Unfortunately, despite their journey, his health was no better and she took an increasingly active editorial role.

Between STC work and household work, Sara extended her

social life. The person she was most pleased to see on her return was a young Irish poet to whom Wordsworth had introduced her in June 1841, just before she left for Belgium. His name was Aubrey de Vere; he was tall, thin and clever and Sara liked him immediately.* She found all the things he wanted to talk about – Dora, Wordsworth, theology and STC – interesting. They began by gossiping about mutual friends. Aubrey had been at Rydal when Dora returned from her honeymoon. He had found her story intriguing. During the visit he'd realised Wordsworth felt betrayed by Edward because he, Wordsworth, had done so much to console his friend after the death of his first wife. De Vere left Rydal with the impression Dora and Edward had been in love for the past fifteen years.[31] He told Sara that Wordsworth expected Dora to live nearby. Neither Sara nor de Vere thought this a good plan, but they could do nothing and their conversation moved on to other topics: the Church, Catholicism, Kant. Eventually, Mrs STC, fearing Sara would exhaust herself, 'fairly turned' him out.[32]

As far as twenty-seven-year-old de Vere was concerned, thirty-eight-year-old Sara was 'scarcely less interesting' than Wordsworth himself. 'She is a most singularly beautiful as well as attractive person,' he wrote to his sister, 'with great blue eyes into which Coleridge looked down till he left there his own lustre, a brow that puts you in mind of the "rapt one of the godlike forehead" and an air of intellect and sweetness more interesting from being shadowed over with the languor of pain.'† His view of Sara is romance itself and he half-fell in love with her, as men often did. Her beauty attracted, her aura of illness

* De Vere (the 'Bard of Curragh Chase') was hailed in America at the end of his life as 'the greatest living English poet' despite being unrecognised (and Irish). His reputation has diminished even further today. Like many others before him, he made a pilgrimage to see Wordsworth. Again, like Edward and like de Quincey all those years before, he was invited to stay.
† In his 'Extempore Effusion upon the Death of James Hogg', written in 1835, Wordsworth had paid tribute to STC:
        The rapt One, of the godlike forehead,
        The heaven-eyed creature sleeps in earth:

inspired protection, and her paternity made her additionally fascinating. But for de Vere, Sara's greatest attraction was her earnest cleverness.

The friendship between Aubrey and Sara was founded 'not only' on their 'delightful conversations about poetry and art' but also on the fact that she seemed always 'glad to talk of her father'.[33] Aubrey's interests overlapped perfectly with Sara's and, at a time in her life when she was interrogating her religious views and STC's, he became her intellectual sounding board. Henry, bowed either by work or by illness, wanted Sara simply to be his wife. He wished she would focus a little less on reading 'discourse on taste and criticism' and a little more on her 'news of wife and children'.[34] Derwent likewise asked for shorter letters.[35] But de Vere encouraged her to give full rein to her exhaustive intellectual curiosity which was having a renaissance after years of dulled spirits.

The Continent had stimulated Sara, and on her return she signed up for a series of lectures. Since the 1830s women had been increasingly attending lectures – mostly religious or phil- anthropic – but Sara attended those given by a Reverend A. J. Scott on the relationship between science and religion. The great theologian F. D. Maurice was amongst the audience in the Marylebone Institute and he and Sara began a correspondence.[36] Sara admired Maurice who in turn was a devotee of STC's. Maurice's religious opinions, she discovered, were closer to hers 'than those of almost anyone with whom I converse'.[37] She also enjoyed a renewed relationship with Derwent, just appointed principal of a training college for elementary teachers in Chelsea and himself a budding theologian.*

She and Henry made little or no mention of Henry's illness to their friends, and planned instead an Easter trip to Oxford. Whether Sara made contact with Cardinal Newman, whose

---

* The college was subsequently rechristened St Mark's College. For more on Derwent's life and career, see Raymonde Hainton and Godfrey Hainton, *The Unknown Coleridge: the Life and Times of Derwent Coleridge, 1800–1883* (London: Janus, 1996).

Tract 90 she had read carefully on publication the year before, is not known. But the Oxford debates were certainly on her mind. Newman's pamphlet had opened the way for his conversion to Catholicism. Sara was as worried about the situation as she was interested; it all became food for thought for her religious essay. She and Henry had been similarly absorbed by a secondary row at Oxford about who should be the next professor of poetry. The Tractarians backed Isaac Williams, their rivals James Garbett; either way, she feared the row would damage religion. Science, religion, philosophy, art, poetry and architecture: all these things were inextricably linked, troubling and fascinating. And Oxford, with all its 'interesting associations' and 'antique buildings', was utterly beautiful.[38] Together, husband and wife toured the colleges – Sara decided Magdalen was her favourite – and they enjoyed the sights of the city in spring.

CHAPTER 17

'HER HUSBAND'S DESIRES'
1842–1843

'A Kindly Fool'

On 17 February 1842, at Lincoln's Inn Court and in the presence
of Sir Lancelot Shadwell, Vice-Chancellor of England, Edward
Quillinan was accused of fraud. He and others stood charged
with illegally making money for various members of his first
wife's family. Jarndyce and Jarndyce-like, the case had been
rumbling through Chancery for over a decade. Wordsworth's
worst fears were about to be realised. People would talk, his
name would be dragged into it and Edward stood to lose both
his money and his reputation. His daughter would, as he'd
predicted, be destitute. Dora was convinced of Edward's honour
and integrity, but the outcome of the trial was by no means a
foregone conclusion. Edward knew now that he had behaved
unwisely; he had to hope the judge would believe he had not
acted with fraudulent intent.

The case revolved around a trust held by the courts for the
Brydges family. Between them, and over a period of many years,
the family persuaded the court that several outlying pieces of
land on the edge of the Lee Priory estate were of little value
and ought to be sold off. They arranged to have them valued
at a vastly deflated rate of £7,600 when, in fact, they were worth
three times that amount. Edward purchased the land and his
money was correctly deposited back in the trust. However, he
then went on to sell the land – as a private individual – at a
more accurate price of £22,000. This money did not have to be

kept within the trust. He was paid back his original 'investment' of £7,600, and the remaining £14,400 was divided between him and various other members of the family. The case had come to court when the mortgagees of the plots of land realised the discrepancy between what the land was sold and bought for, and were justifiably angry.[1]

The ins and outs of the case were immensely complicated, involving many different agents, solicitors, trustees and family members, a number of whom were either dead or mad by 1842.[2] It's still not clear whether Edward was involved in the plotting, or had simply allowed his signature to be used on various deeds which he did not understand. Either way he had been an assenting party to transactions of what Henry Crabb Robinson called a 'most iniquitous character'.[3] The Brydges family were being sued for the £14,400 they had made from the land.[4]

It would not have been a surprise if Wordsworth had once again been furious with his new son-in-law. In fact he could not have behaved more magnanimously. On 1 March – three days into the hearing – he wrote to Edward to reassure him of his support 'and sympathy in your vexations and distresses'. He wanted to assure Edward 'that you need have no anxiety respecting judgement which we are likely to form of your character on these sad proceedings. We have all an entire confidence in your integrity from first to last, in your connection with the Brydges family.'[5]

Every day for the next three weeks, Sir Lancelot listened to the complicated evidence. At the end he said it would take him a long time to consider it all and that they must not expect his verdict for some weeks. Dora and Edward waited anxiously, paying occasional calls to Sara and other London friends. They had taken London lodgings in Upper Spring Street near Baker Street.* Given the trial, it was an unhappy first married home, but one consolation was that it was less than a mile from Chester Place. Dora was all too aware, however, that she and Edward were poor company. She was thin, tired and weak and Edward was nervous and irritable. When they went to dinner with Sara

* Upper Spring St, now known as Montagu Mansions.

and Henry, Edward railed against the stupidity of all Court of Chancery lawyers. He only just remembered to exempt Henry from his condemnation of his profession. Sara pitied him, realising how worried he was 'at the exposure of his connexions [*sic*] and the discredit to himself'.[6] Dora hardly ate a thing.

During this tense period, Dora's life consisted of calming and containing her husband, and trying to stop him reading the newspapers. At the beginning of April Edward spotted an old article in the *Morning Post* which accused him of having acted for his own gain.[7] By this time, he'd been waiting for Sir Lancelot for twenty-two days and his nerves were fraught. He fired off a furious letter. 'Unfortunately,' he told the editor, 'many of those persons of whom my world consists are readers of the Morning Post.' The article would damage his reputation, and he demanded they record his protest. The *Post* printed his letter, but no apology.[8] The whole thing was mortifying; the waiting continued.

It was almost impossible to believe that just a few months before, Dora and Edward had been happily honeymooning in the West Country. For the first time since their 'You man in the Moon' days, they had been able to laugh and relax together. The release of pressure had been extraordinary. They wrote a letter to Jemima, who had not been at the wedding, and all the old banter was back. Edward began by describing the day but gave up when it came to the clothes. He called Dora over to dictate. 'Question. Dora, what did you wear on your head? – Obedient wife answers – A white silk bonnet with a white flower and veil – a bit of orange-flower in the cap . . .' She continued in this vein for a while and then took the pen from her husband: 'As your father has thus trotted me out it is only fair he should be trotted out in his turn.' She described his outfit from the old boots to the old hat by way of the 'whitish waistcoat'. Edward seized the pen again: 'allow me to say that my whitish waistcoat as she calls it, as if it was a dimity waistcoat that I had forgotten to send to the laundry, was a most beautiful rich satin waistcoat . . .' and so it went on. Dora wrote to thank Miss Fenwick for all the kindness she had shown her 'since my Good Angel first put me under your angelic protection at Dover'.[9] It was a brief interlude of wedded bliss.

Edward's was not the only case on Dora's horizon. Her father was plagued by legal suits at that moment. In June, Thomas Noon Talfourd's long awaited copyright bill was finally due to come to the House of Commons for the fifth time. Talfourd, a backbench MP (and Dickens' prototype for Tommy Traddles in *David Copperfield*), wanted to extend the length of the copyright term, which was then set at twenty-eight years. The outcome of this case was as uncertain as Edward's; a less ambitious bill had been repeatedly rejected. In an attempt to make Wordsworth drop the case, he was offered a personal extension to his own rights (on the understanding he would cease campaigning); he rejected it as unfair. Dora was proud of her father but hated that her position had put him in the path of temptation. The new bill aimed to protect writers from piracy and defend their rights internationally.* It mattered to Wordsworth. If copyright were extended, he could provide more for his children after his death.

Just then, Wordsworth was worried about the financial position of all three of his children. Dora seemed to be on the brink of ruin. Willy, aged thirty-one, had been trying and failing to forge a career for the past decade. It had become clear after some years of trying to prepare for university that Willy was not suited to the academic life. He then tried for several years to get into the army, but scuppered his chances by ill-advisedly seeking a favour, rather than using the proper channels. Instead he went to study in Germany for a number of years. On his return, he thought variously of being a landscape gardener or a banker, a Tithe Commissioner or Secretary to the new Birmingham Railway. All had come to nothing. Even John,

---

* Talfourd had been widely supported by most of the leading authors of the day and none more vehemently than Wordsworth (some have suggested the bill was in fact Wordsworth's idea). See also Catherine Seville, *Literary Copyright Reform in Early Victorian England* (Cambridge: Cambridge University Press, 1999).

whom they all thought had done so well in marrying the heiress, Isabella Curwen, was facing an uncertain future. John now had six children, but the Curwens' mining empire had collapsed and Isabella's fortune with it. John attempted to support his family on his curate's salary, but his wife, used to a different lifestyle, succumbed to a nervous illness. To top it all, John himself fell sick with typhus – the doctors recommended a spell in France which he could ill afford – and the strain was telling on all the family.

In addition to the worries about the copyright bill, Wordsworth was still attempting, after years of campaigning, to persuade Sir Robert Peel to allow him to resign the Stamp Office in favour of the impoverished Willy. Just a generation before, such a transfer would have been unproblematic. But times had changed, and however keen he was to help Wordsworth, the Prime Minister did not want to be criticised for acting corruptly. Wordsworth knew that even if he persuaded Peel, there was no guarantee the government would give him a pension to replace his own Stamp income. It was horrible for Dora to imagine her parents' 'much straitened' old age.[10] She realised full well the implications if Edward should lose the case, yet her father was all loving concern for Edward and Dora. 'I cannot suffer the morning of my Birth-day to pass without telling you that my heart is full of you and all that concerns you,' he wrote from Rydal on 7 April.[11]

Nine days later Sir Lancelot gave his verdict. Having laid out in some detail the facts of the case, he proceeded to a lengthy statement about the defendants. He quickly made it clear he regarded Edward as a fool. 'Mr Quillinan', pronounced the Vice-Chancellor, 'took an active part in the transaction. It seems from what he states in his answer, that he must have known that he was taking on himself a false character.' This was not what they had hoped to hear. The suspense was acute. However, he went on, 'I do not impute to him any knowledge of the fraud, or any wish to defraud; he acted thoughtlessly, out of kindness to his brother-in-law.'[12] So, Edward was a kindly fool, not a corrupt one, and thus avoided criminal charges. Nonetheless, he was held responsible and therefore ordered, with the other surviving defendants, to pay back the £14,400 plus costs. With this verdict, Edward's hopes of ever being able to support Dora disappeared. The truth was, as Crabb Robinson saw, he had at best behaved 'incautiously and weakly' in signing the various deeds.[13] And, as Crabb Robinson further noted, 'it is, after all, a melancholy mode of escaping from an imputation to one's honour by allowing that the fault must be transferred to the head'.[14] The whole affair seemed to confirm Wordsworth's opinion of Edward as a good man but an unwise one and a financial dolt to boot.

Sara, who had been following the case closely, updated her acquaintances: 'the Vice-Chancellor cleared Mr Q's character in his judgement in a moral point of view – but said he had acted foolishly in the business'.[15] She had been concerned about Dora throughout the trial, but almost as soon as judgment had been passed – and while the Quillinans were licking their wounds – the Coleridges suffered a disaster of their own. In May 1842, Henry succumbed to a major relapse of the illness which had precipitated the trip to Belgium. He suffered a horrible bout of 'internal' sickness, but the more worrying symptom – and the one that would not go away – was a form of paralysis. It began in his legs and quickly affected his whole spine until he was bedridden. For a month Sara was consumed with anxiety and remained constantly at Henry's side.

Her first social visit after the immediate crisis had passed was to see Dora at Spring Street. Wordsworth and Mary were also in town. They had come to London at the start of June in order to offer Dora support after the trial and to allow Wordsworth to resolve various concerns. The vote on the copyright bill was imminent and Wordsworth was lobbying hard. He was now hopeful he'd be able to pass the Distributorship on to Willy, but nothing was guaranteed. In the meantime, Gladstone was advising him that it would be politically astute to wait a while before receiving a government pension.[16] With Edward's fortunes worse than ever, the financial implications – and hence anxiety – surrounding the pension and the copyright bill were acute. Sara wouldn't have believed Dora could get any thinner, but when she saw her friend she was shocked. 'Dear Dora, whom I saw today,' she told Hartley, 'looks very emaciated – her waist being about an inch round.' She spoke to Edward about Dora's appearance. He confided to her his frustration and conviction that her state was 'owing to pure inanition and that she ought to do – what she will not – that is feed like a baby – on soft food a little at a time and often'. Sara concurred and left several 'excellent strengthening diet receipts for her', but she knew Dora would ignore them.[17]

Mary was terrified. She described with hopeless weariness Dora's dinner on a typical day: 'about as much bacon as a sparrow might pick, no liquid for she is afraid of wine, with a little rice'. The word 'afraid' is telling, as is the way Mary described Dora retiring to bed early 'to hide or to keep off greater suffering'. Sara and Mary agreed Dora was starving herself: 'for really the food she takes, is insufficient one would imagine to sustain life'.[18] Dora refused to consider herself as an invalid. Evidently she could not, or would not, see what everyone else saw when they looked at her. Instead, said Sara, 'she sits so upright, not lying on the sofa . . . pursuing her usual occupations briskly and with no air of languor or invalidism of expression, that it is hard to address her, or think of her when present as one that is ill'.[19] Dora's doctor, Dr Fergusson, went out of his way to visit her at home many times, but could not find any specific illness or way of improving her condition.

In mid-July, when they were as confident as they could be that the Distributorship would be passed to Willy, Wordsworth and Mary eventually departed for Rydal, leaving Dora with strict instructions to visit as soon as possible. Amongst the few bright spots in either Dora or Sara's summers were Dora's visits to Chester Place. On these occasions, Sara was 'bright and cheerful and agreeable'. The two women gossiped about childhood friends. Sara felt Edith Southey had been snubbing her; they touched on the family's dispute and Southey's own illness. Discussing the Southeys' troubles was a relief, of sorts, from living their own.[20] Sara was increasingly worried about Henry's illness; Dora was weak, worried about money and under assault from her parents to return home to the north. Mary wrote to Miss Fenwick as though she were writing about the small obstinate child her daughter had once been. 'I trust, if Dora can but reconcile herself to being absent from the girls – who will ever be a clog, (in spite of her husband's desire to the contrary), to her feelings – and her own diseased clinging to home – this lovely spot and this fine air and kind friends, could not but benefit her health – yet I must fear that it may not be so – and that she will be grateful when she gets back to Sp[ring] St.'[21]

Oddly enough, Edward's relationship with Wordsworth had improved since the trial. Wordsworth seemed to trust him more rather than less. In August, while the poet was still waiting to hear whether he would get his pension, he received a letter from his illegitimate daughter Caroline's husband, Monsieur Baudouin, demanding more money. Caroline's mother Annette had died in January 1841. Having read about the Distributorship in the newspapers and assuming that Wordsworth had been granted a pension, M. Baudouin now demanded more money. Up to this point Wordsworth had settled nearly £1000 on Caroline. It had been received with gratitude, and considered generous. Now he didn't know what to do, and more or less put the whole affair into the care of Edward and Crabb Robinson. On 9 August the two men had a conversation and Edward wrote a letter in French which formed the basis of the reply which Crabb Robinson then sent to France on behalf of Wordsworth. Edward and Crabb Robinson told Baudouin, in no uncertain terms, that 'Wordsworth had not the means of doing anything further'.[22] Despite her husband's involvement, there is still no evidence Dora knew about her French half-sister. Sara, on the other hand, did know, and had long been of the opinion that Dora should have been told: 'such awkwardness should be disclosed on the first favourable op – they otherwise – ten to one – disclose themselves at an unfavourable one and with aggravating circes to the feelings of those interested'.[23]

Wordsworth and Mary continued to fret about Dora as winter approached. They so mourned the loss 'of our companion

child' that on long walks and in dark evenings their main topic
of conversation was their anxiety about her. In November, Dora
finally surrendered and went to Rydal. Edward did not fight
hard for his wife to stay at home. He had seen much less of her
during the autumn than he had in the summer, having been
away on a number of trips and visits. When she left, he simply
said he would follow in due course. Edward eventually arrived
just in time for Christmas. He intended his stay to be temporary.
Mary and Wordsworth, however, began a campaign to make the
arrangement permanent.

'The Prop of My Spirits'

As Christmas 1842 approached in Chester Place, the Coleridges
were having a sorry time. Henry, taking vast amounts of opium
to relieve his pain, was suffering all the side effects with which
Sara was so familiar: insomnia, constipation and disturbed sleep.
She was frightened by her husband's illness and additionally
anxious that people might think he had lost his mind. Writing
to her friend Louisa Plummer (née Powles), Sara tried to make
sure his symptoms would not be confused with those of the
'common brain palsy'. It's possible she hoped to divert suspicion
from the idea that Henry might have syphilis. As everyone
who had read his West Indies book knew, when Henry was a
young man abroad he'd had wild adventures and enjoyed
dancing, at the very least, with Creole women. 'Henry's infection', Sara wrote in a clear hand, 'is wholly in the lower part of
the spinal cord which is a <u>continuation</u> of the nervous matter
of the brain – but produces very different symptoms when
diseased. It does not affect the mind – the intellect at least – &
this makes a wide difference betwixt the two.' He was subject
to spasms and convulsions, she explained, as well as pain in his
back and chest, but in his mind he was *quite* well. She empha-
sised his patience in suffering: 'he is quiet and resigned and
derives quiet comfort from devotional reading, from prayer
and religious ministrations'.[24]

Aside from his physical condition, Henry grew almost neurotically anxious about finances. He worried about a debt of Derwent's, and about executors. Most of all he worried about his wife and children. It was now he, housebound and jobless, who spent all his time preoccupied with STC and his publications. He took it into his head that Pickering, STC's publisher, made too much profit relative to the Coleridge estate: he ought to split the proceeds more fairly. Two thirds rather than half should go to Sara and her brothers. When Pickering refused, Henry asked how much it would cost to buy their way out of the deal. Henry wanted Wordsworth's publisher, Moxon, to take over. Pickering, reasonably enough, was reluctant to relinquish the rights he held, and demanded a huge sum.* Henry, 'now too ill to think of any trying point of law', could not afford to pay.[25] Unhappy letters shot back and forth, and all the while Henry was sinking. Sara had her work cut out to calm and console him.

While her husband's world shrank, Sara's expanded. She took over – without much pleasure – the running of the household finances. Herbert came home for the holidays towards the end of December. He had started at Eton in the autumn of 1841 (he was not much happier there than he had been at St John's Wood) and Sara tried to make preparations for a happy Christmas for the children. But, though he enjoyed hearing them play, Henry did not want to see his son or daughter. In the middle of the month, Edy was struck down with the whooping cough and there were no more games. Henry grew worse. Sara was miserable – not with a nervous depression but a more rational sadness. She struggled to explain the difference: 'this is not all heaviness – it is a seriousness'. When carol singers made their way down the frosty road to call, Sara noted: 'never before did

* Pickering told Henry he would only consider selling if Henry bought the complete inventory at trade price and half the total value of the stock. His argument was that he had for years taken risks on Coleridge and would need to be compensated for loss of future earnings (see Alan Vardy, *Constructing Coleridge*, p. 142).

I hear them with so heavy a heart'. Yet even at this stage, she was curious about how and why her mind created and experienced nostalgia. She speculated about the difference between the happiness of youth and age, and the way 'periodical music knits together all our past years as with a running thread'.[26]

Christmas came and went. Sara refused to give up hope that Henry would recover. She sent Herbert back to school and attended, with the help of Nuck, to her sick husband and daughter. Poor Edy now had the chicken pox on top of the whooping cough and, if that were not enough, Mrs STC was sick and confined to bed. Henry's brothers John Taylor Coleridge and James Coleridge (the vicar and youngest brother) visited on an almost daily basis. It was not until the start of January that Sara finally accepted what Sir Benjamin Brodie had been telling her for some time: her husband would not get better. She did not want to tell Henry. 'He does not know what Brodie has said', she told Derwent, 'and still has hopes of life.'[27] Weeks passed, and she barely left his side, praying with him and talking to him constantly.

But eventually, husband and wife had the conversation both had been avoiding. Henry broached the subject. 'This – he said – must destroy my life – I know I am to die – but I thank God I am quite tranquil quite happy.'[28] They wept. Henry was still anxious about the family's finances; Sara assured him she would try to withdraw STC's books from the long-standing publishing deal with Pickering. He was also worried about their project to republish and reposition STC. Sara tried to reassure him she would finish what he had started: she would ask her brothers to help. In particular, she would issue a new edition of Coleridge's complex *Biographia Literaria* which Henry had been working on until illness forced him to put aside his pen. He had begun to write a defence of STC's character for the introduction. Sara promised to complete the task.

On the morning of 17 January, Henry had a serious coughing fit and later that day he 'had strange dying sensations – languor yet not languor – faintness and sense of inaction'. After the faintness wore off, Henry – not for the first time – 'was very strange in his manner stared vacantly and talked – not with positive incoherency but with a disproportiateness and wildly'. He was being chased by robbers; Sara was not looking after him. He pleaded with her, asking how she could suffer him to be confined with madmen.[29] She told no one about his symptoms, but recorded them in her journal.

Within a week Henry was mostly rambling and delirious. On 21 January she wrote in her diary: 'He looks worn – but his countenance is quiet – though with more ghastliness about it. He talks a little – slowly + at intervals. He embraced and kissed me this morning . . . Alas is this the prelude to the sleep of the grave?'[30] On 25 January, while he was either unconscious or asleep – Sara couldn't tell – he had a violent flush and his breathing grew harder. Sara prayed aloud, willing him to hear, willing him to join in the familiar words. For a moment she thought he was speaking the Lord's Prayer with her, but then his words became senseless ramblings. His brother James spoke the last rites and, at the end, Henry lapsed into unconsciousness. Sara 'kissed his beloved face – over and over again' and then watched him die. She sat for a while beside his body, and from there she wrote to Herbert at Eton to tell him 'your excellent father, is no more in this world'.[31]

When Sara saw Henry's remains in his coffin, 'it seemed as if the prop of my spirits had fallen away + all was crushed to flatness'.[32] The body was placed in the dining room. 'How often at the head of that little dinner table', she reflected, 'have I seen him radiant with smiles and glowing cheeks – and full of wit and glee.' The room was alive with her memories of him, while she stood uncomprehending beside 'his cold remains in their double coffin'.[33] She felt certain the best part of her life was over and could not bear to think 'the sun rises every morning, and he does not see it'.[34] Sara assumed the next stage would be a return to the 'heavy black cloud' she knew so well. 'I am resigned to the blackness and desolation of feeling I must go through', she confided in her diary, and 'I must finish my journey alone.'[35]

On a bleak February morning in Highgate churchyard, the assembled mourners bowed their heads. As the minister spoke,

Sara, dressed in sombre black crepe, could hear crying, as though at a great distance. During the funeral she shed some tears, but did not weep aloud. The laudanum she'd taken to calm her nerves contributed to a sensation of detached otherworldliness: 'When the voice of the minister ceased I drew nearer to the brink of the grave and looked down fixedly into my future home – the receptacle of all that earth will hold of me a few years hence.' James, who had tended Henry faithfully through his final illness, gently took her elbow and guided her away from the edge. Sara returned to Chester Place without her husband, convinced she would fall apart. Such happiness as she had been able to find between the hysteria and heartache of the last ten years 'was gone forever'.[36]

In fact, she went on to experience pure, simple and enormous grief; but she continued to function, driven by the need to make Chester Place as happy a place as possible for her children. Her father's writing, always important, helped her survive those first deep days of sadness. Pickering delivered the proofs of the new edition of *Aids to Reflection* – which included Sara's essay 'On Rationalism' – for her to go through. During the initial mourning period, checking them was exactly the occupation she needed. It was time-consuming labour, which required concentration without much thought. Given she and Henry had worked on her father's book together, getting it ready for the press was something she could do for (and almost with) not only Henry but also her father. She could quite legitimately shut herself away in her room, 'wrapped up' in the words. Here she discovered she could induce a state of mind where she was 'partly out of this world', which was the most 'comfortable' place to be.[37]

When the news of Henry's death reached the Lakes, everyone worried about Sara. Wordsworth, in particular, was deeply concerned. 'Towards Sara', he told Henry's brother John Taylor Coleridge, 'I have much of the tenderness of a Father, having had her so near to us and so long under our eye . . . a more excellent Creature is not to be found.'[38] The Wordsworths had no news to cheer her. Their lives were dominated by the sad unfolding of events at Keswick: Southey was dying. For some time the Poet Laureate had been losing his mind, and for the last six months or so had been suffering from an acute form of what we would probably call senile dementia. On 21 March, less than two months after Henry, Southey breathed his last. He had been more of a real father to Sara than STC had ever been. He was her 'uncle-father', her protector and teacher. He left behind him a divided family; Sara's links to her childhood were well and truly severed.

By contrast, Dora was back in her childhood role, financially dependent upon, and scribe for, her father. Edward had agreed not to return to London and he and Dora moved to lodgings near Rydal and continued, more or less, as part of the Wordsworth household. It was not a comfortable set-up for Edward, but for the time being he had little choice. He and Dora would live on in the dying embers of the once great triumvirate of Romantic poets. Almost before Southey was dead, Sir Robert Peel wrote to Wordsworth to try to persuade him to accept the now vacant Laureateship. Several times Wordsworth refused – but eventually he accepted on the understanding he would not actually have to write any poetry. It seemed that the stories of what remained of Dora and Sara's lives had already been written. The Quillinans would presumably care for Dora's parents through old age and death. Sara would live out her widowhood in London and, in all likelihood, slip into the state of miserable nervousness that everyone (herself included) feared.

PART FOUR

CHAPTER 18

FOR TRUTH AND JUSTICE: THE CALUMNIATED POET

1843–1844

The snow on the mountains above Grasmere had melted, and in the gardens of Rydal Mount the daffodils and celandines 'tossed & reeled & danced'.[1] Swallows and martins, newly returned from African deserts, filled the air with song. One afternoon, a steady stream of little girls, each carrying her own tin mug, made its way up the hill past Rydal Church to Wordsworth's house. It was April 1843 and Edward and Dora were throwing a birthday party for Wordsworth. They had invited 150 schoolgirls to a 'tea-drink' in the field adjoining Rydal's garden. (They hadn't asked boys, on the grounds they would be 'too boisterous'.) The Quillinans exhausted themselves as the 'only managers; & the nominal entertainers of all that young rabble'. They arranged for a fiddler and the little girls danced the spring afternoon away. Wordsworth and Mary sat and watched them play: the very essence of the Bard's pastoral idyll conjured up for his pleasure. The munificent Miss Fenwick, who had given Dora money to pay for the event, joined them on the terrace. The children, delighted by their free tea and licence to run and shriek, had only two well-meaning adults to curb their excesses. Dora, though she looked frail, rushed about in their midst, shepherding the girls and chatting to the adults. The months she had spent working at the Dowlings' school still counted amongst the happiest in her life, and she was in her element with the children and their teachers. At the end of the day, Dora and Edward returned exhausted but happy to their little house in Ambleside. Edward cheerfully concluded it had been a suitably 'royal' affair.*²

Dora and Miss Fenwick had been trying all winter to cheer up the newly crowned Poet Laureate; finally their efforts had at least made him smile. Official confirmation of his position, just weeks before, had been the culmination of the twelve unhappy months which had begun with Edward's trial and ended with Southey's death. One of the things eating away at Wordsworth – even on days like his birthday – was anxiety about his posthumous reputation. After his death, he believed there would be nothing but failure and lies. The biographers had already begun. Only a few years before he had fought to stop a friend of Crabb Robinson's, Barron Field, writing about him.³ Wordsworth was not keen on biography full stop. But he recognised that for men who had played an 'active part' in history, a case could be made for the genre. The world thought it needed a 'thorough knowledge of the good and bad qualities' of such people: a scrutiny of their private lives could be justified to 'explain not only their own public conduct, but that of those with whom they have acted'. Yet, he argued, 'Nothing of this applies to authors, considered merely as authors. Our business is with their books, – to understand and to enjoy them. And, of poets more especially, it is true – that, if their works be good, they contain within themselves all that is necessary to their being comprehended and relished.'⁴

Despite this, by 1843, Wordsworth knew it was inevitable people would write about him. He had seen what had happened to STC: there had been a rash of inaccurate and sometimes downright immoral biographies and critical essays, including the intentionally critical, like de Quincey's; the vicious, like Ferrier's; and in some ways worst of all, those which aimed to venerate but which in fact misinterpreted, like Henry Nelson Coleridge's *Table Talk*, and, more recently, Gillman's memoir

---

* 'Royal', too, in that the party had been delayed until a couple of weeks after Wordsworth's actual birthday.

of STC. Dora minded almost as much as her father. She worried about what had happened to STC, and what might happen to Wordsworth. Malicious gossip, disloyalty and misrepresentation were amongst the few things that could rouse her to anger.

Wordsworth, like so many great men before and since, had started to view his life as a failure. No matter he was Poet Laureate, no matter he had written verses to put him into a class with Shakespeare and Milton – he had failed to complete *The Recluse*. For the last four decades his ambition had been to write this poem, a work inspired by a 'greater muse' than Milton's. It was supposed to present his views 'On Man, on Nature, and on Human Life'. Instead, he had composed only an incomplete and unpublished beginning of a poem on the growth of his own mind. '*The Recluse* has never been written except a few passages,' he'd told his sister a few years before, 'and probably never will.'[5] He berated himself for having under-taken a task that was 'beyond his powers to accomplish'.[6] Periodically, he had promised his family he was just about to finish it, but it had not happened. Dora and Mary kept him hard at work when they could, but to no avail. Though Dora was willing, she did not know how to be a living staff to her father. Ironically, without intending to, she increased his own feeling of failure. She no longer believed *The Recluse* would be written. Her father had failed and so had she.

Once again, Miss Fenwick came to Dora's rescue and helped her make a plan. They would get the old man to go through all his volumes of poetry and tell them the history of each poem's composition and those parts of his own history which he deemed to be relevant or important. Dora assured him it would not tax his eyes; Miss Fenwick had agreed he could dictate to her. Wordsworth, seeing how much his daughter wanted it, agreed to the project. Miss Fenwick was adamant that what she did was 'for Dora'.[7] Thus throughout the long cold January days Wordsworth paced the drawing room at Rydal Mount and remin-isced. It did not precisely make him happy, but it did give him a sense of purpose, and it gave Dora satisfaction to see the piles of notes accumulating. The notes allowed Wordsworth to shape his own biography by producing its raw material.

Wearing her new widow's weeds in Chester Place, as the winter of 1843 turned into spring, Sara did not pay or receive any calls. Instead, day after day, she remained immersed in *Aids to Reflections* which was about to be published. Editing the book drew her back into intellectual thought, and, although she worried it would put her 'out of pocket and not into reputation', she never for a moment regretted the labour. It had given her more 'animated intercourse with some great minds now passed from our own nether sphere than I could have had from merely reading their thoughts without thinking them over again'.

It was not all about retreat. Going through the proofs also meant she had to reread her own religious essay 'On Rationalism', which she had decided to publish in the new volume. In her essay she attempted to walk a tricky path between all the different religious factions – not too close to Newman's dangerously Catholic way of thinking, not too close to the sometimes radical views of the Evangelicals. She re-presented Coleridge as a Church of England man of the 'correct' middle-class kind. Her essay was brave. Jeffrey Barbeau has written brilliantly about it, pointing out that to argue against the great Cardinal Newman as she did was a bold step. 'I do not think it will be much admired by any one,' she told John Taylor Coleridge. 'It makes larger demands on the attention of readers than I, with my power, have perhaps the right to make or replay.'[8]

Having returned her proofs in May, she awaited publication and the verdicts of her readers. Sara knew her reading of STC was more subtle than Henry's. She hoped her essay would go some way to bolstering her father's reputation and allowing him a voice in the ongoing religious debates. In her anxiety about the book, she wrote and confessed to Dora and Wordsworth that she was feeling increasingly isolated by her way of looking at the world which had been formed by 'familiarity and interest' with her father's mind.[9] She would not go along with the simple, unquestioning religious views that people – women in particular – were expected to endorse, and she therefore worried her essay would make her enemies rather than friends. She could 'admire and applaud all the combatants on the theological arena, even the hearty opponents of my father, but I cannot entirely agree with any of them'.[10] She asked Wordsworth for his opinion about Coleridge's religious faith and views.

Pickering published Sara's edition of *Aids to Reflection* in June 1843. On the whole, the responses were gratifying. Henry's earnestly religious younger brother Edward Coleridge worried a little about the impact on her domestic life, but everyone else she heard from was impressed. Henry's nephew, John Duke Coleridge (John Taylor's son), then a student at Balliol, told her he'd heard the essay being discussed by Oxford theologians. She received admiring letters from private and public thinkers, including, most gratifyingly, F. D. Maurice. She was thrilled to hear, by July, that the book was selling well.[11] Perhaps the opinion she most enjoyed was Hartley's: 'Dear Sara's treatise on Rationalism is a wonder,' he wrote to their mother, knowing she would show the letter to Sara. 'I say not a wonder of a woman's work – where lives the man that could have written it? None in Great Britain since our Father died. Poor Henry was perfectly right in saying that she inherited more of our father, than either of us; and that not only in the amount but in the quality of her powers.'[12] It was just the affirmation and confirmation she had needed, and gave her permission to take another, surer, step into that man's world – Literature.

By the end of the summer of 1843, Sara was almost ready to tackle her next 'Esteesian' project: her father's *Biographia Literaria*; the book which had borne the brunt of Ferrier's plagiarism charges. *Biographia*'s reputation was as complex as its subject matter; it would require extraordinary skills of its editor. STC had subtitled the book 'Biographical Sketches of My Literary Life, Principles, and Opinions, chiefly on the subjects of Poetry and Philosophy',* and, so far as it is possible to categorise,

---

* When it was published, the subtitle was shortened to *Biographical Sketches of My Literary Life and Opinions*.

biographer Richard Holmes's term 'literary self-portrait' is the best fit. *Biographia* is a difficult volume but a crucial one in literary history. It is Coleridge at his most Coleridgean: brilliant, complicated, dense and controversial. It is, as Holmes says, a maddening combination of frankness and fraudulence, and is 'part fact, part fiction, part theory'.[13] In this book Coleridge gave the world his definition of the difference between Imagination and Fancy and he also gives us the concept of 'a willing suspension of disbelief'. Its theological musings are by turn revelatory and incomprehensible.

When it was first published in 1817, most critics had seen in it evidence of a mind ruined by opium. Hazlitt had ripped it to shreds in a 10,000-word denunciation, arguing it had been produced from 'the maggots' of his [STC's] brain'.[14] More recent critics have disagreed; it is a cornerstone of what we now call literary criticism and a key text in the history of literature, but it is not an easy read. It is, remarked the poet and critic Arthur Symons, 'the greatest book of criticism in English, and one of the most annoying books in any language'.[15]

When *Biographia* was first published, Sara was fifteen – just the age to feel most painfully the criticisms levelled against her father. The writer John Wilson (erstwhile friend and fan of both STC and Wordsworth, and the man who had tended Dora when she had the whooping cough) had expressed most forcefully the judgements, both intellectual and personal, which Sara hoped to overturn. Reviewing *Biographia* (under his Christopher North pseudonym) in 1817, he had declared: 'We cannot see in what the state of literature would have been different, had [Coleridge] been cut off in childhood, or had he never been born . . .'[16] Furthermore, he sneered, Coleridge gave a 'pretended account of the Metaphysical systems of Kant, of which he knows less than nothing'. And on a personal note, he had concluded: 'A man who abandons his wife and children is undoubtedly both a wicked and pernicious member of society.' But even these criticisms had been put into the shade by the plagiarism charges of Ferrier, de Quincey and others. The accusations had, as Sara knew, at least some justification;

it is undeniable that Coleridge borrowed from Schelling and other German sources.

One of the great ironies of the *Biographia* is that STC had hoped the book would establish Wordsworth's reputation for all time. To this end he incorporated in it a long and serious analysis of Wordsworth's writing, including the much maligned *Excursion*. He had been inspired to write largely by Jeffrey's infamous 'This will not do' criticism of Wordsworth's *Excursion* in the *Edinburgh Review*. Wordsworth never understood the compliment STC had paid him. He only skimmed the *Biographia*, and then felt that where Coleridge had written about his poetry: 'The praise is extravagant, and the censure inconsiderate.' Yet STC's praise did much for Wordsworth's standing as a poet. If *Biographia* had, in recent years, helped secure STC a place as one of the great minds of the century, it had also attracted unprecedented criticism, much of it personal. *Biographia*'s reception, and the effect it had on her father's reputation (in the years when Southey and Wordsworth's stars were rising), haunted Sara.

So, when she took over Henry's editorial work, it was a means of honouring and celebrating what her husband had done, with the hope of defending and celebrating her father. It was also a way to demonstrate her loyalty to Coleridge over Wordsworth. The latter, her 'father-in-feeling', claimed publicly he had never read the book, while privately, hurt by criticism, he dismissed it and said it had given him 'no pleasure'.[17] Sara was almost ready to take on the *Biographia*, but was not quite certain she was the right person. Perhaps Hartley should do it?

While Sara laboured over STC's reputation, Edward Quillinan was engaged in protecting Wordsworth's. *Blackwood's Magazine* had recently published a hurtful and unfair criticism of the poet in the form of a satirical imagined conversation between Southey and the scholar Richard Porson. The article's author, the poet and critic Walter Savage Landor, made his fictional Southey accuse Wordsworth of plagiarism. Throughout the spring, while women surrounded the Bard, encouraging and collecting his spoken words, Edward composed a lengthy defence in the form of a counter-satire against Landor. He corresponded at enormous length with Henry Crabb Robinson and others to make sure he had his facts right, and it took him months to compose. Wordsworth had no idea what Edward was doing until the piece was published.

While the two projects – Miss Fenwick's notes and his own essay – were underway, Edward behaved beautifully. Wordsworth and Mary wanted Dora under their roof as much as possible. Just to be sure, however, they arranged for a carriage to collect her at least three times a week for a hot shower bath in a new-fangled contraption purchased for Rydal. For once, their theories about her health sound genuinely appealing. It must have been lovely to feel warm and clean, if nothing else, and Dora was happy enough to comply. She was so thin that she was almost constantly cold and, aside from any other benefits, the baths energised her. For the sake of the treat she put up with the fashionable 'humbug' of homoeopathy, which her parents also advocated.[18] From Wordsworth and Mary's point of view the shower was a canny purchase. Perhaps an even more generous option would have been to install it in Dora's own house, but Edward held his peace while they were all working on what we now know as *The Fenwick Notes*.

Once Dora and Miss Fenwick had finished taking the dictation, it was the end of June and time for Miss Fenwick to return south. She left Dora and Edward making a fair copy of the notes. Edward did the first half until one day in the summer he stopped mid-sentence and his wife carried on. She signed off neatly on 25 August 1843.[19] If Edward had been inclined towards feeling any resentment at the drudgery of the task, it was lessened by the fact that these were the only set of notes, making him and Dora the Keepers of the Bard. When the time came they – or more probably he – would write Wordsworth's biography. Nothing of significance could now be written by anyone else.

After Wordsworth had finished dictating and summer ended, his low spirits returned: he felt his life was nothing but a series of 'disappointments and distresses and mishaps'.[20] Tensions, which had cooled since the trial, began to simmer again, and over the next eighteen months Edward found it increasingly difficult to bite his tongue. It did not help that Wordsworth had spurned the *Blackwood* defence, into which Edward had poured so much labour. Sara had been thrilled by Edward's satire, and told Dora so: 'how much I am amused & pleased with the Landor & the North Conversation. I think the paper cannot but serve as a moral looking-glass for the arrogant man,' she enthused.[21] Wordsworth, by contrast, frowned on the piece, and said that Edward ought to have known 'very well that I should have disapproved'.[22] On publication, Landor mocked Edward publicly for his 'Quillinanities'. The 'son-in-law of the calumniated poet' withstood the public criticisms manfully,[23] but Edward was a sensitive man, and proud, and Wordsworth's attitude only threw into sharper relief how much all he and Dora did was taken for granted.

Besides this, and for all their fretting about her health, Dora's parents made her work far too hard, and Edward could do nothing about it. They encouraged her to look after her brothers to the detriment of herself – and in looking after her brothers she had her work cut out. Earlier that year Willy had become engaged to – and then disengaged from – a wealthy young woman named Mary Monkhouse. She'd broken it off very publicly and Willy had returned to Rydal to lick his wounds and be looked after by his sister. Meanwhile, John's wife Isabella (née Curwen) had fallen sick and demanded to be taken abroad. In October 1843 John obediently travelled with her and two of their children to Madeira. Dora made regular journeys to visit the four boys who John and Isabella had left in Brigham, ten miles from Rydal. All of which, Edward said, was not good for Dora, and 'very inconvenient & disconsolate for me'.[24] The family dramas and worries meant the mood in the house was tense.

In September 1843, Sara found a project which bridged the gap between *Aids to Reflection* and the *Biographia Literaria*. The miserable summer following Henry's death was ending, and Herbert would soon have to return to school. She decided sea air would do them all good. She took Edith and Herbert with Nuck on the *Prince of Wales* steamer (the 'most vibrating vessel I was ever in') from London Bridge to Margate. On the boat she read Carlyle's collection of essays, *On Heroes, Hero-worship and the Heroic in History.* The steamer made the book shake in her hand, which seemed suitably symbolic, but she did not stop reading for a moment.[25] Carlyle's book explored, through biography, people as diverse as Mahomet and Napoleon, but for Sara it also stirred complicated ideas about the men who had brought her up.

⋅ Edy and Herbert (aged eleven and thirteen) found their mother inattentive but cheerful. With Sara happier, they had permission to be happy themselves. On fine days she took the children down to the beach to wade in the sea while she read. Herbert was allowed – as Edy reported to her grandmother with envy – to bathe in the sea without a machine.[26] When it rained they played with a tabby cat they had found and dragged into the small sitting room: 'Six little mice sat down to spin – Pussy came by and she peeped in,' they chanted, again and again. Sara remained lost in the Carlyle, despite two old ladies in the lodgings irritating her by reading loudly to one another. Almost all she stopped reading for was to hear the children's lessons or to visit various churches in the hopes of finding a preacher with whom she could agree.[27]

The last twelve months had been draining, and Sara had been taking five drops of morphine most nights to sleep. As she pondered Carlyle's definition of heroes, either the book or the sea air improved her health. She sat down to write and tell Dora all about it. 'During the whole of the last week I have done without opium; and though I never have sufficient sleep, & sometimes next to none, or of a very bad sort, yet if I can rest upon the whole as much as at present I will never take another drop of morphine.' Honesty compelled her to continue: 'I have often tried to leave off that, not false friend (for it is not false – it does a real service, which, like chancery law, sometimes costs more than it is worth, but sometimes is worth even more than it costs . . .) – not false but most hurtfully-befriending friend, before, but the medical men, seeing how ill I began to look, have always remanded me to the drug.' By the time they were due to leave Margate, Sara was sleeping and feeling so well that she considered staying on until the end of October. This would have meant sending Herbert to school on his own, and she felt guilty about the idea. In the end, she decided she had better accompany him back to Eton.

From Margate, Sara had written long excited letters to her mother and various others about her reading. But at Eton, for the first time, she had her views challenged. Here, staying with Edward Coleridge (Henry's younger brother and a master at the school), she went to a round of dinner parties. At each, she tried to steer the conversation round to Carlyle. It being Eton, most of the other guests were men (masters, mainly), and most more traditional in their views than Carlyle. Unlike the masters, Sara strongly endorsed the key tenet underlying Carlyle's book: heroes are men who have 'striven for truth and justice'.[28] Whether or not they also lived exemplary personal lives is almost irrelevant. She got into numerous arguments. At dinner on 25 October, things became heated. On one side was Sara; on the other Edward and two of his colleagues, Charles John Abraham and Edward Balston. The next day she reported gleefully to her mother that there had been 'a controversy betwixt the gentlemen and me'.[29] She told Dora and Edward how her brother-in-law, Edward Coleridge, had tried to persuade her to stay: '"You are saving your money by staying here" – he observes – and "and when you go home you will have no one to brush you up with a controversy." You see what a considerate brother I have; but I must not save my money & spend my breath here after next Tuesday. Indeed an occasional meeting with Derwent will suffice to keep my disputatory vein from drying up.'[30]

She returned home, but did not want to drop the subject. By the time she reached Chester Place, she had begun a new essay. This one was entitled 'Reply to the Strictures of Three Gentlemen's Criticisms of her Opinion of Carlyle'. In it she defended Carlyle's views. Sara did not bring her father into the essay but his presence in her thinking is unmistakable. Whole-hearted pursuit of the truth may, at particular times in history, cause heroes – like Voltaire – to be 'misunderstood by the masses of mankind . . . simply because the masses of mankind are not themselves sufficiently wise and good and perspicacious'.[31] The essay is a manifesto not only for venerating heroes but also for educating the 'masses' to become wiser. It can be read as Sara's defence of fulfilling her promise to Henry and taking on STC's *Biographia Literaria*.

Edward Quillinan managed to pay court to Wordsworth with good grace throughout the autumn of 1843. He went on long morning walks 'through the waters & the mists with the Bard who seems to defy all weathers; & who called this a beautiful soft solemn day; & so it was, though somewhat insidiously soft, for a mackintosh was hardly proof against its insinu-ations'.[32] Yet, as he tramped, he grew increasingly resentful. By Christmas, Edward was in a panic about Dora. It seemed she was as thin as it was possible for a living person to be, and yet daily she became even more skeletal: 'within the last fortnight or three weeks', he wrote to tell Sara, 'she has become thinner (you will say that is not possible) and I am not at all easy about her'.[33]

Edward's good behaviour towards his parents-in-law just about lasted through to Wordsworth's seventy-fourth birthday in April 1844. Building on the success of the previous year, Miss Fenwick offered to pay for another party. This time, despite the risk of rowdiness, schoolboys were invited as well as school-girls. Out of nervousness about the boys' behaviour – and because Dora was weaker than she had been the year before – they also invited parents and schoolteachers. The total number of guests was therefore close to five hundred. Even more than the year before, the party was a chance to direct a romantic scene straight from the pages of Wordsworth's early poetry. Under his instructions the stage was set; tables were 'tastefully' arranged in the open air with 'oranges, gingerbread and painted eggs, ornamented with daffodils, laurels, and moss, gracefully mixed'.[34] Preparations made, Wordsworth looked forward to the proud faces the children would turn up to him as they presented themselves from behind the terrace wall. Young and old, rich and poor duly gathered, clutching their own tea cups, to dance before the poet. Towards the end of the afternoon, the children gave Wordsworth three cheers and in return received their Easter eggs and gingerbread. Music was provided by German and Italian 'casual itinerants' as the sun shone down on a soft spring day.[35]

Wordsworth was delighted. 'The treat went off delightfully,' he told Moxon, 'with music, choral singing, dancing and [the children] chasing each other about in all directions.'[36] Apparently without irony, he rejoiced that it was a scene as might have appeared in Goldsmith's novels of almost a century before. Wordsworth was proud of himself for engineering a situation in which he and the 'humbler classes' enjoyed one another's company. Several months later he was using his success to rail sanctimoniously against members of his own class who had too little to do with the people of their neighbourhood. 'They employ them as labourers, or they visit them in charity for the sake of supplying the most urgent wants by almsgiving. But this', he told his friend Henry Reed, 'alas is not enough. – One would wish to see the rich mingle with the poor as much as may be on a footing of fraternal equality.'[37]

But Dora knew Wordsworth never really managed affinity with the working classes. According to the boy who delivered meat to Rydal, Wordsworth himself would never speak to him: 'he'd pass you, same as if you were nobbut a stean'.[38] A man who had worked as a waller at Rydal Mount agreed: 'he wozn't a man as said a deal to common fwoak'.[39] Damningly, a former servant of Wordsworth's concurred: 'There's nea dout but what he was fond of quality and quality was fond of him, but he niver exed fowk aboot their work, not noticed t'floaks, or nowt.' The only kind words he had about Wordsworth were for his generosity if 'fwoaks was sick' – exactly the kind of behaviour Wordsworth had been critical of in his fellow men of 'quality'.[40]

Dora knew her father was as much a figure of fun as of

affection. Wordsworth had taken in his older age to wearing green shades to protect his eyesight. He looked very comic; Harriet Martineau, who came to visit at the end of 1844, described how he would march about lanes 'in his cloak, his scotch bonnet and green goggles attended by a score of cottagers children – the youngest pulling at his cloak or holding his trousers'.[41] (Mind you, she had an ear trumpet, so they made an eccentric pair.) When he noticed children, Wordsworth was as likely to give them a penny as request they recite the Lord's Prayer. But whatever his hopes, 'children was nivver verra fond o' him', pronounced a former servant, because they weren't 'sea sure he was fond of other fowk's bairns, but he was verra fond o' his ain wi'out a doot'.[42]

Dora and Edward kept the festivities alive, encouraging games of hide and seek in the shrubbery and filling children's tea cups. The birthday party ended happily, but it could not dispel the clouds above Rydal. Wordsworth was worrying once again about the question of biography. He was cross that *Chambers' Biographical Encyclopedia* had recently written a notice about him which was full of errors. It might be 'droll' that the editors had married him to his cousin, but he was furious they reported he had been part of the Pantisocrat group. This was 'reprehensible negligence'.[43] Now even little Sara Coleridge was getting involved in the biographical business. It seemed she was attempting to write about the life of her father, which was a foolish notion. Wordsworth had been receiving awkward letters from her and didn't know how to reply. She wanted to know if her father had ever written for a newspaper: ('never') and what Wordsworth thought about STC's religious views: 'I feel incompetent at present to answer.'[44] Meanwhile, his own daughter was a shadow even of what she had been the year before.

When Sara began her edition of *Biographia Literaria*, she had a threefold purpose: to give the volume the editorial attention she believed it deserved, to defend STC against accusations that he had written a plagiarised and 'unintelligible' book, and to defend her father's moral character as an author and a man. She began with the hard graft of editing and glossing the body of text. As she did this, she started to build a defence against the plagiarism charges. In order to complete her editorial work and write the introduction in which she would make the defence, she had not only to redouble her theological studies, but to tackle all of Coleridge's philosophical thinking and reading. All this studying stretched her; it was an irony not lost on her that most of the trouble she took, in editing at least, would never be seen by readers.

Coleridge had quoted from any number of sources, and Sara set out on an intellectual pilgrimage through her father's life. The idea was to follow each trail and, wherever possible, give references and glosses as well as corrections. It was a mammoth task. 'A literary man, who reads and writes on a large scale, would make nothing of the business,' she told Henry Taylor and his wife disingenuously, 'but it makes me feel I had no rest for the sole of my feet and must be continually starting up to look in this or that volume, or find it out in some part of Europe.' *Biographia Literaria* could be described as an autobiography of Coleridge's reading life; as such, there aren't many people – men or women, then or now – who would have the confidence to imagine they could relive it. Sara may have been 'tempted to wish that my father would just have read more *common-place-ishly*, and not quoted from such a number of out-of-the-way books', but this merely gave her permission to do the same.[45] Henry's death had given her the freedom to enter this world and to behave like a 'literary man'. Because Henry had begun the project, and because she had promised, on his deathbed, to complete it, she could claim with honesty that the book was a tribute to both father and husband.

When she came to the introduction, Sara tackled both the charges head-on. She had several arguments in response to the Schelling question. First, that Coleridge always meant the 'borrowings' to be known. He has a footnote early in the book where he acknowledges the debt he owed to his 'German predecessor'. Sara suggested that one of the characteristics of

Coleridge's particular genius was a sort of chaos. It was not that he had intended to mislead, but rather that he did not have the pedantic kind of mind required for the making of footnotes. In order to construct this argument and to edit and gloss the book, Sara mastered all of Schelling, Kant and Fichte in the original German. This done, she made perfect translations from the original Schelling (there was still no English translation) and inserted the relevant attributions.

Secondly, she extended an argument she and Henry had made in the introduction to *Table Talk*. She acknowledged Coleridge did use Schelling 'verbatim' but explained he patched different bits of text together in order to create something new. He did not steal. He did not see thoughts as 'property'. He drove ideas forwards. STC had borrowed, absorbed, integrated and in some cases anticipated arguments made by the German philosophers. While writing, Sara took up a position amongst London's literati and found to her surprise that she loved and needed it. 'I want either society or brisk intellectual occupation.' Either one kept off the brooding, she told Hartley.[46] To her astonishment, she discovered, 'I feel content with singleness and begin, even in some respects to prefer it, which I once thought impossible.'[47]

CHAPTER 19

'YET HOPE STILL LIVES'

1845

'A Change of Air'

To WW, on His Seventy-fifth Birthday, by Hartley Coleridge
Happy the year, the month, that finds alive
A worthy man in health at seventy-five.

On 7 April 1845, Dora sat at the table of a subdued dinner party hosted by Miss Fenwick in Ambleside on the occasion of Wordsworth's seventy-fifth birthday. There were none of the usual festivities: no children, no dancing, no music. Wordsworth was downcast. 'I am in my seventy-sixth year – eheu fugaces,' he wrote melodramatically to his nephew.[1] It was cold and damp, and at dinner there was only one real topic of conversation. A couple of days earlier Dora and Edward had announced they were going to travel to Portugal together. Dora, toying with her food, tried to ignore that her mother looked grave, said very little and eventually stopped speaking altogether.[2] The others made an effort to keep the conversation going, but Mary's silence was impossible to ignore.

Edward was in high spirits, describing his brother's villa near the sea at Oporto and even believing he could persuade his parents-in-law to come and visit. Dora and Edward had been plotting the trip for months – ever since Edward's half-brother, John Quillinan, told them he planned to get married in Portugal. He had not yet set a date, but it would probably be some time in the summer, and he wanted Edward to come.

This much they had told Dora's parents some months before, and William and Mary assumed Edward would travel alone. Privately, however, Dora and Edward discussed travelling to Portugal together. The more they thought about it the, better an idea it seemed. The climate would be good for Dora's health; they could live cheaply yet luxuriously; more importantly, they could have an adventure.

As far as the English were concerned, nineteenth-century Portugal was an undeveloped, largely unknown, dangerous and thus exotic kingdom. Having been stuck at home so long, Dora began to dream, and to admit she had long craved 'foreign novelty'.[3] Insofar as Portugal was known to people in the west, it was through Southey's unfinished history of the region. This early influence, plus her husband's descent and literary interests had combined to mean Dora was captivated by the country's rich and romantic history. Edward was born and partly bred in Portugal, he spoke the language and understood the culture. He was just then translating the sixteenth-century Portuguese poet Luiz Vaz de Camões.* It was an epic undertaking. Dora could not fully know her husband without seeing his homeland, yet from the day she had first met him all those years ago he had always been subsumed into her family. The journey would be good for their marriage, if nothing else.

So, shortly before Wordsworth's birthday, they had broken the news to her parents. They hoped to travel, they said, 'for the benefit of a change of air'. Mary looked at Dora with an expression of such misery and terror that she feared her mother's 'heart would break'.[4] Dora's resolve faltered but Dr Davy and Miss Fenwick pressed William and Mary to approve; and reluctantly they had acknowledged the plan's prudence. Dora wrote excitedly to Sara to give her the news, and she and Edward set about making plans to leave very soon. Perhaps it was too soon.

---

* Edward followed the convention of his time and anglicised Camões' name to Camoens. Where he or the Wordsworths write Camoens, their spelling is left unchanged.

Maybe if Dora had played her cards differently she would not
have been sitting at the miserable dinner watching her disconsolate parents while the others valiantly tried to keep the conversation going.

Edward, looking at his frail wife across the dinner table, was
both afraid for her health and filled with a sense of hope that
finally he might be doing something to improve it. Dora's parents
were not happy, but they had agreed. Edward discussed their
plans with gusto. In the years since they had all been living on
top of one another, the mostly unspoken rivalry between him
and his father-in-law had flared with increasing regularity.
Superficially, the rows were always about Dora's health. The
previous summer, for example, Mary had put pressure on Edward
and Dora to visit the seaside. Neither were especially keen, but
eventually, on hearing that a party of Dora's Brinsop cousins
were taking a house in the coastal village of Flimby, they agreed
to join them for a month. After a few weeks Dora was no better;
if anything she was worse. According to Edward's diary, she was
'knocked up working + starving according to custom'.[5] Foolishly
they wrote to Wordsworth and Mary and let them know she
had also caught a cold, which prevented her from lying down
or sleeping.

Wordsworth, convinced that Edward could not look after
his wife, rushed to Flimby. Quite what he hoped to do for
Dora that Edward or her cousins could not is unclear, and
Edward bristled on being told that if Dora was no better
Wordsworth would whisk her 'home' to Rydal. Fortunately,
by the time Wordsworth reached them Dora was considerably
better. She had submitted to a blistering in the hope of effecting
a cure, and the hope (if not the blister) had worked. Wordsworth
acknowledged himself satisfied with her progress. For the time
being, since she was sleeping at night, he decreed she could
stay.

Wordsworth stayed at Flimby for five days and, despite
the improvement in Dora's health, they were tense days.
Wordsworth did not trouble to hide his disapproval of his
son-in-law. Edward, refusing to pander, stubbornly read the

papers. Wordsworth, working just as hard to ignore Edward, tramped up and down the beach and came back to the house to write notes about the 'warbling' larks.[6] Dora, cooped up inside, coughing and hacking, tried not to feel critical of either and to keep the peace.

Edward knew Wordsworth thought his Camões translation was a waste of time. Even Edward had to admit it was unlikely to bring fame or fortune. Wordsworth thought Edward had approached his translation with such an overblown sense of his own importance that he ended up neglecting his wife. There is an irony to Wordsworth's criticisms, which is drily amusing. Wordsworth had always behaved in this fashion himself. 'I've see'd him a takkin' his family out in a string,' a local farmer would later claim, 'and niver geein' the deariest bit of notice to 'em; standin' by hissel' and stopping; behind agapin', wi' his jaws workin' the whoal time but niver no crackin' wi' 'em, nor no pleasure in 'em, – a desolate-minded man, ye kna . . . it was the potry as did it.'[7] Wordsworth was infamous for this habit of 'bumming and booin' about' the lanes while Dorothy or Mary – or later Dora – scampered along behind, transcribing for him.[8] And of course as a young man he had abandoned wife and children for weeks at a time or locked himself up with Coleridge and their 'potry' which, for many years, had been every bit as unprofitable as Edward's Camões. All these tensions over Edward's lifestyle and Dora's health were bad enough; the final straw, as far as Edward was concerned, had come when Wordsworth refused to give Dora a house he had long promised her.

Miss Fenwick, sitting at the seventy-fifth dinner party, was too astute an observer not to notice William and Mary's unhappiness. In the past few years she had taken to spending winter and spring at Rydal. While her love for the poet – almost maternal in nature – had grown during this time, so too had her frustration with him. Wordsworth's recent treatment of Dora and Edward had upset her. Wordsworth had always promised to build a house that Dora would inherit. After her marriage he changed his mind. He decided to build a house for Miss Fenwick instead – *she* had never wavered in her loyalty to him.* Miss Fenwick was shocked, and refused to countenance the injustice. Wordsworth was adamant: 'I must repeat what I have said to you before,' he told her, 'that building for Dora, situated as she is [i.e. married to Edward], I cannot think of.'⁹ If Miss Fenwick refused the house, he still would not give it to Dora. He thought that if he did (or gave her a fixed allowance), Edward would cease altogether attempting to earn a living. His belief, never quite admitted, that Dora had betrayed him by marrying, was growing rather than diminishing with time.

In a demonstration of how outraged she was by Wordsworth's decision, Miss Fenwick had, that winter, refused his invitations to return to stay at Rydal. The difficulty for Dora and Edward and everyone else was that Wordsworth was desperately sensitive and the very people he hurt found themselves rushing to try and comfort him. 'I do not love others less, because I seem to hate myself more,' he told Miss Fenwick in a letter to try and persuade her to come back.¹⁰ Sure enough, by February – a couple of months before the seventy-fifth birthday – she found herself back in Ambleside, though firmly in lodgings of her own. She did not offer to put on another grand celebration.

Wordsworth hardly pretended to enjoy his birthday dinner. He was old, dying perhaps, and his wretched son-in-law was proposing to take Dora away from him. Wordsworth thought it astonishing that so clever a man as Edward could be so obtuse. He wrote to Miss Fenwick in despair, explaining how Edward poured his energy into the wrong tasks: 'nobody could be kinder

---

* In fact the situation was more complicated than this. There was a plot of land next to Rydal Mount, purchased in 1824, which was known as 'Dora's field'. This was where Wordsworth had always said he would build the house to leave Dora. In 1844, he suggested that once the house was complete, Miss Fenwick should occupy it as a tenant on a long lease. He'd drawn up plans and building had been due to begin in August 1844. However, at the last moment, permission to build had been withdrawn. Wordsworth set about trying to find another piece of land to build a house for Miss Fenwick – even though this was explicitly against the terms of the marriage settlement and Dora would not benefit.

or more ready to serve, or more generally amiable', yet 'neither this nor anything else reconciles me to his course of life'. Miss Fenwick tried in vain to defend Dora's husband but this only irritated the Bard: 'You say he could not procure employment,' Wordsworth thundered. 'I say that he does not try.' Instead Edward persisted with his translation, 'which could not possibly turn to profit of any kind either pecuniary or intellectual'. Edward maddened Wordsworth since he believed him to have literary talents 'greatly superior to many of those who earn a handsome livelihood by literature'. Wordsworth wanted to control his son-in-law's finances and his employment, but found his intractability infuriating. 'The fact is he cannot bring himself to stoop in the direction he ought to stoop in. His pride looks + works the wrong way; and I am hopeless of a cure – but I am resolved not to minister to it, because it ought not to exist; circumstanced as he is.'[11]

It was not just that Edward could not make up his mind to earn any money. When Wordsworth had gone – out of the goodness of his heart – to help them at Flimby the year before, he had been shocked. As soon as he got home, he wrote a furious letter to Miss Fenwick about the 'unpleasantness of a domestic kind' which he had found there. 'Mr Q', he told her, 'seems incapable of reconciling his own temper according to the demands which his wife's indispositions too frequently put upon it. And it is not to be doubted', he continued, warming to his theme, 'that his way of spending his time is little suited to make the day pass pleasantly for others. He never scarcely converses with his wife or children; his papers, his books or a newspaper engross his whole time.' He was jealous and baffled. 'This surely is deplorable,' he concluded, 'yet, poor Creature, she is very fond of him; and this I suppose must happen mostly if married pairs do not positively dislike each other.'[12] How would poor Dora manage in Portugal?

Silent Mary would probably not have accepted the offer of a party even if it had been made. The past year had been wearisome, and she and her husband were both feeling their age. All either had ever wanted was the best for their children, but her entire family seemed to be crumbling. John, having married the dreadful Isabella, was being manipulated into living (vastly beyond his means) in Italy. Willy was heartbroken and ill, and now Dora was worse again. When alone, Dora would not, or could not, look after herself properly; six months before, while William and Mary went to visit relatives, Dora had gone to Rydal to look after Aunt Dorothy. (Edward had refused to accompany her.) When William and Mary returned they found Dora was frighteningly ill. She had not eaten for three days – 'unless', Wordsworth told Miss Fenwick in a state of shock, 'tea may be called so'.[13] The servants had worried and called the doctor twice to the house in one day, but he could not help. Mary, seeing her daughter white with fatigue (Dora had not slept for three days either), had tried to persuade her to go to the seaside. Eventually they had not travelled because the doctor said the trip was not advisable. And now they planned to go all the way to Portugal?

The poem Hartley had written as a present for Wordsworth on the occasion of his seventy-fifth birthday was gratefully received, but Hartley had not captured the current mood of the poet. Hartley was acutely aware of all the different unhappinesses assembled around the table. It wasn't just the Portugal idea and illness. More mundane worries depressed the Rydalians. The railways were expanding and Wordsworth had launched a vehement campaign against extending the line further and further into the Lakes, bringing day-trippers pouring into the landscape he loved. He was depressed not only by the prospect itself, but also by the criticism his own campaign received. From the Board of Trade to anonymous newspaper articles, he was accused of selfishly wishing to deny the working man what he himself enjoyed. It was more tragic than that: he realised that through his poetry he had created a tourist industry that would destroy what he had written. A correspondent of Henry Crabb Robinson's, Barron Field, was typical in wishing that Wordsworth would be quiet about the railways and 'either complete *The Recluse* or lock up his desk'.[14] But of course finishing *The Recluse* was the other great task Wordsworth knew he could not manage. This

knowledge added to the gnawing sense of failure, which was
becoming so hard for everyone to live with.

During dinner, Mary snapped; she simply could not bear the
Portugal plan. Dora buckled. She told Edward to go without her.
He capitulated without a fight, affecting indifference in an unat-
tractively sarcastic fashion. He merely commented that he thought
it selfish of Mary not to 'take more cheerfully to the only plan
likely to restore her daughter's health'. He told Dora she would
now be no use in Portugal since she'd 'be fretting because she
would feel her Mother was fretting'.[15] Once again the subtext was
clear: who loved Dora the most? Who knew Dora the best?

  Wordsworth was in no doubt a journey would be dangerous.
So, having written to all their closest friends about their plans,
Dora and Edward spent the next day writing notes to explain
they were not travelling after all. They told Sara that it was not
Dora but her parents who could not bear the thought of it and
so the 'purpose is given up'.[16] Wordsworth wrote to Moxon with
steely satisfaction. 'Mrs Q has given up the thought of going to
Portugal. Mr Q, however, is going shortly.'[17] One week later
Sara heard the trip was back on. As ever Miss Fenwick was
largely to thank. She had galvanised Dr Davy into pushing the
scheme and it reached the point where Wordsworth and Mary
were made to feel they could be signing Dora's death warrant
if they did not encourage her to go.

Late summer, 1845. On a beach where the River Douro meets
the Atlantic Ocean, Dora is riding a fine Andalucian horse. It
is early evening, and along the length of the beach, in the fading
light, fishermen are mending their nets and drying their sails.
Dora, side by side with Edward, is cantering along the shore.
The horses are 'full of fire and frolic', starting back from each
'half spent foam-crested wave' as it breaks over their hooves.
They've been there for hours and will soon leave, with reluctance, only because the lighthouse keeper has lit his flame and
they can no longer see the squat fort on the coast above. Dora's
face is flushed with excitement and exertion.[18] Her hands are

tanned. Her figure is fuller than it has been in years. Wisps of hair escape from her usual neat braids. As she brings her horse down to a trot and prepares to leave the beach, she looks like her youthful self. If Sara – one of the last people Dora had seen in London – could have seen her, she might have recognised Dora from the days when the pair rode their ponies together, in the hills between Greta and Rydal. Dora just might have been thinking of her friend as the sun set.

'A Strong Hand Grasping'

The ancient beech trees of Windsor Forest were just on the point of turning gold, the oaks were still determinedly green. Autumn was coming, but the day was crisp and fresh. Three horses made their way from Eton College towards Windsor Castle and the Great Forest. Two young girls on ponies called to one another. They'd heard the tales of the ghost of Herne's Oak, 'sometime a keeper of this Forest', who lived somewhere within it and might yet be spied in the still of night walking around his oak with 'ragg'd horns'. But there was no sign of him today. It was more a day for dryads, fawns and fairies, or for royal hunting parties and feasts. The girls trotted cheerfully, laughing and talking. Sara Coleridge, leading them, was an elegant rider with a good seat.[19] Lines were just beginning to trace their way across her face but she was no less beautiful for them.*[20]

Sara was staying with Edward Coleridge at Eton. He had generously taken on Herbert's fees after Henry's death.[21] The boy was not yet fourteen, but already Edward said he had an astonishing 'love of intellectual study'. The only criticism he made was that Herbert was not as devoted to his religion as he was to his scholarship – he had some anxiety about his nephew's preparations for the next world.[22] But then Sara and

---

* The portrait by Richmond depicts a still youthful woman, unquestionably beautiful at forty-two.

Henry had never seen eye to eye with Edward on religious topics. Sara thought him a dear man and a good one, but quite astonishingly zealous. Just now he was consumed with his project to restore the ruins of St Augustine's Abbey in Canterbury and found a Missionary College on the site. He was a key member of the Society for the Propagation of the Gospel in Foreign Parts.* It was all highly admirable, but Sara knew him to be shameless about writing to her friends and relatives to ask for their support. Several times she'd been obliged to write and explain they need not get involved on her account. Aubrey de Vere had been his most recent victim.[23] Still, if Sara had to temper her religious views in his company it was worth it for the care and love he showed her and Herbert.[24]

Whether visiting, riding or reading, Sara had regained a zest for the world which had been missing since her early years of marriage. As her daughter and niece rode ahead of her, she did not look like a woman who was brooding, but as always, a portion of her mind was running on the *Biographia Literaria*. When they turned their horses, Sara headed back to Eton in high spirits: nobody could make her laugh like Edward; he had a mortifying habit of quoting *Pretty Lessons*, but he flattered while he teased. He had recently commissioned a portrait by the great George Richmond, to capture her beauty before she descended 'still further into the vale of a certain age'.[25] Sara was enjoying her stay, but already looking forward to returning to her mother and Nuck and the *Biographia Literaria* at Chester Place. When the time came to turn the horses back, the three women, riding side-saddle as decorum decreed, made an elegant tableau in their tight-waisted jackets and tall hats.

---

* Edward Coleridge remained, essentially, a High Church Anglican (Sara is probably best described as a Broad Church Liberal). The missionary movements needed and gained support from across the Protestant spectrum, including organisations like the Evangelical Church Missionary Society. It was not so much that Sara disagreed with his motives, but she questioned, slightly, his means of achieving them.

Four days later, on 24 September, the date she was due to leave Eton, Derwent arrived unexpectedly. He had driven as fast as he could from St Mark's College in Fulham. Before Sara could exclaim at his presence, he sat her down and quietly broke the news that their mother had died. But Derwent must be mistaken – Sara had received a letter that very morning in which Mrs STC had told her daughter not to worry about her: 'Now, dearest Child, make yourself easy about me . . . and pray do not think of coming home a minute sooner than you first intended.'[26] Derwent gently told his sister that Mrs STC had been woken as usual by Nuck, who had helped her out of bed. The two old women took a couple of steps together and then Mrs STC stumbled and collapsed. She died almost immediately. She had just turned seventy-five. Writing to break the news to Hartley in Ambleside, Derwent's wife said: 'we could not have chosen a calmer end – no pain – not bed-ridden – a thing she so much dreaded – and her faculties clear to the very last!'[27] It did little to assuage Sara's grief – or her guilt. She had been away for only two weeks all year, and yet her mother had died without her.

Sara had lived with Mrs STC for her entire life except for her first year of marriage, when their house had been too small. A world without her seemed impossible. A sombre party made its way back to London. Once again, everyone else, including Sara herself, predicted a relapse to her former hysterical illness. But once again, they were wrong. First, she had to deal with a family crisis. Hartley was proposing to come to London for the funeral and Sara was convinced this would be a disaster; he would get drunk and, besides, the Wordsworths had long ago made her promise *'never to induce* him to come to London'.[28] She wrote to Dora in Portugal – despite knowing the letter could not possibly arrive in time. She trusted Dora's judgement above all others where Hartley was concerned. Then she wrote to the Wordsworths to ask their advice. She managed her brother diplomatically; he did not come, and the funeral passed off as well as anyone could have hoped. Mrs STC was buried beside her husband in Highgate. Sara was, of course, 'very sad and low' and not a little morbid. To her diary (now rechristened a

'Mourning Book'), she predicted it would not be long 'ere the hand that writes this word will be mouldering beside the mortal spoils of my parents and my husband in that vault at Highgate'. Her sadness took on a pining quality. All this thinking of Hartley and the Wordsworths set her longing for her 'native vale'.[29] With her mother and her husband dead, the Wordsworths and Rydal were the closest thing she had to parents and home.

Once the funeral was over, two key things staved off a return to illness. First and most important was the *Biographia Literaria*. Sara agreed to show the introduction to her cousin John Taylor Coleridge and altered it according to his suggestions, but she refused to share it with Derwent. 'I think you may feel confident now that there will not be anything disgraceful in it,' she told him firmly. She couldn't face another round of changes: if she showed it to everyone the whole thing would get blacked out. If anything was wrong with the book it was her name, not her father's and not Derwent's, which would be criticised. Besides, she said in an attempt to appease him, she didn't want to take up too much of his time – he was in mourning for the loss of a baby boy. 'I should be glad to hear that from you that I may print it at once without further criticism', she wrote in a firm hand and then underlined the whole sentence.[30] By October 1845 she had finished the first volume and thought the second should give 'comparatively little trouble'.[31]

Sara had been wondering what to do about some of the more personal charges made against Coleridge – in particular, his dependency on opium. She had not alluded to the habit in her introduction – it did not seem the right place – but she had considered doing so in a biographical essay which she could place at the end of the *Biographia Literaria*. The death of her mother liberated Sara. Mrs STC's loyalty to her husband had remained staunch to the end. Yet for Sara to be truly honest about her father was to address some uncomfortable home truths.

Sara did not deny charges of opium-taking and chaotic living, but still managed to produce a subtle and brilliant portrait of a great – if flawed – man. Other friends and relations would have preferred a whitewashed version be presented to the public, but Sara knew that would be foolish. Instead, her arguments were complicated, biased and occasionally contradictory, but they could not be written off. She had never believed in lying or dissembling and addressed the truth directly: whether it was talking about her own hysteria and opium use or her father's erratic lifestyle. 'If my father sought more from opium than the mere absence of pain,' she wrote in her essay, 'I feel assured that it was not luxurious sensations of the glowing phantasma-goria or passive dreams; but that the power of the medicine might keep down the agitations of his nervous system, like a strong hand grasping the strings of some shattered lyre – that he might once more lightly flash along.'[32] She told Henry Crabb Robinson she wanted to 'make it more & more clearly appear that he was not the *idle man* that he has been represented'.[33]

The second thing – or rather person – to keep her going was Aubrey de Vere. The two had grown very close after Henry's death and it would be easy, reading their letters, to imagine they had formed a romantic relationship. They talked and talked – on paper and in person – about religion, politics and literature and were in touch almost every day. When Sara struggled with her father's thoughts, she wrote to tell Aubrey about it and he was sympathetic and helpful. One result of their closeness was that Sara began to write poetry again. One of her poems, written in 1845, is particularly important. Entitled 'For my Father on his lines called "Work Without Hope"', it is in fact a poem to her husband and about herself. It begins:

> Father, no amaranths e'er shall wreathe my brow,–
> Enough that round thy grave they flourish now:–
> But Love mid' my young locks his roses braided,
> And what car'd I for flowr's of deeper bloom?
> Those too seem deathless – here they never faded,
> But, drench'd and shatter'd dropp'd into the tomb.
>
> Ne'er was it mine t'unlock rich founts of song,
> As thine it was ere Time had done thee wrong:
> But ah! how blest I wander'd nigh the stream,
> Whilst Love, fond guardian, hover'd o'er me still!

It ends, with more optimism than STC's poem, by concluding:

> Nought can for me those golden gleams renew,
> The roses of my shattered wreath repair.
> Yet Hope still lives and oft, to objects fair
> In prospect pointing, bids me still pursue
> My humble tasks: – I list – but backward cast
> Fain would mine eye discern the Future in the Past.[34]

The poem is Sara's epitaph to her husband and a way of accepting, without bitterness or self-deprecation, that although she would never live up to her father's genius as a writer, she had nonetheless created her own legacy. Unlike her father, she had built a loving marriage and stable family. It is a calm and mature poem; a song for the ordinary life, no less noble than the great. And, ironically, it's the first of her poems to assure her at least a minor place in literary history in her own right.

CHAPTER 20

'SHE SHINES WITH A LIGHT OF HER OWN'

1847

'My Father was Faultless in this Line'

Sara was wrong to say that completing the second volume of *Biographia Literaria* would give little trouble, but by the start of 1847, nearly two years after her amaranths poem, she could finally say she had almost finished. She now had just one task left: a favour to ask Wordsworth. Would he agree to have the book dedicated to him? His reply was not overwhelmingly enthusiastic: 'I shall be pleased to have my name united with your dear Father's in the way you suggest,' he told her, but, he continued, 'Some regret I feel that I have not seen you previous to preparing the Edit. of the B.L. – as I might probably have mentioned a few particulars which you might have deemed worthy of being recorded, and corrected others in which you may have been innocently misled.'[1] This was irritating. Sara *had* tried to get Wordsworth to engage in the editorial process, but it was too late now – the book was practically at the printers. Still, he'd agreed and, apart from anything else, his endorsement would bolster the book's reception. She humbly noted his corrections to the text of the proposed dedication and accepted his ungracious response.

By this time Sara was thoroughly exhausted. She never wanted to see another proof-sheet in her life, and vowed she would never 'scribble or search in books' ever again.[2] So when,

in March, Miss Fenwick asked her and Edy to come and stay
at a house she had taken in Bath, Sara was delighted to get out
of London. Miss Fenwick, who was in the West Country caring
for relatives, had already persuaded the Wordsworths to come
and visit. Sara had some fears about the journey itself and worried
there might be some final *Biographia Literaria* checks to make,
but on balance 'the opportunity of being once more under the
same roof with my dear old friends' simply could not be passed
up.³ Sara had been following the sad breakdown of John
Wordsworth's marriage to Isabella. She feared it would be
preying heavily on his father's mind. Moreover, Edy was delirious
with excitement at the idea of visiting both fashionable Bath
and the famous poet. Now Brunel had finished his Great Western
Line, the express train to Bath took just two hours and twenty
minutes from Paddington Station.* Pickering could have the
title-sheet sent to Bath if necessary. She accepted.

On seeing the white-haired Wordsworths, Sara was initially
most shocked by Mary: she appeared to have aged dramatically.
Sara reported sadly to Hartley that her face was pale, 'sunken
and insubstantiative; the features seem all falling together'.⁴ This
made her even more concerned about Mary's extreme asceticism.
Despite her frailty Mary was proposing to fast on every holy
day over Easter and it was only Wordsworth putting his foot
down and saying – in the Lakeland voice that took Sara straight
back to her childhood – 'Doont be so foolish, Mary' that made
her give up the idea. Dora had certainly learned her self-restraint
and self-denial from her mother. Wordsworth seemed to have
fared better. His physical health was impressive, and at nearly
eighty it was unsurprising if he tired in the evening.

Within a day or two, however, Sara realised that her first
impressions had been mistaken. Mary was as sharp and animated
as ever, but Wordsworth was 'dozy and dull during a great part
of the day'. Sara sensed that he 'seems rather to recontinue
his former self, and repeat by habit what he used to think and

---

* The London to Bristol line had been completed six years earlier in 1841.
Sara took the 9.50 from Paddington and arrived at Bath at 12.10.

feel, than to think anything new'.[5] He was at his best in the mornings. Then he and Sara would go for long walks together – unaccompanied, he tended to get bewildered and lost – to discuss poetry.[6] On these walks she could still see flashes of the younger man, but only 'as if he remembered what he used to think and say'. By the afternoon he was 'the faintest possible shadow of his former self'.[7]

Despite this, she still minded desperately what he thought of her. She was touched he treated her 'parentally', pleased when he endorsed her opinion, and frustrated when he would not engage in her arguments. She wrote to tell Nuck: 'Mr W quite behaves as if he considered me indeed his child as he always calls me.'[8] Sara wanted to talk theology and poetry; Wordsworth did not. She suspected that when she proffered an opinion, he agreed with her because it was easier than arguing. He preferred to gossip about domestic matters – 'the concerns and characters of the maids, wives and widows'. Sara wanted to talk about 'the state of the nation, or the people of history', or more particularly the situation in Ireland.'[9] It was an expression of discontent movingly close to that of the seven-year-old Sara who, all those years before, had longed for Wordsworth, STC and de Quincey to stop 'discussing the affairs of the nation, as if it all came home to their business & bosoms' and play with her and Dora.[10]

Part of the reason for Sara's assessment of Wordsworth's mind was nothing to do with his age but the fact he was distracted by other concerns. His professional problem was that Prince Albert had half-bullied and half-flattered him into promising to write an Installation Ode. The Queen's Consort was becoming Chancellor of Cambridge, and Wordsworth was already regretting that he had agreed. He had always hated producing poetry on demand; now he saw himself as in retirement, so he wrote nothing but fretted about the Ode. Sara realised it was an 'incubus' upon him and encouraged him to give it up. Eventually Mary, Sara and Miss Fenwick persuaded him to write and ask Edward Quillinan to produce a first draft.

Greater yet than the demands of poetry was the problem of his children: John and Dora in particular. Having spent a little over a year abroad, Dora and Edward had returned to England in June 1846. Sara knew her friend had come home, in part, because of John. Not only was his marriage disintegrating, but one of his six children – four-year-old Edward – had died while the Quillinans were in Portugal. Isabella and John had returned to England from Italy in March 1846, but Isabella had since gone to live on the south coast. John, with his five surviving children, returned to his newly built – and as yet barely habitable – rectory in Brigham. As a result, he had spent almost as much time at Rydal as at Brigham. Dora wished that John had made his rectory more comfortable. She knew it would not have kept Isabella there, but at least 'she would have had no good reason to throw in *his face* for leaving her home'.[11]

But it was Dora, not John, who Wordsworth talked about with anxiety to Sara. Dora was just then at Rydal, with Edward, looking after Aunt Dorothy. Separated from his daughter, Wordsworth worked himself into a frenzy about her health. Repeatedly he told Sara that Dora was suffering from a troubling cold – she'd gone to help her newly-wed brother, Willy, set up home before Christmas and had caught an infection. Sara did not take Wordsworth's concerns too seriously. She had been one of the first to see Dora on her return from Portugal. They met at a dinner given by their mutual friend Mrs Hoare to welcome the Quillinans home, and Sara was amazed by her friend's appearance: 'Dora looks like a rose', she exclaimed with delight in a letter to Crabb Robinson.[12] Dora was stronger and healthier than she had been since their teenage years. She had colour in her cheeks, her skin was tanned, and though still very thin, she no longer looked emaciated. Sara was able to see the bones in Dora's neck, but not the actual muscles, which had been so frighteningly visible when she left.[13] Her friend had clearly been invigorated by her time abroad. Yet despite this, Wordsworth could not relax. He was convinced she was 'not stouter in appearance' than when she had left.[14] Sara grew increasingly disappointed with the old man; she found his worrying about Dora neurotic, and his pomposity irritating.

Worse still, Sara realised with sadness that Wordsworth was

not only worried about Dora but furious with her. He was still reeling from the shock of discovering his daughter was going to publish a book. It had begun with a journal: when Dora returned to Ambleside from Portugal, Wordsworth was pleased to see she had kept a diary. It was what travelling ladies ought to do. He fondly indulged her scribbling and editing. Sometimes she read him extracts. Yet, to Wordsworth's consternation, Moxon had somehow got wind of the existence of Dora's journal and had written to ask Wordsworth whether, in his opinion, it was publishable. Wordsworth had not yet read the complete journal, but said it was not. 'Women observe many particulars', he mused to Moxon, 'of manners and opinions which are apt to escape the notice of the Lords of Creation', yet the journal was too insignificant to be made public.[15] But Dora wrote, secretly, to Moxon and one October morning, Wordsworth was astonished to receive a letter from his publisher discussing terms for the forthcoming publication.

Wordsworth dissembled frantically, telling Moxon: 'We were not aware that Mrs Q. had actually made up her mind to publish her journal.' He thought Moxon must be offering to do it as a favour to him and made it clear he would not take it as a kindness. 'Please do not speak of this publication . . . in connection with her. Her mother and I don't like it, and *she* would shrink from notoriety.'[16] Besides, he argued, surely Moxon would lose money?

Eventually he resigned himself to what he could not prevent. Since Moxon had 'induced' Dora to prepare the book, Wordsworth insisted it at least be anonymous. He thought Dora had not had enough chance to travel in Portugal to make the book worthwhile. In this opinion, Edward supported him; it was a 'mere clever journal', which could never appeal because the English had so little interest in Portugal. Edward had tried to help beef it up by adding in a whole lot of history, but Wordsworth thought his insertions made it worse rather than better. Wordsworth's judgement was correct. Edward's historical additions are heavy, dull and poorly integrated into what otherwise would be a light and energetic journal.

Sara had not yet read the book, so could not comment on the content, but she utterly approved of the concept and thus disapproved of Wordsworth's response. She was infuriated that 'Mrs W. exclaimed when Mr W spoke of Dora's book as if she could not bear such publicity'.[17] Sara knew how brave Dora was being: 'Mrs Wordsworth has all her life wished her daughter to be above both marriage & authorship', she told Crabb Robinson with scorn, '& finds it hard to submit to these vulgarities on her behalf in this stage of her life career.' Sara, on the other hand, was proud of her friend: 'Dora deserves success & happiness . . . in every stage of it; I admire her and love her for *her own* sake, and consider it a great proof of sterling merit in her, that she shines with a light of her own & is more than a mere portion of parental radiance.'[18] It might just as well have been a statement of her own ambition.

Sara must have realised that Wordsworth objected as much to Sara's *Biographia Literaria* as he did to Dora's journal and this merely strengthened her resolve to improve Coleridge's reputation relative to his. Wordsworth remained convinced she was making a mistake. 'I rather tremble for the Notice she is engaged in giving of her father's life,' he told Miss Fenwick. He thought 'her opportunities of knowing any thing about him were too small for such an Employment, which would be difficult to manage for anyone'.[19] The year before, Sara had written to ask Wordsworth for help identifying some STC quotations. He had reported to Crabb Robinson, with cruel condescension, that 'If Mrs C – had been a reader of Milton she would have known . . . [where one quote came from] and if of Akenside, she would not have been ignorant . . . [of another].'[20] Her entire project was ill-conceived and would be biased. He implied Sara was arrogant to believe she could manage it and shameless to court the attention. He did not think much of her arguments and he thought even less of her being the one to make them.

It was around this time that Sara began working on an essay entitled 'Reasons for not placing "Laodamia" in the First Rank of Wordsworthian poetry'.[21] The essay was perhaps a response to her disillusionment with Wordsworth at Bath and inspired by Dora's act of rebellion. She had never been so critical of Wordsworth, and it was yet another measure of her growing confidence. Sara's central argument was that when Wordsworth tried to invent or empathise he was far less imaginative than when he wrote about people and places he observed. In 'Laodamia' he retells the dramatic tale of a woman who loved her husband so much she could not accept his death, and ultimately died of misery. Sara felt it lacked conviction. Many critics agree it has a certain artificiality.[22] But Sara's particular analysis is interesting; she believed the reason Wordsworth could not inhabit the mind of Laodamia was because he 'was never *in love*, properly speaking'. She argued that because he could not 'sympathise with a certain class of feelings in consequence – he cannot realise them' in poetry.

Sara's literary opinion may be justifiable, but her supporting evidence hints at something more complicated than pure scholarly criticism. She never published the essay but sent it to Aubrey de Vere – an interesting gesture in itself. He disagreed about the poem, so, to persuade him, Sara explained that Wordsworth used to 'boast' of never having been in love 'in [the] presence of his wife, who smiled angelically, delighted that her husband should be superior to common men'.* Sara thought as a result that in his love poems Wordsworth 'stalks along with portentous stride & then stamps his great wooden foot down, in the clumsiest manner imaginable'. In contrast, 'My father', she told de Vere, 'was perfect in this line – faultless as Shakespeare, in his representation of women, & the relationship of men to women.'[23] It was essential that people should recognise this truth about Wordsworth and Coleridge – hence the need for her edition of the *Biographia Literaria*.

Sara stayed in Bath for almost a month – a week or so longer than Wordsworth and Mary – and it was 15 April before

---

* Of course there were many other reasons why Wordsworth might have smiled at his wife, not least the fact that he was deeply in love with her as his letters show. Sara had clearly misinterpreted, as a young woman, a conversation between husband and wife.

she followed them to London. On the late-running train home she mused with nostalgic pleasure on her time in Bath. 'I shall ever remember [the visit] with deep interest + satisfaction,' she told Miss Fenwick, 'and not the less of interest because it brought many a sad thought to mind, both remembrance of what is past from our eyes and anxiety reflecting what is left us of the world's best blessings: our friends and the well being of friends.'[24]

When she reached London, Sara saw the Wordsworths on several more occasions. Wordsworth had received his copy of Dora's journal, but said he had not yet found time to do more than 'glance' at it. This horribly neglectful response was exactly the one Sara feared for her own book. Publication was a gamble in which her reputation was bundled up with her father's – and, to some extent, with her husband's – and she was desperate for it to succeed. She had shown very few people the final draft of her long introduction and was nervous. On 26 April Sara finally received the first copies of the *Biographia Literaria* printed in two cloth-bound volumes. Flicking anxiously through it, she found various printing mistakes, which infuriated her, and she sat down to correct them in copies she wanted to send to friends and relatives.

Wordsworth, the book's dedicatee, received his copy on the same day. At ten that morning he was sitting for a talented young artist called Leonard Wyon in the cloisters of Westminster Abbey. Wyon, who was employed by the London Mint, was drawing his profile. It was a second study for what would eventually become a medallion. The subject, never keen on sitting still and quiet, had asked Henry Crabb Robinson to come and keep him company. As Wyon worked and Crabb Robinson chatted, Wordsworth was called away to read a letter. Crabb Robinson and Wyon waited – but Wordsworth had gone. The letter was from Edward; three days before, the Ambleside surgeon Dr Fell had examined Dora and expressed deep concern – for the first time he talked in terms of fearing for her life. Wordsworth and Mary raced for home. By the time Sara heard they had left, they were halfway to Rydal.

'The Sea is Like Music'

A narrow bed, sunlight streaming through the window, shadows playing across white walls. A smell of sickness. Dora Quillinan, emaciated, lies propped up in bed in her childhood bedroom at Rydal, surrounded by cushions carefully arranged to alleviate the pressure of bedsores. She's not asleep, but her eyes are closed. Dr Gough, the second doctor in as many days, has finished examining her. She hears him make his way along the corridor and down the stairs, which creak slightly. He crosses the hall and gives his verdict to Edward in hushed tones.

Dora closes her eyes and returns to Portugal.

From the verandah of her brother-in-law John Quillinan's house at Foz, she watches fearless open boats tossing with their brave fishermen among the waves. The sun sinks into the ocean, a ball of fire; the moon shines brightly through the branches of a fig tree. The last sunlight is reflected by clouds to the east and thrown back upon the sea as the waves roll in crested with pink foam. The grandeur of the sea is like music.*

Dawn. She lies in bed beneath a print of her father placed there by John Q. – who has given up his bedroom for her and Edward. She sips a hot cup of chocolate while a maid prepares a salt bath.

She sits with her journal and her sketchbook on the verandah. Edward, John and Rotha will be with her in a moment for breakfast. She is watching Camilla, the *aquadeira* (water-carrier), a tall, handsome young woman who has just arrived in the garden below, bearing on her head all the goods the house will need that day except coal. Camilla left the house at four that morning and has already walked six miles to the nearest village and back. She joins the other servants for a large and noisy breakfast. The working women in Portugal are like another species. They do not expect to be treated differently to the men; indeed, they

---

* This section draws heavily on the text of Dora's Portuguese journal as well as the letters she wrote home. Slight liberties with the text have been taken to piece together her various descriptions, but the words and images are Dora's.

assume they will have to work harder. Even before the plates
are cleared, Camilla is off again. This time to the fountain to
collect water for the day. Dora scribbles in her journal. A servant
brings her breakfast: an egg, a little milk, a couple of Carr's
water biscuits sent by her mother.

She watches the bathers on the beach below. Portuguese men
and women with flashing black eyes lead overdressed tourists
into the sea from decorous changing huts. The bathers emerge
gasping and spluttering, full of sea-water, clutching at their guides.
A man in a scarlet hat bobs seriously up and down in a rock
pool, cork boards attached to his hands, surrounded by a gaggle
of fascinated children. Dora laughs and points them out to John
and Edward.

She sits with John Q. while Edward, inside, labours away at
his Camões. John's brow is furrowed as he explains his worries.
He *is* in love with the girl he is engaged to, truly he is, but not
certain he should actually marry her. Dora, who has the measure
of her charming, flirtatious, irresponsible and impulsive brother-
in-law, is certain he should not. She is not sure he is ready to
make anyone a good husband, but particularly not the pretty
twenty-year-old Portuguese girl he has chosen. She holds her
own counsel and listens as John talks himself backwards and
forwards in the heat of the Portuguese morning. She eats
breakfast.

Early evening. The Quillinans are out riding: she on a
donkey, he walking beside with the donkey man. They take the
road towards Oporto. The Douro runs beside them and women
and children carry pitchers to the water and *lavandeiras* wash
linen in it, rubbing and beating its life out on the hard stones,
and singing. Old-fashioned Douro boats, pointed at each end
like Chinese shoes, bob up and down. The ascent grows steep,
the donkey labours, Edward smiles. Men and boys are driving
carts drawn by oxen, heavy wooden wheels creaking. Cottages
line the route with children darting in and out of doors like
rabbits, racing across the road, without a rag of covering, to
plunge headlong into the water. There they play for hours like
water-spaniels, laughing when half a dozen of them get knocked

down by a great wave, which carries them high up on the shore and leaves them there, sprawling on the sand, until a second wave comes to make more sport. Fish girls and fruit girls with baskets on their heads shout cheerful greetings to the foreign couple.

At Rydal, Dora shifts uncomfortably in her bed and dreams.

She is in a boat. She, Edward, Jemima and a friend are on an adventure. For over a week they have been travelling about the countryside, staying in small inns and riding long distances every day. Today is different. Today they are floating down the River Lima, a cool breeze accompanying them. The sail is arranged over the centre of the boat, as a covered awning, and under it are cushions for Dora and Jemima and a basket laden with cakes and wine. The riverbed is soft and barely a foot beneath them, so from time to time, despite their boat's shallow hull, the men are obliged to dig channels for it to pass through. Dora drifts. On the shore she can see her horse and their mules wending their way along the riverside. She makes notes in her journal, describing the oaks and olive trees, the chapels and stone cottages, and she and Jemima and Edward chat lazily as the world passes them by. Nightingales sing and cuckoos call to one another.

They pass a group of men spear-fishing and soon afterwards she sits up with surprise to see men carrying baskets on their heads as they walk across the river; she has come to regard this as women's work in Portugal. Blue, green and gold dragon-flies hover. The surface of the water is myriads of diamonds, dancing.

Evening. The light is beginning to fade. They've been riding since early afternoon in open countryside along sandy roads but now must pass into a thick pinewood forest. Bats flutter above them; it becomes increasingly hard to pick out the path: the stars are the only light in a moonless sky. The inn, when they finally reach it, is detestable. But Edward knows someone and a party is arranged in their honour. There is singing, guitar-playing and dancing. At midnight Dora pleads fatigue and heads to bed. After weeks in flea-ridden inn beds, she has a mattress which, though hard, is clean, and she sleeps as well as if it had been stuffed with down. Her body is tired and sore.

At Rydal, Dora wakes and hears Edward downstairs.

Winter. They leave the villa for John Q.'s town house in Oporto. Forty girls, laughing and joking, carry the furniture, food and clothes to the town. Dora and Edward travel by horse through Oporto's camellia and orange groves, and the markets of Via Flores – Oporto's answer to Bond Street.*

The hauntingly beautiful fourteen-year-old *aquadeira* at a fountain in Oliveira. The troop of bakers at Avintes rowing bread across the river, singing as they go. Dora, dressed in her finest clothes, rides a donkey to the opera. Her mother would laugh to see her.

Long walks with Edward. Wild flowers like nothing she has seen before but as they turn down narrow lanes – rich in lichens, mosses, ferns, rocks, fine old pollard oak trees – she is reminded of home. Under the simple stone bridge a bunch of primroses grow on the river's edge reflecting themselves in the glassy pool. They ford a brook where a blind man feels his way with his long stick. Far away, a range of purple and blue hills. Primroses make her long for Rydal.

Unhappy letters from John and Isabella.

So home. Not by sea this time but overland. One last adventure. Wordsworth sends them £20 as a contribution. Instead of heading north, they make their way by sea further down the coast of Portugal and from there they will turn inland into Spain. They leave Oporto in spring, ahead of them Sintra, Cordoba, the Alhambra, southern France, Paris, the Channel and Grasmere.

She is in the gardens and groves of Sintra; she and Edward have gone for an evening walk in the lanes and find themselves surrounded by hundreds of goats and kids. The landscape

---

* Dora always uses the word 'camilla' but was presumably referring to the camellia. Camellias were popular with the fashionable Portuguese from the first half of the nineteenth century. They were imported from Asia and cultivated with care in the gardens of the wealthy (see Helena Attlee, *The Gardens of Portugal*, London: Frances Lincoln, 2008, p. 27).

resembles her beloved Easedale – with its crags, woods, water and freshness – but the arabesque castle in the town belongs to dreams.

At Rydal, Dora turns in her bed, shivers and draws the covers closer.

In Seville they go to a dance which reminds her of the balls of Penrith. Courteous bands of black-robed monks. The horror of a bullfight. At Gibraltar's market Jews, Moors, Christians and Turks all contrive to cheat one another; the Moors are the most gentlemanly looking.

The rock of Gibraltar reminds her of Nab Scar, just under the screes, on the mountain road to Grasmere. They meet monkeys. Waiting for the carriage to depart one day, she begins to draw the outline of the Rock to while away the time. An officious redcoat appears: 'Pray, ma'am, have you a permit from the governor to sketch?'

She lingers in the enchanted palace of Alhambra: cool marble floors, murmuring fountains and walls covered with the finest lacework. From the fairy windows of the Sala de las Dos Hermanos, she can hear children clicking castanets and night-ingales singing. The air is perfumed with cypress, aloe and prickly pear.

When Dora and Edward reached England in June 1846, the smells were of new beginnings: drying paint and carpenter's dust. Soon after arriving, they saw Miss Fenwick and Sara, and then they travelled north. By the end of July they were installed in their new home, Loughrigg Holme Cottage in Ambleside. They enjoyed the pun: Loughrigg Holme – their home. Wordsworth had agreed to pay the rent. The house had been extended while they were away, and Crabb Robinson had paid for smart book-shelves to be put up as a belated wedding present. Dora went to visit a beloved cousin who was dying of consumption, and her brother Willy. Jemima and Rotha with their dresses and mirrors and hairbrushes came to visit. Dora and Edward wrote to Sara – whom they addressed as 'the essence of a brick' – to tell her the gossip: Willy was about to be married, but Sara was sworn to secrecy on the details. They told her about their new donkey, Dr Dabble, 'the vicar of Bray' for he would shout all night long. In the evenings, the Quillinans dined together. Every day they visited Rydal Mount, just a short walk away. They spent long hours writing about Portugal. Edward discussed its poetry and history and Dora span a tale about horseback adventures and romantic landscapes. Eventually they began to thread the strands of their writing together.

In February 1847, Wordsworth and Mary went on their visit to Miss Fenwick and Sara in Bath. Edward and Dora decided Loughrigg Holme needed repainting. Dora had not managed to shake off her cold, which had become a painful cough, and Edward would not hear of her staying in the house while the work was being done, so they went to stay at Rydal with poor mad Aunt Dorothy. Once again Dora was thin and weak. Now her tan had faded, she looked as much of an invalid as before their travels. Edward wrote to Miss Fenwick to tell her about Dora's troublesome cough and regular fevers. He reassured her that the doctors did not foresee any danger, but already, he confessed, he was steeling himself for battle. 'I shall hardly dare to let Dora remain here through the next winter,' he told Miss Fenwick but asked her not to mention it to Wordsworth.[25]

CHAPTER 21

'STRONG FLIGHT HOME AGAIN'

1847

Sara's *Biographia Literaria* reached the bookshops in April 1847. It is a breathtakingly accomplished volume. Modern critics agree, 'she produced what are still the standard versions for the purposes of editing *Biographia Literaria*, and she remains the Germanist of record for subsequent scholars'.[1] In her own time, *Biographia Literaria*'s reception was mixed. Sara was not certain how her own brothers would react, but she knew it was unlikely that Henry's brothers, John Taylor Coleridge and Edward Coleridge, would entirely approve. John was, as she feared, worried. He had never wanted her to write the introduction in the first place. He thought it made her look arrogant and before publication had suggested that if she *insisted* on publishing, then she should make her tone more self-effacing by inserting apologies and deferential clauses throughout her text. He made various other small pedantic points about content, which Sara was happy to address, but against his main criticism she made a characteristically sharp defence. 'If I was justified in attempting to defend my father's opinions at all, what could have been the use of perpetually interspersing modest <u>phrases</u>, which after all mean very little – for the arrogance – if such there be – counts in doing the thing at all – not in doing it, as I have done it, plainly and straight-forwardly.'[2] Derwent was still disgruntled not to have been consulted, but Hartley was full of sheepish admiration: he had failed to provide any text despite promising to contribute.

Later, when de Quincey read her introduction, he changed his mind about Coleridge's plagiarisms. So much so that he added notes to an essay about Coleridge in his own literary reminiscences. The book by 'Coleridge's admirable daughter', he said, 'placed this whole subject in a new light'. The brilliance of her defence was that, wherever the 'plagiarism was undeniable, she allowed it; whilst palliating its faultiness by showing the circumstances under which it rose'. She made him look at Coleridge's writing differently; she had revealed his spirit.* De Quincey reiterated her arguments: other people had attributed ideas and arguments to Coleridge that he never himself claimed. Coleridge did not believe thoughts belonged to individuals. De Quincey now acknowledged the truth as Sara had stated it: 'if he took he gave. Continually he fancied other men's thoughts his own but such were the confusions of his memory that continually and with even greater liberality he ascribed his own thoughts to others.'³ Even Ferrier, in a private letter towards the end of his life, softened his verdict on STC's plagiarisms: they 'should rather be attributed to forgetfulness than wilful plagiarism'.⁴ But there is no evidence Sara knew of the impression her work had made on the two people who had most goaded her into it.

As Sara had predicted, most people had no idea how much labour it had cost her, or how important the task would prove to be in the construction of Coleridge's afterlife. It was 'a filial phenomenon; nobody will thank me for it, and no one will know or see a twentieth part of it. But I have done the thing *con amore*, for my father's book.'⁵ The *North British Review*, damning with faint praise, commented that her book contained a 'considerable number of corrections' for a new edition, and also several MS notes . . . one or two of them to us of much interest'.⁶ Worse, the *Edinburgh Review* wrote of the *Biographia Literaria* (in parenthesis while discussing something else): 'we are glad to have a new edition, though we should have preferred it less burdened with commentary'.⁷ Other than that, it was barely noticed at all.

---

* De Quincey had genuinely never intended the endless Coleridge vilification which he had unleashed in the media. He never doubted Coleridge was a genius and he always tried, however cackhandedly, to defend him.

Sara tried to teach herself to be philosophical. Whilst writing the *Biographia* she had addressed a poem to de Vere called 'Toil not for burnished gold that poorly shines'. Strive not after 'Honour's purple robe' or 'treacherous fame', she counselled. The important thing was to avoid 'unfilled leisure': the 'worst load' that life can lay upon a 'mortal breast'.[8] Despite her poem, Sara would have liked a little gold – or recognition – but she was not surprised the book did not get the reception it deserved at the time. However, her reputation amongst Coleridge academics has been growing ever since.*

Meanwhile, Sara was pleased when Dora's book on Portugal appeared. Dora's circle was just as ambivalent about publication as Sara's had been. Wordsworth had always been against the idea of publishing at all: 'I don't like it,' he pronounced.[9] Edward believed no one would read Dora's book unless it received a push from a leading journal; but feared any leading journal would slate it. Only Miss Fenwick was wholly supportive and convinced the book would be of interest to the general public.[10] She was correct. The book was surprisingly widely and positively reviewed. There was no guidebook to Portugal, but there was a growing awareness that it was a country people knew too little about. By the time the reviews appeared, however, they hardly mattered. Dora was dying.

Edward wrote to Sara. 'Everything that I love seems dearer to me now that I am going to lose the dearest of all,' he explained. 'Ever since I first saw you . . . you have been one of the friends whom I have most cherished as one of the earliest and most constant friends of Dora. I therefore write to you though I have little heart to write to anyone – You know', he continued, 'by your own sorrow what mine is; and what it must be from this time forth.'[11] In Bath, Sara had been sure Wordsworth's concern was unwarranted; he was being his normal, over-protective self.

---

* In 2010, Alan Vardy's excellent *Constructing Coleridge: The Posthumous Life of the Author* did much to reinstate Sara's contribution to Coleridgean scholarship. Peter Swaab's recent book, *The Regions of Sara Coleridge's Thought, Selected Literary Criticism* (2012), has raised her profile still further.

'I was not prepared for this,' she told Miss Fenwick in shock.[12] She felt her life in London ought to change, but still income tax forms had to be wrestled with, calls made, cards left, meals organised, lessons supervised and servants managed. Yet the entire time, as she told Hartley, all she could think about was Dora. Always the greater part of her mind was in her oldest friend's bedroom, imagining.

When the Wordsworths had left London without even saying goodbye to Crabb Robinson, they had rushed home. Thirty-six hours later, having travelled without stopping, they were greeted by a pale-faced Edward. Dora was in a pitiful state, though of course pity was the last thing she wanted. Dr Fell had given Edward a bleak report, so Wordsworth sent for a second opinion from a Kendal physician, Dr Gough. His assessment was worse. Having examined Dora, Gough went downstairs to talk to her anxious husband and parents. He could give them no hope. It was, he said, 'a question only of time'; they should let people know. Wordsworth could not think of writing to anyone.

For the first couple of weeks after Dr Fell and Dr Gough delivered their verdicts, Edward, Wordsworth and Mary tried, with Dora, to act as though nothing had changed. Sara, who they kept up to date in London, thought this plan was best. 'I am relieved to think that <u>she</u> does not yet think her case hopeless,' she told Edward, 'I have a strong opinion on this point.'[13] It would be rash and unfair to deprive Dora of all hope. So her family kept up an energetic performance. Edward sat in her room and read selections of his letters to their friends. 'I told Dora just now cheerfully "I have not written to Mr Robinson for a long time, I think I shall write today" – "Do, do," she answered and give him my love".' Edward put the dreadful news in a part of the letter he did not read aloud.[14] But despite the charade, Dora knew. Less than two weeks after Dr Gough's visit, while Edward sat with her, she asked questions which he 'answered faithfully; so she was put in full possession of the truth'.[15]

Dora had returned from Portugal just in time to see her thirty-one-year-old cousin John, who was dying of consumption.

John, son of her father's brother Richard, had been living in Keswick for several years. Dora and the rest of her family took it in turns to nurse him while his body wasted away. They fetched him a waterbed and made him as comfortable as they could until his painful death on 18 August 1846. The process had taken a toll on Dora. It was by way of a more cheerful occupation, that in October she had gone to Briscoe, near Carlisle, to visit her brother Willy. She had helped him to chose furniture and set up home before his wedding. When she returned, she had caught a cold which she had not managed to shake off. Her family feared either the nursing or the visit to John's unfurnished house was the cause of her decline. Either way, Keswick John had shown her what to expect.

Dora made preparing for death a conscious activity. She and Mary shared a faith that grew stronger and bound them together. Mary felt blessed to be able to help and house her daughter in this final, crucial task, and she was grateful the separation would not be for long. Dora set her life in order by drawing up a will and then, when not racked with pain, worked to keep faith. She read a book called *Horne's Manual for the Afflicted* and filled the margins with notes and quotations. Helpful chapters covered the full range of topics under headings such as: 'On the Design of God in the Permission of Afflictions', 'Examples of Persons who Rejoiced Amidst Afflictions' and 'A Prayer for a Blessed Death'. She kept the book tucked under her pillow when she slept.[16]

Dora's brother John visited for what she assumed would be the last time on 18 May. The following day, he delivered the final sacrament. 'Take, eat, this is my body, which is given for you. Do this in remembrance of me.' But unlike Mary and Dora, Wordsworth, Edward and John still dreamed of Dora's recovery. When a Dr Fergusson mentioned that a new drug called 'cod's liver oil' might do some good, Wordsworth and Edward sent John rushing off to Kendal to find some. Dora swallowed the medicine but only, as she told her mother, 'as a duty to those who clung to earthly hope'.[17] She herself tried hard not to hope. She knew she would not recover, wished she might live long enough to see the summer, but expected to be 'snatched' at any moment. She was, said Edward, 'so willing to love, yet so resigned to die; and so loving withal, and so considerate'.[18] Between awful bouts of coughing and diarrhoea, Dora, with the help of her mother, made herself ready for death.

Dora wrote letters of farewell to friends, and read theirs to her. On 22 May, she wrote to Sara. Folded in with her note was a much older piece of writing: one of Coleridge's Asra poems. 'This original MS of your father's was transcribed for aunt Sarah [*sic*] – my Mother gave it to me on my Aunt's death: and I give it to you knowing how precious it must be to you for all their sakes, and being sure it will be prized for mine also as a memorial of a lifelong friendship, and of my undying love.'[19] It was Dora's quiet way of letting go all the complications which had arisen from Coleridge's infatuation with her Aunt Sara. What she could not know was that Sara did not receive the letter.*

Two days later she wrote to her 'Good Angel'. 'My Beloved Miss Fenwick I must with my own hand send you one line of loving farewell.' The surviving version of the letter is a transcript; there is nothing to be discovered in the neat, unfamiliar handwriting. 'But I must stay my pen – I know I have your prayers and that you will not cease to pray for me and my beloved parents and my broken-hearted husband.'[20] Crabb Robinson, in his final letter to Dora, told her of his sorrow but also of his 'envy'. She would, he reminded her, soon pass into a better world. He admired and encouraged her 'cheerfulness', which he said would be a help to her family. Then he asked to take 'farewell of you with assurance of my perfect esteem'.[21]

Sara wrote again to Mary, to tell her Dora should not be told she was dying. Mary replied, slightly testily, to tell her of the 'state of heavenly composure and preparation in which your early friend remains awaiting her dismissal'. Mary wanted Sara to approve, for, as she told her, you 'were her first-companion friend – you a babe were in the house when she was born'.[22]

---

* It is possible that she received the letter at some point, but not until after Dora's death.

Sara tried to understand and felt it a 'privilege to be admitted to dwell on such a dying bed as hers'.[23]

Encouraged by the success of the cod-liver oil hunt, John left for his parochial duties, with promises to return. But Mary and Dora could see the medicine had effected no change. Dora tried to look heavenward, tried to express love for her family, and waited. But she did not die. The painful routine continued. Dora had her long hair cut off. It was kept in a plait for Edward. Wordsworth spent his days weeping. He could not bear to go into Dora's room without Mary to lean on. Mary, exhausted and stoic, criticised his lack of 'self command'. Dora completed her letter to Miss Fenwick – 'Oh may God in his mercy grant us all in his good time a joyful meeting in heaven!'[24] She did not want to see Miss Fenwick or Sara or any of the others who wrote. She feared that if she saw the faces of old friends she would be 'drawn from that tranquillity which she has endeavoured to preserve ever since she was aware of her real state'.[25] She could bear hideous bedsores and living practically without food, but she told her mother she could not 'trust' herself not to lose her resignation or her faith.

On 1 June, despite her precautions, faith disappeared anyway. Alone in her room (for she insisted that the rest of the household should eat their meals at their usual time and place 'without fuss'), Dora panicked. It was as though a black cloud of terror had settled over her – 'a fear and cold trembling as if she had lost the support of her saviour', she told Edward. She did regain her composure, but recognised she needed to 'think and wrestle less in order to retain the needful Christian fortitude to the last'.[26]

Dora's dying was an exhausting struggle, and it dragged on and on. Every day, at some point, everyone would think she was about to die. When present, John would deliver the sacrament again, and then she would somehow pull through. As the days turned into weeks, her body in agony, she continued to hear from friends, but only admitted the same small circle into her bedroom: her immediate family, the doctor, the servant and Hannah Cookson, an old friend of Aunt Sara's, who was a skilled nurse.

Many people sent Dora advice about 'how to die' well.* Most of it irritated Mary and Edward, but one hymn, sent by Edith Warter (née Southey), was admitted to the sickroom. The words, by the poet Charlotte Elliott, gave Dora great comfort: 'That's the very thing for me,' she said, and asked Edward to write it down in *Horne's Guide*:

> Just as I am – without one plea,
> But that Thy blood was shed for me,
> And that Thou bidst me come to Thee,
> O lamb of God, I come.†

In the days to come Dora asked for it to be read again and again, sometimes as often as ten times a day. She called it 'my prayer'; and it was always the first thing she heard in the morning and the last at night.[27]

In London, Sara was struggling to let go of her own hope for Dora. Like Wordsworth, who spent his days in tears, Sara hoped. 'May she not even yet rise up again?' she asked Miss Fenwick, who loved them both; might not 'the physicians be mistaken'? She tried to resign herself. 'Who would have thought, when Dora and I played as children together that she would be taken first and I left behind for a time.'[28] Like Dora, Sara found consolation in poetry. She sat down to do the only practical thing she could, and composed a poem for Dora: 'Prayer for Tranquillity'. It was as much to comfort herself as her friend. 'Dear Lord, who at thy blessed will,/Could'st make the raging sea be still,' she begged, 'smooth the tossing of the sea' and at the end bring us 'With Thee to dwell, supremely blest,/Anchored on everlasting rest.'[29]

John delivered the sacrament for a third time and still Dora

---

* The manuals, letters and prayers are fascinating in that they accept and confront death in a way that is so strikingly different from today.

† Perhaps, as much as the words, she empathised with the poet. Elliott was a chronic invalid herself and when the poem was set to music as a hymn it achieved huge popularity. It was a reminder of the power of the pen; thousands of people wrote to Elliott to tell her how the hymn had touched their lives.

lived. In another world, reviews were appearing of her journal. Mary had strongly disapproved of Dora publishing, but perhaps, in spite of this, she allowed the newspaper and journal reviews into her daughter's room. Notwithstanding Edward's fears, the book was widely and (mostly) favourably reviewed; it is true that everyone who wrote about it commented upon its lack of sophistication, but they found this charming. No one could pretend it was likely to be remembered long after its time: her book would 'have its little day of popularity, to be shoved aside and forgotten as other and more recent tourists enter with their "Journals" . . . to be replaced by later travellers in turn', wrote J. A. Heraud in an otherwise complimentary article.[30] It was all Dora had ever wanted: 'My main inducement, indeed, to the publication of this desultory Journal is the wish to assist in removing prejudices which make Portugal an avoided land by so many of my roving countrymen and countrywomen.' They might, she argued, 'find much to gratify them if they could be persuaded that it does not deserve the reproach of being merely a land of unwashed fiery barbarians and over-brandied port wine'. After all, it has 'to most of our travellers who have been everywhere else, the grand recommendation of being new. It is to this "great fact," the possibility of finding novelty even yet in the Old World, and in a quarter within three days' voyage from the Isle of Wight, that I would call their attention.'[31]

By the time the book was published, many people seemed to know that she – that is to say Wordsworth's daughter – had written it. Therefore, those reviews which were particularly pleasing were the ones which were unaware of her identity, or at least did not disclose it to their readers. The *John Bull*, the *Morning Post* and the *Spectator*, for example, only commented that the author of the journal was 'a lady' and an 'invalid'. All these reviewers liked her 'lightsome brave and spirited tone' and 'spontaneity', so judged her book a simple, unaffected success.[32] Like the *Edinburgh Review*, they enjoyed her 'eye for all that is picturesque and sublime in scenery'.[33]

Those reviewers who did mention her father (or hint at who he was) tended to compare her kindly. *The Atlas* was convinced she had inherited 'poetical feeling', and pleased that, as a woman, she had not tried to 'step out of her proper sphere to solve problems or social perplexities'.[34] And though we might wish otherwise, Dora had no ambition to do anything of the kind. In general the critics were gentle, but one hopes Crabb Robinson's plausible theory about why she'd garnered good notices did not occur to her. He recorded in his journal that he had 'read a very favourable review of Mrs Quillinan's book in the *Edinburgh Review*. Such is the effect of a name! The Edinburgh makes up for the injustice to the father by overpraise of the daughter.'[35] Equally, one hopes a review from an unidentified paper (now in the archives at Dove Cottage) was kept from her: 'A pious and gifted author laid them [the journals] at the feet of an illustrious parent. Alas! A vain offering.'[36] Assuming no one showed this one to Dora, the reviews might have brought some pleasure as her health deteriorated. Crabb Robinson feared they all came too late.[37]

If Dora read the articles, they would not have brought simple comfort, but something closer to triumph at having pulled off a remarkable deception. Because the journal Dora claimed was nothing more than a 'record' was in fact a work of fiction. The reviewer in the *John Bull* paraphrased Dora's own assertion that she had not given her journal 'the attraction of a Story book'. There is, the critic agreed, 'no book making in it . . . no artifice'.[38] But he was wrong. There was plenty of bookmaking in it. *The Britannia* gave another positive review of her 'descriptive scenes, anecdotes and occurrences', praising her accuracy in writing while events 'were fresh in the author's recollection'.[39] He was wrong too: many of the events described were fictional too. The *John Bull* thought the book was 'what the dedication says it is, – written for the gratification of a domestic circle'.[40] But while her private diary may have been kept to please her parents, the public book had done the opposite, and was absolutely not what the dedication said it was. Perhaps Edward read the reviews aloud and there was laughter at Rydal, despite everything.

In so far as Dora's book tells a story, it is that of an invalid made well by Portugal. Dora described herself as 'an invalid stranger who had only left my native hills for a warm climate, as a rain-vexed bird comes out from the wood to dry its feathers in the sun and take a strong flight home again'.[41] The narrator arrives by sea and is unwell. In Portugal she is soon able to go on long and arduous horseback rides, and walk and enjoy the climate, countryside, food and people. By the end, she leaves on a long trip overland through Portugal, Spain and France. Dora did not bother to write about France because, as she said, 'We left a world that is nobody's when we left the serras of Portugal . . . In France we were in a world that is everybody's, *pace Galliæ*.'[42] She wanted to make her compatriots see the wonder of Portugal, as her father had shown them the wonder of the Lakes.

Much of the first half of the journal is a description of a great adventure through Portugal on horseback and by boat. Dora's expedition, made in the company of Edward, Jemima and an unnamed friend, 'Mr H', lasted from 24 May to 9 June 1845. Like most of the first volume, Dora presented her text as a diary: a record of each day's travel – where they stayed, what they ate, what they saw and what they talked about. (The entries are bulked out by Quillinan's historical insertions.) The trip was energetic, with late nights, early starts, long rides and uncomfortable inns. Yet while Dora was supposedly exploring the Portuguese countryside, she was in reality ill in bed in John Quillinan's villa.

On the dates she gives in the journal, Dora was confined to her room. She had received a bitter, cruel and unhappy letter from her sister-in-law Isabella within days of arriving in Portugal, and Edward was furiously convinced that the letter was the cause of the setback to her health. The 'harassing correspondence', he told his parents-in-law on 27 May, had been a 'very torch to the fever' and he had never been so disappointed in his life.[43] The doctor – Dr Jebb – visited ten times between 28 May and 24 June and was paid £6 for his troubles. Edward's accounts were meticulously kept. He updated both Dora's family and his own journal on his wife's progress. It was not until 9 July (a month after Dora had supposedly returned from her expedition) that Edward was finally delighted to report that her appetite was better than he had ever known it.[44] She had been out several times on a donkey and was no longer an invalid. Throughout the rest of her time in Portugal, Dora did indeed get better and explore the region on long daytime rides by horseback, but she never made the journey she described in her journal. She did want to – and made tentative plans to go on a trip in the autumn – but was prevented by bad weather. In October, the Quillinans left the villa and went to the city of Oporto for the winter.

Even if we did not have Edward's letters, journal and account book, there could be no doubting the timing of Dora's illness, since it was precipitated by Isabella's letter. Dora was often ill, but she was no fainting novel-heroine, liable to be sent to her bed by a disagreeable correspondence or conversation. What had happened with Isabella was a truly shocking moment in her life, and indeed, the lives of all the Wordsworths. John had done a terrible thing and taken a sixteen-year-old mistress in Rome. Rather like the Vallon scandal, it has been effectively covered up by later generations of Wordsworths. Kate Summerscale, in *Mrs Robinson's Disgrace*, was the first to make the facts public. As she points out, Wordsworth's biographers have characterised Isabella as the spoilt heiress and John as the upstanding family man doing his best to support her and their children.[45] No one will ever know the full story, but by 1845 Isabella knew about her husband's affair. She learned, too, that he had promised to marry the girl when his wife died (an event he assured his mistress was imminent). How much of this Dora discovered in Portugal is unclear, but Isabella's letter accused Dora of deceit and of interference – in it Isabella was hysterical, accusatory, miserable and confused.[46]

Dora was devastated. Edward was furious and posted the letter on to Wordsworth and Mary – someone has since thoroughly blacked out most of his letter. By New Year, Wordsworth had disinherited his son, having received a strongly worded letter from Isabella's father. All John's portion of Wordsworth's money would go directly to his children. Whatever else Dora was thinking about in May and June 1845, it was not an expedition along the Douro River.

Precisely where truth ends and fiction begins in Dora's Portuguese book is unclear. She must have seen many of the sights she describes at some point, and had many of the conversations she reports – but not at the end of May when she was in bed. It makes one question the whole diary. Her botanical details, however, are spot on. She describes Portugal's yellow jessamine, the nightingales, the wild mignonette. Why did she do it? Perhaps there was some gossip about her illness, perhaps she'd been briefly pregnant, perhaps . . . we can never know. But when we read she was on a boat eating cakes, she was actually lying sick in bed under her father's portrait. When we are told she was riding through woods in the moonlight, she was actually feverish and weak, neither sleeping nor eating. It is every bit as much a fantasy as Sara's *Phantasmion*: honest Dora is more complicated than she seems. So, just as she is about to slip from life, Dora escapes our grasp. But as a piece of fiction, the journal is a far more interesting book than its readers have realised.

Dora did not read the opinion in *The Guardian*, which would have pleased her beyond all others. According to that paper, 'so cheerful and buoyant is the tone of the writer, that the cursory reader would never suspect that he was perusing the composition of an invalid'.[47] He was right. Dora's journal is defiantly, creatively, and loudly full of life, health and good humour. It is how she wanted to be remembered. By the time she came to write it, she probably knew she would never recover. She wrote her story and then set about dying.

Now her mother bustles into the room and we cannot follow. There are more prayers, gentle hands. No fuss, she murmurs. *Just as I am – without one plea*. Dora makes a feeble joke about her 'fatness' – the illness has caused strange swellings. *And that thou bidst me come to Thee*. The sportive wit of the girl in the 'Triad' splutters and fades. Her pale face with the 'childishness that always hung upon her' loses expression. And the girl at the ball smiles at Edward, nods her head, and is gone. *O lamb of God, I come*. It is 9 July 1847.

CHAPTER 22

'BUCKLAND IN PETTICOATS'

1847–1850

To think about Sara in the years after Dora died is to imagine two different people. She splits into the 'Good Genius' and 'Invalid' personas of her 'On Nervousness' essay. In both roles, Sara's passion and intellect shine out, but the Good-Genius Sara is also wise, capable and grounded with her children, household and writing at 10 Chester Place. Then there is the dark Invalid Sara of morphine drops, hysteria, long nights and nostalgia. She was consumed with grief for her oldest friend: during the day she could force herself to be practical but 'at night, in my sleepless hours, I am ever with her, or dwelling on my own future deathbed'.[1] Sara plunged into her dark self: a pool of self-doubt and bitter mourning.

Dora had forgotten her. On her deathbed, her oldest friend had sent no final message of farewell. Now Sara fears she has 'always seen that there was something in my frame of mind that did not suit' Dora. Yet surely, she beseeches Miss Fenwick, who *had* received a letter from Dora, 'she ever considered me one of her principal friends'?[2] She is filled with the addict's self-doubt. Had she been as good a friend as she might? Could she have 'done more to please and be of use' to Dora? She needs morphine. She does not write to Rydal Mount; she cannot find the words. Everyone she loves dies.[3]

Within a month of Dora's funeral, Sara at last received a message from her dead friend. At the start of August, grief-stricken Edward sent Sara a manuscript of STC's great fantasy poem, *Christabel*. He told Sara that Dora had been able to 'think of nothing in her possession likely to be so precious to you, and therefore selected that as the best token she could leave with you of her deep true love. I cannot write more today.'⁴ Dora had acknowledged Sara's role as Coleridge's editor and the keeper of his memories. Practical Sara, calm again, wrote to Edward to tell him how pleased she was that Dora had 'thought of me, and with earnest satisfaction, in her last illness when she was raised so far above this earth in her frame of mind'.⁵ This Sara talked of her 'dear departed' friend in suitably mournful tones. Perhaps Edward told her about the Asra manuscript and final letter Dora had tried to send. She resolved to try to take less opium. Life carried on.

In September, Miss Fenwick came to stay, bringing with her a copy of Dora's book which Sara had not yet seen. Her STC research had put her so in debt to her bookseller that he had refused her more credit until his bills were paid. She was grateful to Miss Fenwick, but it was almost two more months before she could face reading Dora's words. 'I have at last found the courage', she told Miss Fenwick, 'though at times I can scarce bear it – thoughts of <u>her</u> mingle so affectingly with thoughts of the scenes in which she places the reader.' For the most part she enjoyed it: she found the 'Dorian' parts beautiful and often funny. However, she thought it would have been 'more interesting without the Quillinan bits, which <u>seem like</u> insertions. I cannot fancy Dora, from herself, quoting Claudian, and Ariosto and criticising Camoens and sporting a knowledge of Politics.' She was right of course, but was there just a hint of the old rivalry? 'She never had a habit of quoting poetry,' she told Miss Fenwick, 'except her father's or that of some <u>friend,</u> she had no literary ways.'⁶

Amongst the disadvantages of being a widow were, for Sara, the constant and increasing worries about money. She tried hard to manage her affairs sensibly, but finances had always been Henry's department. Educating Herby properly was an expensive business. Sara felt keenly the responsibility of bringing up her children alone. Herby had turned into a brilliant scholar. Aged sixteen he had just published an article in Eton's magazine on the 'estate of the female character as developed in the writings of the Ancients'. Nothing could have been a better tribute to his mother; as she said, it 'showed his knowledge of books and his admiration of ladies, and places both in as strong a light as possible'.[7] He had one year left before university. Sara wanted him to follow family tradition and go to Cambridge but he had set his heart stubbornly on Oxford. She was not sure how she would pay for either.

Sara had not made money from *Biographia Literaria*. She continued to receive an income from the Coleridge estate and from Henry's savings, but her Hampstead life was not cheap.* As well as Herbert, she had the servants, Martha and Caroline, Old Nuck (more of a companion now than a nurse), Cook and Edy to support – and a house to run. She tried to send regular amounts to Hartley and the church, and was constantly in debt to tradespeople. She worried Edy was bored and needed more entertainment and instruction than she could afford. Therefore, in January 1848 she wrote to John Gibson Lockhart, editor of the *Quarterly Review*, to ask if she might be paid for writing some reviews for him. He offered her Tennyson's recently published 'The Princess' which she set about critiquing with energy.† Within weeks she was in a great tangle.

When she sent the piece to Lockhart it was three times as long as he wanted. Worse, as far as he was concerned, Sara's reading of Tennyson was intelligent and nuanced. Tennyson was a controversial and divisive poet. His admirers loved him, his detractors – like Lockhart – hated him, and put him in the same excessively soupy category of poets as the late Keats. Sara not only praised Tennyson (with qualifications) but she also made favourable references to Keats. Of course the *Quarterly* had

---

* SC generally had around £550 per year. It is notoriously difficult to give a suggestion of what this translates to today. Certainly she lived well above the average income in London – but this was a time of great poverty for many. It is perhaps equivalent to around £30–50,000 today. About £85 went on the rent for Chester Place.

† It is ironic to think that Lockhart was the man who, on meeting Sara as a young woman, had thought her beautiful, but not intelligent.

published the terrible review of Keats' *Endymion* which his friends melodramatically claimed had killed him.* Lockhart set to work chopping and changing. The version of the article he published was severely cut. He removed all Sara's positive comments about Keats and inserted the odd vitriolic comment about Tennyson for good measure. The published article was far more critical of Tennyson than Sara had intended. The review now described Princess Ida as a 'Buckland in petticoats' – not particularly cheering for an academically minded woman. Sara had written the piece anonymously and in the masculine third person as was conventional (and sensible), but Lockhart's editing made her sound far more male and reactionary than her original.[8] She had to try to be pragmatic, since she couldn't turn to other journals; she refused to deal with *Blackwood's*, the *Edinburgh Review* or any other which she felt had treated STC unfairly. Also, she'd already agreed to write another article for Lockhart and needed the twenty-five guineas he'd promised her.[9]

Nonetheless, the whole affair stuck in her craw and strengthened her feeling that journalism was a miserable trade. One result of her stint as a critic, however, was to send her back to her Esteesian projects with a renewed faith in their intrinsic value. The first thing she did was to look again at the four volumes of *The Literary Remains* which Henry had worked so hard to produce. Neither Pickering nor Sara ever directly said it, but Henry's volumes were not well done. All the different categories of writing were, as Sara delicately put it, 'mingled'.[10] She drew up a plan to rescue them with a series of new publications. Pickering agreed, and so, with surprising ease, Sara managed to put together the first of these: two volumes of STC's literary criticism which she called *Notes and Lectures Upon Shakespeare and Some of the Old Poets and Dramatists*. They were so little trouble in comparison to the *Biographia Literaria* that she began to think about doing the same for STC's political

---

* The idea of Keats as a poet 'killed by a review' endures today. Keats clearly died of TB but the suffering the review caused him is not to be doubted and it certainly did not help his health – not least because it curtailed his income.

writings. These were in a very muddled state. No one knew even how many essays there might be. If she were to undertake the project to put her father in his rightful place as one of the great political and philosophical thinkers in history, it would be a huge amount of work. As she contemplated the idea she could feel herself struggling with her old nervousness.

February 1848. Sara yearns for the landscape of her childhood: Prince Phantasmion's rugged mountain crags, the clear lake, which never seems so bright as when it sleeps, and the song of a lark soaring above dark cypress trees. This is the landscape of her 'sleeping or waking dreams'. She remembers the maypole at Keswick. So many of those laughing children are dead.[11] Winter drags on, politics frighten her. There is talk of a violent uprising. The Chartists are coming. She reads her father's essays. She cannot sleep and takes more laudanum. In the long poppy-sweet nights, she dreams a joyful 'conscious dream', but it fades into a 'mass of cheerless, starless shade'. She tries to hold the vision but it was a 'phantom dream-light, full of strife'.[12] Violence is marching through her dreams with blazing eyes. There are riots in Brazil, Romania, Schleswig, Belgium, and barricades in Paris. The Irish are coming, thundering crowds cheering them on.

Nevertheless Sara's sense of responsibility for her children prevented her from allowing the Good Genius to be consumed by her Invalid self. After all, as she said: 'One cannot brood with children to care for.'[13] The practical Sara decided to leave London. In the middle of March 1848, the Chartists announced they would present their third petition to Parliament on 10 April. They would hold a 'monster rally' on Kennington Heath and carry the petition from there to Parliament. Sara decided to go to Eton, taking Martha, Caroline and Edy with her. Poor old Nuck was left to hold the fort against the mob. Though Sara was broadly sympathetic to Chartist aims,* she could not

---

* Chartism was a movement for political reform named after the 'People's Charter' of 1838. The Charter's demands included universal male suffrage and an end to property qualification for MPs.

accept their methods. Like so many of her class, she felt 'changes there must be, but they must be brought about with us, in a gradual orderly manner and not through intimidation of the mob'.[14]

Sara was a product of her times, and the entire middle class was in a state of panic.[15] The Royal Family was evacuated to the Isle of Wight, though even there the government feared they could still be vulnerable. What if the rebels seized a warship? Ridiculous as it may seem, Wellington, the victor of Waterloo, was drafted in to fight the mob if necessary. The tenth of April was a rainy day and far fewer protesters than the movement had hoped for turned out; in the end the petition was carried to Westminster in a cab. Historians tend to describe this moment as the day the Chartist movement died. Sara was delighted with the outcome. Wellington was again a hero, just as he had been in her youth. 'How gloriously for our country the whole affair ended,' she exclaimed. She returned to London just as bluebells appeared in the park and things were looking up.

The previous autumn Sara had learned to her delight that Herbert had been elected a scholar at Balliol: she could not have been more proud. (The Master of Balliol College 'complimented him on not being like his family'; three of his cousins had all recently been sent down from Oxford.)[16] Sara knew he needed to get to university as soon as possible. For all his brilliance, Herbert was not especially happy at school. He excelled not only in the classics and history, but also modern languages, maths and science; he even went so far as to study Icelandic. But he was a hopeless athlete, which did not endear him to his peers, who celebrated physical over intellectual prowess.* In April 1848, to crown his academic triumphs at school, Herbert won the Newcastle Scholarship – Eton's most prestigious academic prize, and one of considerable monetary value (£50 per year for three

---

* Defenders of Eton might argue this is not entirely true at this time: they had just founded prizes for French, German and Italian, and William Johnson Cory had recently arrived to take up a teaching position.

years).* Sara was justifiably proud and it also slightly eased her financial worries. Herbert went up to Oxford in the autumn of 1848 and Sara was relieved to see that he was far happier there than he had been at school. He continued to consult his mother about his studies in a way that was unusual and moving. It was no great surprise he eventually obtained a double first in classics and mathematics.[17] Sara felt she lived in the 'second spring' of her life.[18] She could enjoy her children, look forward to grand-children and absorb herself in her work.

One of her chief confidantes was Edward Quillinan. Since Dora's death she and Edward had exchanged ever-longer letters. As Aubrey de Vere leant dangerously towards Catholicism, Edward's importance to her as a correspondent grew. She wrote about her hopes for the work she was doing, he told her about his everlasting Camões, they talked about books (she had been convinced the anonymous author of 'Jane Ayre [sic]' was a man, and was astonished to discover the truth).[19] They reminisced about Dora and Edward tried to persuade her to come and stay. She kept refusing, telling him she was nervous of the journey itself – but in fact she feared disturbing her idyllic memories of the Lakes with reality.

Just as she began work on the political essays, she was plunged back into despair. On 6 January, her brother Hartley died at the age of fifty-two. Despite his drinking, his death came as a shock. As far as possible the Wordsworths had kept an eye on him and helped to monitor his behaviour as they monitored his money. Perhaps without Dora their vigilance was reduced. Perhaps his grief for Dora played a role. In any event, during December 1848 he had several evenings of heavy drinking with friends, after which he insisted on walking home in the cold and dark. On one such night he got lost and wandered about in the rain for five hours. He caught a chill, which turned into an infection, and by Christmas was desperately ill. Derwent went up to be with him, and sent Sara regular bulletins, ending with a

* The prize was so significant that the winner was announced in *The Times* newspaper.

description of his laying out and funeral. Grief for Hartley mingled with grief for Dora who had 'never mentioned his name but to say something of praise or affection'.[20] Sara was pleased that his remains should lie 'beside those of dear, bright-minded, kind-hearted Dora', but it was scant comfort. For Sara, Hartley was still the young man she'd last seen two decades ago. 'I always thought he would live to old age,' she wrote in horror, 'and that, perhaps, in our later years, we might cherish each other.'[21] It 'rends my heart' that he should be gone.[22] She had hoped that Edith would come to know and love her uncle.[23]

More strongly than before, Sara has a presentiment of her own approaching demise. 'Scarce any death would make me anticipate my own with such vividness as would his. Children + parents belong each to a different generation; but as a brother, a few years older who has never suffered from any malady – in him I should seem in some sort to die myself.'[24] For the first time, she is convinced she will never live to old age; his death has shaken her 'hold upon earth'.[25]

This time, it took anger about the thorny old subject of biography to rouse her. Sara wanted to have Hartley's poems collected up and published with an honest memoir. She thought Derwent could do justice to their brother's 'genius' without dissembling about his life. But her friends and family resisted revealing the truth about Hartley's dissolute habits. Wordsworth was not alone in thinking Hartley's life was not worthy of 'any high eulogy'.[26] Sara was furious. It was hypocrisy: the Sage of Rydal Mount and his family had conspired to cover up the facts about his illegitimate daughter while STC and Hartley had been troubled, certainly, but never duplicitous. 'There are some who bear a high name for respectability of conduct,' she wrote, incensed, to Derwent, 'whose history it would be almost as difficult to write quite <u>truthfully</u> as Hartley's – whose history <u>never will be written truthfully</u> by any relation wife, or friend.'[27]

Sara was also more attuned to the times. She saw what Wordsworth did not want to see: the age of the dutifully respectful Victorian memoir was dead. 'It is not to be expected in these days', she explained to John Taylor Coleridge, 'that what is to be lamented in Hartley's life and character can be "veiled in silence", . . . at least, if his prose and verse live, his personal history will live also.'[28] She believed passionately in truth – and poetry. Hartley's biography was not for his Ambleside friends but 'for all persons now and hereafter who take an interest in the products of his genius'. Therefore, 'It is politic to tell our own story, for if we do not, it will surely be told for us, and always a degree more disadvantageously than truth warrants.'[29] Derwent wearily agreed to undertake the project, but Sara had to draw up detailed plans and nag him. Sara's 'own story' meant, of course, the story of her brothers and father, not herself.

Sara was cross about the aspersions that continued to be cast upon STC as a husband and father. She felt there was a constant, implicit, unfavourable comparison of her parents and the Wordsworths. 'As for my father's faults as a husband,' she wrote, 'I believe that with a wife who humoured him as some would have done [i.e. Mary Wordsworth] he would have been faithful – [as]others who have clung to their better half would not had they not been humoured.'[30] Angrily she worked harder than ever collecting her father's political writing, for a volume she would call *Essays on His Own Times*. Perhaps she also suspected what the Wordsworths thought. Mary wrote to Crabb Robinson, in March 1849: 'I do wish poor dear indefatigable Sara would let her Father's character rest. Surely that great spirit has left sufficient to gratify the craving for literary fame in any one, without that dear Creature worrying her brain in her endeavours to increase, or justify it – which with all her pains she will never accomplish.'[31]

In January 1849, Sara had read an article in the *Edinburgh Review* which argued she should not edit or write about STC because of her relationship to him.* In fact, she fumed in her

* The article was first published in the *Edinburgh Review* in April 1848. It spoke of 'how disqualified even the gifted daughter of a gifted parent may be for the strict responsibilities of a judge, in a case like the present, – no less, how vain her affectionate endeavours to clear the memory of her father from all, and even heavy blame'.

diary, no one could be better suited. After all, she could 'set forth the true character of a person nobody else could have seen so much'.[32] Perhaps the criticism was particularly painful because, while intellectually speaking she was absolutely the right editor, actually she had hardly known him. Defiant, Sara spent the best part of 1849 working on the *Essays*. She had come to expect the hard editorial graft, but this time she also spent long days in coffee shops and the British Museum poring over old copies of newspapers, hunting down obscure references and lost articles. Sometimes Nuck accompanied her, sometimes Edy. It was slow, painstaking labour. 'I am beleaguered with piles of the *Morning Post* of near fifty years since, and with *Couriers* above thirty years old.' She vowed it would be 'the last editing work, I trust, in which I shall engage that will be very laborious and confining. The mere bodily exertion which it involves is not small; and if I were as weak in muscle as I am disordered and uneasy in nerves, I could not get on with my task at all.'[33] She worked hard with her pen, and just as hard lifting, fetching and finding heavy bundles of old newspapers, while the curious proprietor of Peel's Coffee Shop looked on.

Her purpose in collecting and editing the essays was to 'form part of the materials, out of which a future biographer may frame the history of his life. They will show how he was employed during certain portions of his time, & why he was not then given up to some work of more permanent interest . . . the world knew nothing of his labours & he was set down, even amongst those who should have known better, as a man of genius, who from indolence and bad habits, frittered away in mere talk the gifts with which God had endowed him.'[34]

Sara had high standards for herself. She wanted to complete the volume 'in the exact, complete sort of way in which it is my nature to execute whatever I undertake', but she endured 'a deal of pains-taking and jog-trot drudgery'. Helpful friends assured her the essays would not sell. She hoped they were wrong because she fervently believed what she was doing mattered. In everything STC had ever said, 'however transient the immediate topic, he always referred it to the permanent, and shed the steady light of the past, and the bright gleams of the future, on every present of which he treated'.[35]

Throughout 1849–50, Sara took increasing amounts of morphine and suffered from all the usual horrible side effects. She was sharp with the servants: it shouldn't have been a total surprise when, as Sara sat eating supper one Saturday in March 1849, Caroline gave notice. Both Caroline and Martha had worked for Dora before she went to Portugal, and Dora had been anxious to find them a place when she left the country. Sara had tried to follow Dora's maxim on servants: 'To all their faults a little blind, to all their virtues a little kind', but, when Caroline told her she would need to find a replacement, her mistress snapped back that she would be 'only too happy to do so'.[36] Martha left shortly afterwards. Sara took more morphine for the sleepless nights and every day resolved to take less.

Her friendship with Aubrey de Vere provided both comfort and complication. If the age difference had not existed, perhaps Sara might have considered a relationship with de Vere, for she certainly felt something close to love for him. Soon after becoming friends, she wrote a poem, 'Time's Acquittal', in which she reflects on seeing her once beautiful face in the looking glass.[37] 'I vow, ev'n I myself can scarce recall/ Its heavenly charm!' She bargains with the mirror against time: 'Come, thou canst bring it forth again', but the 'the wasted form, wan cheek and sunken eye' are unchanging. The poem is a meditation on her own ageing and engages in a dialogue with her father's 'Youth and Age'. Where STC's poem has a melancholic ending, Sara's concludes that Time has not, in fact, cheated her: her youth is in 'my children's faces'. But nonetheless, the time had come to 'wane', not to think about remarriage. Instead, in poetry, she found a parallel world to speak to Aubrey. 'The union of thy heart and mine', she recognised, is 'but a dream'. She is 'dark, in life's decline' while round him 'noon day splendours beam'.[38] The dream staved off the darkness, but when she ceased to dream, 'What darkness will my soul invade?'

Sara suffers a nightmare about Aubrey's dead and naked body.[39] She worries about de Vere's 'Romanish' leanings. She wakes in a cold sweat to feel her dead husband's arm around her.[40] Nurse is ill and the servants are abandoning her. There is a pain in her right breast. She will take less morphine. There is gossip: Herbert has fallen in love. Sara does not know the girl or her family. Herbert is too young to throw his life away on a pretty face.

It took her almost a year, but by late spring 1850 Sara had managed to engage two new servants – Hannah and Harriet – and she liked them both. Even more importantly, Nuck seemed to be recovering. Together they went for long, slow walks in the park and the demons began to fade. As summer approached, she tackled *Essays on His Own Times* with vigour. She wanted people to re-evaluate her father's story. But the introduction to the volume was proving to be more difficult than anything she'd done before. This was because, when it came to politics, Sara hoped to demonstrate the 'Consistency of the Author's career of Opinion'.[41] The problem was that, if she had been brutally honest with herself, Coleridge had no such consistency.

Aubrey's companionship and advice at this time proved invaluable, despite his worrying Catholic leanings. The pair exchanged extended complicated letters and discussed Irish politics, religion and Coleridge. Being a widow held certain advantages a single woman could not have enjoyed. She was more or less free to see whom she chose, including a younger man, without causing gossip. She disagreed with Aubrey's views on baptism and regeneration, but since she loved arguing with him, the disagreements were no bad thing.

Eventually, for the introduction to *Essays on His Own Times*, Sara created a piece of fiction that was every bit as imaginative as Dora's Portuguese journal. Where Sara's *Biographia Literaria* introduction had been over-complex but astonishingly honest, she now presented the father she had always wanted. He was close enough to the 'real' man, but turned brilliantly to Sara's light, he became something rather different. A genius, flawed certainly, but at core a philosopher with a true line – an 'essence' – which she revealed and described.[42] More than this, STC became a seer or prophet, and Sara began to imagine what he might have thought of the major questions of the day. Ireland, for example, a subject she and Aubrey discussed non-stop. Endeavouring to prove her father's political and religious opinions were 'ever the same' despite various 'boyish enthusiasms' for revolution, she moved on to the situation across the Irish Sea.

'In the foregoing sections', she remarked, 'I have noticed some salient points of my Father's opinions on politics, – indeed to do this was alone my original intent; but once entered into the stream of such thought I was carried forward almost involuntarily by the current. I went on to imagine what my Father's view would be of subjects which are even now engaging public attention. It has so deeply interested myself thus to bring him down into the present hour, – to fancy him speaking in detail as he would speak were he now alive.'

Clearly Coleridge, who had been dead for sixteen years, did not have an opinion on Ireland in the past decade, but nonetheless Sara wrote a great deal about her views upon the subject. She felt justified because: 'I have come to feel so unified with him in mind, that I cannot help anticipating a ready pardon for my bold attempt.'[43] Sara felt 'assured' she knew what STC would have said about the Irish crisis. In fact the essay becomes a defence of Aubrey and a book he had recently published on Ireland, as well as a robust statement of her own opinions. Her 'introduction' took up one hundred and fifty-three pages. She wrote about the situation in Ireland, proposed remedies for the future, and from time to time ranged across the Atlantic to topics such as the British in America. Sara's conclusion about her father was simple. In politics, religion and morals, 'the spirit of his teaching was ever the same amid all the variations and corrections of the letter'.[44]

This time the reviewers did engage. Not as fully as Sara might have hoped, but they did comment. Most agreed with the *Literary Examiner*'s view that, impressive as Sara's volumes were, they could not 'concede to Mrs Sara Coleridge that she has established even the "virtual consistency" of their author'.[45] Sara was resigned. But she was struck one day by a comment in one of Edward's letters which suggested – to her astonishment – that even he did not fully understand STC. Edward seemed to think that only those who had studied metaphysics could follow STC's political arguments. Sara tried to put him right in a long letter. 'I have always been enraged at talk of my father's abtruseness,' she scribbled furiously in the margin just before posting it.[46] Still, she began to accept it would take time before her father was as renowned as he should be in her lifetime. In any case, by the time the reviews appeared, she had other concerns.

CHAPTER 23

'BRIGHT ENDOWMENTS OF A NOBLE MIND'

1850–1852

England learned the news in the morning papers on Thursday, 25 April 1850. *The Times* article began: 'It is with great regret that we announce to-day the death of William Wordsworth.' Sara opened her letters before her newspapers and so learned the news from Edward. Wordsworth was eighty years old, and had been the most constant father-figure in Sara's life. She wept bitterly. She had known him 'perhaps as well as I have ever known any one in the world – more intimately than I knew my father, and as intimately as I knew my Uncle Southey'.[1] He was 'the last, with dear Mrs W of that lovely and honoured circle of elder friends who surrounded my childhood and youth – and I can imagine no happiness in any state of existence without the restoration of that circle'.[2] There was a pain in her chest and she could feel her heart palpitating. Since Dora's death, Wordsworth had lost interest in the world – there had been no more poetry. In his last illness, she learned, the old poet had repeatedly mistaken a niece for his beloved Dora. As he died, Mary told him: 'William, you are going to Dora.' Sara was touched to hear it had brought comfort. His last reported words were 'Is that Dora?'[3]

'I feel stunned to think that my dear old friend is no more in this world,' Sara wrote back to Edward. Since Dora's death, he had grown ever more important to her and had become the link back to Dora and her youth. 'You have long been [a true friend],' she told him, '– and yet I feel as if you had become twice as much so of late as ever before.'[4] He was easy to talk to; occasionally she wrote to him so frankly that she regretted it afterwards. In her letters she reconstructed her lost world in the mountains of the Lake Country. 'O those days of youth,' she exclaimed to him, remembering a race she had run against John Wordsworth at the age of sixteen, 'will heaven be a glorified youth hood?'[5] All her thoughts and memories flew northwards as she imagined Wordsworth being buried in Grasmere churchyard next to his daughter. Keswick, she told Emily Trevenen, was 'where I long to be and which to my imagination is a sort of terrestrial Paradise'.[6]

Sara confided three great hopes to Edward. The first was her wish to defend her father and secure for him the place she believed he deserved in history. The second was that her children might be well married before she died, and the third was that Edith should visit the north. There was little Edward could do about the first two; but as her desire for the third seemed to grow in urgency, he cheerfully offered to have Edy to stay at Loughrigg Holme. Sara was delighted and her spirits lifted.

While they were making plans, Sara heard that Mary Wordsworth was in the process of having a new work of Wordsworth's, *The Prelude*, published. As far as Sara understood, this was another fragment of *The Recluse* to add to the already published *Excursion*. In June, just before Edith left, Sara received her copy of Wordsworth's autobiographical poem. She immediately recognised it as what it is: one of the greatest pieces of writing in the English language. *The Prelude* is arguably Wordsworth's highest achievement, even though he thought it was proof of his own failure. In spite of everything, *The Prelude* was addressed to Sara's father, as *The Excursion* had been. Wordsworth declared, from beyond the grave, that STC was the only man to whom it was worth dedicating his whole life (Mary subtitled *The Prelude* 'Growth of a Poet's Mind').* It

* Wordsworth left the poem untitled, though he sometimes referred to it as 'the poem to Coleridge'. Mary chose to call it *The Prelude* and took the subtitle from the fact that Wordsworth had described it as 'the growth of a poet's mind' in letters to Dorothy.

made the two poets equal again. Sara only wished her father could have known; he had gone to his grave believing that Wordsworth would remove his name from the poem.

Edy went to stay with Edward on 20 July 1850. Only then, once Edy was safely away and Sara had received happy letters describing her mother's old haunts, did Sara finally face facts. Her heart was not sore; there was a lump in her breast. It was growing and she was scared. She wrote to tell Edward. He replied immediately to say he was coming to London. He claimed he wanted to consult a doctor about his own health. Also, there were people and exhibitions he wanted to see: could he stay in Chester Place? Edward arrived on 31 August, having arranged for Edy to visit other friends and relations in the north. Edward and Sara plotted various cultural excursions and she found him as 'interesting and agreeable as ever'. Edward wrote to ask the eminent Dr Benjamin Brodie to examine some odd little bumps on his arm that he said bothered him. Perhaps the doctor might see Sara at the same time?

Brodie came to Chester Place at 2 p.m. on 6 September and saw them both. In all likelihood, the doctor feared the worst the moment he saw Sara's painful and inflamed breast. Nonetheless, he reassured her that it might well be a simple glandular swelling and told her he would return in a week or two. Edward had probably invented his peculiar bumps, for the doctor would not accept payment from either of them. For as long as Edward stayed, Sara persuaded herself to believe Brodie's assessment that the lump might simply disappear. Perhaps she was just starting the change of life – Emily Trevenen had apparently had a lump in her breast during the menopause. And even if it was a tumour, she could probably have an operation once it had settled.[7]

Sara and Edward walked in the park together. Autumn 'with its rich yellowing foliage and its mellow atmosphere' was the time which 'connects itself most with my remembrances of youth, the pleasures of out of door social entertainment of my girlish days'.[8] While they walked in the park and spoke of Keswick and Rydal, Sara felt content and almost young again.

As soon as Edward was away for any length of time, visiting other friends, she grew anxious. She resented his leaving; his presence seemed to stave off the terror. When he returned they discussed metaphysics, Leibniz and Grasmere, and everything was all right.

On 24 September, less than three weeks after the initial consultation and shortly after Edward had left, Sir Benjamin Brodie returned. The breast was worse. Sara's children were still away, and this beautiful woman must have suddenly seemed very alone to the old doctor. He was unsure what to do, so told her he could not give any definite opinion. He went to talk to J. H. Green, an old friend and collaborator of Coleridge's. Green called on Sara the next day and gave her the doctor's verdict. There was a chance, he told her, that the tumour might 'remain in an inert state for many years and not shorten her life', but it would, if left untreated, eventually kill her.[9] Sara's world reeled. Having heard what might be a death sentence, Invalid Sara returned with a vengeance and was given full rein in her journal. 'Alas! I live in constant fear – like the Ancient Mariner with the Albatross hung about his neck, I have a weight always upon me.'[10]

She lost her faith in the two things she had always believed in most: her father's poetry and her God. It seemed to her she had been 'wasting herself' in fighting the 'STC fight'.[11] She had isolated herself and no one would understand what it had cost her. She should have written more of her own poetry. 'I began a wild poem once,' she told Derwent wistfully, 'I sometimes wish I had not been diverted from it, and spent so much time on theology.'*[12]

As she wrestled with her own crisis, it seemed that England's foundation stone, the Church of England, was under threat. Sara had been devastated by Cardinal Newman's conversion to Catholicism five years before; now his act appeared symbolic of a church on the verge of collapse. Newman himself had been

---

* According to Swaab, the wild poem was probably 'Howithorn'; see her *Collected Poems*, pp. 199–211 and pp. 242–5. Even in failure she aligned herself with her father who left a wild, unfinished poem, namely 'Christabel'.

influenced by Coleridge's writing: it had led him to argue for religion based on individual faith and inward conviction. Like STC, he believed in the supremacy of imagination as a means to self-examination. A Coleridgean way of thinking took Newman to Rome and, having converted, he began to deny he had ever read Coleridge. His highly influential voice asked people to look into their souls (as STC had), but then inspired hundreds of other conversions to Catholicism. The conversions, as well as the proliferation of other sects and congregations, further eroded the authority of the Anglican institution in which STC had believed so strongly. Sara had to work hard to cling on to her own faith. She did not have Mary or Dora's solid conviction, and the realisation frightened her. Once again she poured her agony into her diary: 'What shall I do to be saved?' . . . 'A question full of trembling fear' . . . 'Is there salvation to be had?' . . . 'Alas! 70 drops' . . . '90 drops Alas!'[13] 'A Letter from Mr de Vere – very Romeward . . .'[14]

She took herself back to her father's essays, working through Coleridge's reasoning and setting down her interpretations of his arguments: could chance really 'produce order and unveiled symmetry'?[15] In the act of writing she grew calmer. Yet she could not quite *feel* her father's proof – that Christianity meets a human need precisely because it is true. She knew rational arguments could be made in either direction. Pure faith was a different concept and still necessary – though hers was not quite solid. She began to cast about for earthly salvation and hit upon Mesmerism, which several friends had recommended as a miracle cure. Mesmerism was *the* great medical fad of the mid-nineteenth century. Made famous by Harriet Martineau, Charles Dickens and Henry C. Atkinson, it was both fashionable and popular, particularly among middle-class women. When Sara proposed it to Dr Newton, her regular doctor, he advised that an operation would be of more use than Mesmerism and sent her to Sir Benjamin again.*

* Mesmerism, invented by Anton Mesmer in the late 1770s, had been undergoing a revival in popularity since the 1830s. It might best be described as an esoteric version of hypnosis; the theory underpinning the practice had to do

The consultation with Brodie was devastating. He agreed Mesmerism was mere 'quackery and nonsense' but he also removed all hope of a medical cure. There was no longer any doubt that the tumour was cancerous, he said, but it had progressed too far for an operation. Her best chance lay in keeping the tumour. As in the Ilchester days, the single word 'Alas' becomes the refrain of her diaries. Her breast was hot, heavy and sore against new specially constructed stays. 'O Woe is me! A cloud is come upon my life never to pass away . . .'[16]

Meanwhile more friends recommended mesmerism. She determined to try it but was shocked by the cost: she wrote to tell Miss Fenwick all about it and received a letter and a present of £100 from 'my Angel, Miss Fenwick'.[17] She had the treatment but the breast did not seem to improve; it had to be drained daily. Her wine bill increased; she couldn't sleep and it did not help that her next-door neighbours had bought a piano, or that Herbert, home for the holidays, competed with them by practising his cornet.

By the late spring of 1851, Sara, by sheer force of will, pulled herself at least some way out of the despair into which she had sunk. The excitement of that season was the Great Exhibition and the Crystal Palace which housed it in Hyde Park.* So many people asked Sara whether she had seen it that eventually she set off to have a look – if only to have an opinion and 'escape the perpetual question, "Have you seen the great wonder!"'[18] On 24 May she spent four hours wandering the galleries. Sara was transfixed. The beauty and innovation of the building itself overwhelmed her even more than the 14,000 wonders of the British Empire it housed. Joseph Paxton's building made of light was the physical realisation of the 'triumphal arch of light and

---

with mesmeric or magnetic fluid that circulated in the body and could be harnessed by the Mesmerist. For an interesting survey of Mesmerism at this period, see: 'All I Believed Is True: Dickens and the Mesmerism System', a talk by Steven Connor at Dickens and Science, Dickens Day, Birkbeck, 10 October 2009; <http://www.stevenconnor.com/mesmerism/mesmerism.pdf>
* The Palace was later moved to Sydenham, an area of south London which was subsequently renamed Crystal Palace. It was destroyed by fire in 1936.

architecture' she'd imagined for her fairy-tale.[19] Almost a million
square feet of glass supported by iron girders, and under them
Sara (and six million other visitors – a third of the population)
wandering from the giraffes of Africa to the Laocoön of Ancient
Greece by way of the Sphinxes of Egypt. She went back time
and again. Sara was struck by the fact it was full of people finding
hope. 'I saw so many Bath chairs, and invalids in them,' she
reported to Miss Fenwick, and the invalids all seemed uplifted
by the experience.[20] The 'sun cast prismatic colours and rays
and silver sparks along the walls and azure arches'.[21] Each time,
she left feeling rejuvenated. It was Kubla Khan's Pleasure Dome
and King Phantasmion's 'palace of pleasure' all rolled into
one.[22]

And then, without anyone expecting it, Edward died, aged
fifty-five. This relentless roll call. Edward had not been ill, and
he died on 8 July with his pen in his hand, still trying to finish
his doomed Camões translation. Also unfinished was an edition
of Wordsworth's poems he had hoped to put together using the
Fenwick Notes. He had been desperately disappointed when, in
1848, Wordsworth had asked his nephew Christopher, and
not Edward, to write his authorised biography. Christopher
asked Edward for the notes he, Dora and Miss Fenwick had
made. Edward stalled for a year before sending 'those precious
Notes; to be dealt with at his discretion and then returned to
me'.[23] He had been afraid of what Christopher would do with
his 'treasure' – 'What if he uses them up?' Christopher produced
a dull whitewashed biography at the end of 1850 and sent the
notes back. Edward had only had them for a matter of months
before he died. For Sara his death, in Loughrigg Holme, brought
not only grief but powerful memories of Dora and her youth.

Edith Warter, whom Sara still thought of as Edith Southey,
came to visit at Chester Place. It was the first time Sara had
seen her in years and she simply could not reconcile this red-
faced old-looking woman with the Edith of her childhood.[24] It
seemed 'as if the present Life were passing away and leaving me
for a while behind'. Only the loss of her father was 'less felt
than the rest' because she had the sense he was more with her,

not less. 'Indeed he seems ever at my ear, in his books, more especially his marginalia, speaking not personally to me and yet in a way so *natural* to my feelings, that *finds me* so fully and awakens such a strong echo in my mind and heart, that I seem more intimate with him now than I ever was in life.'[25] The echo reverberated when, in August, Mary Wordsworth sent Sara a parcel and note to give to her daughter Edy. Inside was 'a much prized relic of your Grandfather, a Watch that was given by him to my beloved Sister Sarah; as you will see by the date, 44 years ago'. Mary told Edy: 'Before your dear Mother was Mistress of a watch, my Sister used to say that she would leave it to her; and remembering this, since it came into my possession I have designed it for you. You will not value it the less I hope, for its having been worn 15 years by my side, as a treasured Memorial, whence, it was only removed, alas! to give place to a more sacred Trust.'[26]

By the autumn of 1851 Sara had accepted her tumour would eventually kill her. Her best hope was that it would take years, but she also knew it could be weeks and she still had so much to do. She *would* complete her final project, and in doing so 'leave the Esteesian House in order'.[27] She had to prioritise. There were some things, which, with a bit of guidance, Derwent could do after her death. To this end, she gave him detailed notes for a scheme of work that would leave the public with the entire corpus of STC's writings. Some of Henry's editions of her father's volumes ought to be redone; he had made mistakes and errors of judgement and, without expressing disloyalty to her husband, she pointed them out to her brother. But what she was certain Derwent could not do alone was a new collection of all their father's poems.

This sounds straightforward but was in fact editorially complex, and it quickly became clear that Derwent and Sara had strong differences of opinion. Derwent was, for the most part, keen to take the simplest path. Sara was not and, moreover, she wanted to take brave and sometimes controversial editorial decisions. First she wanted to rearrange the poems completely; they ought to be placed in chronological order. Derwent disagreed, thinking they should be left as they had been in STC's lifetime. Secondly, Derwent wanted to remove poems that might be criticised for being indecent. Sara disagreed with the idea of rejecting anything on these grounds.

For a while Sara seemed to acquiesce on the question of chronology. 'I regret very much your arrangement,' she told him at the start of 1852. 'But one or other must yield – therefore have your way.'[28] Then she reminded her brother she was dying and Derwent caved in. Contented, she reassured him the chronological approach was now considered most academically rigorous. 'Students of poetry', she explained, 'are beginning more and more to approve the ordering of poetry according to the date of production.' Besides, here was a chance to do better for her father than had been done for Wordsworth; lovers of *his* poetry were now 'longing for a regular chronological arrangement of his poems', and yet no such volume existed.[29]

Sara told Derwent to get on with writing a preface for the new edition while she returned to the poems. But in winning the chronology battle she had created an enormous challenge for herself. STC had left his papers in undated chaos, and he himself had never given a 'thought to the arrangement of the poems'.[30] Figuring out when he had written them was immensely difficult and took 'longer than you could imagine'.[31] Sara was not prepared to take the simplest path and place the poems into broad sequential order. Derwent hoped that within STC's different collections – the *Sybilline Leaves*, for example, published in 1817 – they could leave the poems as STC had presented them. Sara disagreed. STC had merely 'thrown' the poems into any old order. To her it was 'obvious' the book had not been 'designed by STC on any principle – any internal principle – but dictated by the 3 vol. form', and she believed that to 'adhere to him in some things when we depart from him in others' was mere superstition.[32] Derwent reluctantly acquiesced.

Both Sara and Derwent wanted to leave some poems out of the new edition, but they had very different criteria for doing so. Derwent wanted to exclude poems he thought were disreputable. Sara only wanted to exclude poems where she felt their father had been uncharacteristically unkind (such as his satire 'Two Round Spaces' about Sir James Mackintosh). She lectured her brother sternly: STC would never be entirely fit for schoolroom or drawing room. His poetry was so sensuous and impassioned that she had never, for example, put it into Edy's hands and never planned to until the girl was married; nonetheless, this was what made STC's poetry great and should *never* be grounds for censorship.*[33] Sara was looking to the long-term reputation and not the next day's book sales.

Correcting and proof-reading; arguing with Derwent; thinking about the preface; issuing instructions about other STC volumes – all these activities distracted Sara from the business of dying. On Derwent's arrival at Chester Place he would rush upstairs and plunge 'at once into Moxon-Pickering-Hartley-STC-ism and such topics which do me good by taking my mind off my uncomfortable *self*', she told John Taylor Coleridge.[34] But when Sara wasn't writing or thinking or seeing people, she turned to her diary and her terror flooded on to the page. The tumour was oozing an unpleasant-smelling discharge; the doctor showed the servants how to drain it. Despite this, she kept hoping. After all, old Mrs Jacobson, an aunt of Derwent's wife, 'had a tumour for 30 years & died of old age at 80'.[35]

Sara took up mesmerism again and thought that perhaps it was doing some good this time. She ate raw egg and saline powder, wore a silk vest and a mercurial plaster, stopped lifting her arm to dress her hair and drank any number of recommended tonics. Until September 1851, hope was strong enough, more or less, to sustain her. Then she discovered another tumour. 'Alas! Alas! another bud of my sad malady right in the middle of my chest! O life thou art a series of disappointments.'[36] The new tumour hurt and she counselled herself, without much success, not to fear death. It caused a second total crisis of faith, not helped by thoughtless friends writing letters wishing her

---

* Interestingly, she also said she would never have been able to 'pore over' her father's poems with de Vere.

farewell. Such missives might have helped Dora, but they almost destroyed Sara.

Everything seemed to be collapsing. Herbert came to her and confessed that the gossip she had heard was true. He was, at the tender age of twenty-one, engaged. Her name was Ellen Phillips and she had no money, but hadn't his parents' example taught him this was unimportant? Miss Phillips' parents knew all about it, so Sara thought they were being duplicitous.[37] 'Oh! that Edy were the engaged one and not Herbert!' On top of that, Derwent had just sent his son, Dervy, to Australia. The boy had managed to get himself sent down from Oxford. His family had struggled throughout his adolescence to control his wild behaviour, but this was the final straw. They decided to exile him, despite the fact that they would almost certainly never see him again. Sara had tutored Dervy as a child, loved him dearly, and mourned his loss. And then Aubrey de Vere wrote to tell her he had converted to Catholicism. She was distraught. John Taylor Coleridge's son Henry seemed to be leaning dangerously in the same direction. To lose a son to Rome would be at least as great a loss as exiling one to the New World. There was another lump on her left breast now and the right was bleeding.

The crisis lasted until November. 'The first ray of hope and relief and improvement that I have had for a weary time,' she recorded in her diary. 'Mr Newton finds the tumour improved.'[38] But less than a month later, she slumped again: 'now I feel that I am dying . . . Dearest Derwent has just administered the Holy Communion to me.'[39] She read *Pride and Prejudice* for the third time, fully expecting it to be the last thing she ever read. (She still could not believe they would all have looked after Lydia in the way they did.)[40] Sara wished she could be buried in Grasmere church. She wished she could 'live thro' life's evening in that lovely native vale'.[41] She wrote her will. She worried about where the children would live after her death and wept to think how Edy would manage without her. She fretted for the future of her only son and his foolishness in having made a choice of wife based on looks alone. But Christmas approached and with it 'thoughts of the Prince of Peace'. Sara decided she would not play the same 'unwise game' Wordsworth had played with Dora.[42] Herbert must marry whomever he wanted and the Phillipses were at least respectable. Emily Trevenen sent Sara a new-fangled inflatable Macintosh cushion and she was able to sleep a little. Again, Brodie gave grounds for some hope. Sara veered between hope of life and conviction of imminent death.

Strangely, it was at this point that Sara's sense of humour – never her defining characteristic – came to the fore. This was not the uncomfortable black humour of a dying woman, but a certain playful spirit of fun which lived alongside her fear. For all she was a difficult co-editor for Derwent, she maintained a stream of cheery banter with him. When she learned that he intended to put a picture of her on the frontispiece of the book, instead of the one of STC they had agreed on, 'without saying a word to poor I', she wrote to him in mock protest, satirising the way their entire collaboration had worked. Is that 'the way a poor drudge of a painstaking slave of a co-editor is to be served by her "*elder brother*" [*sic*]', she asked. She wrote him a poem: 'Darran was a bold man', she began,

> And Darran was a bad –
> Darran came to my house
> And stole away my Dad.[43]

And so she continued for several poorly scanning verses. She read *David Copperfield* and laughed. She composed rhymes for Edy teasing her about how many partners she'd danced with at a ball.

Her sense of humour failed, however, when Derwent sent his preface towards the end of January. 'It's a bonny skeleton,' she told him, 'but it seemeth to me that the flesh and some of the muscle require a little re-edification.'[44] A couple of weeks later she wrote to ask him whether *she* might write some of it. Her reasoning was that, if she did not, 'it will be concluded by all men, under the circumstances, that I am joined with you as co-editor in the title page merely out of courtesy and condescension on your part'. In fact, as he knew, 'the bulk' of the editorial labour had been done by her. Once again she reminded him of her illness: 'You will allow for the feelings of an invalid unwilling to be supposed incapable more than needs must. No one likes to be shelved – to be considered *hors de combat* . . . the public – hearing that I am shut up with a serious malady – out of society – not seeing any but a very few intimate friends, will never dream that I can be capable of <u>composition</u> or Editorship in any shape. And this, I own, would be painful to me. All I ask', she repeated, 'is to be allowed to write a small part.'[45]

Derwent did not have much of a choice and told his dying sister to write the entire preface. She did so in an incredibly short time. She defended all the editorial decisions she had made and explained why Coleridge would have approved. Finally, she was the author of her father. When the volume came to be printed, Derwent composed a single-page 'Advertisement' in which he wrote of his sister: 'At her earnest request, my name appears with hers on the title-page, but the assistance rendered by me has been, in fact, little more than mechanical. The preface, and the greater part of the notes, are her composition; – the selection and arrangement have been determined almost exclusively by her critical judgement, or from records in her possession.'

Sara's two selves, Invalid and Good Genius, lived side by side now. She had good days and terrible ones. All the while, she was aware of racing against time, 'when there is still much to do'.[46] At the start of March, she thought her health was 'decidedly better'.[47] By the middle of March, she and Derwent were putting the finishing touches to the poems. By the end of March, the tumour was growing again. She simply did not have time for it and took chloroform at night to sleep. She composed a brave and witty charm: 'To a little lump of malignity, on being medically assured that it was not a fresh growth, but an old growth splitting': 'Split away, split away,/split away, split!' it began.[48]

Throughout April, she tried her best to make sure Derwent understood her plans for the future volumes of STC's works. She criticised his introduction to *Lay Sermons* and lectured him about Fichte and Kant. She told him what to do about the *Theological Marginalia* and how she thought he should spell Shakespeare (with three 'e's). She approved his introduction to *Lay Sermons*. She scolded him for his 'Uriah 'umbleness', and made him promise to put his own name as editor.

Derwent visited frequently, but Sara still wrote to him most days. When she was too weak to write, Edy held the pen. At the end of April she thought the tumours had decreased again.[49] Yet her house was continually full with a stream of friends and relatives bringing jellies and strawberries, tongue and celery. She kept a record of their names in her diary and wished they would not refer to her invalidism. She began to draft a new defence of the plagiarism accusation. She was running out of time.

Only at the very end did she stop. She wrote a final letter to Derwent: 'I had thought of adding the date of my Father's birth to the Preface. But, dear Derwent, I am dying. I feel it.'[50] Her brother delivered the final sacrament again.

Sara died on 3 May 1852.

EPILOGUE

In 2010 Peter Swaab published a new edition of Sara Coleridge's poetry. Her reputation as an editor and scholar continues to grow:

'Sara Coleridge was probably the most learned of her father's editors; and she is one who cannot, so far as I know, be charged with tampering with any text.'

Kathleen Coburn, 1971[1]

'Sara Coleridge's intelligence, energy, learning, and above all her willingness to lay damaging materials clearly before the reader, have not only never received anything like the praise they deserve, but she has sometimes been patronized by professional scholars. Her sensitivity to the distorting pressures of personal bias, all the more remarkable in her acutely difficult psychological position as the poet's daughter, has not been approached by any subsequent editor.'

Norman Fruman, 1985[2]

'[S]he was determined to lay the evidence she had before the reader. Sara has never received anything like the credit she deserves.'

Norman Fruman, 1989[3]

'Out of the complex web of Sara Coleridge's motives was born the first major scholarly edition [of *The Collected Coleridge*] – the very model of rigorous editing.'

Alan Vardy, 2010[4]

'Sara Coleridge was among the best literary critics of the Early
Victorian years.'

Peter Swaab, 2012[5]

Sara wrote a poem once in which she argued against the idea
that love will necessarily blind the beholder.

> Passion is blind, not Love: her wond'rous might
> Informs with threefold pow'r man's inward sight:
> To her deep glance the soul at large display'd
> Shows all its mingled mass of light and shade:
> Then call her blind when she but turns her head,
> Nor scans the fault for which her tears are shed.
> Can dull Indifference or Hate's troubled gaze
> See through the secret heart's mysterious maze?
> Can Scorn and Envy pierce 'that dread abode,'
> Where true faults rest beneath the eye of God?
> Not theirs, 'mid inward darkness, to discern
> The spiritual splendours shine and burn.
> All bright endowments of a noble mind
> They, who with joy behold them, soonest find;
> And better now its stains of frailty know
> Than they who fain would see it white as snow.[6]

She was right – it is better to see 'stains of frailty' than not
– and in being right Sara wrote her finest poem. Scholars will
continue to disagree about her editing of STC, but her love
for him did not blind her to his faults. She is arguably still the
greatest editor he has had: she created the poet we know today.
And if Virginia Woolf was right, that she lived in the light of
her father, then by the end of her life she was shining that
light forward for our benefit. Like Dora, it no longer blinded
her.

Throughout her life Dora kept an album, in a blue silk cover,
to which she asked friends and family to contribute poems,
autographs and sketches. Sixty people – from Coleridge and

Sir Walter Scott by way of Edward and Sara – contributed. On the final page of the book was Sara's 'Prayer for Tranquillity'. Amongst the most touching entries, in 1832, was Aunt Dorothy's. Though she could be critical, she loved her niece dearly and she knew how much Wordsworth owed his daughter, even then.

> **'To my niece Dora'**
> But why should *I* subscribe my name
> No poet I – no longer young?
> The ambition of a loving heart
> Makes garrulous the tongue.
>
> Memorials of thy aged Friend,
> Dora! Thou dost not need
> And when the cold earth covers her
> No flattery shall she heed.
>
> Yet still a lurking wish prevails
> That when from Life we all have passed,
> The friends that loved thy Father's name
> On hers a thought may cast.[7]

Dora's Portugal book continued to be read and republished until the end of the nineteenth century. After a gap of more than a century, it was reprinted in 2009. The first proper travel guide to Portugal was published in England in 1853.*

Christopher Wordsworth, Wordsworth's first authorised biographer, was the first to reproduce most of Isabella Fenwick's notes and Jared Curtis finally published *The Fenwick Notes of William Wordsworth* as a book in its own right in

---

* In 1855 John Murray finally printed one of his famous red handbooks for Portugal. Finally travellers had a guide to the country which Murray acknowledged in his first sentence was 'less known to Englishmen than any other in Europe'.

2007. Since Wordsworth's death, however, all serious scholars of the poet have depended on the notes collected by Dora. In their different ways, she and Sara had tended the legacies of their fathers and helped shape the poetry of Wordsworth and Coleridge for posterity.

Isabella Wordsworth died in Italy in 1848. After her death, **John Wordsworth** went on to marry three more times. With his third wife, Mary Ann Dolan, he had one daughter whom he named Dora. He died in 1875.

Aunt Dorothy partially came back to her senses after her brother died. She and Mary lived together at Rydal until Dorothy's death in 1855.

Miss Isabella Fenwick, Dora and Sara's Good Angel, died in 1856.

Mary Wordsworth died, quietly and quickly, in 1859. She was buried with her husband.

Herbert Coleridge died in 1861 at the age of thirty having married in 1853. In his short life he became a renowned philologist. As a member of the Philological Society, he formed a committee whose efforts eventually led to the development of the Oxford English Dictionary.

Henry Crabb Robinson died in 1867. In 1851, when Christopher Wordsworth's biography of his uncle was about to be published, Robinson performed a final act of kindness towards the Wordsworth family. Somehow he fended off Caroline Baudouin's husband, who had threatened to expose the secret of Wordsworth's French mistress.

John Taylor Coleridge became a member of the Privy Council in 1858. He died at Ottery St Mary in 1876.

Edward Quillinan's daughters lived on together in Loughrigg Holme until their deaths in 1876 (Rotha) and 1891 (Jemima). Neither Rotha nor Jemima married.

Derwent Coleridge died in 1883 at the age of eighty-two, after a long and successful career at St Mark's College, Fulham, and as the rector of Hanwell. He published a number of scholarly works.

Willy Wordsworth died in 1883, the same year as Derwent. He and his wife Fanny had four children, three of whom outlived him.

Aubrey de Vere lived on until 1902. After Sara's death he returned to live in Ireland, where he remained until his death. He never married.

Edy Coleridge died at the age of seventy-eight, in 1911, never having married. She published a memoir of her mother in 1873, which was popular for a while.

NOTES

List of Abbreviations used in the notes

B of O	Molly Lefebure, *S. T. Coleridge: Bondage of Opium* (Worcester and London: The Trinity Press, 1974)
Barker	Juliet Barker, *Wordsworth: A Life* (London: Viking, 2000)
Biographia	Samuel Taylor Coleridge, *Biographia Literaria; or, Biographical Sketches of My Literary Life and Opinions*, second edition prepared for publication in part by the late Henry Nelson Coleridge, completed and published by his widow, Vol. 2 (London: William Pickering, 1847)
BL	British Library
Coleridge Fille	Earl Leslie Griggs, *Coleridge Fille: A Biography of Sara Coleridge* (London, New York and Toronto: Oxford University Press, 1940)
Dove Cottage	Wordsworth Trust at Dove Cottage
EOT	Samuel Taylor Coleridge, *Essays on His Own Times*, ed. Sara Coleridge, 3 vols (London: W. Pickering, 1850)
HCRBW	Henry Crabb Robinson, *Henry Crabb Robinson on Books and Their Writers*, ed. Edith J. Morley, 3 vols (London: J. M. Dent and Sons, 1938)
HCR Diary	Henry Crabb Robinson, *Diary, Reminiscences and Correspondence* ed. Thomas Sadler, 3 vols (London: Macmillan, 1869)

HCRWC	Henry Crabb Robinson, *The Correspondence of Henry Crabb Robinson with the Wordsworth Circle (1808–1866)*, ed. Edith J. Morley, 2 vols (Oxford: Clarendon Press, 1927)
Holmes *DR*	Richard Holmes, *Coleridge: Darker Reflections* (London: Harper Collins, 1998)
Holmes *EV*	Richard Holmes, *Coleridge: Early Visions* (London: Penguin, 1990)
HRC	Harry Ransom Center, University of Texas at Austin
Jones	Kathleen Jones, *A Passionate Sisterhood: The Sisters, Wives and Daughters of the Lake Poets* (London: Virago, 1997)
LCRS	Robert Southey, *The Life and Correspondence of the Late Robert Southey*, ed. Rev Charles Cuthbert Southey, 6 vols (London: Longman, Brown, Green & Longmans, 1849–50)
LHC	Hartley Coleridge, *Letters of Hartley Coleridge*, ed. Grace Evelyn Griggs and Earl Hartley Griggs (London: Oxford University Press, 1936)
LMW	Mary Wordsworth, *The Letters of Mary Wordsworth 1800–1855*, ed. Mary E. Burton (Oxford: Clarendon Press, 1958)
Low	Dennis Low, *The Literary Protégées of the Lake Poets* (Hampshire: Ashgate, 2006)
LSH	Sara Hutchinson, *The Letters of Sara Hutchinson, 1800–1835*, ed. Kathleen Coburn (Routledge & Kegan Paul, 1954)
MS	Manuscript
Memoir	Sara Coleridge, *Memoir and Letters of Sara Coleridge*, ed. Edith Coleridge, 2 vols (London: Henry S. King & Co., 1873)
Minnow	Sara [Fricker] Coleridge, *Minnow among Tritons: Mrs. S. T. Coleridge's Letters to Thomas Poole, 1799–1834*, ed. Stephen Potter (London: Nonesuch Press, 1934)

Mudge	Bradford Keyes Mudge, *Sara Coleridge: A Victorian Daughter* (New York and London: Yale University Press, 1989)
NLRS	Robert Southey, *New Letters of Robert Southey*, ed. Kenneth Curry, 2 vols (New York and London: Columbia University Press, 1965)
Phantasmion	Sara Coleridge, *Phantasmion* (London: William Pickering, 1837)
Quincey Lit Rem	Thomas De Quincey, *Literary Reminiscences from the Autobiography of an English Opium-Eater*, 2 vols (Boston: Ticknor, Reed & Fields, 1851)
SCCP	Sara Coleridge, *Collected Poems*, ed. with an introduction by Peter Swaab (Manchester: Carcanet Press Ltd, 2007)
SLRS	Robert Southey, *Selections from the Letters of Robert Southey, &c &c &c*, ed. John Wood Warter, 4 vols (London: Longman, Brown, Green, Longmans, & Roberts, 1856)
STCCL	Samuel Taylor Coleridge, *Collected Letters*, ed. Earl Leslie Griggs, 6 vols (Oxford: Clarendon Press, 1956–71)
STC *Notebooks*	Samuel Taylor Coleridge, *The Notebooks of Samuel Taylor Coleridge 1772–1834*, ed. Kathleen Coburn, 5 vols (London: Routledge & Kegan Paul, 1958–2002)
Vardy	Alan Vardy, *Constructing Coleridge: The Posthumous Life of the Author* (New York: Palgrave Macmillan, 2010)
Vincent	Dora Wordsworth, *Letters of Dora Wordsworth*, ed. with an introduction by Howard P. Vincent, limited edition of 450 copies (Chicago: Packard and Company, *c.* 1944)
WLMS	Wordsworth Library manuscripts
WW EL	William Wordsworth, Dorothy Wordsworth, *The Early Letters of William and Dorothy Wordsworth (1787–1805)*, ed. Ernest De Selincourt (Oxford: Clarendon Press, 1935)

| *WW LLY* | William Wordsworth, *The Letters of William and Dorothy Wordsworth: The Later Years*, 2nd edn, ed. Ernest De Selincourt and revised and ed. Alan G. Hill, 4 vols (Oxford: Clarendon Press, 1939) |
| *WW LMY* | William Wordsworth, *The Letters of William and Dorothy Wordsworth: The Middle Years*, 2nd edn, ed. Ernest De Selincourt and revised by Mary Moorman, 2 vols (Oxford: Clarendon Press, 1937) |

Other abbreviations

Dora	Dora Wordsworth
DW	Dorothy Wordsworth
HC	Hartley Coleridge
HCR	Henry Crabb Robinson
HNC	Henry Nelson Coleridge
IF	Isabella Fenwick
JTC	John Taylor Coleridge
Mrs STC	Sarah Coleridge (Sara's mother)
MW	Mary Wordsworth
SC	Sara Coleridge
SH	Sara Hutchinson (Dora's aunt)
STC	Samuel Taylor Coleridge
WW	William Wordsworth

Foreword

1. Virginia Woolf, 'Sara Coleridge', in *Death of the Moth and Other Essays* (New York: Harcourt Brace Jovanovich, 1970), p. 111. The essay originally appeared in the *New Statesman and Nation* (26 October 1940).

Prologue

1. STC *Notebooks*, III, January 1804, note #1801. • **2**. STC to Mrs STC, 23 November 1802; *STCCL*, II, p. 889. • **3**. STC to WW, 30 May 1815; *STCCL*, IV, p. 574. • **4**. WW to James Tobin, 6 March 1798; *WW EL*, p. 188.

1 'The Shadow of a Shade', 1808

1. STC to Mrs STC [9 September 1808]; *STCCL*, III, p 120. • **2.** DW to Lady Beaumont, 20 June 1804; *WW EL*, p. 395. • **3.** SC Autobiography, in Mudge, pp. 262–3. • **4.** SH to Mr Monkhouse, 28 March [1812]; *LSH*, p. 45. • **5.** SH to Miss Monkhouse [October 1808]; *LSH*, p. 9. • **6.** SC Autobiography, in Mudge, pp. 262–3. • **7.** Robert Southey, *The Doctor &C in one Volume*, ed. John Wood Warter (London: Longman, 1865), pp. 681–6. • **8.** See, for example, SC to Mary Stanger, 27 March 1851; Dove Cottage, WLMS Moorsom/55/1/71, in which SC talks of her longing for Keswick and the north: 'It's a privilege dear Mary to live as you do and look to live thro' life's evening in that lovely native vale of ours.' • **9.** STC to Thomas Wedgwood, 20 October 1802; *STCCL*, II, p. 876. • **10.** Southey to John Rickman, mid April 1807; *NLRS*, I, pp. 448–9. • **11.** STC to Southey, 25 December 1802; *STCCL*, II, p. 902. • **12.** SC Autobiography, in Mudge, p. 262. • **13.** SH to Miss Monkhouse [30 November 1808]; *LSH*, p. 12. • **14.** SC to EQ, 5 to 10 September 1846; Dove Cottage, WLMS A/Coleridge, Sara/43. • **15.** SC Autobiography, in Mudge, p. 261. • **16.** *Coleridge Fille*, p. 79. • **17.** All quotes from SC Autobiography, in Mudge, pp. 260–63. • **18.** SC to EQ, 5 to 10 September 1846; Dove Cottage, WLMS A/Coleridge, Sara/43. • **19.** All quotes from SC Autobiography, in Mudge, pp. 260–66. • **20.** *Phantasmion*, p. 133. • **21.** SC Autobiography, in Mudge, pp. 260–62. • **22.** STC to Mrs STC [9 September 1808]; *STCCL*, III, p. 121. • **23.** 25 December 1835; *HCR Diary*, II, p. 79. • **24.** WW to Richard Sharp, February 1805: *WW EL*, p. 445. • **25.** De Quincey, *Collected Writings, New and Enlarged Edition, in Fourteen Volumes*, ed. David Masson (Edinburgh: Adam and Charles Black, 1889), II, pp. 231–6. • **26.** WW to STC, 24 December 1799; *WW EL*, p. 236. • **27.** See Margaret and Robert Cochrane, *Housekeeping with Dorothy Wordsworth at Dove Cottage* (Beverley: Highgate Publications, 2001), especially pp. 17–21. See also DW to Mrs John Marshall, 10 and 12 September 1800; *WW EY*, pp. 245–54. • **28.** See Derek Roper, *Reviewing before the Edinburgh, 1788–1802* (Newark: University of Delaware Press, 1978), p. 94. • **29.** For the best overview of the early reception of *Lyrical Ballads*, see Roper, pp. 94 –101. • **30.** The article was by John Stoddart, an acquaintance of Wordsworth's. See Roper, p. 99. • **31.** Francis Jeffrey,

'Review of Southey's *Thalaba*', *Edinburgh Review*, 1 (October 1802), 63–83. • **32.** Mary Spaulding and Penny Welch, *Nurturing Yesterday's Child: A Portrayal of the Drake Collection of Paediatric History* (Toronto: Natural Heritage/Natural History Inc., 1994), p. 266. • **33.** DW to Lady Beaumont, 23 September 1804; *WW EL*, p. 503. • **34.** DW to Lady Beaumont, 24 August 1804; *WW EL*, p. 496. • **35.** WW, 'Address to my Infant Daughter, Dora, On being Reminded That She was a Month Old That Day, September 16'. • **36.** DW to Catherine Clarkson, 16 June 1811; *WW LMY*, II, p. 497. • **37.** All previous quotes from DW to Catherine Clarkson, 12 April 1810; *WW LMY*, II, pp. 397–9. • **38.** STC to Robert Southey, [8] January 1803; *STCCL*, II, p. 910. (Thomas Grattan also mentioned STC eating eggs cooked in this way over twenty-five years later, when he met him during a continental tour in 1829.) • **39.** DW to Catherine Clarkson, 16 June 1811; *WW LMY*, II, p. 495. • **40.** DW to Catherine Clarkson, 12 April 1810; *WW LMY*, II, p. 399. • **41.** STC to de Quincey, 2 February 1808; *STCCL*, III, p. 53. • **42.** SC Autobiography, in Mudge, p. 262. • **43.** DW to Richard Wordsworth, 23 March 1810; *WW LMY*, I, p. 394, and DW to Richard Wordsworth, 9 May 1810; *WW LMY*, I, p. 403. The rent on Allan Bank was £15 which included the right to cut as much peat as they wanted. Coal cost around £8 per year in addition. • **44.** STC to Thomas Poole, 12 January 1810; *STCCL*, III, p. 273. • **45.** WW to Lady Beaumont, 21 May 1807; *WW LMY*, II, p. 150. • **46.** WW, 'Ode: Intimations of Immortality from Recollections of Early Childhood'. • **47.** Francis Jeffrey, 'Review of Wordsworth Poems in Two Volumes', *Edinburgh Review*, 11 (October 1807), 214–31. • **48.** George Gordon Noel Byron, *The Works of Byron, Complete in One Volume*, 3rd edn (Frankfurt: H. L. Broener, 1837), p. 686 (review is reprinted from *Monthly Literary Recreation*, August 1807), p. 686. • **49.** Francis Jeffrey, 'Review of Wordsworth Poems in Two Volumes', *Edinburgh Review*, 11 (October 1807), 214–31, pp. 222 and 231.

2 'The Aunt-Hill', 1810

1. W. A. Speck, *Robert Southey: Entire Man of Letters* (New Haven and London: Yale University Press, 2006), p. 97. • **2.** STC to

Southey, Note [16 February 1807]; *STCCL*, III, p. 3. • **3**. Mrs STC to SC, Note [16 February 1807]; *STCCL*, III, p. 3. • **4**. Mrs STC to Thomas Poole, February 1814; *Minnow*, p. 65. • **5**. Southey to Thomas Southey, 25 February 1807; *NLRS*, I, p. 439. • **6**. H. D. Rawnsley, *Literary Associations of the English Lakes* (Glasgow: James MacLehose and Son, 1894), I, pp. 52–3. • **7**. Holmes *DR*, p. 201. • **8**. Southey to John Rickman [mid-April] 1807; *NLRS*, I, pp. 448–9. • **9**. Mrs STC to Thomas Poole, 3 August 1810; *Minnow*, p. 11. • **10**. STC to Mrs STC [19 February 1810]; *STCCL*, III, p. 284 [note written in the manuscript by Mrs STC]. • **11**. STC to Mrs STC [19 February 1810]; *STCCL*, III, p. 285. • **12**. Holmes *DR*, p. 200. • **13**. Holmes *DR*, p. 230. • **14**. 'Harum Scarum': SH to Miss Monkhouse [October 1808]; *LSH*, p. 10. 'Windermere Gentlemen': DW to Catherine Clarkson, 3 August 1808; *WW LMY*, II, p. 263. • **15**. DW to Catherine Clarkson, 30 October 1810; *WW LMY*, II, p. 440. • **16**. STC Notebooks, III, October 1810, note #3991. • **17**. STC to J. J. Morgan, 23 February 1812; *STCCL*, III, p. 376. • **18**. Molly Lefebure, *The Bondage of Love: A Life of Mrs. Samuel Taylor Coleridge* (London: Victor Gollancz, 1986), p. 202. • **19**. *Quincey Lit Rem*, II, pp. 21–2. • **20**. Christopher Wordsworth, *Memoirs of William Wordsworth, Poet-Laureate*, ed. Henry Reed, 2 vols (Boston: Ticknor, Reed, and Fields), 1851, I, p. 260. • **21**. H. D. Rawnsley, *Literary Associations of the English Lakes*, 2 vols (Glasgow: James MacLehose and Son, 1894), I, pp. 73–4. • **22**. Southey to Grosvenor C. Bedford, 14 September 1814; *SLRS*, III, p 270. • **23**. 'When Herbert's Mama was a Slim Little Maid', *SCCP*, p. 97. • **24**. Southey to Grosvenor C. Bedford, 14 September 1814; *SLRS*, III, p. 272. • **25**. 'When Herbert's Mama was a Slim Little Maid', *SCCP*, p. 97. • **26**. All previous quotes from SC Autobiography, in Mudge, pp. 258–9. • **27**. DW to Catherine Clarkson, 27 December 1811; *WW LMY*, II, p. 526. • **28**. DW to Catherine Clarkson, 18 November 1809; *WW LMY*, II, pp. 373–4. • **29**. DW to Catherine Clarkson, 16 June 1811; *WW LMY*, II, p. 497. • **30**. SH to Miss Monkhouse, 3 December 1811; *LSH*, p. 35. • **31**. DW to Catherine Clarkson, 14 August 1811; *WW LMY*, II, p. 501.

3 *'An Agony of Tears'*, *1812*

1. STC to J. J. Morgan, 23 February 1812; *STCCL*, III, p. 375.
• **2**. STC to J. J. Morgan, 11 February 1812; *STCCL*, III, pp. 368–9.
• **3**. Mrs STC to Thomas Poole, 30 October to 14 November 1812;
Minnow, p. 16. • **4**. Mrs Clarkson to WW, 4 May 1812; Dove Cottage,
WLL/Clarkson, Thomas/16. • **5**. Southey to WW [April 1812];
NLRS, I, pp. 32–3. • **6**. STC to J. J. Morgan [27 March 1812]; *STCCL*,
III, pp. 381–2 and notes. • **7**. STC to J. J. Morgan [23 February
1812]; *STCCL*, III, p. 375. • **8**. Mrs STC to Thomas Poole, 30
October to 14 November 1812; *Minnow*, p. 17. • **9**. DW to Jane
Marshall, 13 April 1810; *WW LMY*, II, p. 400. • **10**. DW to Catherine
Clarkson, 11 June 1812; *WW LMY*, III, p. 24. • **11**. WW to
Catherine Clarkson, 6 May 1812; *WW LMY*, III, p. 16. •
12. All previous quotes from DW to Catherine Clarkson, 23 June
[1812]; *WW LMY*, III, pp. 31–4. • **13**. MW to De Quincey, 20 August
1810; *WW LMY*, II, p. 429. • **14**. 'little Darling': MW to De Quincey,
20 August 1810; *WW LMY*, II, p. 428; 'dear Innocent': DW to De
Quincey, 5 June 1812; *WW LMY*, III, p. 23; 'spirit of infancy': *Quincey
Lit Rem*, p. 216; 'uncommonly good-tempered': DW to Catherine
Clarkson, 27 December 1811; *WW LMY*, II, p. 525; 'the purest spirit
in heaven': DW to Catherine Clarkson, 23 June [1812]; *WW LMY*,
III, p. 31. • **15**. DW to Catherine Clarkson, 23 June 1812; *WW
LMY*, III, p. 31. • **16**. De Quincey, *Confessions of an English Opium-
Eater* (London: The Bodley Head Ltd, 1930), p. 72. • **17**. All previous
quotes from De Quincey, *Collected Writings*, II, pp. 442–3. • **18**. DW
to Catherine Clarkson, 24 April 1814; *WW LMY*, III, p. 141. • **19**.
DW to Catherine Clarkson, 10 August 1812; *WW LMY*, III, p. 42.
• **20**. All previous quotes from DW to Catherine Clarkson, 5 January
1813; *WW LMY*, III, pp. 63–5. • **21**. DW to Elizabeth Threlkeld
and Jane Marshall, 19 January 1813; *WW LMY*, III, p. 71. • **22**. DW
to Catherine Clarkson, 5 January [1813]; *WW LMY*, III, pp. 60–61.
• **23**. DW to Elizabeth Threlkeld and Jane Marshall, 19 January 1813;
WW LMY, III, p. 71. • **24**. DW to Mary Hutchinson, 1 February
1813; *WW LMY*, III, p. 78. • **25**. DW to Catherine Clarkson, 31
July 1812; *WW LMY*, III, p. 40. • **26**. DW to Mary Hutchinson, 1
February 1813; *WW LMY*, III, p. 78.

4 'These Dark Steps', 1816

1. WW, 'The French Revolution: As It Appeared To Enthusiasts At Its Commencement'. • **2.** WW, 'It is a Beauteous Evening Calm and Free'. • **3.** DW to Sara Hutchinson, 8 April 1815; *WW LMY*, II, p. 223. • **4.** *SCCP*, p. 97. • **5.** SC to Mrs STC, 9–10 September 1843; HRC MS. • **6.** SC Autobiography, in Mudge, p. 265. • **7.** Aubrey de Vere, Diary, 6 August 1841; *Aubrey de Vere, A Memoir, Based on his Unpublished Diaries and Correspondence*, ed. Wilfrid Ward (London: Longmans Green and Company, 1904), p. 88. • **8.** MW to DW, 29 October 1814; *LMW*, p. 24. • **9.** SH to Miss J. Hutchinson, 24 November 1815; *LSH*, p. 87. • **10.** 'terrible Battles': DW to Catherine Clarkson, 31 July 1812; *WW LMY*, II, p. 40; cold baths and obstinacy: DW to Catherine Clarkson, 15 August 1815; *WW LMY*, II, p. 246; unsteady at her books is a repeated claim, e.g. DW to Mary Hutchinson, 1 February 1813; *WW LMY*, III, p. 80, or DW to Priscilla Wordsworth, 27 February 1815; *WW LMY*, III, p. 208; 'fits of obstinacy with pride': DW to Catherine Clarkson, 4 April 1816; *WW LMY*, III, p. 294. • **11.** DW to Catherine Clarkson, 31 July 1812; *WW LMY*, III, p. 40. • **12.** DW to Catherine Clarkson, 4 April 1816; *WW LMY*, III, p. 294. • **13.** Mrs STC to Thomas Poole, February [1814?], *Minnow*, p. 26. • **14.** Mrs STC to Thomas Poole, 20 September [1815?], *Minnow*, pp. 41–2. • **15.** 'The Narrow Escape', *SCCP*, p. 104. • **16.** DW to Catherine Clarkson, 24 April [1814?], *WW LMY*, III, p. 141. • **17.** SC to Frank Coleridge, 1 February 1844, HCR MS. • **18.** DW to Catherine Clarkson, 4 April 1816; *WW LMY*, III, p. 294. • **19.** 'January brings the blast', *SCCP*, p. 83. • **20.** Southey to Sharon Turner, 2 April 1816; *LCRS*, IV, p. 154. • **21.** Southey to WW, 28 April 1816; *LCRS*, IV, p. 168. • **22.** *Memoir*, I, p. 30. • **23.** See DW to SH [11 September 1813?]; *WW LMY*, III, pp. 109–13 and DW to Catherine Clarkson [about 14 September 1813]; *WW LMY*, III, p. 114. • **24.** SH to Thomas Monkhouse, 23 June [1813?]; *LSH*, p. 55. • **25.** DW to Catherine Clarkson [about 14 September 1813]; *WW LMY*, III, p. 114. • **26.** WW to Thomas Poole, 13 March 1815; *WW LMY*, III, p. 209. • **27.** SC to HNC, 29 September to 2 October 1838, HCR MS. • **28.** WW, Poems of Sentiment and Reflection, XXIV, lines 54–7. • **29.** Francis Jeffrey, 'Wordsworth's Excursion', *Edinburgh Review*, 24 (November 1814),

1–4. • **30**. 24 May 1812; Henry Crabb Robinson, *Henry Crabb Robinson on Books and Their Writers*, ed. Edith J. Morley, 3 vols (London: J. M. Dent and Sons, 1938), I, p. 85. • **31**. WW to John Scott, 18 April 1816; *WW LMY*, III, p. 304. • **32**. STC to WW, 30 May 1815; *STCCL*, IV, p. 575. • **33**. David Higgins, *Romantic Genius and the Literary Magazine: Biography, Celebrity, and Politics* (Oxon: Routledge, 2005), p. 96. • **34**. William Hazlitt, *The Spirit of the Age, or, Contemporary Portraits: and 'My first Acquaintance with Poets'*, introductory essays by Robert Woof; Foreword by Michael Foot (Grasmere: The Wordsworth Trust, 2004), p. 203. • **35**. WW to unknown correspondent, no date, probably between 1804 and 1808; *WW LMY*, I, pp. 284–8. • **36**. DW to Jane Marshall, 25 June [1817]; *WW LMY*, II, p. 395. • **37**. SC to DW, 25 May 1818; Dove Cottage, WLMS A/Coleridge, Sara/1.

5 *'Like the Graces', 1821–1822*

1. Sarah Harriet Burney, *Country Neighbours*, 2nd edn, 3 vols (London: Henry Colburn, 1820), I, p. 79. • **2**. MW to John Kenyon, 28 December [1821]; *WW LLY*, I, pp. 100–101. • **3**. *The Times*, Tuesday, 16 July 1816, p. 2. • **4**. Note, STC to John Taylor Coleridge [9 February 1823]; *STCCL*, V, p. 268. • **5**. 'Namput': HC to Mrs STC, 1829, *LHC*, p. 98; 'Snimpet': H. W. Howe, *Greta Hall: Home of Coleridge and Southey*, with revisions by Robert Woof (Norfolk: Daedalus Press, 1977), p. 35 and 'butterfly's wing': SC to Derwent Coleridge, 12 October 1821; *LSH*, note p. 233. • **6**. DW to Catherine Clarkson, 24 October 1821; *WW LLY*, I, p. 89. • **7**. DW to Catherine Clarkson, 19 December 1819; *WW LMY*, III, p. 571. • **8**. DW to Catherine Clarkson, 26 May [1816]; *WW LMY*, III, p. 320. • **9**. SH to John Monkhouse, 7 September [1820]; *LSH*, p. 195. • **10**. SH to MW, 11 September [1820]; *LSH*, p. 198. • **11**. SH to John Monkhouse, November–December 1819; *LSH*, p. 167. • **12**. Compared to Edith, SH wrote, 'Sara C is more of the Piano . . . she is far less indifferent to admiration than Edith': SH to John Monkhouse, 7 September [1820]; *LSH*, p. 195. • **13**. SH to John Monkhouse, 7 September [1820]; *LSH*, p. 195. • **14**. SH to Mrs

Hutchinson, 27 February 1820; *LSH*, p. 177. • **15**. MW to DW [9 May 1839]; *LMW*, p. 238. • **16**. Mrs STC to Thomas Poole [20 September 1820]; *Minnow*, p. 82. • **17**. Mrs STC to Thomas Poole [11 March 1820]; *Minnow*, p. 88. • **18**. EQ Diary, 1821; Dove Cottage, WLMS/13/1/5/a, pp. 13–15. • **19**. WW and MW to John Kenyon, 22 September 1821; *WW LLY*, I, p. 83. • **20**. SH to Thomas Monkhouse [5 February 1822]; *LSH*, p. 233. • **21**. WW, 'The Triad'. • **22**. DW to EQ, 31 December 1821; Dove Cottage, WLL/ Wordsworth, Dora/1/1a. • **23**. 'An Account of the Abipones, an Equestrian People of Paraguay. Translated from the Latin of Martin Dobrizhoffer, Eighteen Years a Missionary in that Country', *Quarterly Review*, 26, 52 (January 1822), 277–323. • **24**. Charles Lamb to Southey, 19 August 1825; *The Letters of Charles Lamb Complete in One Volume With a Sketch of his Life*, ed. Sir Thomas Noon Talfourd (Philadelphia: Henry Carey Baird, 1857), p. 158. • **25**. SH to Thomas Monkhouse [5 February 1822]; *LSH*, p. 233. • **26**. SC to Dora, April 1822; Dove Cottage, WLMS/Coleridge, Sara /5. • **27**. SH to Thomas Monkhouse [5 February 1822]; *LSH*, p. 233. • **28**. SH to Thomas Monkhouse, 22 February 1822; *LSH*, p. 237. • **29**. DW to EQ, 6 August 1822; *WW LLY*, I, p. 148. • **30**. Mrs STC to Thomas Poole, 7 November 1821; *Minnow*, p. 90. • **31**. SC to Dora, 13 April 1822; Dove Cottage, WLMS A/Coleridge, Sara/5. • **32**. Henry Nelson Coleridge, *Specimens of the Table Talk of Samuel Taylor Coleridge*, 2 vols (London: John Murray, 1835), II, p. 81. • **33**. HC to Derwent, 30 August [1830]; *LHC*, pp. 108–109. • **34**. Southey to WW, 11 April 1822; *NLRS*, II, p. 235. • **35**. DW to HCR, 3 March 1822; *WW LLY*, I, p. 114. • **36**. 'Memorials of a Tour on the Continent by William Wordsworth', *Edinburgh Review*, 37 (November 1822), 449–556. • **37**. Originally an introduction and accompaniment to the engravings in Joseph Wilkinson's *Select Views in Cumberland, Westmoreland, and Lancashire* (1810). Wordsworth's *Guide* reappeared in expanded texts in 1820, 1822, 1823 and 1835; the full title in 1835 was *A Guide through the District of the Lakes in the North of England, with a Description of the Scenery, &c. for the Use of Tourists and Residents*. • **38**. WW to Walter Savage Landor, 20 April [1822]; *WW LLY*, I, p. 126. • **39**. DW to EQ, 19 November [1822]; *WW LLY*, I, p. 167.

6 'Prime and Pride of Youth', 1823

1. Morton D. Paley, *Portraits of Coleridge* (Oxford: Oxford University Press, 1999), p. 53. • **2**. Byron to Thomas Moore, 27 September 1813; George Gordon Noel Byron, *Byron's Letters and Journals*, ed. Leslie Marchand, 12 vols (London: John Murray, 1982), III, p. 428. • **3**. *Coleridge Fille*, p. 43; for the lines of verse, see *SCCP*, pp. 30–31. • **4**. Mudge, p. 32. • **5**. E. V. Lucas, *The Life of Charles Lamb*, 2nd edn, 2 vols (London: Methuen & Co., 1905), II, p. 101. • **6**. John Gibson Lockhart to Mrs Lockhart, 25 August 1825; *The Familiar Letters of Sir Walter Scott*, ed. David Douglas, 2 vols (Boston: Houghton Mifflin, 1894), II, p. 342. • **7**. Kathleen Coburn, *In Pursuit of Coleridge* (Oxford: Bodley Head, 1977), pp. 28–9. • **8**. JTC, Journal, 19 March 1822; BL Add MS 47558. • **9**. Holmes *DR*, p. 359. • **10**. All previous quotes from HNC to Revd James Coleridge, 11 January 1823; BL Add MS 47558. • **11**. 'garrulous': JTC, Journal, 1 February 1823; BL Add MSS 86027–86060 and 'tyrant': HNC to Revd James Coleridge, 11 March 1823; BL Add MS 47558. • **12**. HC to Mrs STC [1829]; *LHC*, p. 98. • **13**. Mrs STC to DC, 6 October 1826; HRC MS. • **14**. *Coleridge Fille*, p. 45. • **15**. DW to EQ, 17 June 1823; *WW LLY*, I, p. 200. • **16**. SH to EQ, 15 or 18 March 1823; *LSH*, p. 248. • **17**. DW to Mary Laing, 26 August 1823; *WW LLY*, I, p. 214. • **18**. DW to Elizabeth Crumpe, 31 August 1823; *WW LLY*, I, p. 219.

7 'Budding, Billing, Singing Weather', 1823

1. Penrith racecourse was built in 1814. For an interesting account of Penrith's history, see *Penrith Town and Parish*, <http://www.stevebulman. f9.co.uk/cumbria/penrith_f.html> [accessed 12 November 2011]. • **2**. DW to Catherine Clarkson, 11 or 12 November 1823; *WW LLY*, I, p. 230. • **3**. SH to EQ, 1 November [30 October 1823]; *LSH*, p. 267. • **4**. Dora to Joanna Hutchinson, quoted in note to letter: DW to Mary Laing, 25 November 1823; *WW LLY*, I, p. 234. • **5**. DW to Mary Laing, 28 December [1823]; *WW LLY*, I, pp. 239–40. • **6**. Tom Monkhouse to Mrs Tom Hutchinson, 26 March [1823]; Dove Cottage, WLMS H/1/15/7. • **7**. Dora to EQ, 22 March 1824;

Dove Cottage, WLL/Wordsworth, Dora/1/4. • **8**. WW, 'The Parrot and the Wren', XXI, 'The Contrast' from Poems of the Fancy. • **9**. Dora to Maria Jane Jewsbury, 21 May [1828]; Vincent, p. 39. • **10**. When Dorothy wrote to Quillinan to update him with news of Rydal, she did not bother to tell him anything of Dora because she knew he would have been in more recent and regular contact than Dorothy herself. • **11**. DW to John Monkhouse, 16 April 1824; *WW LLY*, I, p. 261. • **12**. DW to EQ, 19 April 1824; *WW LLY*, I, p. 264. • **13**. Horace Walpole to Miss Mary Berry, 23 June 1790; Horace Walpole, *The Letters of Horace Walpole*, eds Helen Wrigley Toynbee and Paget Jackson Toynbee, 16 vols (Oxford: Clarendon Press), 1905, XIV, pp. 270–71. • **14**. Dora to Maria Jane Jewsbury [September 1825], Vincent, p. 26. • **15**. Dora to EQ, 11 May 1824; Dove Cottage, WLL/Wordsworth, Dora/1/5. • **16**. DW to Thomas Monkhouse, 20 May 1824; *WW LLY*, I, p. 267. • **17**. DW to EQ [3 May 1824]; *WW LLY*, I, p. 266. • **18**. Poem by Edward Quillinan, 'To The Poet', 30 April 1824; Dove Cottage, WLMS 11/9–50/19. • **19**. SC to DC, 27 June 1824; HCR MS. • **20**. DW to Lady Beaumont, 18 September 1824; *WW LLY*, I, p. 274. • **21**. SC to JTC, 17 August 1824; HCR MS. • **22**. Henry Reed, 'The Daughter of Coleridge', *The Literary World* (January 1853); reprinted in *Sara Coleridge and Henry Reed*, ed. L. N. Broughton (New York: Ithaca, 1937), p. 86. Sara made the comment in the margin of Volume II, p. 367, of *The Memoirs of William Wordsworth*, compiled by Revd Christopher Wordsworth. • **23**. SC to JTC, 17 August 1824; HRC MS. • **24**. 'Oh, how, Love, must I fill', *SCCP*, p. 49. • **25**. SC to Elizabeth Crumpe, 19 October 1832; Dove Cottage, WLMS 16/365.39.

8 *'The Parrot and the Wren'*, 1826

1. 'My cousin . . . almost my sister': Henry Nelson Coleridge, *Six Months in the West Indies in 1825* (London: John Murray, 1826), p. 117; 'fair and languid shape': HNC, *Six Months*, p. 39. • **2**. HC to DC [1826]; *LHC*, p. 93. • **3**. HNC, *Six Months in the West Indies in 1825* (London: John Murray, 1826), p. 251. • **4**. 1 Corinthians 15:58. • **5**. Southey to Edith May Berth and Katherine Southey, 19 July 1826; *LCRS*, V, pp. 255 – 9. • **6**. Advertisements & Notices, *Liverpool Mercury*,

Friday, 4 August 1826. • **7**. All previous quotes from SH to EQ, 23 August 1826; *LSH*, pp. 322–3. • **8**. Mrs STC to Thomas Poole, 28 August 1826; *Minnow*, pp. 131–2. • **9**. *Coleridge Fille*, p. 61. • **10**. *Coleridge Fille*, p. 61. • **11**. HNC, *Specimens of the Table Talk of Samuel Taylor Coleridge*, 2 vols (London: John Murray, 1835), I, p. 54. • **12**. SC to DC, 6 January 1826; HCR MS. • **13**. WW, 'The Parrot and the Wren'. • **14**. SH to EQ, 28 September 1826; *LSH*, pp. 328–9. • **15**. Dora to Maria Jane Jewsbury, 17 July 1829; Vincent, p. 58; Dora to Maria Jane Jewsbury, 12 April 1829; Vincent, p. 46. • **16**. All previous quotes from Bertha Hill to Mary Stanger, 6 March unknown year; Dove Cottage, WLMS/Moorsom/59/1/13. • **17**. Dora to Maria Jane Jewsbury, 21 July 1831; Vincent, p. 90. • **18**. SH to EQ, 23 August 1826; *LSH*, p. 323. • **19**. WW to Mrs Richard Wordsworth [? early 1827]; *WW LLY*, I, p. 502. • **20**. Henry Reed, 'The Daughter of Coleridge', *The Literary World* (January 1853); reprinted in *Sara Coleridge and Henry Reed*, ed. L. N. Broughton (New York: Ithaca, 1937), p. 86. • **21**. HC to Derwent, 30 August 1830; *LHC*, p. 112. • **22**. WW and MW to John Kenyon, 25 July 1826; *WW LLY*, I, p. 474. • **23**. HC to Derwent, 30 August 1830; *LHC*, p. 112. • **24**. DW to HCR, 18 December 1826; *WW LLY*, I, p. 500.

9 *Bridesmaid and Bride, 1828–1829*

1. George Eliot, *Middlemarch* (London: William Blackwood & Sons, 1871), p. 188. • **2**. Dora to Maria Jane Jewsbury, 21 May [1828]; Vincent, p. 39. • **3**. WW, 'The Triad'. • **4**. Dora to Maria Jane Jewsbury, 21 May [1828]; Vincent, p. 39. • **5**. HC to Thomas Blackburne [1847]; *LHC*, p. 293. • **6**. Henry Reed, 'The Daughter of Coleridge', *The Literary World* (January 1853); reprinted in *Sara Coleridge and Henry Reed*, ed. L. N. Broughton (New York: Ithaca, 1937), p. 86. • **7**. Thomas Grattan, *Beaten Paths and Those Who Trod Them*, 2 vols (London: Chapman and Hall, 1862), II, p. 110. • **8**. SC to Elizabeth Wardell, 10 July [1828]; Dove Cottage, WLMS A/ Coleridge, Sara/22. • **9**. All quotations from Dora Wordsworth, *Journal of a Tour of the Continent*; Dove Cottage, unpublished MS 110. • **10**. Grattan, *Beaten Paths*, II, p. 119. • **11**. *Journal of a Tour of the*

Continent; Dove Cottage, MS 110. See also Judith Page, 'Neatly-Penned Memorials: Dora Wordsworth's Journal of 1828 and the Community of Authorship', *A/B: Autobiography Studies*, 17 (2002), 65–80. Page is particularly interesting on the way in which Dora envisioned the world. • **12**. Barker, p. 540. • **13**. Dora, *Journal*; Dove Cottage, MS 110. • **14**. Grattan, *Beaten Paths*, II, p. 115. • **15**. Quoted in Barker, p. 602. • **16**. Dora to EQ [19 December 1829]; Dove Cottage, WLL/Wordsworth, Dora/1/25. • **17**. SC to Elizabeth Wardell (née Crumpe), 2 February 1829; Dove Cottage, WWL, WLMS A/Coleridge, Sara/20. • **18**. WW to HCR, 26 April 1829; *WW LLY*, II, p. 69. • **19**. SC to Elizabeth Wardell (née Crumpe), 13 April 1829; Dove Cottage, WLMS A/Coleridge, Sara/23. • **20**. SC to Elizabeth Wardell (née Crumpe), 5 July 1828; Dove Cottage, WLMS A/Coleridge, Sara/21. • **21**. SC to Louisa Powles, 27 March 1829; BL Add MS 85958. • **22**. SC to Elizabeth Wardell (née Crumpe), 2 February 1829; Dove Cottage, WWL, WLMS A/Coleridge, Sara/20. • **23**. SC to Louisa Powles, 27 July 1829; BL Add MS 85958. • **24**. SC to Louisa Powles, 27 March 1829; BL Add MS 85958. • **25**. See William Wordsworth, *The Fenwick Notes of William Wordsworth*, ed. Jared Diamond (Bristol: Bristol Classical Press, 1993; and newly corrected edition, Jared Curtis, HumanitiesEbooks.co.uk, 2007), pp. 157–8. Wordsworth gave Felicia Hemans, the poet, a gift of a set of scales since 'she was totally innocent of housewifery'. • **26**. SC to Louisa Powles, 27 March 1829; BL Add MS 85958. • **27**. SC to Elizabeth Wardell (née Crumpe), 2 February 1829; Dover Cottage, WWL, WLMS A/Coleridge, Sara/20. • **28**. SC to Louisa Powles, 1829; BL Add MS 85958. • **29**. SC to Elizabeth Wardell (née Crumpe), 2 February 1829; Dover Cottage, WWL, WLMS A/Coleridge, Sara/20. • **30**. HC to Mrs STC [July 1829]; *LHC*, p. 98. • **31**. WW to George Huntly Gordon, 16 June 1829: *WW LLY*, II, p. 86. • **32**. Mrs STC to Thomas Poole, 15 July 1829; *Minnow*, pp. 148–9. • **33**. Mrs STC to Thomas Poole, 15 July 1829; *Minnow*, pp. 148–9. • **34**. MW to Dora [9 May 1839]; Dove Cottage, WLL/Wordsworth, Mary/2/132. • **35**. SC to Louisa Powles, 27 March 1829; BL Add MS 85958. • **36**. SC to Louisa Powles, 31 July 1829; BL Add MS 85958. • **37**. Coleridge had pledged to give Sara a copy of the book in his will. The last revision of his will was dated 29 September 1929 but did not reflect the fact that Sara had, at that stage, been married two weeks. Presumably he had written it some time before and did not alter it after her wedding. • **38**. HC to Mrs STC, 1829; *LHC*, p. 101. • **39**. SC to Louisa Powles, 8 September 1829; BL Add MS 85958. • **40**. Mrs STC to Thomas Poole, 15 July 1829; *Minnow*, p. 147. • **41**. Southey to Mrs Septimus Hodson, 10 September 1829; *NLRS*, p. 344. • **42**. DW to Jane Marshall, 15 September 1829; *WW LLY*, II, p. 131. • **43**. WW to SC [late 1829 date uncertain]; *WW LLY*, II, p. 186. • **44**. DW and Dora to Maria Jane Jewsbury, 11 September 1829; *WW LLY*, II, p. 127. • **45**. HNC in SC's commonplace book, December 1826; Mudge, p. 48. • **46**. *Coleridge Fille*, pp. 62–3.

10 'Sorrows of the Night', 1834

1. Weather from Thomas Carlyle to Jean Carlyle Aitken, 6 July 1834; *The Carlyle Letters Online*, 2007. Available at <http://carlyleletters.org> [accessed 12 January 2012]. • **2**. SC and Mrs STC to DW [16 July 1834]; Dove Cottage, WLMS A/Coleridge, Sara/33. • **3**. SC to Elizabeth Wardell (née Crumpe) [18 February 1830]; Dove Cottage, WLMS A/Coleridge, Sara/26. • **4**. SC to Louisa Powles, 7 April 1830; BL Add MS 85958. • **5**. Sara Coleridge, *Pretty Lessons in Verse for Good Children with some Lessons in Latin in Easy Rhyme*, 3rd edn (London: John W. Parker, 1839), p. 95. • **6**. SC to Elizabeth Wardell, 25 February 1831; Dove Cottage, WLMS A/Coleridge, Sara/27. • **7**. *Coleridge Fille*, p. 74. • **8**. SC and Mrs STC to Emily Trevenen, 27 February 1832; HRC MS. • **9**. *Coleridge Fille*, p. 74. • **10**. SC, 'Diary of her Children's Early Years', 1 May 1833; HRC MS. • **11**. Alexander Hamilton, *A Treatise on the Management of Female Complaints* (Edinburgh: George Ramsay & Company, 1813), pp. 47–50. • **12**. Elisabeth Young-Bruehl, *Subject to Biography: Psychoanalysis, Feminism, and Writing Women's Lives* (Cambridge, MA: Harvard University Press, 1998). The book discusses the far greater complexity of the issue than it is possible to encompass here; see, for example, pp. 203–4 on some of the parallels between eating disorders and hysteria. • **13**. SC, 'Diary of her Children's Early Years', March 1833; HRC MS. • **14**. SC to Elizabeth Wardell (née

Crumpe), 29 March 1833; Dove Cottage, WLMS A/Coleridge, Sara/31. • **15**. SC to HNC, 21 March 1833: HRC MS. • **16**. STC to the Wordsworths, 4 April 1804; *STCCL*, II, pp. 1115–16. • **17**. STC *Notebooks*, II, note #2085. • **18**. Holmes *DR*, p. 14. • **19**. STC *Notebooks*, II, note #2091. • **20**. 'Verses written in sickness 1833, before the Birth of Berkeley and Florence', in *SCCP*, pp. 62–3. • **21**. Aubrey de Vere, Diary, 6 August 1841; *Aubrey de Vere, A Memoir, Based on his Unpublished Diaries and Correspondence*, ed. Wilfrid Ward (London: Longmans Green and Company, 1904), p. 89. • **22**. SC, 'Diary of her Children's Early Years', 12 January 1834; HRC MS. • **23**. SC, 'Diary of her Children's Early Years', 7 February 1834; HRC MS. • **24**. SH to EQ, 17 March [1834]; *LSH*, p. 407. • **25**. HNC to SC, 20 March 1834; BL Add MS 47558. • **26**. HNC to Louisa Powles, 18 May 1834; BL Add MS 86340. • **27**. SC Autobiography, in Mudge, pp. 210–11.

11 *'What is to Come of Me?'*, *1834*

1. WW to HNC, 29 July 1834; *WW LLY*, II, pp. 727–9. • **2**. WW to HNC, 29 July 1834; *WW LLY*, II, p.728. • **3**. SC to Dora [July 1834]; Dove Cottage, WLMS A/Coleridge, Sara/33. • **4**. See Heidi Thomson, 'Sara Coleridge's Annotation in Pretty Lessons in Verse for Good Children', in *Notes and Queries* (2011) 58 (4), 548–9. • **5**. SC to Dora, [July 1834]; Dove Cottage, WLMS A/Coleridge, Sara/33. • **6**. DW to EQ, 1 June 1835; Dove Cottage, WLL/Wordsworth, Dora/1/64. • **7**. WW to DW [8 November 1830]; *WW LLY*, II, p. 338. • **8**. SC to DW, 16 June 1835; Dove Cottage, WLMS A/Coleridge, Sara/37. • **9**. SC to William Wardell, December 1834; Dove Cottage, WLMS A/Coleridge, Sara/35. • **10**. SH to Mary Clarkson, 28 June 1834; *LSH*, p. 419. • **11**. Dora to EQ, 26 June, 1832; Dove Cottage, WLL/Wordsworth, Dora/1/41. • **12**. WW and Dora to EQ, 26 June 1832; Dove Cottage, WLL/Wordsworth, Dora/1/41. • **13**. WW to EQ, 10 July [1832]; *WW LLY*, II, p. 541. • **14**. WW to EQ [26 June 1832]; *WW LLY*, II, p. 539. • **15**. Dora to EQ, 26 June [1832]; Dove Cottage, WLL/Wordsworth, Dora/1/41. • **16**. WW to EQ, 11 June [1834]; *WW LLY*, II, pp. 718–20. • **17**. EQ to WW, 12 September 1834; Dove Cottage, WLL/Quillinan, Edward/1/52. • **18**. SH to EQ,

8 January 1835; *LSH*, p. 437. • **19**. EQ to DW, 10 March 1835; Dove Cottage, WLL/Quillinan, Edward/1/54. • **20**. DW to Lady Beaumont [5 January 1834]: *WW LLY*, II, p. 684. • **21**. Dora to EQ, 3 October 1832; Dove Cottage, WLL/Wordsworth, Dora/1/44. • **22**. SH to Mrs STC [9] February [1833]; *LSH*, p. 391. • **23**. WW to Christopher Wordsworth, 1 April 1832: *WW LLY*, II, p. 517. • **24**. Dora to Maria Jane Jewsbury, 3 December 1831; Vincent, p. 93. • **25**. WW to Eliza Hamilton, 10 January 1833; *WW LLY*, II, p. 581. • **26**. WW to HCR [*c*. 14 November 1833]; *WW LLY*, II, pp. 657–8. • **27**. Dora to Maria Jane Jewsbury, 28 December 1828; Vincent, p. 45. • **28**. Dora to Christopher Wordsworth, 12 November 1833; Dove Cottage, WLL/Wordsworth, Dora/56. • **29**. Dora to Jemima Quillinan, 6 October 1833; Dove Cottage, WLL/Wordsworth, Dora/1/54. • **30**. DW to Lady Beaumont, 13 January [1834]; *WW LLY*, II, p. 683. • **31**. Dora to Maria Jane Jewsbury 20 October 1831; Vincent, pp. 90–91.

Interlude, 1834–1835

1. Rosemary Hill, *God's Architect: Pugin and the Building of Romantic Britain* (London: Penguin), 2007, p. 128. • **2**. All previous quotes from SC to HNC, 7 October 1834; HRC MS. • **3**. SC to HNC, 3 January 1835; HRC MS. • **4**. J. A. Heraud, 'Coleridgeana', *Fraser's Magazine for Town and Country*, 13 (January 1835), 50–58, p. 50. • **5**. SC to HNC, 3 January 1835; HRC MS. • **6**. SH to Thomas Hutchinson [3 or 10 August 1834]; *LSH*, p. 428. • **7**. Dora to EQ, 1 October 1834; Dove Cottage, WWL/Quillinan, Edward/1/52. • **8**. *Specimens of the Table Talk of Samuel Taylor Coleridge*, ed. Henry Nelson Coleridge, 2 vols (London: John Murray, 1835), I, p. ix. • **9**. *Coleridge Fille*, p. 100. • **10**. Mudge, p. 76. • **11**. SC to Louisa Plummer, 1835; *Memoir*, I, pp. 123–4. • **12**. 'On Nervousness', in Mudge, p. 213. • **13**. 'On Nervousness', in Mudge, p. 205. • **14**. SC to Louisa Plummer, October 1834; *Memoir*, I, p. 115. • **15**. SC to Louisa Plummer, October 1834; *Coleridge Fille*, p. 107. (Interestingly this part of the letter is not included in Edith Coleridge's Memoir – her collection of her mother's letters.) • **16**. MW to Isabella Fenwick, 13 May [1835]; *LMW*, p. 145. • **17**. SH to EQ, 8 January 1835; *LSH*,

p. 437. • **18**. SC to William Wardell, December 1834; Dove Cottage, WLMS A/Coleridge, Sara/35. • **19**. WW to Southey [24 June 1835]: *WW LLY*, III, p. 66. • **20**. WW to HCR, 24 June [1835]: *WW LLY*, III, p. 65. • **21**. SC to Dora [1835]; Dove Cottage, WLMS A/Coleridge, Sara/38. • **22**. WW to Catherine Clarkson, 6 August 1835; *WW LLY*, III, p. 83. • **23**. Dora to EQ, 1 June 1835; Dove Cottage, WLL/Wordsworth, Dora/1/64.

12 *A Moment's Blaze Across the Darkness, 1836*

1. WW to his Family [early June 1836]; *WW LLY*, III, p. 239. • **2**. WW and Dora to HCR, 27 April 1836; *WW LLY*, III, p. 208. • **3**. MW and DW to Jane Marshall [mid-December 1835]; *WW LLY*, III, p. 140. • **4**. Robert Gittings and Jo Manton, *Dorothy Wordsworth* (Oxford: Oxford University Press, 1985), p. 273. • **5**. WW to HCR, 6 July [1835]; *WW LLY*, III, p. 78. • **6**. WW to his family [22 May 1836]; *WW LLY*, III, p. 224. • **7**. WW to his family [*c.* 17 June 1836]; *WW LLY*, III, pp. 253–4. • **8**. WW to his family [early June 1836]; *WW LLY*, III, p. 239. • **9**. WW to his family [25 June 1836]; *WW LLY*, III, p. 261. • **10**. WW to his family [30 June 1836]; *WW LLY*, III, p. 271. • **11**. WW to his family [24 June 1836]; *WW LLY*, III, p. 260. • **12**. WW to his family [?29 June 1836]; *WW LLY*, III, p. 269. • **13**. WW to his family [27 June 1836]; *WW LLY*, III, p. 266. • **14**. WW to his family [?29 June 1836]; *WW LLY*, III, p. 270. • **15**. WW to his family [30 June 1836]; *WW LLY*, III, p. 272. • **16**. WW to EQ [5 July 1836]; *WW LLY*, III, p. 278. • **17**. WW to his Family, 4 [June 1836]; *WW LLY*, III, p. 241. • **18**. WW to his Family [5 July 1837]; *WW LLY*, III, pp. 423–4. • **19**. Southey to John May, 1 August 1835; *LCRS*, VI, p. 272. • **20**. MW to HCR, 6 November 1836; *WW LLY*, III, p. 315. • **21**. See MW to HCR [28 September 1836]; *WW LLY*, III, note, pp. 297–8. • **22**. MW to HCR [28 September 1836]; *WW LLY*, III, pp. 297–8. • **23**. HC to Mrs STC, 21 August [1836]; *LHC*, p. 195. • **24**. EQ to Dora, 22 April 1838; Dove Cottage, WLL/Quillinan, Edward/1/79. • **25**. EQ Diary, 13 September 1836; Dove Cottage, WLMS 13/3/1.2. • **26**. EQ Diary, 16 September 1836; Dove Cottage, WLMS 13/3/1.2.

• **27**. EQ to MW, 29 October 1836; Dove Cottage, WLL/Quillinan, Edward/1/65. • **28**. EQ to Dora, 25 November 1836; Dove Cottage, WLL/Quillinan, Edward/1/67. • **29**. WW to Christopher Wordsworth Jnr, 9 January [1837]; *WW LLY*, III, p. 343.

13 *'This Filial Likeness'*, 1836

1. SC to HNC [17 October 1836]; HRC MS. • **2**. SC to Emily Trevenen, 8 October 1836; HRC MS. • **3**. SC to HNC [19 October 1836]; HRC MS. • **4**. SC Autobiography, in Mudge, p. 215. • **5**. SC, 'Diary of her Children's Early Years', 23 October 1836; HRC MS. • **6**. SC to HNC, 21 [October 1836]; HRC MS. • **7**. SC, 'Diary of her Children's Early Years', 7 November 1836; HRC MS. • **8**. SC to HNC, 19 October [1836]; HRC MS. • **9**. SC to HNC, 22 [October 1836]; HRC MS. • **10**. SC to Mary Stanger, 25 October 1835; Dove Cottage, Moorsom 55/1/10. • **11**. SC to Arabella Brooke, 29 July 1837; HRC MS. • **12**. *Phantasmion*, p. 186. • **13**. SC to Arabella Brooke, 29 July 1837; HRC MS. • **14**. Brian Stableford makes this argument in his *Historical Dictionary of Fantasy Literature* (Lanham, Maryland, Toronto and Oxford: The Scarecrow Press, Inc., 2005), as does Roger C. Schlobin in *The Literature of Fantasy: A Comprehensive, Annotated Bibliography of Modern Fantasy Fiction* (New York: Garland Publishing, 1979). • **15**. Holmes *EV*, p. xvi. • **16**. HC to HNC, 8 May 1836; *LHC*, p. 189. • **17**. *Coleridge Fille*, p. 100. • **18**. In her essay about Sara Coleridge, Virginia Woolf described Sara as a 'heaven-haunter', like her father. Virginia Woolf, 'Sara Coleridge', *The Death of the Moth and Other Essays* (New York: Harcourt Brace Jovanovich, 1970), pp. 111–18; p. 114. • **19**. SC to HNC, 15 November 1836; HRC MS. • **20**. SC to Derwent, 20–22 [October] 1825; HRC MS. • **21**. SC to Derwent, 2 February 1826; HRC MS. • **22**. Vardy, pp. 92–3. • **23**. SC to HNC, 29 September 1837; HRC MS. • **24**. Dennis Low, *The Literary Protégées of the Lake Poets* (Hampshire: Ashgate, 2006), p. 141. • **25**. From STC's Notebooks, quoted in Low, p. 137. • **26**. SC to HNC, 4 September 1834; HRC MS. • **27**. SC to HNC, 6 November 1836; HRC MS. • **28**. *Phantasmion*, p. 14. • **29**. SC to HNC, 10 November 1836; HRC MS. • **30**. SC to HNC, 13

November 1836; HRC MS. • **31**. SC, 'Nervousness', in Mudge, p. 214. • **32**. For more information about emmenagogues, see Etienne van de Walle and Elisha P. Renne (eds), *Regulating Menstruation: Beliefs, Practices, Interpretations* (Chicago: University of Chicago Press, 2001). • **33**. Malcolm Potts and Martha Campbell, 'History of Contraception', in *Gynecology & Obstetrics*, 6 (2004), Chapter 8. • **34**. SC, 'Diary of her Children's Early Years', 16 November 1836; HRC MS.

14 Saudades *and the Dread Voice that Speaks from Out the Sea, 1837–1838*

1. Dora to Miss Fenwick, 19 April 1838; Dove Cottage, WLL/Wordsworth, Dora/1/68. • **2**. EQ to Dora, 11 April 1837; Dove Cottage, WLL/Quillinan, Edward/1/69. • **3**. EQ to Dora [25] March 1837; Dove Cottage, WLL/Quillinan, Edward/1/68. • **4**. WW to MW, 17 July [1837]; *WW LLY*, III, p. 429. • **5**. WW to Dora, 8 August 1837; *WW LLY*, III, p. 431. • **6**. WW to his Family [9 August 1837]; *WW LLY*, III, p. 432. • **7**. WW to EQ, 20 September [1837]; Dove Cottage, WLL/Wordsworth, W and D/7/537. • **8**. WW to Christopher Wordsworth Jnr, 5 October [1837]; *WW LLY*, III, pp. 468–9. • **9**. SC to HNC, 11 October 1837; HRC MS. • **10**. EQ to WW, 25 October 1837; Dove Cottage, WLL/Quillinan, Edward/1/70. • **11**. EQ Diary, 25 October 1837; Dove Cottage, WLMS 13/3/2. • **12**. An inside ticket from London to Brighton, for example, would have cost 18s and an outside seat 9s. See William C. A. Blew, *Brighton and its Coaches – A History of London to Brighton Road* (London: John C. Nimmo, 1894), p. 213. • **13**. Henry Taylor, *Autobiography of Henry Taylor, 1800–1875*, 2 vols (London: Longmans, Green and Co., 1885), I, p. 52. • **14**. Thomas Carlyle to Alexander Carlyle, 27 February 1835; *The Carlyle Letters Online*, 2007; available at <http://carlyleletters.org> [accessed 12 January 2012]. • **15**. Dora to MW and WW, 7 March 1846; Dove Cottage, WLL/Quillinan, Dora/2/26. • **16**. For details of Dover in 1837, see W. Batcheller, *A Descriptive Picture of Dover, or: the Visitor's New Guide: Being a Concise Outline of the History, Antiquities, and Present State of the Town and Castle* (Dover: W. Batcheller, 1837). • **17**. EQ Diary, 15 November 1837; Dove Cottage, WLMS 13/3/2. • **18**. All previous quotes from EQ to Dora,

5–7 December 1837; Dove Cottage, WLL/Quillinan, Edward/1/72. • **19**. EQ to Dora, 8 December 1837; Dove Cottage, WLL/Quillinan, Edward/1/73. • **20**. EQ to Dora, 24 December 1837; Dove Cottage, WLL/Quillinan, Edward/1/74. • **21**. EQ to Dora, 8 December 1837; Dove Cottage, WLL/Quillinan, Edward/1/73. • **22**. EQ to Dora, 24 December 1837; Dove Cottage, WLL/Quillinan, Edward/1/74. • **23**. EQ to Dora, 8 December 1837; Dove Cottage, WLL/Quillinan, Edward/1/73. • **24**. EQ to Dora, 27 December 1837; Dove Cottage, WLL/Quillinan, Edward/1/75. • **25**. Quoted in EQ to Dora, 24 December 1837; Dove Cottage, WLL/Quillinan, Edward/1/74. • **26**. Referenced in EQ to Dora, 24 December 1837; Dove Cottage, WLL / Quillinan, Edward/1/74. • **27**. EQ to Dora, 24 December 1837; Dove Cottage, WLL/Quillinan, Edward/1/74. • **28**. EQ to Dora, 27 December 1837; Dove Cottage, WLL/Quillinan, Edward/1/75. • **29**. EQ to Dora, 19 [January] 1838; Dove Cottage, WLL/Quillinan, Edward/1/ 77. • **30**. The letter no longer exists, but Edward described its effect on Dora in a letter of his own the following year: EQ to Dora, 17 April 1839; Dove Cottage, WLL/Quillinan, Edward/2/85. • **31**. WW to Dora, 8 February 1838, *The Letters of William and Dorothy Wordsworth: A Supplement of New Letters*, ed. Alan G. Hill (Oxford: Clarendon Press, 1993), p. 238. • **32**. EQ to Dora, 20 March 1838; Dove Cottage, WLL/Quillinan, Edward/1/78. • **33**. EQ Diary, 20 March 1838; Dove Cottage, WLMS 13/4/1. • **34**. See Henry Taylor, *Autobiography of Henry Taylor, 1800–1875*, 2 vols (London: Longmans, Green and Co., 1885), I, pp. 213–23, for a full account of the affair and Miss Fenwick's role in it. • **35**. WW to Dora [*c.* 5 April 1838]; *WW LLY*, III, pp. 548–9. • **36**. EQ to Dora, 20 March 1838; Dove Cottage, WLL/Quillinan, Edward/1/78. • **37**. STC, 'Reflections on Having Left a Place of Retirement'. • **38**. From *The Wye Tour of Joseph Farington* (1803). • **39**. All previous quotes, Dora to Miss Fenwick, 18 April 1838; Dove Cottage, WLL/Wordsworth, Dora/1/68. • **40**. EQ to Dora, 22 April 1838; Dove Cottage, WLL/Quillinan, Edward/1/79. • **41**. EQ to Dora, 22 April 1838; Dove Cottage, WLL/Quillinan, Edward/1/79. • **42**. EQ to Dora, 8 December 1838; Dove Cottage, WLL/Quillinan, Edward/1/73. • **43**. EQ to Dora, 22 April 1838; Dove Cottage, WLL/Quillinan, Edward/1/79. • **44**. Dora to RQ, 2 July 1838; Dove Cottage, WLL/Wordsworth, Dora/1/69. • **45**. The bill was brought by Thomas Noon Talfourd.

15 'Hopes & Fears', 1838–1840

1. SC to Mrs STC, 13–16 September 1838: HRC MS. • **2**. SC to HNC, 6 October 1838; HRC MS. • **3**. *Memoir*, I, p. 223. • **4**. SC to Emily Trevenen, 9 April 1838; HRC MS. • **5**. SC to HNC, 8 October 1837; HRC MS. • **6**. SC to HNC, 19 September 1839; HRC MS. • **7**. SC, 'The Five Declensions', in Sara Coleridge, *Pretty Lessons in Verse for Good Children with some Lessons in Latin in Easy Rhyme*, 3rd edn (London: John W. Parker, 1839), p. 107. • **8**. SC, 'Mary I, or Queen Mary Tudor (vulgarly "bloody Queen Mary")', in *SCCP*, p. 151. • **9**. SC to Louisa Plummer (née Powles), November [1839]; BL Add MS 85958. • **10**. *Coleridge Fille*, p.127. • **11**. SC to Louisa Plummer (née Powles), 26 August 1837; *Memoir*, I, p. 180. Regent's Park was opened to the public, two days per week, from 1838. • **12**. SC to HNC, 14 October 1840; HRC MS. • **13**. SC to Henry Reed, 19 May 1851; *Memoir*, II, p. 410. • **14**. EQ to Dora, 17 April 1839; Dove Cottage, WLL/Quillinan, Edward/2/85. • **15**. WW to EQ [early February 1839]; *WW LLY*, III, p. 660. • **16**. EQ to Dora, 17 April 1839; Dove Cottage, WLL/Quillinan, Edward/2/85. • **17**. EQ to Dora, 17 April 1839; Dove Cottage, WLL/Quillinan, Edward/2/ 85. • **18**. WW to Southey, 18 February [1839]; *WW LLY*, III, p. 663. • **19**. EQ to Dora, 20 February 1839; Dove Cottage, WLL/Quillinan, Edward/2/83. • **20**. WW to Southey, 18 February [1839]; *WW LLY*, III, p. 663. • **21**. EQ to Dora, 20 February 1839; Dove Cottage, WLL/Quillinan, Edward/2/83. • **22**. All previous quotes from EQ to Dora, 17 April 1839; Dove Cottage, WLL/Quillinan, Edward/2/85. • **23**. WW to EQ, 13 April [1839]; *WW LLY*, III, p. 682. • **24**. EQ to Dora, 17 April 1839; Dove Cottage, WLL/Quillinan, Edward/2/85. • **25**. MW to Dora, 19–23 April 1839; *LMW*, p. 229. • **26**. EQ to Dora, 17 April 1839; Dove Cottage, WLL/Quillinan, Edward/2/85. • **27**. EQ to Dora, 5 June 1839; Dove Cottage, WLL/Quillinan, Edward/2/87. • **28**. MW to Dora, 19 April 1839; *LMW*, p. 229. • **29**. WW to Dora, 9 June 1839; *WW LLY*, III, pp. 702–703. • **30**. EQ to JQ and RQ, 25 November 1839; Dove Cottage, 2001.85.16 [from Woods-Higginsbottom facsimile]. • **31**. All previous quotes from EQ to Dora, 10 June 1839; Dove Cottage, WLL/Quillinan, Edward/2/88.

• **32**. WW to HCR, 22 June 1839; *WW LLY*, III, p. 709. • **33**. SC to Mary Stanger, 11 December 1839; Dove Cottage, Moorsom 55/1/15. • **34**. HCR Diary, 22 February 1840: *HCRBW*, II, p. 580. • **35**. SC to Mary Stanger, 3 April 1840; HRC MS. • **36**. SC, 'Journal of Bertha Fanny Coleridge's death', July 1840; HRC MS. • **37**. 'The Plagiarism of ST Coleridge', *Blackwood's Edinburgh Magazine*, 47 (March 1840), 287–308. • **38**. HC to HNC, 10 July 1840, *LHC*, p. 241. • **39**. All previous quotes from SC, 'Journal of Bertha Fanny Coleridge's death', July 1840; HRC MS.

16 'A New Hat with an Old Lining', 1841

1. EQ to RQ, 1 September 1840; Dove Cottage, WLL/Quillinan, Edward/2/101. • **2**. Available at <http://www.lake-district-attractions.co.uk/_images/striding-edge.jpg> • **3**. EQ to Dora, 28 September 1840; Dove Cottage, WLL/Quillinan, Edward/2/102. • **4**. EQ to Dora, 26 February 1841; Dove Cottage, WLL/Quillinan, Edward/2/111. • **5**. EQ to Dora, 30 September 1840; Dove Cottage, WLL/Quillinan, Edward/2/103. • **6**. WW to Christopher Wordsworth, 16 February [1841]; *WW LLY*, IV, p. 181. • **7**. EQ to Dora, 26 February 1841; Dove Cottage, WLL/Quillinan, Edward/2/111. • **8**. EQ to Dora [December 1840?]; Dove Cottage, WLL/Quillinan, Edward/2/110. • **9**. Dora to SC, 26 [January] 1841; Victoria University Library, Part III, Correspondence, 1020 (S MS F5.4). • **10**. WW to Edward Moxon, 4 March [1841]; *WW LLY*, IV, p. 183. • **11**. SC to Mary Stanger, 12 April 1841; Dove Cottage, Moorsom 55/1/24. • **12**. SC to Mrs Henry Jones, 31 March 1841; HRC MS. • **13**. Christopher Wordsworth, *Memoirs of William Wordsworth, Poet-Laureate*, ed. Henry Reed, p. 86. SC made the comment in the margin of vol. II, p. 367, of HCR's copy of *Memoirs of William Wordsworth*. • **14**. SC to Mary Stanger, 12 April 1841; Dove Cottage, Moorsom 55/1/24. • **15**. SC to Mary Stanger, 4 April 1841; Dove Cottage, Moorsom 55/1/24. • **16**. See Barker, p. 716. • **17**. Miss Fenwick to Henry Taylor, 6 May 1841; Henry Taylor, *Autobiography of Henry Taylor, 1800–1875*, 2 vols (London: Longmans, Green and Co., 1885), I, p. 337. • **18**. Christopher Wordsworth to WW, 1 May 1841; Dove Cottage; WLL/Wordsworth,

Christopher /101. • **19**. WW to Christopher Wordsworth [3 or 4 May 1841]; *WW LLY*, IV, p. 196. • **20**. EQ to JQ, 21 May 1841; Dove Cottage, WLL/Quillinan, Edward/2/116. • **21**. EQ to RQ, 12 May 1841; Dove Cottage, WLL/Quillinan, Edward/2/115. • **22**. EQ to JQ, 21 May 1841; Dove Cottage, WLL/Quillinan, Edward/2/116. • **23**. EQ to JQ, 21 May 1841; Dove Cottage, WLL/Quillinan, Edward/2/116. • **24**. Eliza Hutchinson to JQ [mid-May 1841]; Dove Cottage, WLMS H/2/5/15. • **25**. EQ to JQ, 21 May 1841; Dove Cottage, WLL/Quillinan, Edward/2/116. • **26**. SC to Emily Trevenen, 27–29 October 1841; HRC MS. • **27**. *Coleridge Fille*, p. 133. • **28**. SC to Emily Trevenen, 27–29 October 1841; HRC MS. • **29**. SC to Mary Stanger, 6 December 1841; Dove Cottage, WLMS Moorsom/55/1/28. • **30**. *Coleridge Fille*, p. 133. • **31**. Aubrey de Vere, *Aubrey de Vere, A Memoir, Based on his Unpublished Diaries and Correspondence*, ed. Wilfrid Ward (London: Longmans Green and Company, 1904), p. 65. • **32**. Aubrey de Vere, Diary, 1 August 1841; *Aubrey de Vere, A Memoir*, p. 88. • **33**. All previous quotes from Aubrey de Vere, to his sister, 25 June 1841; *Aubrey de Vere, A Memoir*, p. 66. • **34**. HNC to SC, 15 September 1834; quoted in Mudge, p. 98. • **35**. *Coleridge Fille*, p. 122. • **36**. See Hensleigh Wedgwood, *On the Development of the Understanding* (London: Taylor and Walton, 1848), p. 4, for location of lectures. • **37**. SC to Emily Trevenen, 17 January 1842; HRC MS. • **38**. SC to Mrs Thomas Farrar, Easter, 1842; *Memoir*, I, p. 256.

17 'Her Husband's Desires', 1842–1843

1. For an overview of the case see, Mary Katharine Woodworth, *The Literary Career of Sir Samuel Egerton Brydges* (Oxford: Blackwell, 1935), pp. 28–30. • **2**. David Chambers, 'The Private Library: Quarterly Journal of the Private Libraries Association', 5th series, 5 (Summer 2002), 111–40, see particularly pp. 116–19. • **3**. HCR, Diary, 14 March 1842; *HCRBW*, II, p. 613. • **4**. E. Fitch Smith, *Reports of cases decided in the High Court of Chancery: with notes and references to both English and American decisions*, XXXV (New York: Banks Gould and Co.), 1864, pp. 313–32. • **5**. WW to EQ, 1 March 1842; *WW LLY*, IV, pp. 294–5.

• **6**. SC to Mary Stanger, March 1842; Dove Cottage, Moorsom 55/1/31. • **7**. *Morning Post*, 11 March 1842. • **8**. *Morning Post*, 2 April 1842. • **9**. Dora to IF, 8 June 1841; Dove Cottage, WLL/Quillinan, Dora/74. • **10**. WW to DW and IF, [24 May 1842]; *WW LLY*, IV, p. 338. • **11**. WW to Dora, 7 April 1842; *WW LLY*, IV, p. 319. • **12**. E. Fitch Smith, *Reports of cases decided in the High Court of Chancery: with notes and references to both English and American decisions*, XXXV (New York: Banks Gould and Co.), 1864, p. 331. • **13**. HCR Diary, 14 March 1842; Henry Crabb Robinson, *Books and their Writers*, ed. Edith Morley, 3 vols (London: J. M. Dent and Sons, 1938), II, p. 613. • **14**. HCR Diary, 14 March 1842; *HCRBW*, II, p. 613. • **15**. SC to Mary Stanger, 29 April 1842; Dove Cottage, WLMS Moorsom/55/1/32a. • **16**. Gladstone's advice turned out to be quite right: see Barker, p. 737, for more details. • **17**. SC to HC, 13 June 1842; HRC MS. • **18**. MW to IF [21 May 1842]; *LMW*, p. 252. • **19**. SC to HC, 13 June 1842; HRC MS. • **20**. Dora discussed her visit in a letter to Mary Stanger: DW to Mary Stanger, 22 September 1842; Dove Cottage, WLMS Moorsom/62/4/10. • **21**. MW to IF, 21 June 1842; *LMW*, pp. 258–9. • **22**. Edith Batho, *The Later Wordsworth* (Cambridge: Cambridge University Press, 1933), p. 394. • **23**. SC to HNC, 6 October 1833; HRC MS. • **24**. SC to Louisa Plummer, 7 December 1842; BL Add MS 85958. • **25**. HNC to Pickering [postmarked 13 February 1843]; HRC MS. Sara sent the letter three weeks after HNC had died. • **26**. *Coleridge Fille*, p. 137. • **27**. SC to Derwent [January 1843]; HRC MS. • **28**. SC to unidentified recipient [no date]; HRC MS. • **29**. SC, 'Book of Mourning', Diary, 18 January 1843; HRC MS. • **30**. SC, 'Book of Mourning', Diary, 21 January 1843; HRC MS. • **31**. *Coleridge Fille*, p. 139. • **32**. SC 'Book of Mourning', Diary, 27 January 1843; HRC MS. • **33**. *Coleridge Fille*, pp. 139–40. • **34**. SC to Revd H. Moore, 13 February 1843; *Memoir*, I, p. 268. • **35**. Jones, p. 307, and SC, 'Book of Mourning', Diary, 26 January 1843; HRC MS. • **36**. SC, 'Book of Mourning', Diary, 2 February 1843; HRC MS. • **37**. SC to Emily Trevenen , 1843; HRC MS. • **38**. WW to Sir John Taylor Coleridge, 11 November 1842; *WW LLY*, IV, pp. 386–7.

18 *For Truth and Justice: The Calumniated Poet, 1843–1844*

1. DW, 15 April 1802; Dorothy Wordsworth, *The Grasmere and Alfoxden Journals* (Oxford: Oxford University Press), 2002, p. 85. • 2. EQ to HCR [9/19] April 1843; HCR Wordsworth Correspondence, I, p. 496. • 3. See WW to Barron Field, 16 January 1840; *WW LLY*, IV, pp. 6–7, and note to the letter. The biography was eventually published in 1975. • 4. William Wordsworth, *A Letter to a Friend of Robert Burns: Occasioned by an Intended Republication of The Account of the Life of Burns, by Dr. Currie; and of the Selections made by him from the Letters* (London: Longman, Hurst, Rees, Orme, and Brown), 1816, p. 17. • 5. Aubrey de Vere to his sister, 25 June 1841; *Aubrey de Vere Memoir*, p. 66. • 6. Stephen Gill, *Wordsworth: A Life* (Oxford: Clarendon Press, 1989), p. 73. • 7. Miss Fenwick to EQ, 11 February 1848; Dove Cottage, WLMS A/Fenwick, Isabella/6. • 8. All previous quotes from SC to JTC, 22 March 1843; HRC MS. [Misdated in vol. I, p. 282 for July 1843.] • 9. SC to WW [1843]; HRC MS. • 10. SC to JTC, 22 March 1843; HRC MS. • 11. SC to JTC, 15 July 1843; HRC MS. • 12. HC to Mrs STC, 25 October 1843; *LHC*, p. 267. • 13. Holmes *DR*, pp. 378–9. • 14. 'Review of Coleridge's Biographia Literaria', *Edinburgh Review*, 28 (August 1817) 488–515. • 15. Samuel Taylor Coleridge, *Biographia Literaria* (J. M. Dent & Co.: London, 1906), pp. x–xi. • 16. 'Observations on Coleridges Biographia Literaria', *Blackwood's Edinburgh Magazine*, Volume 2, No. 7 (October 1817), 3–18, p. 6. • 17. HCR Diary, 4 December 1817; *HCRBW*, I, p. 213. • 18. EQ to HCR, 19 April 1843; *HCRWC*, I, p. 496. • 19. *The Fenwick Notes of William Wordsworth*, ed. Jared Diamond (Bristol: Bristol Classical Press, 1993; newly corrected by Jared Curtis, HumanitiesEbooks.co.uk, 2007), p. 22. • 20. WW to Dora, 14 [October 1843]; *WW LLY*, IV, p. 483. • 21. SC to Dora, 13 September, 1843; Dove Cottage, WLMS A/Coleridge, Sara/40. • 22. WW to Sir William Rowan Hamilton, April 1843; *WW LLY*, IV, p. 438. • 23. EQ to HCR, 1 June 1843; *HCRWC*, I, p. 500. • 24. EQ to HCR, 25 August 1843; *HCRWC*, I, p. 517. • 25. SC to Mrs STC, 1 September 1843; HRC MS. • 26. SC and Edith Coleridge to Mrs STC

[September 1843]; HRC MS. • **27**. SC to Mrs STC [2–3 September 1843]; HRC MS. • **28**. SC, 'Reply to the Strictures of Three Gentlemen's Criticisms of her Opinion of Carlyle', in Mudge, p. 240. • **29**. For the essay and its origins, see Mudge, pp. 236–44 and note p. 236. • **30**. SC to EQ, 24 October 1843; Dove Cottage, WLMS A/Coleridge, Sara/42. • **31**. SC, 'Reply to the Strictures of Three Gentlemen . . . Carlyle', Mudge, p. 240. • **32**. EQ to HCR, 9 December 1843; *HCRWC*, I, p. 532. • **33**. EQ to SC, 9 December 1843; HRC MS. • **34**. Christopher Wordsworth, *Memoirs of William Wordsworth, Poet-Laureate*, ed. Henry Reed, 2 vols (Boston: Ticknor, Reed, and Fields, 1851), II, p. 456. • **35**. WW to Henry Reed, 5 July 1844; *WW LLY*, IV, pp. 560–61. • **36**. WW to Moxon, 15 April 1844; *WW LLY*, IV, p. 546. • **37**. WW to Henry Reed, 5 July 1844; *WW LLY*, IV, pp. 560–61. • **38**. H. D. Rawnsley, *Lake Country Sketches* (Glasgow: James MacLehose and Sons, 1894), p. 9. • **39**. Rawnsley, *Lake Country Sketches*, p. 17. • **40**. Rawnsley, *Lake Country Sketches*, p. 50. • **41**. Harriet Martineau, *Harriet Martineau's Autobiography, with Memorials by Maria Weston Chapman*, 2nd edn, 3 vols (London: Smith, Elder and Co., 1877), II, p. 236. • **42**. Rawnsley, *Lake Country Sketches*, p. 49. • **43**. WW to Edward Moxon, 20 April 1844; *WW LLY*, IV, p. 548. • **44**. WW to SC, 2 May 1843; *WW LLY*, IV, pp. 440–42. • **45**. SC to Mrs Henry Taylor, 8 December 1845; *Memoir*, I, p. 346. • **46**. SC to HC, 16 February [1846]; HRC MS. • **47**. SC to HC, 20–21 January 1845; HRC MS.

19 *'Yet Hope Still Lives'*, 1845

1. WW to Christopher Wordsworth Jnr, 10 April 1845; *WW LLY*, IV, p. 666. • **2**. EQ to HCR, 8 April 1845; *HCRWC*, II, p. 597. • **3**. Dora Wordsworth, *Journal of a Few Months Residence in Portugal etc* (London: Edward Moxon, 1847), I, p. xii. • **4**. EQ to HCR, 4 April 1845; *HCRWC*, II, p. 594. • **5**. EQ Diary, 13 June 1844; Dove Cottage, WLMS 13/5/3. • **6**. WW to IF, 17 July 1844; *WW LLY*, IV, p. 575. • **7**. H. D. Rawnsley, *Lake Country Sketches* (Glasgow: James MacLehose and Sons, 1894), p. 42. • **8**. Rawnsley, *Lake Country Sketches*, p. 7. • **9**. WW and MW to IF, 19 September 1844; *WW LLY*, IV, p. 596.

• **10**. WW to IF, 17 July 1844; *WW LLY*, IV, p. 575. • **11**. WW and MW to IF, 19 September 1844; *WW LLY*, IV, p. 597. • **12**. WW to IF, 17 July 1844; *WW LLY*, IV, p. 576. • **13**. WW and MW to IF, 19 September 1844; *WW LLY*, IV, p. 597. • **14**. Barron Field to HCR, 16 February 1845; *HCRWC*, II, p. 592. • **15**. EQ to HCR, 8 April 1845; *HCRWC*, II, p. 597. • **16**. HC to DC, 12 April 1845; *LHC*, p. 279. • **17**. WW to Edward Moxon, 10 April 1845; *WW LLY*, IV, II, p. 666. • **18**. Dora Wordsworth, *Journal of a Few Months Residence in Portugal*, II, p. 8. • **19**. SC to Mrs STC, 19 September [1845]; HRC MS. • **20**. SC to Mrs STC, 30 October 1845; HRC MS. • **21**. *Coleridge Fille*, p. 224. • **22**. SC to Mrs STC, 20 November 1844; HRC MS. • **23**. SC to IF, 23 September 1845; HRC MS. • **24**. SC to Mrs STC, 30 October [1843]; HRC MS. • **25**. *Coleridge Fille*, p. 218. • **26**. Lefebure, *The Bondage of Love: A Life of Mrs. Samuel Taylor Coleridge*, pp. 259–60. • **27**. Mary Coleridge to HC, 24 September 1845; HRC MS. • **28**. *Coleridge Fille*, p. 231. • **29**. SC, 'Book of Mourning', Diary, 26 September 1845; HRC MS. • **30**. SC to DC [18 October 1845]; HRC MS. • **31**. SC to HC [October 1845]; HRC MS. • **32**. Samuel Taylor Coleridge, *Biographia Literaria; or, Biographical Sketches of My Literary Life and Opinions*, second edition prepared for publication in part by the late Henry Nelson Coleridge, completed and published by his widow, 2 vols (London: William Pickering, 1847), II, p. 410. • **33**. SC to HCR [28 March 1847]; *HCRWC*, II, p. 642. • **34**. *SCCP*, p. 156.

20 *'She Shines with a Light of Her Own'*, 1847

1. WW to SC [*c.* 4 February 1847]; *WW LLY*, IV, pp. 831–2. • **2**. SC to IF [1847]: HRC MS. • **3**. SC to Aubrey de Vere, April 1847; *Memoir*, II, p. 106. • **4**. SC to HC, 30 March 1847; HRC MS. • **5**. All previous quotes from SC to Aubrey de Vere, April 1847; *Memoir*, II, pp. 106–107. • **6**. SC to Emily Trevenen , 9 April 1847; HRC MS. • **7**. SC to HC, 30 March [1847]; HRC MS. • **8**. SC to Ann Parrott, 29 March 1847; HRC MS. • **9**. SC to Aubrey de Vere, April 1847; *Memoir*, II, p. 107. • **10**. SC Autobiography, Mudge, p. 262. • **11**. Dora to Willy, 15 October 1846; Dove Cottage, WLL/Wordsworth,

Dora/93. • **12**. SC to HCR, 27 June 1846; *HCRWC*, II, p. 631. • **13**. Dora to MW, 9 August 1845; Dove Cottage, WLL/Quillinan, Dora/2/12. • **14**. WW to HCR, 22 June 1845; *WW LLY*, IV, p. 788. • **15**. WW to Edward Moxon, 1 October 1846; *WW LLY*, IV, pp. 803–804. • **16**. WW to Edward Moxon, 12 October 1846: *WW LLY*, IV, p. 805. • **17**. Christopher Wordsworth, *Memoirs of William Wordsworth, Poet-Laureate*, ed. Henry Reed, 2 vols, p. 104. Sara made the comment in the margin of vol. II, p. 409, of the *Memoirs of William Wordsworth*. • **18**. SC to HCR [28 March 1847]; *HCRWC*, II, pp. 643–4. • **19**. WW to IF [early November 1846]; *WW LLY*, IV, p. 813. • **20**. WW to HCR, 22 June 1846; *WW LLY*, IV, p. 788. • **21**. SC, 'Reasons for Not Placing "Laodamia" in the First Rank of Wordsworthian Poetry', Mudge, pp. 245–8. • **22**. Matthew Arnold for example. Many others have disagreed, George Maclean Harper thought it a perfect work of art; see <http://www.jstor.org/pss/4173731> • **23**. SC, 'Reasons for Not Placing "Laodamia" in the First Rank of Wordsworthian Poetry', Mudge, p. 247. • **24**. SC to IF [April 1847]; HRC MS. • **25**. EQ to IF, 21 April 1847; Dove Cottage, WLL/Quillinan, Edward/2/130 April.

21 *'Strong Flight Home Again'*, 1847

1. Vardy, p. 120. • **2**. SC to JTC [April 1847]; HRC MS. • **3**. *Quincey Lit Rem*, 2 vols (Boston, Ticknor, Reed, & Fields, 1851), II, pp. 342–3. • **4**. Ferrier wrote the letter around 1860. See also Vardy, p. 166, quoting A. Thomson, *Ferrier of St Andrews: An Academic Tragedy* (Edinburgh: Scottish Academic Press), 1985. • **5**. SC to IF [1847]; HRC MS. • **6**. 'Bibliomania', *The North British Review*, 79, February–May 1864, 70–93, p. 87. • **7**. 'Article II', *Edinburgh Review*, 87, April 1848, 321–68, p. 371. • **8**. *SCCP*, p. 175, See Swaab's commentary, pp. 233–4, for an excellent analysis of this poem. • **9**. WW to Edward Moxon, 12 October 1846: *WW LLY*, IV, p. 805. • **10**. EQ to IF, 21 April 1847; Dove Cottage, WLL/Quillinan, Edward/2/130. • **11**. EQ to SC, 29 April 1847, HRC MS. • **12**. SC to IF [April 1847]; HRC MS. • **13**. SC to EQ [May?] 1847 [misdated at Dove Cottage, must be first two weeks of May]; Dove Cottage, WLMS

A/Coleridge, Sara/45. • **14**. EQ to HCR, 30 April 1847; *HCRWC*, II, p. 645. • **15**. Edward Quillinan, *Poems by Edward Quillinan with a Memoir by William Johnson* (London: Edward Moxon, 1853), p. xxxvii. • **16**. Thomas Hartwell Horne, *A Manual for the Afflicted: Comprising a Practical Essay on Affliction, and a Series of Meditations and Prayers, etc.* (London: E. Cadwell, 1832). • **17**. MW to IF [24 May 1847]; *LMW*, p. 278. • **18**. Edward Quillinan, *Poems by Edward Quillinan with a Memoir by William Johnson* (London: Edward Moxon, 1853), p. xxxvii. • **19**. *Coleridge Fille*, p. 234. • **20**. Dora to IF, 24 May 1847; Dove Cottage, Transcription of letter, Reference 2004.130.1.40. • **21**. HCR to Dora, 20 May 1847; Dove Cottage, WLL/Robinson, Henry Crabb/8. • **22**. MW to SC, 25 May 1847; *WW LLY*, IV, p. 849. • **23**. SC to Miss Morris, *Memoir*, II, p. 117. • **24**. Dora to IF, 24 May 1847; Dove Cottage, WLL/Wordsworth, Dora/1/99. • **25**. MW to SC, 25 May 1847; *WW LLY*, IV, p. 848. • **26**. EQ to IF, 2 June 1847; Dove Cottage, WLL/Quillinan, Edward/2/131. • **27**. Charlotte Elliott, *Selections From the Poems of Charlotte Elliott. With a Memoir by Her Sister*, E.B (London: The Religious Tract Society, 1873), Appendix, pp. 245–6. • **28**. SC to IF [June 1847]; HRC MS. • **29**. *SCCP*, p. 183. • **30**. J. A. Heraud, 'Literary Register', *Tait's Edinburgh Magazine*, 14 (1847), 496–8, p. 498. • **31**. Dora Wordsworth, *Journal of a Few Months Residence in Portugal*, I, p. xii. • **32**. *Morning Post*, 3 May 1847; *John Bull*, 28 May 1847; and *The Spectator*, 8 May 1847. • **33**. 'Article VIII', *Edinburgh Review*, 84, July 1847, 177–87, p. 179. • **34**. *The Atlas*, 8 May 1847; Dove Cottage, WLMS 1/5a/7. • **35**. HCR Diary, 10 July 1847; *HCRBW*, II, p. 667. • **36**. Dove Cottage, WLMS 15/10, DC. (The article has been scribbled on, presumably by a relative who objected to its content.) • **37**. HCR Diary, 6 July 1847; *HCRBW*, II, p. 667. • **38**. *John Bull*, 28 May 1847. • **39**. *The Britannia*, 12 June 1847; Dove Cottage, WLMS 1/5a/8. • **40**. *John Bull*, 28 May 1847. • **41**. Dora Wordsworth, *Journal of a Few Months Residence in Portugal*, I, p. 201. • **42**. Dora Wordsworth, *Journal of a Few Months Residence in Portugal*, II, p. 238. • **43**. EQ and Dora to MW, 27 May 1845; Dove Cottage, WLL/Quillinan, Dora/2/6. • **44**. Dora to WW and MW, 9 July 1845; Dove Cottage, WLL/Quillinan, Dora/2/9. • **45**. See Kate Summerscale, *Mrs Robinson's Disgrace* (London:

Bloomsbury, 2012), pp. 95–6. • **46**. The letter seems not to exist any longer. • **47**. *Guardian*, 4 August 1847.

22 'Buckland in Petticoats', 1847–1852

1. SC to Miss Morris, 31 May 1847; *Memoir*, II, p. 117. • **2**. SC to IF, 7 June 1847; HRC MS. • **3**. See entries in SC's 'Book of Mourning', Diary; HRC MS. • **4**. EQ to SC, 7 August 1847; HRC MS. • **5**. SC to EQ [1847]; Dove Cottage, WLMS A/Coleridge, Sara/46. Date of the letter must be August 1847 as she mentions the fact that Derwent is tutoring at Merivale (see SC to IF, 2 August 1847; HRC MS). SC's letter to Edward makes clear that the first she knew that Dora had thought of her on her deathbed was when she received the MS of *Christabel*. • **6**. SC to IF, 30 October 1847; HRC MS. • **7**. SC to Mary Moorsom, 3 October 1847; Dove Cottage, WLMS Moorsom/55/1/56. • **8**. For an excellent article on this review see Joanne Wilkes, 'Snuffing Out an Article: Sara Coleridge and the Early Victorian Reception of Keats', in Joel Faflak and Julia M. Wright, eds, *Nervous Reactions: Victorian Recollections of Romanticism* (New York: State University of New York Press, 2004), pp. 189–206. Also SC to Mrs Derwent Coleridge, September 1848; HRC MS: 'What I grieved to part with – (the only passage I cared much about) was a critique upon Keats, doing him, as I thought, due honour.' • **9**. SC to Mrs Derwent Coleridge, 3 December [1848]; HRC MS. • **10**. Vardy, p. 153. • **11**. SC to Mary Moorsom, 2 February 1848; Dove Cottage, WLMS Moorsom/55/1/58. • **12**. 'Dream Love', *SCCP*, pp. 168–9. • **13**. *Coleridge Fille*, p. 223. • **14**. SC to IF [April 1848]; HRC MS. • **15**. Alan Vardy is interesting in his criticisms of Sara and her 'ilk' for their 'hysteria' over the Chartists: see Vardy, pp. 128–31. • **16**. *Coleridge Fille*, p. 228. • **17**. For an account of Herbert's education, see the obituary in *Macmillan's Magazine*, IV (7 September 1861), 56–60. • **18**. SC, 'Diary, 9 January 1849–31 August 1849', 9 January 1849; HRC MS. • **19**. SC to EQ, 21 December 1849; Dove Cottage, WLMS A/ Coleridge, Sara/48. • **20**. SC to EQ, 15 January 1849; HRC MS. • **21**. SC to Miss Morris, 17 January 1849; *Memoir*, II, p. 209. • **22**. SC to John Taylor Coleridge, 8 January 1849; HRC MS. • **23**. SC to

Derwent [January 1849]; HRC MS. • **24**. SC to IF, 7–8 January 1849; HRC MS. • **25**. SC to John Taylor Coleridge, 8 January 1849; HRC MS. • **26**. SC to John Taylor Coleridge [March 1849]; HRC MS. • **27**. *Coleridge Fille*, p. 241. • **28**. SC to John Taylor Coleridge [March 1849]; HRC MS. • **29**. SC to John Taylor Coleridge [February 1849]; HRC MS. • **30**. SC, 'Diary, 9 January 1849–31 August 1849', 31 January 1849; HRC MS. • **31**. MW to HCR, 24 February 1849; *WW LLY*, IV, pp. 888–9. • **32**. SC, 'Diary, 9 January 1849–31 August 1849', 31 January 1849; HRC MS. • **33**. SC to John Taylor Coleridge [July 1849]; HRC MS. • **34**. SC to Mary Stanger, 17–18 August 1849; Dove Cottage, Moorsom 55/1/63. • **35**. SC to John Taylor Coleridge [July 1849]; HRC MS. • **36**. 'To all their faults a little blind': SC to IF, 13 April 1849; HRC MS. 'Only too happy': SC, 'Diary, 9 January 1849–31 August 1849', 12 March 1849; HRC MS. • **37**. 'Time's Acquittal', *SCCP*, pp. 160–61. • **38**. 'Dream Love', *SCCP*, pp. 168–9. • **39**. SC, 14 August 1850, quoted in *SCCP*, pp. 228–9. • **40**. SC, 'Diary, 9 January 1849–31 August 1849', 3 April 1849; HRC MS. • **41**. The second chapter of SC's Introduction to *EOT*, 'On the Consistency of the Authors Opinions', I, pp. xxii–xxv. • **42**. See Vardy, p. 126. • **43**. *EOT*, p. lxxxiv. • **44**. *EOT*, p. xxv. • **45**. Anonymous, *Literary Examiner*, Saturday, 25 May 1850. • **46**. SC to EQ, 29 March 1850; Dove Cottage, WLMS A/Coleridge, Sara/52.

23 *'Bright Endowments of a Noble Mind'*, 1850–1852

1. SC to Professor Henry Reed, 19 May 1851; *Memoir*, II, p. 407. • **2**. SC to EQ, 25 March 1850; Dove Cottage, WLMS A/Coleridge, Sara/50. • **3**. Christopher Wordsworth, *Memoirs of William Wordsworth, Poet-Laureate*, ed. Henry Reed, 2 vols, II, p. 517. • **4**. SC to EQ, 8 October 1850, Dove Cottage, WLMS A/Coleridge, Sara/70. • **5**. SC to EQ, 30 September 1850, Dove Cottage, WLMS A/Coleridge, Sara/68. • **6**. *Coleridge Fille*, p. 244 • **7**. SC to EQ, 8 October 1850; Dove Cottage, WLMS A/Coleridge, Sara/70. • **8**. SC to Emily Trevenen, 20 March 1850; HRC MS. • **9**. *Coleridge Fille*, p. 246. • **10**. SC, 'Diary, 8 September 1850–20 Aug 1851', 5 December 1850; HRC MS. • **11**. SC, 'Diary, 12 June 1848–January 1849', 28 October

1848; Diary, HRC MS. • **12**. SC to Derwent Coleridge, 7 November 1851; HRC MS. • **13**. SC, 'Diary, 8 September 1850–20 Aug 1851', 3-6 November 1850; HRC MS. • **14**. SC, 'Diary, 8 September 1850–20 Aug 1851', 21 November 1850; HRC MS. • **15**. SC, 'Diary, 8 September 1850–20 Aug 1851', 3 November 1850; HRC MS. • **16**. SC, 'Diary, 8 September 1850–20 Aug 1851', 12 November 1850; HRC MS. • **17**. SC, 'Diary, 8 September 1850–20 Aug 1851', 4 October 1850; HRC MS. • **18**. SC to IF, 29 April 1851; HRC MS. • **19**. The palace of Diamanthine: *Phantasmion*, p. 199. • **20**. SC to IF, 29 April 1851; HRC MS. • **21**. Edmondo de Amicis, *Jottings about London, 1883*, quoted in *Victorian London* <http://www.victorian-london.org/buildings/crystalpalace.htm> [accessed 14 November 2011]. • **22**. *Phantasmion*, p. 164. • **23**. William Wordsworth, *The Fenwick Notes of William Wordsworth*, ed. Jared Diamond (Bristol: Bristol Classical Press, 1993; newly corrected edition by Jared Curtis, HumanitiesEbooks.co.uk, 2007), pp. 24–5. • **24**. SC, 'Diary, 8 September 1850–20 Aug 1851', 31 July 1851; HRC MS. • **25**. SC to EQ [April] 1851; Dove Cottage, WLMS A/Coleridge, Sara/53. • **26**. *Coleridge Fille*, p. 235. • **27**. SC to Derwent Coleridge, 28 September 1851; HRC MS. • **28**. SC to Derwent Coleridge [January 1852]; HRC MS. • **29**. SC to Derwent Coleridge, 24 January 1852; HRC MS. • **30**. SC to Derwent Coleridge, 22 January 1852; HRC MS. • **31**. SC to Derwent Coleridge [January 1852]; HRC MS. • **32**. 'Designed by STC . . .': SC to Derwent Coleridge, 24 January 1852; 'adhere to him in some . . .': SC to DC, 22 January 1852; HRC MS. • **33**. SC to Derwent Coleridge, 18 January [1852]; HRC MS. • **34**. SC to John Taylor Coleridge, quoted in Mudge, p. 173. • **35**. SC to EQ, 8 October [1850]; Dove Cottage, WLMS A/Coleridge, Sara/70. • **36**. SC, 'Diary from 21 August 1851', 23 September 1851; HRC MS. • **37**. SC to John Taylor Coleridge, 24 October 1851; HRC MS. • **38**. SC, 'Diary from 21 August 1851', 10 November 1851; HRC MS. • **39**. SC, 'Diary from 21 August 1851', 5 December 1851; HRC MS. • **40**. SC, 'Diary from 21 August 1851', 24 November 1851; HRC MS. • **41**. SC to Mary Stanger, 6 October 1851; Dove Cottage, Moorsom 55/1/72. • **42**. SC to JTC, 7 December 1851, HRC MS. • **43**. SC to Derwent, January 1852, quoted in *SCCP*, pp.197–8, 22 January 1852. • **44**. SC to Derwent, 23 January 1852,

HRC MS. • **45**. SC to Derwent, 2 February 1852, HRC MS. Where SC underlines, she uses a thick pen and three lines. • **46**. SC to Derwent, 10 February [1852]; HRC MS. • **47**. SC, 'Diary from 21 August 1851', early March 1851; HRC MS. • **48**. 29 March 1852; *SCCP*, p.198. The full title of the poem is 'To a little lump of malignity, on being medically assured that it was not a fresh growth, but an old growth splitting'. • **49**. SC, 'Diary from 21 August 1851', 18 April 1852; HRC MS. • **50**. SC to Derwent [May 1852]; HRC MS.

Epilogue

1. Shirley Watters, 'Sara Coleridge and *Phantasmion*', *The Coleridge Bulletin*, New Series, No. 10 (Autumn 1997), 22–38, p. 33. • **2**. Norman Fruman, 'Review Essay: Aids to Reflection on the New "Biographia"', *Studies in Romanticism*, 24 (Spring 1985), 141–73, pp. 141–2. • **3**. Norman Fruman, in Frederick Burwick (ed.), *Coleridge's Biographia Literaria: Text and Meaning* (Columbus: Ohio State University Press, 1989), p. 9. • **4**. Vardy, p. 121. • **5**. Peter Swaab, *The Regions of Sara Coleridge's Thought: Selected Literary Criticism* (New York: Palgrave Macmillan, 2012), p. ix. • **6**. *SCCP*, pp. 186–7. • **7**. Verse in Dora's Book, dated May 1832; Dove Cottage, Reference DCMS 122.23.

BIBLIOGRAPHY

MANUSCRIPT SOURCES
Dove Cottage Manuscripts held by the Wordsworth Trust
British Library Manuscripts
Harry Ransom Research Center, University of Texas at Austin
Victoria University Library in Toronto

BOOKS AND ARTICLES
Primary sources
Anderson, William John, *Hysterical and Nervous Affections of Women Read Before the Harveian Society* (London: John Churchill, London, 1853)

Austen, Jane, *Northanger Abbey* (London: Penguin, 1995)

Batcheller, W., *A Descriptive Picture of Dover, or: the Visitor's New Guide: Being a Concise Outline of the History, Antiquities, and Present State of the Town and Castle* (Dover: W. Batcheller, 1837)

Blew, William C. A., *Brighton and its Coaches – A History of London to Brighton Road* (London: John C. Nimmo, 1894)

Burney, Sarah Harriet, *Country Neighbours*, 2nd edn, 3 vols (London: Henry Colburn, 1820)

Burton, Mary E. (ed.), *The Letters of Mary Wordsworth: 1800–1855* (Oxford: Clarendon Press, 1958)

Byron, George Gordon Noel, *Byron's Letters and Journals*, ed. Leslie Marchand, 12 vols (London: John Murray, 1982), vol. III

Byron, George Gordon Noel, *The Works of Byron, Complete in One Volume*, 3rd edn (Frankfurt: H. L. Broener, 1837), p. 686 (reproduced from *Monthly Literary Recreation*, August 1807)

Coleridge, Christabel R., *Charlotte Mary Yonge, Her Life and Letters* (Detroit: Gale Research Co., 1969)

Coleridge, Hartley, *Letters of Hartley Coleridge*, ed. Grace Evelyn Griggs and Earl Hartley Griggs (London: Oxford University Press, 1936)

Coleridge, Henry Nelson, *Six Months in the West Indies in 1825* (London: John Murray, 1826)

Coleridge, Henry Nelson, *Specimens of the Table Talk of Samuel Taylor Coleridge*, 2 vols (London: John Murray, 1835)

Coleridge, Samuel Taylor, *The Literary Remains of S. T. Coleridge*, 4 vols, ed. Henry Nelson Coleridge (London: W. Pickering, 1836)

Coleridge, Samuel Taylor, *Biographia Literaria; or, Biographical Sketches of My Literary Life and Opinions*, second edition prepared for publication in part by the late Henry Nelson Coleridge, completed and published by his widow, 2 vols (London: William Pickering, 1847)

Coleridge, Samuel Taylor, *Essays on His Own Times*, ed. Sara Coleridge, 3 vols (London: W. Pickering, 1850)

Coleridge, Samuel Taylor, *Unpublished Letters of Samuel Taylor Coleridge*, ed. Earl Leslie Griggs, 2 vols (London: Constable & Co. Ltd, 1932)

Coleridge, Samuel Taylor, *Collected Letters*, ed. Earl Leslie Griggs, 6 vols (Oxford: Clarendon Press, 1956–71)

Coleridge, Samuel Taylor, *The Notebooks of Samuel Taylor Coleridge 1772–1834*, ed. Kathleen Coburn, 5 vols (London: Routledge & Kegan Paul, 1958–2002)

Coleridge, Samuel Taylor, *Selected Letters*, ed. H. J. Jackson (Oxford: Oxford University Press, 1987)

Coleridge, Sara, *Memoir and Letters of Sara Coleridge*, ed. Edith Coleridge, 2 vols (London: Henry S. King & Co., 1873)

Coleridge, Sara, *Pretty Lessons in Verse for Good Children: With Some Lessons in Latin in Easy Rhyme*, 3rd edn (London: John W. Parker, 1839)

Coleridge, Sara, *The Right Joyous and Pleasant History of the Feats, Gests, & Prowesses of the Chevalier Bayard* (London and New York: Newnes Ltd & Charles Scribner & Sons, n.d. but *c.* 1910)

Coleridge, Sara, *Phantasmion* (London: William Pickering, 1837)

Coleridge, Sara [Fricker], *Minnow among Tritons: Mrs. S. T. Coleridge's Letters to Thomas Poole, 1799–1834*, ed. Stephen Potter (London: Nonesuch Press, 1934)

De Quincey, Thomas, *Collected Writings, New and Enlarged Edition in Fourteen Volumes*, ed. David Masson (Edinburgh: Adam and Charles Black, 1889)

De Quincey, Thomas, 'Samuel Taylor Coleridge by the English Opium Eater', *Tait's Edinburgh Magazine*, New Series, 1 (Edinburgh: William Tait, 1834)

De Quincey, Thomas, *Literary Reminiscences from the Autobiography of an English Opium-Eater*, 2 vols (Boston: Ticknor, Reed & Fields, 1851)

De Quincey, Thomas, *The Confessions of an English Opium-Eater* (London: The Bodley Head, 1930)

De Quincey, Thomas, *Autobiographical Sketches* (Boston: Ticknor, Reed & Fields, 1851)

De Vere, Aubrey, *Aubrey de Vere, A Memoir, Based on his Unpublished Diaries and Correspondence*, ed. Wilfrid Ward (London: Longmans Green and Company, 1904)

Dobrizhoffer, Martinus, *An Account of the Abipones, an Equestrian People of Paraguay. From the Latin of M.D.*, trans. by Sara Coleridge (London: John Murray, 1822)

Eliot, George, *Journals of George Eliot*, ed. Margaret Harris and Judith Johnston (Cambridge: Cambridge University Press, 1998)

Eliot, George, *Middlemarch* (Los Angeles: IndoEuropean Publishing, 2010)

Elliott, Charlotte, *Selections From the Poems of Charlotte Elliott. With a Memoir by Her Sister, E.B* (London: The Religious Tract Society, 1873)

Ferrier, J. F., 'The Plagiarism of S. T. Coleridge', *Blackwood's Edinburgh Magazine*, 47 (March 1840), 287–308

Grattan, Thomas, *Beaten Paths and Those Who Trod Them*, 2 vols (London: Chapman and Hall, 1862)

Griggs, Earl Leslie (ed.), *Collected Letters of Samuel Taylor Coleridge*, 6 vols (Oxford: Clarendon Press, 1956)

Griggs, Grace, and Earl Leslie Griggs (eds), *Letters of Hartley Coleridge* (London, New York and Toronto: Oxford University Press, 1941)

Hamilton, Alexander, *A Treatise on the Management of Female Complaints* (Edinburgh: George Ramsay & Company, 1813)

Hazlitt, William, *The Spirit of the Age, or, Contemporary Portraits: and 'My first Acquaintance with Poets'*, introductory essays by Robert Woof, foreword by Michael Foot (Grasmere: The Wordsworth Trust, 2004)

Heraud, J. A., 'Coleridgeana', *Fraser's Magazine for Town and Country*, 13 (January 1835), 50–58

Heraud, J. A.,'Literary Register', *Tait's Edinburgh Magazine*, 14 (1847), 496–8

Hutchinson, Sara, *The Letters of Sara Hutchinson from 1800–1835*, ed. Kathleen Coburn (Routledge & Kegan Paul, 1954)

Jeffrey, Francis, 'Review of Southey's *Thalaba*', *Edinburgh Review*, 1 (October 1802), 63–83

Jeffrey, Francis, 'Review of Wordsworth Poems in Two Volumes', *Edinburgh Review*, 11 (October 1807), 214–31

Jeffrey, Francis, 'Wordsworth's Excursion', *Edinburgh Review*, 24 (November 1814), 1–4

Jeffrey, Francis, 'Memorials of a Tour on the Continent by William Wordsworth', *Edinburgh Review*, 37 (November 1822), 449–556

Lamb, Charles, *The Letters of Charles Lamb Complete in One Volume With a Sketch of his Life*, ed. Sir Thomas Noon Talfourd (Philadelphia: Henry Carey Baird, 1857)

Martineau, Harriet, *Harriet Martineau's Autobiography, with Memorials by Maria Weston Chapman*, 2nd edn, 3 vols (London: Smith, Elder and Co., 1877)

Morley, F. V., *Dora Wordsworth: Her Book* (London: Selwyn & Blount, 1924)

Potter, Stephen (ed.), *Minnow Among Tritons: Mrs. S. T. Coleridge's Letters to Thomas Poole, 1799–1834* (London: Nonesuch Press, 1934)

Quillinan, Edward, *The Conspirators, or a Romance of Military Life*, 3 vols (London: Henry Colburn, 1841)

Quillinan, Edward, *Poems by Edward Quillinan with a Memoir by William Johnston* (London: Edward Moxon, 1853)

Rawnsley, Hardwicke Drummond, *Lake Country Sketches* (Glasgow: James MacLehose and Sons, 1894)

Rawnsley, Hardwicke Drummond, *Literary Associations of the English Lakes*, 2 vols (Glasgow: James MacLehose and Sons, 1894)

Robinson, Henry Crabb, *Diary, Reminiscences and Correspondence*, ed. Thomas Sadler, 3 vols (London: Macmillan, 1869)

Robinson, Henry Crabb, *The Correspondence of Henry Crabb Robinson with the Wordsworth Circle (1808–1866)*, ed. Edith J. Morley, 2 vols (Oxford: Clarendon Press, 1927)

Robinson, Henry Crabb, *Henry Crabb Robinson on Books and Their Writers*, ed. Edith J. Morley, 3 vols (London: J. M. Dent and Sons, 1938)

Scott, Sir Walter, *The Familiar Letters of Sir Walter Scott*, ed. David Douglas, 2 vols (Boston: Houghton Mifflin, 1894)

Smith, E. Fitch, *Reports of cases decided in the High Court of Chancery: with notes and references to both English and American decisions*, XXXV (New York: Banks Gould and Co., 1864)

Southey, Robert, 'An Account of the Abipones, an Equestrian People of Paraguay. Translated from the Latin of Martin Dobrizhoffer, Eighteen Years a Missionary in that Country', in *The Quarterly Review*, 26, 52 (January 1822), 277–323

Southey, Robert, *The Doctor &C in one Volume*, ed. John Wood Warter (London: Longman, 1865)

Southey, Robert, *Sir Thomas More or Colloquies on the Progress and Prospects of Society*, 2 vols (London: John Murray, 1829), vol. 1

Southey, Robert, *The Life and Correspondence of the Late Robert Southey*, ed. Revd Charles Cuthbert Southey, 6 vols (London: Longman, Brown, Green & Longmans, 1849–50)

Southey, Robert, *Selections from the Letters of Robert Southey, &c &c &c*, ed. John Wood Warter, 4 vols (London: Longman, Brown, Green, Longmans, & Roberts, 1856)

Southey, Robert, *New Letters of Robert Southey*, ed. Kenneth Curry, 2 vols (New York and London: Columbia University Press, 1965)

Tate, George, *A Treatise on Hysteria* (London: Highley, 1830)

Taylor, Henry, *Autobiography of Henry Taylor, 1800–1875*, 2 vols (London: Longmans, Green and Co., 1885)

Walpole, Horace, *The Letters of Horace Walpole*, ed. Helen Wrigley Toynbee and Paget Jackson Toynbee (Oxford: Clarendon Press, 1903–1905)

Wilson, Herbert, 'Phantasmion', *The Examiner* (11 April 1874)

Wordsworths, *Letters of the Wordsworth Family: From 1787 to 1855*, ed. William Knight, 3 vols (Boston and London: Ginn and Company, 1907)

Wordsworth, Christopher, *Memoirs of William Wordsworth, Poet-Laureate*, ed. Henry Reed, 2 vols (Boston: Ticknor, Reed & Fields, 1851)

Wordsworth, Dora, *Journal of a Few Months Residence in Portugal etc.* (London: Edward Moxon, 1847)

Wordsworth, Dora, *Letters of Dora Wordsworth*, ed. with an introduction by Howard P. Vincent, limited edition of 450 copies (Chicago: Packard and Company, *c.* 1944)

Wordsworth, Dorothy, *The Grasmere and Alfoxden Journals* (Oxford: Oxford University Press, 2002)

Wordsworth, Mary, *The Letters of Mary Wordsworth 1800–1855*, ed. Mary E. Burton (Oxford: Clarendon Press, 1958)

Wordsworth, William, 'The Ecclesiastical Sonnets XXI. Sponsors', in *The Complete Poetical Works*, ed. John Morley (London: Macmillan and Co., 1888)

Wordsworth, William, *The Fenwick Notes of William Wordsworth*, ed. Jared Diamond (Bristol: Bristol Classical Press, 1993; newly corrected edition by Jared Curtis, HumanitiesEbooks.co.uk, 2007)

Wordsworth, William, *A Letter to a Friend of Robert Burns: Occasioned by an Intended Republication of The Account of the Life of Burns, by Dr. Currie; and of the Selections made by him from the Letters* (London: Longman, Hurst, Rees, Orme, and Brown, 1816)

Wordsworth, William, *Lyrical Ballads, with Other Poems, In Two Volumes* (London: T. N. Longman and O. Rees, 1800)

Wordsworth, William, and Dorothy Wordsworth, *The Early Letters of William and Dorothy Wordsworth (1787–1805)*, ed. Ernest De Selincourt (Oxford: Clarendon Press, 1935)

Wordsworth, William, and Dorothy Wordsworth, *The Letters of William and Dorothy Wordsworth: The Middle Years*, ed. Ernest De Selincourt and revised by Mary Moorman, 2nd edn, 2 vols (Oxford: Clarendon Press, 1937)

Wordsworth, William, and Dorothy Wordsworth, *The Letters of William and Dorothy Wordsworth: The Later Years*, ed. Ernest De Selincourt and revised and ed. Alan G. Hill, 2nd edn, 4 vols (Oxford: Clarendon Press, 1939)

Wordsworth, William, and Dorothy Wordsworth, *The Letters of William and Dorothy Wordsworth: A Supplement of New Letters*, ed. Alan G. Hill (Oxford: Clarendon Press, 1993)

Wordsworth, William, and Mary Wordsworth, *The Love Letters of William and Mary Wordsworth*, ed. Beth Darlington (London: Chatto & Windus, 1982)

Wordsworth, William, and Samuel Taylor Coleridge, *Lyrical Ballads and Other Poems*, ed. with an introduction by Martin Schofield (Hertfordshire: Wordsworth Poetry Library, 2003)

Secondary sources

Anon., 'Article II', *Edinburgh Review*, 87, April 1848, 321–68

Anon., 'Article VIII', *Edinburgh Review*, 84, July 1847, 177–87

Anon., 'Bibliomania', *The North British Review*, 79, February–May 1864, 70–93

Anon., *Literary Examiner*, Issue 2280, Saturday, 25 May 1850

Anon., 'Obituary', *Macmillan's Magazine*, 5 (1861–2), 56–60

Appignanesi, Lisa, *Mad, Bad and Sad: A History of Women and the Mind Doctors From 1800 to the Present* (London: Virago, 2008)

Ashton, Rosemary, *The Life of Samuel Taylor Coleridge* (Oxford: Blackwell, 1996)

Attlee, Helena, *The Gardens of Portugal* (London: Frances Lincoln, 2008)

Barker, Juliet, *Wordsworth: A Life* (London: Viking, 2000)

Batho, Edith, *The Later Wordsworth* (Cambridge: Cambridge University Press, 1933), p. 394

Beal, Oleana, *Dora Wordsworth: A Poet's Daughter* (Cumbria: Wren's Nest Press, 2009)

Berridge, V., and G. Edwards, *Opium and the People: Opiate Use in Nineteenth Century England* (London: Allen Lane, 1981)

Blanshard, Frances, *Portraits of Wordsworth* (London, George Allen & Unwin, 1959)

Bloom, Harold, *Deconstruction and Criticism* (New York: Seabury Press, 1980)

Bloom, Harold, *The Visionary Company: A Reading of English Romantic Poetry* (London: Faber and Faber, 1962)

Bloom, Harold, and Lionel Trilling (eds), *The Oxford Anthology of English Literature* (New York and London: Oxford University Press, 1973)

Brears, Peter, *Cooking and Dining with the Wordsworths: From Dove Cottage to Rydal Mount* (Ludlow: Excellent Press, 2011)

Broughton, Leslie Nathan (ed.), *Sara Coleridge and Henry Reed* (New York and London: Cornell University Press and Oxford University Press, 1937)

Burwick, Frederick (ed.), *Coleridge's Biographia Literaria: Text and Meaning* (Columbus: Ohio State University Press, 1989)

Byatt, A. S., *Unruly Times: Wordsworth and Coleridge in Their Time* (London: Vintage, 1997)

Carey, Hilary M., *God's Empire: Religion and Colonialism in the British World, c.1801–1908* (Cambridge: Cambridge University Press, 2011)

Chambers, David, 'The Private Library: Quarterly Journal of the Private Libraries Association', 5th series, 5 (Summer 2002), 111–40, see particularly pp. 116–19

Clarke, Norma, *Ambitious Heights: Writing, Friendship, Love – the Jewsbury Sisters, Felicia Hemans and Jane Welsh Carlyle* (London: Routledge, 1990)

Cochrane, Margaret, and Robert Cochrane, *Housekeeping with Dorothy Wordsworth at Dove Cottage* (Beverley: Highgate Publications, 2001)

Coleridge, Sara, *Collected Poems*, ed. with an introduction by Peter Swaab (Manchester: Carcanet Press Ltd, 2007)

Connor, Steven, 'All I Believed is True: Dickens and the Mesmerism System', a talk given at Dickens and Science, Dickens Day, Birkbeck College, London, 10 October 2009

Dally, Peter, *Elizabeth Barrett Browning: A Psychological Portrait* (London: Macmillan, 1989)

Davies, Hunter, *Walk around the Lakes: A Visit to the Lake District* (London: Orion, 1979)

Davies, Hunter, *William Wordsworth: A Biography* (London: Weidenfeld and Nicolson, 1980)

Faflak, Joel, and Julia M. Wright (eds), *Nervous Reactions: Victorian Recollections of Romanticism* (New York: State University of New York Press, 2004)

Fruman, Norman, 'Review Essay: Aids to Reflection on the New "Biographia"', *Studies in Romanticism*, 24 (Spring 1985), 141–73

Gill, Stephen, *Wordsworth: A Life* (Oxford: Clarendon Press, 1989)

Gill, Stephen, *Wordsworth and the Victorians* (Oxford: Clarendon Press, 1998)

Gillis, John R., *A World of Their Own Making: A History of Myth and Ritual in Family Life* (Oxford: Oxford University Press, 1997)

Gilman, Sander L., Helen King, Roy Porter, G. S. Rousseu and Elaine Showalter (eds), *Hysteria Beyond Freud* (Berkeley, Los Angeles and London: University of California Press, 1993)

Gittings, Robert, and Jo Manton, *Dorothy Wordsworth* (Oxford: Oxford University Press, 1985)

Gordon (Wilson), Mary, and Mackenzie Shelton, *'Christopher North' A Memoir of John Wilson* (New York: W. J. Widdleton, 1863)

Grantz, Carl L., 'Letters of Sara Coleridge: A Calendar and Index of Her Manuscript Correspondence in the University of Texas Library', Dissertation, University of Texas (June 1986)

Griggs, Earl Leslie, *Coleridge Fille: A Biography of Sara Coleridge* (London, New York and Toronto: Oxford University Press, 1940)

Griggs, Earl Leslie. *Wordsworth and Coleridge; Studies in Honor of George Mclean Harper* (New York: Russell & Russell, 1962)

Hainton, Raymonde, and Godfrey Hainton, *The Unknown Coleridge: The Life and Times of Derwent Coleridge 1800–1883* (London: Janus Publishing Company, 1996)

Hartman, Geoffrey H., *The Unremarkable Wordsworth* (Minneapolis: University of Minnesota Press, 1987)

Higgins, David, *Romantic Genius and the Literary Magazine: Biography, Celebrity, and Politics* (Oxford: Routledge, 2005)

Hill, Rosemary, *God's Architect: Pugin and the Building of Romantic Britain* (London: Penguin, 2007)

Holmes, Richard, *Coleridge: Darker Reflections* (London: Harper Collins, 1998)

Holmes, Richard, *Coleridge: Early Visions* (London: Penguin, 1990)

Hoppin, James M., 'The Letters of Sara Coleridge', *The New Englander*, 34 (1875), 201–21

Horne, Thomas Hartwell, *A Manual for the Afflicted: Comprising a Practical Essay on Affliction, and a Series of Meditations and Prayers, etc.* (London: E. Cadwell, 1832)

Howe, H. W., *Greta Hall: Home of Coleridge and Southey*, with revisions by Robert Woof (Norfolk: Daedalus Press)

Hughes Hallett, Penelope, *Home at Grasmere: The Wordsworths and the Lakes* (London: Collins & Brown, 1993)

Hurd, Douglas, *Robert Peel: A Biography* (London: Weidenfeld & Nicolson, 2007)

Jackson, J. R. de J., *Samuel Taylor Coleridge: The Critical Heritage*, 2 vols (London: Routledge and Kegan Paul, 1970–92)

Jones, Kathleen, *A Passionate Sisterhood: The Sisters, Wives and Daughters of the Lake Poets* (London: Virago, 1997)

Jump, Harriet Devine (ed.), *Women's Writing of the Romantic Period, 1789–1836: An Anthology* (Edinburgh: Edinburgh University Press, 1997)

Lane, Steven Mark, 'How Wordsworth became Wordsworth: A Dialogic Study of a Poet and his Audience' (unpublished doctoral thesis, University of Victoria, 2007)

Lefebure, Molly, *S. T. Coleridge: Bondage of Opium* (Worcester and London: The Trinity Press, 1974)

Lefebure, Molly, *The Bondage of Love: A Life of Mrs. Samuel Taylor Coleridge* (London: Victor Gollancz, 1986)

Legouis, Emile, *William Wordsworth and Annette Vallon* (London and Toronto: J. M. Dent and Sons, 1922)

Lindop, Greville, *A Literary Guide to the Lake District* (London: Chatto & Windus, 1993)

Lister, W. B. C., *A Bibliography of Murray's Handbooks for Travellers and Biographies of Authors, Editors, Revisers and Principal Contributors*, introduction by John R. Gretten (Norfolk: Dereham Books, 1993)

Low, Dennis, *The Literary Protégées of the Lake Poets* (Hampshire: Ashgate, 2006)

Mahoney, Paul, *Wordsworth and the Critics: The Development of a Critical Reputation* (Suffolk, Camden House, 2001)

Mason, Emma, *Cambridge Introduction to William Wordsworth* (Cambridge: Cambridge University Press, 2010)

Matthew, Colin (ed.), *The Nineteenth Century: The British Isles: 1815–1901* (Oxford: Oxford University Press, 2000)

Mazzeo, Tilar J., *Plagiarism and Literary Property in the Romantic Period* (Philadelphia: University of Pennsylvania Press, 2007)

McLeod, Sheila, *The Art of Starvation* (London: Virago, 1981)

McNulty, John Bard, 'Autobiographical Vagaries in "Tintern Abbey"', *Studies in Philology*, 42, No. 1 (January 1945), 81–6

Miles, Alfred H. (ed.), *The Poets and the Poetry of the Century*, vol. 7 (London: Hutchinson & Co., 1891)

Mudge, Bradford Keyes, 'On Tennyson's *The Princess*: Sara Coleridge in the *Quarterly Review*', *Wordsworth Circle*, 15 (1984), 51–4

Mudge, Bradford Keyes, *Sara Coleridge: A Victorian Daughter* (New York and London: Yale University Press, 1989)

Page, Judith W., *Wordsworth and the Cultivation of Women* (Berkeley: University of California Press, 1994)

Page, Judith, 'Neatly-Penned Memorials: Dora Wordsworth's Journal of 1828 and the Community of Authorship', *A/B: Autobiography Studies*, 17 (2002), 65–80

Paley, Morton D., *Portraits of Coleridge* (Oxford: Oxford University Press, 1999)

Porter, Roy, *The Greatest Benefit to Mankind: A Medical History of Mankind* (London: HarperCollins, 1997)

Potts, Malcolm, and Martha Campbell, 'History of Contraception', in *Gynecology & Obstetrics*, 6 (2004), Chapter 8

Purton, Valerie, *A Coleridge Chronology* (Suffolk: Ipswich Book Co. Ltd., 1993)

Reed, Henry, 'The Daughter of Coleridge', *The Literary World* (January 1853); reprinted in *Sara Coleridge and Henry Reed*, ed. L.N. Broughton (New York: Ithaca, 1937)

Roper, Derek, *Reviewing before the Edinburgh, 1788–1802* (Newark: University of Delaware Press, 1978)

Rubinstein, W. D., *Britain's Century: A Political and Social History 1815–1905* (London: Arnold, 1998)

Schlobin, Roger C., *The Literature of Fantasy: A Comprehensive, Annotated Bibliography of Modern Fantasy Fiction* (New York: Garland Publishing, 1979)

Seville, Catherine, *Literary Copyright Reform in Early Victorian England: The Framing of the 1842 Copyright Act* (Cambridge: Cambridge University Press, 1999)

Shattock, Joanne (ed.), *Women and Literature in Britain 1800–1900* (Cambridge: Cambridge University Press, 2001)

Shorter, Edward, *A History of Women's Bodies* (London: Allen Lane, 1983)

Shorter, Edward, 'Paralysis: The Rise and Fall of a "Hysterical" Symptom', *Journal of Social History*, 19, No. 4 (Summer 1986), 549–82

Silver, Anna Krugovoy, *Victorian Literature and the Anorexic Body* (Cambridge: Cambridge University Press, 2002)

Sisman, Adam, *The Friendship: Wordsworth and Coleridge* (London: Viking Books, 2007)

Skultans, Vieda, *Madness and Morals: Ideas on Insanity in the Nineteenth Century* (London and Boston: Routledge & Kegan Paul, 1975)

Smith, Christopher J. P. A, *Quest For Home: Reading Robert Southey* (Liverpool: Liverpool University Press, 1997)

Spaulding, Mary, and Penny Welch, *Nurturing Yesterday's Child: A Portrayal of the Drake Collection of Paediatric History* (Toronto: Natural Heritage/Natural History Inc., 1994)

Speck, W. A., *Robert Southey: Entire Man of Letters* (New Haven and London: Yale University Press, 2006)

Stableford, Brian, *Historical Dictionary of Fantasy Literature* (Lanham, Maryland, Toronto and Oxford: The Scarecrow Press, Inc., 2005)

Stuart, Dorothy Margaret, 'Coleridge Fille, A Biography of Sara Coleridge', *English* (1941) 3(16), 187–8

Summerscale, Kate, *Mrs Robinson's Disgrace* (London: Bloomsbury, 2012)

Swaab, Peter, *The Regions of Sara Coleridge's Thought, Selected Literary Criticism* (Hampshire and New York: Palgrave Macmillan, 2012)

Thomson, A., *Ferrier of St Andrews: An Academic Tragedy* (Edinburgh: Scottish Academic Press, 1985)

Thomson, Heidi, 'Sara Coleridge's Annotation in Pretty Lessons in Verse for Good Children', in *Notes and Queries* (2011) 58 (4), 548–9

Tobin, Shelley, Sarah Pepper and Margaret Willes, *Marriage à la Mode: Three Centuries of Wedding Dresses* (London: National Trust, 2003)

Tosh, John, *A Man's Place: Masculinity and the Middle-Class Home in Victorian England* (New Haven and London: Yale University Press, 1999)

Towle, Eleanor A., *A Poet's Children: Hartley and Sara Coleridge* (London: Methuen, 1912)

Van de Walle, Etienne, and Elisha P. Renne (ed.), *Regulating Menstruation: Beliefs, Practices, Interpretations* (Chicago: University of Chicago Press, 2001)

Vardy, Alan, *Constructing Coleridge: The Posthumous Life of the Author* (Hampshire and New York: Palgrave Macmillan, 2010)

Vickery, Amanda, *Behind Closed Doors: At Home in Georgian England* (New Haven and London: Yale University Press)

Watters, Sarah, 'Sara Coleridge and Phantasmion', *Coleridge Bulletin*, New Series, No. 10 (1997), 22–38

Wedgwood, Hensleigh, *On the Development of the Understanding* (London: Taylor and Walton, 1848)

Wilson, A. N., *The Victorians* (London: Hutchinson, 2002)

Wilson, Frances, *The Ballad of Dorothy Wordsworth* (London: Faber and Faber, 2008)

Wolf, Naomi, *The Beauty Myth* (London: Vintage, 1990)

Woodworth, Mary Katharine, *The Literary Career of Sir Samuel Egerton Brydges* (Oxford: Blackwell, 1935)

Woolf, Virginia, 'Sara Coleridge', *The Death of the Moth and Other Essays* (New York: Harcourt Brace Jovanovich, 1970), pp. 111–18

Wordsworth, Jonathan, M. H. Abrams and Stephen Gill (eds), *William Wordsworth, The Prelude 1799, 1805, 1850: Authoritative Texts, Context and Reception, Recent Critical Essays* (New York and London: W. W. Norton & Company, 1979)

Wu, Duncan (ed.), *A Companion to Wordsworth* (Oxford: Blackwell Publishing, 2001)

Wu, Duncan, *Wordsworth: An Inner Life* (Oxford: Blackwell Publishing, 2002)

Wu, Duncan, *Romanticism: An Anthology*, 3rd edn (Oxford: Blackwell Publishing, 2006)

Young-Bruehl, Elisabeth, *Subject to Biography: Psychoanalysis, Feminism, and Writing Women's Lives* (Cambridge, MA: Harvard University Press, 1998)

Websites

Penrith Town and Parish, <http://www.stevebulman.f9.co.uk/cumbria/penrith_f.html> [accessed 12 November 2011]

The Carlyle Letters Online, 2007, available at <http://carlyleletters.org> [accessed 12 January 2012]

Edmondo de Amicis, *Jottings about London, 1883*, quoted in *Victorian London*, <http://www.victorianlondon.org/buildings/crystalpalace.htm> [accessed 14 November 2011]

ACKNOWLEDGEMENTS

I would like to thank all those who have given me advice and support while writing this book. I owe particular thanks to Jeff Cowton, Rebecca Turner and John Coombe at Dove Cottage for being so generous with their time and support. I am grateful too, to the staff at The Harry Ransom Centre at the University of Texas at Austin; the Victoria University Library in Toronto and the British Library. In particular, at the British Library, I am grateful to Arnold Hunt for his generosity with his research about John Taylor Coleridge. I am also grateful to Jeronime Palmer for showing me her house and for a stimulating conversation. Likewise thank you to Priscilla Cassam, both for permission to print from Sara Coleridge's letters and for showing me some of Sara's possessions. For permission to quote from manuscript sources and reproduce images I am grateful to the Trustees at Rydal Mount and Dove Cottage and to the Harry Ransom Center at the University of Texas at Austin. Thank you to the various members of staff at each institution who have given their help in this respect: Peter Elkington, Chelsea Weathers and Richard Watson.

Anyone who writes about Wordsworth or Coleridge owes a debt of gratitude to the editors of their letters and those of their families. I have been especially grateful for the scholarship of Earl Leslie Griggs, Ernest de Selincourt, Kathleen Coburn, Mary Moorman and Alan G. Hill. I have also drawn inspiration from many excellent biographies, in particular, of Coleridge by

Richard Holmes; of Wordsworth by Juliet Barker; and of Sara Coleridge by both Bradford Keyes Mudge and Griggs.

I would like to thank my agent Peter Straus as well as the talented and patient team at Hutchinson: in particular, Jocasta Hamilton, Paulette Hearn, Emma Mitchell and Caroline Gascoigne as well as Caroline Knight, Sarah Rigby and Jane Robertson. Thank you for bearing with me and teaching me so much.

Many brilliant people have helped me research, write and shape this book. Richard Holmes, Alan Vardy, Arnold Hunt, Peter Swaab, Robin Schofield, Liza Waldegrave and many members of The Friends of Coleridge Society, have all given invaluable advice. For your comments and intelligence: thank you. The mistakes are, of course, all mine.

Without the constant support, good humour and intelligence of Kathryn Hughes, I could not have written this book. I would also like to thank the Lorna Sage Memorial Fund at the University of East Anglia for giving me the means to travel to the University of Texas at Austin.

Thank you to all the wonderful writers, young and old, whom I have met and been inspired by at First Story.

Above all, I am grateful to friends and family, who read drafts along the way. They managed to give me indispensable critical feedback, as well as the confidence to keep going. They include: Indrojit Banerji, Colleen Burns, William Fiennes, Victoria Gray, Sarah Marsh, Mónica Parle, Caroline and William Waldegrave, Harriet Waldegrave and Frances Wilson.

Finally, Dro, who has lived with Dora, Sara and me for a long time – and put up with us all: I will never be able to thank him for all his 'little, nameless, unremembered acts of kindness and love'.

INDEX

'WW' indicates William Wordsworth and 'STC' Samuel Taylor Coleridge.